From the reviews of *Disraeli*:
'A thoroughly enjoyable read . . . [by] a superbly skilful historical writer'
JANE RIDLEY, *Spectator*

'A fine new biography . . . acute and insightful' ANDREW ROBERTS, *Daily Telegraph*

'A fine study of the most intriguing man, in every sense, ever to lead Britain' *Sunday Times*

'In this shouty world, Christopher Hibbert's account of the private life of Benjamin Disraeli comes as an immensely dependable relief. Hibbert is a popular historian of the old school, reticent, scholarly and modest . . . Innumerable younger historians owe him an immense debt' STELLA TILLYARD, *Sunday Times*

'Dizzy swaggers his way through the law courts, the literary Establishment, high society and Parliament in a most enjoyable fashion . . . A rollicking triumph of anecdote and selected braggadocio' SAMUEL BLAKE, *Times Literary Supplement*

'Mr Hibbert has painted, with admirable clarity and thoroughness, a warts-and-all picture of one of Britain's most gifted Prime Ministers. The result is a biography of substance, and one that is never lacking in fascinating personal detail' BERNARD PALMER, *Church Times*

By the same author

CHRISTOPHER HIBBERT

DISRAELI

The Victorian Dandy Who Became Prime Minister

palgrave
macmillan

DISRAELI
© Christopher Hibbert, 2006.

First published in hardcover in 2006 by
PALGRAVE MACMILLAN™
175 Fifth Avenue, New York, N.Y. 10010 and
Houndmills, Basingstoke, Hampshire, England RG21 6XS.
Companies and representatives throughout the
world.

PALGRAVE MACMILLAN is the global academic imprint of the Palgrave Macmillan division of St. Martin's Press, LLC and of Palgrave Macmillan Ltd. Macmillan® is a registered trademark in the United States, United Kingdom and other countries. Palgrave is a registered trademark in the European Union and other countries.

ISBN-13: 978–1–4039–7896–7 paperback
ISBN-10: 1–4039–7896–4 paperback

Library of Congress Cataloging-in-Publication Data is available from the Library of Congress

Hibbert, Christopher, 1924–
    Disraeli : the Victorian Dandy who became prime minister / Christopher Hibbert.
        p. cm.
    Includes bibliographical references and index.
    ISBN 1–4039–7270–2 (cloth)
        1. Disraeli, Benjamin, Earl of Beaconsfield, 1804–1881. 2. Great Britain—Politics and government—1837–1901. 3. Prime ministers—Great Britain—Biography. I. Title.

DA564.B3H5 2006
941.081092—dc22
[B]   2006041220

First published in 2005 by Harper Perennial

First PALGRAVE MACMILLAN paperback edition: June 2007

10 9 8 7 6 5 4 3 2 1

Printed in the United States of America.

For John Rae
with affection

CONTENTS

Photosection appears between pages 180 and 181.

ILLUSTRATIONS

Daniel Maclise's "The author of Vivian Grey." © *John Hammond/ The National Trust Photographic Library*

C. Bone. Watercolor of Disraeli in 1828. © *National Portrait Gallery*

Mary Anne Disraeli in 1840 by A. E. Chalon. © *John Hammond/ The National Trust Photographic Library*

Sir Leslie Ward's cartoon of Disraeli with his secretary. © *Nick Pollard National Trust Photographic Library*

Confidential Letter to private secretary Montague Corry, *Dep. Hughenden 41/1, fols 88–9*

Pages from Disraeli's Mutilated Diary. *Dep. Hughenden 11/1/4, pp. 18–19*

Disraeli when Chancellor of the Exchequer by Sir Francis Grant. © *John Hammond/The National Trust Photographic Library*

A caricature of "Dizzy" in *The Hornet* of 19 July 1871.

A caricature of Dizzy in the Hornet of 19 July 1871. © *John Johnson Collection, Political General 1(33)/Bodeleian Library, University of Oxford*

Queen Victoria visits Disraeli at Hughenden. © *Mary Evan Pictures Library*

The Earl of Beaconsfield in 1877, a portrait after Von Angeli. © *John Hammond/The National Trust Photographic Library*

Disraeli in the House of Lords with Montagu Corry looking over his shoulder. An engraving after a sketch by Harry Furniss

ACKNOWLEDGEMENTS

For their help in a variety of ways I wish to thank the late Lord Blake, my editor in the US, Alessandra Bastagli, Richard Johnson of HarperCollins in the UK, Bruce Hunter of David Higham Associates, Dr Francis Sheppard, Dr Philip Unwin, Captain Gordon Fergusson, Diana Cook, Richard Ogden, the National Trust's property manager at Hughenden Manor, Christopher Hurley of the London Library, the editors of the *Benjamin Disraeli Letters*, University of Toronto, the staff of the Bodleian Library, University of Oxford and Helen Langley, Head of Modern Political Papers at the Bodleian Library.

Juliet Davis helped me choose the illustrations for the book and Marian Reid edited it, while Emily Leithauser secured the files and rights for the art in the US edition. Hamish Francis has been good enough to read the proofs and my wife has made the comprehensive index.

CHRISTOPHER HIBBERT

PART ONE

1804–46

I

BOYHOOD

'He had a taste, not uncommon
among schoolboys, for little acts of
bargaining and merchandise.'

IN CONVERSATION WITH HIS FRIEND, Lord Barrington, Benjamin
Disraeli once observed, 'I was born in a set of chambers in the Adelphi
– I may say in a library, for all my father's rooms were full of books.'
Like many of the accounts he gave in later years of his family, his
childhood and youth, this was not, in fact, true. His father's rooms were
certainly full of books, which Isaac D'Israeli, a bibliophile if not a great
scholar, would take pleasure in arranging and rearranging, constantly
adding to his collection until it numbered no fewer than twenty-five
thousand volumes, taking notes from them on scraps of paper which
he would tuck between their leaves, peering at the print shortsightedly,
his eyes behind thick spectacles, his chin concealed behind the folds of
his white neckcloth, a small black velvet cap over his long curly hair,
emerging from his library to talk loquaciously and disjointedly over his
meals.

His eldest son, Benjamin, was not, however, born in these chambers
in the Adelphi which the Adam brothers had built on land granted to
them by the Duke of St Albans not long before. Isaac D'Israeli had lived
there as a bachelor; but, not long after his marriage, he had moved to
Bloomsbury, to 6 King's Road, Bedford Row, now 22 Theobald's Road,
and it was here, in a house overlooking Gray's Inn Garden, that Benjamin
was born at half past five on the morning of 21 December 1804.

On the eighth day of his life, a large group of men in black hats and morning coats assembled at 6 King's Road for the celebration of the *brit milah*, the circumcision. The baby was placed on one of the two ceremonial chairs which had been brought over from the Bevis Marks synagogue, the other being occupied by the baby's paternal grandfather. The *mohel*, the child's uncle, then performed the operation. After prayers had been said, the baby was returned to the women, who were waiting with coffee, wine, tea and cakes in a nearby room. Here also was Benjamin's small sister, Sarah, whose second birthday was to be celebrated the following day.[1]

For these relations Benjamin was to provide an exotic and largely fictitious ancestry. They were, he liked to think and to say, of Italian descent 'from one of those Hebrew families whom the Inquisition forced to emigrate from the Spanish Peninsula at the end of the fifteenth century, and who found a refuge in the more tolerant territories of the Venetian republic . . . They assumed the name of DISRAELI, a name never borne before, or since, by any other family, in order that their race might be for ever recognised . . . They flourished as merchants for more than two centuries under the protection of the Lion of St Mark.'[2]

Proud of his Jewish ancestry, Disraeli, in his novel, *Contarini Fleming,* was to ask if the 'mixed population of Saxons and Normans, among whom he had first seen the light of day, was of purer blood than he? Oh no, he was descended in a direct line from one of the oldest races in the world, from that rigidly separate and unmixed Bedouin race who had developed a high civilization at a time when the inhabitants of England were going half-naked and eating acorns in their woods.'

What at least could be said for certain about his forebears was that Disraeli's grandfather, also Benjamin, and spelling the name D'Israeli, came to England at the age of eighteen in 1748, the twenty-first year of the reign of King George II, leaving behind two sisters who presided over a school for fellow-Jews in the Venetian ghetto.

A bright young man, Benjamin D'Israeli soon found employment in a Jewish firm in Fenchurch Street which imported goods from Italy. After working for this firm for some years, he married a Spanish Jewess – whose family, so his grandson liked to suppose, was far more distinguished than it was – and, soon afterwards, he set up his own business as an importer of coral and of those fashionable straw hats from Leghorn so often to be seen in portraits of young ladies by Thomas Gainsborough.

His wife having died in 1764, Benjamin D'Israeli married again within four months and, as with the first wife, his grandson chose to ascribe to the second a more distinguished lineage than she possessed. She was a grumpy, dispiriting woman and her grandson – comparing her to those imperious women, Catherine the Great, Sarah, Duchess of Marlborough and the loftily intimidating Frances Anne, Marchioness of Londonderry – ever afterwards recalled the dreaded weekly visits to her house where there was 'no kindness, no tea, no tips – nothing'. In her eighty-third year she came to stay in her son's house and behaved in a kindly manner that astonished all. 'Depend upon it,' her daughter-in-law suggested with well-founded prescience, 'she is going to die.'

After an initially unsuccessful diversification of his business into that of financial speculation, Benjamin D'Israeli became sufficiently prosperous as a stockbroker to buy an impressive country house, attributed to Sir Christopher Wren, at Enfield, where his grandson described him as eating macaroni with his dear friend Sir Horace Mann, for forty-six years British envoy at Florence, although, in fact, the Mann referred to was Sir Horace's nephew and heir, Horatio, Member of Parliament for Sandwich.

After a contented life, which would have been even more so had not his second wife been almost as difficult and demanding as his first, Benjamin D'Israeli, known to his neighbours as 'Old Mr Israel', died in 1816, leaving what was then an extremely large fortune of £35,000 which, in today's terms, would have been worth well over £1 million.

His only son, Isaac D'Israeli, was then forty years old. He had been a difficult, rather morose child, showing little or no interest in his father's business and apparently, on one occasion, had run away from home and been found lying on a tombstone in Hackney churchyard. His kindly father, profoundly relieved, hugged him and gave him a pony, much, no doubt, to the annoyance of his stricter mother who firmly believed that to spare the rod was to spoil the child.[3] It was evidently through her influence that the boy was taken away from the school near his family's house at Enfield and sent to work in the counting-house of his father's agent in Amsterdam and thence to a firm in Bordeaux. Having shown not the least aptitude for business, taking no interest in politics which he claimed not to understand, and, in the words of his son, Benjamin, being 'lost in reverie and . . . seeking no better company than a book', he declared that he had written a poem celebrating the evils of business and that he had decided to become a man of letters, despite the ridicule which his mother poured upon the idea. The death of his maternal grandmother, who bequeathed him a handsome legacy, enabled him to fulfil his ambition.[4]

He was certainly industrious and, despite the diffidence of his manner, assuming. He left one of his poems at Bolt Court for the approval of Samuel Johnson, who was too ill to take notice of it; he approached Vicesimus Knox, master of Tonbridge Grammar School, with the suggestion that he might become a clerkly member of his household in the medieval manner; he sent examples of his work to the topographer and antiquary, Richard Gough; he sought the patronage of Henry James Pye, the future Poet Laureate, whose talents, slender as they were, had been recognized by the Prime Minister, William Pitt, for his support in the House of Commons; and he made the acquaintance of Samuel Rogers, the witty poet and generous host. He also met the antiquary, Francis Douce, on one of his regular visits to the British Museum.

Poems and plays, novels, short stories, oriental romances, satires, biographies and book reviews flowed from his pen as well as publications with such titles as *An Essay on the Literary Character*; *A Dissertation on Anecdotes*; *Miscellanies or Literary Recollections*; *Calamities of Authors*; *Genius of Judaism*, and *Curiosities of Literature*. This last, a collection of sketches, anecdotes and brief essays on all manner of subjects from 'Men of Genius Deficient in Conversation' to 'The Custom of Saluting after Sneezing', was the most successful of all his books and was reissued in its twelfth edition in 1841.

Samuel Rogers said of him, 'There is a man with only half an intellect who writes books that must live';[5] and, while never renowned for his wit or striking intelligence, Isaac D'Israeli was a welcome enough guest at such dinner tables as that of the publisher, John Murray, while Sir Walter Scott flattered and astonished him by repeating some of his verses when first introduced to him.

Byron was another admirer. Having read *Quarrels of Authors*, he described it as being 'most entertaining'; and he told Murray, after reading and annotating a copy of the diligent author's *Essay on the Literary Character*, 'I have a great respect for Israeli and his talents, and have been amused by them greatly and instructed often . . . I don't know a living man's book I have taken up so often or lay down more reluctantly than Israeli's.'

When the two men first met, Byron treated him with so much respect that D'Israeli thought he was being teased. 'The fact is', he wrote complacently, 'that my works being all about literary men were exceedingly interesting to him. They contained knowledge that he could get nowhere else. It was all new to him.'[6]

By the time of the appearance of the twelfth edition of *Curiosities of Literature*, Isaac D'Israeli had become an easily recognized figure in the streets of Bloomsbury. Some years before, an American author, who saw him from time to time in the British Museum, described him as being 'a dapper little gentleman in bright coloured clothes, with a chirping, gossipy expression of countenance, who had all the appearance of an author on good terms with his bookseller'.

He was also by then a contented family man. At the age of thirty-five he had married Maria Basevi, the pretty daughter of an Italian Jew, a merchant in a good way of business, who had come to England from Verona in 1762. Maria's mother was of distinguished Jewish stock, one of whose illustrious forebears was a leader of the great exodus of his race from Spain in 1492. Maria's son, Ben, was extremely proud of his Jewish ancestry, considering himself of highly aristocratic birth, exaggerating, in a characteristically romantic way, the family's past glories and – unaware of his mother's distinguished descent – making unwarranted claims for that of his father.[7]

His mother's nephew was George Basevi, the architect, whose works included the Fitzwilliam Museum at Cambridge and large parts of Belgravia in London which his cousin, Benjamin Disraeli, was unfairly to condemn as being 'as monotonous as Marylebone, and so contrived as to be at the same time insipid and tawdry'.

Maria D'Israeli's first child, Sarah, was born in December 1802; two years later came Benjamin, then three more boys, none of whom became in any way distinguished. Napthali died in infancy; Ralph, five years younger than Benjamin, was born in 1809; James, known as Jem, born in 1813, was almost ten years younger.

Benjamin had little in common with either of these two surviving brothers. To his sister, however, he was as devoted as she was to him; and he was to write to her with a fond and frank intimacy which endured until her death.

Benjamin was also deeply and unreservedly attached to his father, of whom he wrote affectionately, 'He was a complete literary character ... Even marriage produced no change; he rose to enter the chamber where he lived alone with his books, and at night his lamp was ever lit within the same walls ... He disliked business, and he never required relaxation ... If he entered a club, it was only to go into the library. In the country he scarcely ever left his room but to saunter in abstraction upon a terrace, muse over a chapter, or coin a sentence.'[8]

When he was six years old, Benjamin was sent to a school in Islington kept by a Miss Roper; and from there he went to a school in Blackheath kept by a nonconformist minister, John Potticary, who numbered several Quakers among his pupils as well as at least one Jew with whom Benjamin was required to stand at the back of the class during Christian prayers. On Saturdays these two Jewish boys were also singled out to receive instruction from a Hebrew rabbi. At the end of term, so one of his fellow pupils said, 'Disraeli went home for the holidays in the basket of the Blackheath coach, [firing] away at the passers-by with his pea-shooter'.[9]

There is no record of Benjamin's father having objected to his son's instruction in the faith of his ancestors by the rabbi at Blackheath. But when, in 1813, Isaac was elected warden of the Bevis Marks synagogue, he declined to take office. A fine of £40 was imposed, he refused to pay it, requiring the elders to accept that 'a person who had lived out of the sphere of [their] observations, of retired habits of life who [could] never unite in [their] public worship, because, as now conducted, it disturbed instead of excited religious emotions ... Such a man never could accept the solemn function of an elder of your congregation'.

Having broken with the synagogue, Isaac might well have allowed the matter to rest there, content for his son to be the non-practising Jew that he was himself. But a friend, Sharon Turner, a fellow frequenter of the British Museum, a solicitor, historian, devout Anglican and adviser on legal matters to the publisher John Murray, persuaded him to allow his four children to be baptised. The ceremony of baptism accordingly took place at St Andrew's, Holborn on the last day of July 1817. Benjamin was then twelve years old.

His brothers were to go to Winchester, the public school founded in 1382 by William of Wykeham; and it seems that their father would have liked his eldest son to go to Eton. But it was, perhaps, as with the mother in *Vivian Grey*, that Ben's mother – being 'one of those women whom nothing in the world can persuade that a public school is anything but a place where boys are roasted alive' – was firmly against this proposal and, as was commonly the case, her views prevailed. So Benjamin was sent instead to Higham Hall, a school near Walthamstow in Epping Forest which was kept by the nonconformist minister and Greek scholar, the Revd Eli Cogan, and at which, as at all similar schools in those days, the classics, with a little arithmetic, formed almost the only, and certainly the main, subject on the curriculum.

According to Mr Cogan, Benjamin did not shine as a scholar. 'I do not like D'Israeli,' Cogan was quoted as having said. 'I never could get him to understand the subjunctive.'

'I looked up to him as a big boy,' an elderly clergyman said, recalling his days at school with Disraeli, 'and very kind he was to me, making me sit next to him in play hours, and amusing me with stories of robbers and caves, illustrating them with rough pencil sketches which he continually rubbed out to make way for fresh ones. He was a very rapid reader, was fond of romances, and would often let me sit by him and read the same book, good-naturedly waiting before turning a leaf till he knew I had reached the bottom of the page.'

Other former pupils remembered Ben as a lively, carefree boy who took scant trouble over his lessons, who amused his companions on wet half-holidays by reciting romantic adventures of his own composition, and who 'had a taste, not uncommon among schoolboys, for little acts of bargaining, and merchandise'.[10] Much later, Cogan's daughter told Beatrix Potter that the boy Disraeli 'used to keep the other boys awake half the night romancing'.

But Benjamin seems not to have been happy at Mr Cogan's, and if the schooldays of Contarini Fleming and Vivian Grey as described in his novels can be supposed to bear some resemblance to his own, they were certainly far from being contented ones. However, in his early days at the school, his idiosyncracies seem to have been tolerated at least: it was recorded of him that he suggested that he and his fellow Anglicans – who, having to walk some way to the local church and back to attend morning service, were late for dinner, which was half over by the time they returned to the school – should therefore become Unitarians during term time.

In *Vivian Grey*, the eponymous hero does not acquire the classical knowledge which has been dinned into the heads of the other boys but in 'talents and various accomplishments' he is 'immeasurably the superior of them'. This leads him into a fight with another boy which is described with a lyricism and an evident pride in the author's boxing skills acquired in those lessons which Disraeli was given in the holidays at home.

There is a great fight also in *Contarini Fleming* in which the hero enjoys a passionate friendship with another boy, a boy of sublimely beautiful countenance named Musaeus, after the semi-legendary poet whose verses had the authority of oracles.

> 'I beheld him: I loved him [Disraeli has Fleming say]. My friendship was a passion ... Oh! days of rare and pure felicity, when Musaeus and myself, with arms around each other's neck, wandered together ... I lavished on him all the fanciful love that I had long stored up; and the mighty passions that yet lay dormant in my obscure soul now first began to stir...'[11]

So Contarini endures the homosexual yearnings of youth but his passion for Musaeus soon cools and he, like Vivian Grey, is provoked into a fight which he wins. Thereafter he is shunned and persecuted by the other boys, as, no doubt, Disraeli was himself for being so obviously Jewish, as well as foppish with his ringlets and dandified clothes.

To his obvious relief he was taken away from Mr Cogan's school when he was fifteen years old and allowed to continue his studies at home.

> Questions have been sometimes raised as to the extent of Disraeli's classical acquirements [wrote his biographer, William Flavelle Monypenny], and he has been accused in this connexion of pretending to knowledge which he did not really possess. The truth would seem to be that he contrived at this time to make himself

a fair Latin scholar and retained in after life a moderate familiarity with the great Roman authors; but that his Greek was scanty at the beginning, and, in spite of his efforts after leaving school, remained scanty to the end.

He was conscientious in his studies, keeping a notebook in which he recorded his progress, listing the works he read and his precociously confident opinions of them. In one week he mentions having read Lucien and Livy, Terence and Virgil, Webb 'on the Greek metres – the author is not very profound' – and the 'sensible preface of M. [J.-F.] Marmentel to the Henriade'. 'Prepared my Greek,' he goes on. 'Finished the Speech of Camillus . . . made Latin verses . . . writing . . . ciphering . . . grammar.' 'Euripides,' his notes continued. 'Latin exercises. Drawing. Began with myself the *Iliad* . . . Again at the Greek metres – bewildered! – lost! . . . Gibbon, vol ix . . . Demosthenes is indeed irresistible . . . Read [William] Mitford's *History of Greece*. His style is wretched, scarcely English.' From one of the books he read, he copied out a passage from Petrarch and wrote it on the end-paper: 'I desire to be known to posterity; if I cannot succeed, may I be known to my own age, or at least to my friends.'[12]

He had already made up his mind, so he afterwards declared, that he would one day make his way into the House of Commons; and his brother, Ralph, related how fond he was of 'playing Parliament', always reserving for himself the part of Prime Minister or at least of a senior member of the Cabinet, relegating his siblings to the benches of the Opposition.

Lord Byron, Sir Walter Scott and Samuel Rogers were but three of the literary men whom Isaac D'Israeli met at John Murray's house in Albemarle Street, the great literary salon of Regency London. Also to be encountered here were Byron's intimate friend, the Irish writer, Tom Moore, and the prolific author, Robert Southey, who said that Isaac D'Israeli looked like 'a Portugee, who being apprehended for an assassin, is convicted of being circumcised. I don't like him.' He grew to love him, however; he was, he eventually decided, 'the strangest mixture of information, cleverness and folly'.

When he was considered old enough, Ben D'Israeli was occasionally taken by his father to these dinners at Murray's, and he gave a description of one of them:

November 27th 1822. Wednesday. Dined at Murray's ... Moore [who had recently returned from abroad] very entertaining.

Moore. This is excellent wine, Murray.

D'Israeli. You'll miss the French wines.

M. Yes, the return to port is awful.

D. I am not fond of port, but really there is a great deal of good port in England, and you'll soon get used to it.

M. Oh! I've no doubt of it. I used to be very fond of port – but French wines spoil one for a while. The transition is too sudden from the wines of France to the port of Dover ...

D. Pray, is Lord Byron much altered?

M. Yes, his face has swelled out and he is getting fat; his hair is gray and his countenance has lost that 'spiritual expression' which he so eminently had. His teeth are getting bad, and when I saw him he said that if ever he came to England it would be to consult Wayte about them.

B.D. Who is since dead, and therefore he certainly won't come ...

M. I certainly was very much struck with an alteration for the worse. Besides, he dresses very extraordinarily.

D. Slovenly?

M. Oh, no! no! He's very dandified, and yet not an English dandy. When I saw him he was dressed in a curious foreign cap, a frogged great coat, and had a gold chain round his neck and pushed into his waistcoat pocket. I asked him if he wore a glass and he took it out, whereupon I found fixed to it a set of trinkets. He had also another gold chain tight round his neck, something like a collar. He had then a plan of buying a tract of land and living in South America. When I saw Scrope Davies and told him that Byron was growing fat he instantly said, 'Then he'll never come to England.' ...

M. Rogers is the most wonderful man in conversation that I know. If he could write as well as he speaks he would be matchless, but his faculties desert him as soon as he touches a pen.

D. It is wonderful how many men of talent have been so circumstanced.

M. Yes! Curran, I remember, began a letter to a friend thus: 'It seems that directly I take a pen into my hand it remembers and acknowledges its allegiance to its mother goose.' ...

D. Have you read the *Confessions of an Opium Eater*?

M. Yes.

D. It is an extraordinary piece of writing.

M. I thought it an ambitious style and full of bad taste.

D. You should allow for the opium. You know it is a genuine
work.

M. Indeed.

D. Certainly. The author's name is De Quincey. He lives at the
lakes. I know a gentleman who has seen him.

Murray. – I have seen him myself. He came to me on business
once ... There never was a man so ignorant of the world's
ways.[13]

The conversation at Murray's often turned to Byron, and it was
upon the romantic poet that the young Disraeli, as he grew into man-
hood, chose to model himself, both in his clothes and in his dandiacal
gestures as suggested in the portrait of him, drawn some time later, by
Daniel Maclise. In this portrait he is depicted leaning on a chimney-
piece, beringed left hand on hip, right hand playing with his luxuriant
curled hair.

A YOUNG MAN OF
HIGH FASHION

'You have too much genius for
Frederick's Place. It will never do.'

DISRAELI WAS SEVENTEEN YEARS OLD when he began to record the conversations in Murray's dining-room. He had already become an occasional consultant of the publisher, who from time to time sought his advice on manuscripts that were sent to 50 Albemarle Street in the hope of their acceptance for publication; and it was on Disraeli's recommendation that Murray published *Fairy Legends and Traditions in the South of Ireland* by the Irish antiquary, Thomas Crofton Croker, a book highly praised by Sir Walter Scott, which became a bestseller.

By then Disraeli, as he had begun to sign himself, dropping the apostrophe, had become an articled pupil in a leading firm of solicitors in Frederick's Place, Old Jewry. The senior partner, Thomas Maples, was a friend of Isaac D'Israeli; and it seems to have been agreed between them that, in due course, Benjamin should be admitted into partnership and marry Maples's daughter.

Benjamin himself had not been at all taken with this arrangement; but his father was 'very warm' about the business. Indeed, it was 'the only time in his life', so his son records, 'in which he exerted authority'. Benjamin accordingly went to work in the office of one of the partners, Mr Stevens, who, Benjamin recalled, 'dictated to me every day his correspondence which was as extensive as a Minister's; and when the clients arrived I did not leave the room, but remained not only to learn my business but to become acquainted with my future clients. They were in general men of great importance – bank directors, East India directors, merchants . . . it gave me great facility with my pen and no inconsiderable knowledge of human nature.'[1]

Disraeli, however, became 'pensive and restless'. He could not reconcile himself to the thought of being a lawyer; and when he returned to Bloomsbury Square of an evening he did not take up the legal textbooks which he was meant to be studying, but helped himself to more interesting books from the tightly packed shelves of his father's library.

When he went out in the evening he was careful not to dress as the articled clerk he was determined not long to be, setting himself apart from his colleagues by a style of dress – a black velvet suit with ruffles and black stockings with red clocks – as well as a manner which was considered flamboyant, even in those early years of the reign of King George IV. 'You have too much genius for Frederick's Place,' a lady pleased him by suggesting one day. 'It will never do.'[2]

His manner, so another lady remarked, was entirely fitted to his 'rather conspicuous attire' and his theatrical gestures as he 'delivered himself of high-flown compliments and sharp asides'. He performed his duties in Frederick's Place adequately; but, like Charles Dickens, who was to start work in a smaller firm of solicitors a few years later, he yearned for other things. The books he read in his father's library, the distinguished men he met at work and the conversations he had heard at Murray's dinner table stirred his imagination and ambition. He felt himself worthy of a more dramatic future than that promised by the testaments and conveyances and ledgers of Frederick's Place, Old Jewry.

Visitors to the house at 6 Bloomsbury Square, where his family had moved in 1817, described him as looking as though he were bored to death by the life that was led there. William Archer Shee, then a boy some years younger than himself, who had come to a children's party at the D'Israelis' house, recalled seeing him 'in tight pantaloons with his hands in his pockets, looking very *pale*, *bored* and *dissatisfied*, and evidently wishing that we were all in bed. He looked like Gulliver among the Lilliputians, suffering from chronic dyspepsia.'[3]

In the office as well as at home, Disraeli spent as much time as he could in writing to please himself rather than the partners of Messrs Swain, Stevens, Maples, Pearse and Hunt. One of the earliest, if not perhaps the first, of his completed productions was a melodramatic play in verse, *Rumpel Stilts Kin*, based on the German folk tale about a deformed dwarf, Rumpelstiltskin, written in collaboration with William George Meredith, his sister Sarah's rather staid and tedious fiancé, an undergraduate at Oxford and heir to a rich uncle.

A few months after *Rumpel Stilts Kin* was finished – and perhaps performed by the D'Israeli and Meredith families – Disraeli delivered to John Murray the manuscript of a novel to which he had given the title *Aylmer Papillon*, a short work intended, as its author said, to be a satire on 'the present state of society'. Murray evidently did not rate the novel very highly but, reluctant to offend his young protégé, could not bring himself to write a letter of rejection. After a month had elapsed, Disraeli approached the publisher again; and, alluding impertinently to Murray's burning of Byron's *Memoirs* as being too salacious for publication, Disraeli wrote, 'And, as you have some small experience in burning MSS, you will perhaps be so kind as to consign [mine] to the flames.'[4]

In the summer of 1824, Benjamin, by now aged nineteen, and his father, both of whom had been in indifferent health of late, decided to go away for six weeks on holiday on the Continent with Sarah's fiancé, William Meredith, who by then had taken his degree at Oxford. They went by steamer to Ostend and thence by diligence to Bruges, where Benjamin wrote the first of several long letters to his sister describing the places they visited, the sights they saw and, in some detail, the meals they ate. Both Benjamin and his father were enthusiastic trenchermen and Sarah was regaled with accounts of memorable meals which they enjoyed in the *estaminets* on their route through the Low Countries and the Rhine Valley.

Writing from Antwerp on 2 August, Benjamin told Sarah that 'the hostess' at Ghent had seemed 'particularly desirous to give us a specimen of her cookery and there was a mysterious delay. Enter the waiter. A *fricandeau*, the finest I ever tasted, perfectly admirable, a small and very delicate roast joint, veal chops, a large dish of peas most wonderfully fine, cheese, a dessert, a salad pre-eminent even among the salads of Flanders which are unique for their delicate crispness and silvery whiteness ... Cost only six francs, forming one of the finest specimens of exquisite cookery I ever witnessed.'

In Antwerp, the travellers stayed at the Grand Laboureur where there was unfortunately no table d'hôte, but they enjoyed 'capital private feeds . . . the most luxurious possible'. 'And my mother', he added, 'must really reform her table before our return. I have kept a journal of dinners for myself, and in doings in general for my father, so I shall leave the account of churches, cathedrals and cafés till we come home . . . love to Mère and all, Your affectionate Brother, B. Disraeli.'

'The dinner was good,' he added after describing with enthusiasm the pictures by Rubens in the Museum at Antwerp. 'The Grand Laboureur is *un hôtel pour les riches*. The vol au vent of pigeons was admirable. The peas were singularly fine.' The table d'hôte at the Belle Vue in Brussels was equally commendable – 'dinner excellent – frogs – *pâté de grenouilles* – magnificent! – sublime'. He was most thankful that the English at the table d'hôte in Brussels shared a 'vulgar but lucky prejudice against frogs. So had the pâté to myself,' he recorded in his journal. 'Eat myself blind.' At Mechlin, the 'oysters were as small as shrimps but delicately sweet'. 'We always put up at the crack hotels,' he wrote from Mainz, 'and live perfectly *en prince*. The Governor allows us to debauch to the utmost, and Hochheimer, Johannisberg, Rudesheimer, Assmannshauser and a thousand other varieties are unsealed and floored with equal rapidity.' At Frankfurt, the 'Gâteau de Pouche' was 'superb beyond conception'.[5]

Occasionally Disraeli's accounts of their travels were more than a little facetious. Describing their crossing by steamer to Ostend, he writes: 'We had a very stiff breeze, and almost every individual was taken downstairs save ourselves who bore it all in the most manly and magnificent manner . . . The Governor was quite frisky on landing, and on the strength of mulled claret, etc., was quite the lion of Ostend . . . We rode on the Spa ponies to the distant springs . . . The Governor was particularly equestrian . . . I have become a most exquisite billiard player . . . Meredith and I talk French with a mixture of sublimity and *sang-froid* perfectly inimitable.'[6]

The sketches he provided for Sarah of individuals his party came across in their travels are more entertaining. He tells her, for instance, about an Irish tourist 'who would have made an inimitable hero for [the comedian, Charles] Mathews. It was his first debut on the Continent, and, with a most plentiful supply of ignorance and an utter want of taste ... I met him two or three times afterwards in different places, and his salutations were exceedingly rich. It was always "How do you do, Sir. Wonderful city this, Sir, wonderful! Pray have you seen the Crucifixion by Vandyke, wonderful picture, Sir, wonderful picture, Sir". '[7]

At Darmstadt, Disraeli sees the Grand Duke at a performance of *Otello*. He is an 'immense amateur'. His 'royal box is a large *pavillon* of velvet and gold in the midst of the theatre. The Duke himself in grand military uniform gave the word for the commencement of the overture, standing up all the time, beating time with one hand and watching the orchestra through an immense glass with the other.'

Occasionally, the diary reveals some inner thought or emotion:

> Ghent, Sunday – High Mass. A dozen priests in splendid unity. Clouds of incense and one of Mozart's sublimest Masses by an orchestra before which San Carlo might grow pale. The effect is inconceivably grand. The host raised and I flung myself on the ground.[8]

In another entry in his journal he wonders if German beggars would prove to be even more tiresome than Belgian ones: 'But the traveller is well trained in Flanders ... for your carriage never leaves an inn yard without a crowd of supplicating attendants and three old women, a dozen young ones, half a dozen men and all the children of the village attending you on your whole journey. The old women seem to have the best breath.'

There is, in the diary, a rare political observation. 'The Belgians', he wrote, 'seem extremely hostile against the Dutch. It may be questioned whether, in case of a war, they may not rebel against the present authorities.'

This seems to have been the first comment of its kind that he made. He had not at that time seriously considered a career in politics. He had, however, come to one decision that was to upset 'the Governor': 'I determined when descending those magical waters [of the Rhine] that I would not be a lawyer.' 'The hour of adventure had arrived. I was unmanageable.'[9]

Although determined not to return to the office in Frederick's Place, or to go up to Oxford as his father had wanted him to do, Benjamin, on his return to London, did submit to his father's wishes by not abandoning his legal training altogether: he followed Meredith in reading for the bar at Lincoln's Inn. But he did not relish the thought of becoming a barrister any more than he had taken to the idea of becoming a solicitor. 'Pooh!' he has his character Vivian Grey say. 'Pooh! THE BAR! Law and bad jokes till we are forty, and then, with the most brilliant success, the prospect of gout and a coronet. Besides, to succeed as an advocate, I must be a great lawyer, and, to be a great lawyer, I must give up my chance of being a great man.'[10] And, as though to emphasize his rejection of the idea of becoming successful as an advocate, he appeared one day in the Old Square chambers of his precise and pedantic cousin, Nathaniel Basevi, with a copy of Edmund Spenser's *Faerie Queene* prominently displayed.

He was soon to decide that 'in England personal distinction is the only passport to the society of the great. Whether the distinction arises from fortune, family or talent is immaterial; but certain it is, to enter high society, a man must either have blood, a million or be a genius.' He also decided that he himself must have both '*Riches and Power*'.

On his return to England Disraeli had found London's financial houses and moneyed classes excited by that prospect of making such fortunes as they had hoped to do at the time of the fever of speculation resulting in the financial crisis known as the South Sea Bubble in 1720. On this later occasion, the excitement arose from the perceived opportunity of acquiring great riches from the exploitation of the gold and silver mines of South America and the profits to be derived from such companies as the Columbian Mining Association, the Chilean Mining Association and the Anglo-Mexican Mining Association which were promoted by John Powles, a persuasive merchant banker of rather dubious reputation whom Disraeli had come across while working in Frederick's Place and who appears as the character Premium in *Vivian Grey*. 'It immediately struck me', Disraeli was later to say, 'that, if fortunes were ever to be made, this was the moment and I accordingly paid great attention to American affairs.'

He threw himself into the business of acquiring a fortune with almost demonic energy. Although he had so very little money of his own, he bought shares in South American companies on credit, and further shares on John Murray's behalf. The value of the shares increased enormously; but Disraeli declined to take an immediate profit in the hope of making yet more money; and then, inevitably, the share prices fell dramatically. Disraeli, however, remained optimistic and he wrote an anonymous and seriously misleading pamphlet, published by Murray, contradicting gloomy reports that drew a parallel between the present speculation and the South Sea Bubble. He produced accounts claiming that both he and John Murray had made handsome profits. He hoped to make more with money borrowed from both his uncle, George Basevi, and Robert Messer, the son of a rich stockbroker.

Not content with his endeavours to make a fortune, Disraeli planned at the same time to found a daily newspaper with the help of John Powles's money and John Murray's publishing expertise. With extraordinary rashness, Disraeli himself undertook to put up a quarter of the necessary capital. Meanwhile, he set out on the four-day journey to Scotland to see Sir Walter Scott and Scott's shy and crabby son-in-law, John Gibson Lockhart, a journalist who had trained as a lawyer, whom he hoped to persuade to become the proposed newspaper's editor. It was no wonder that he felt, as he told Robert Messer, 'acutely dizzy'.

He found both Scott and Lockhart initially wary of committing themselves to the fortunes of a non-existent newspaper; and Disraeli, spending almost three weeks in Scotland – and 'revelling in the various beauties of a Scotch breakfast of cold grouse and marmalade'[11] – did all he could to persuade them that the editor of this new paper would not be just an editor but the 'Director General of an Immense Organ and at the head of a band of high-bred gentlemen and important interests'. A seat in Parliament would also surely be found for him.

To give authority and encouragement to Disraeli's approach, John Murray wrote to Lockhart:

> I left my young friend Disraeli to make his own way with you
> ... But as you have received him with so much kindness and
> favour, I think it right to confirm my good opinion which you
> appear so early to have formed of him, by communicating to you
> a little of my own. And I may frankly say that I never met with a
> young man of greater promise ... He is a good scholar, hard
> student, a deep thinker, of great energy, equal perseverance and
> indefatigable application, and a complete man of business. His

knowledge of human nature ... [has] often surprised me in a young man who has hardly passed his twentieth year, and, above all, his mind and heart are as pure as when they were first formed.[12]

John Murray's high opinion of Disraeli was reinforced by the young man's father:

I know nothing against him but his youth, a fault which a few seasons of experience will infallibly correct; but I have observed that the habits and experience he has acquired as a lawyer often greatly serve him on matters of business. His views are vast, but they are based on good sense and he is most determinedly serious when he sets to work.[13]

A more cautious note was sounded by one of Murray's legal advisers, William Wright, who warned Lockhart that, while Disraeli was 'a clever young fellow', his judgement wanted 'settling down'. 'He has never had to struggle with a single difficulty,' Wright continued. 'Nor has he been called on to act in any affairs in which his mind has been necessarily forced to decide and choose in difficult circumstances. At present his chief exertions as to matters of decision have been with regard to the selection of his food, his enjoyment and his clothing. I take it that he is wiser than his father but he is inexperienced and untried in the world ... You cannot prudently trust much to his judgement.'[14]

Wright went on to suggest that 'whatever our friend D'Israeli [might] say ... on this subject', Lockhart's acceptance of the editorship of a newspaper 'would be *infra dig*, and a losing of caste'. This was 'not the case in being editor of a Review like the *Quarterly* [*Review*, Murray's Tory journal]. That was the office of a scholar and a gentleman.'

The longer Disraeli remained in Scotland, the closer he grew to Lockhart.* Scott, however, was less sure about the young man. He described him as a 'sprig of the rod of Aaron', 'a young coxcomb'; and, when Lockhart came down to London to meet Murray, the meeting

---

* The early friendship was not to survive. Lockhart was to remain editor of the *Quarterly* for twenty-eight years and, for all that time, did his best to ensure that Disraeli's name was not mentioned in it. When Disraeli's novel, *Coningsby*, was published in 1844, Lockhart commented, 'That Jew scamp has published a very blackguard novel' (Andrew Lang, *Life and Letters of J.G. Lockhart*, ii, 190; Robert Blake, *Disraeli*, 48).

with the publisher was not a success since Murray was rather drunk – as he not infrequently was in moments of stress.

Eventually, however, it was arranged that Lockhart, who declined the editorship of the proposed new newspaper, should become editor of the *Quarterly Review* at a handsome salary of £1,000 a year while at the same time contributing articles for an even more generous sum to the newspaper.

Meanwhile, Disraeli occupied himself with the establishment of this paper, writing to proposed correspondents in Britain and abroad,* searching for premises, settling upon a house in Great George Street as suitable offices, employing George Basevi as architect for their conversion, getting himself increasingly involved in matters his experience did not qualify him adequately to deal with, and making outrageously false claims as to the correspondents he had enlisted, including Dr Edward Copleston, Provost of Oriel College, Oxford; then, having suggested a name for the newspaper, *The Representative* – which made its long-delayed appearance in January 1825 – he had nothing more to do with it.[15]

Murray wished heartily that he had not had anything to do with it either. Editor followed editor of a newspaper which was a disaster from the beginning. After six months he had lost over £25,000 and felt compelled to call a halt. Publication ceased, its closure unlamented even by those few readers who had troubled to peruse its tedious pages.[16] Murray blamed Disraeli and, in *Vivian Grey*, Disraeli was later to describe a scene which was, no doubt, based on one which took place at 50 Albemarle Street and in which the character whom Murray took to be based upon himself 'raved' and 'stamped' and 'blasphemed', levelling 'abuse against his former "monstrous clever" young friend . . . who was now . . . an adventurer – a swindler – a young scoundrel – a base, deluding, flattering, fawning villain etc. etc. etc.'[17]

---

* A characteristically fulsome letter was that addressed to the proprietor of the Trierche Hof in Coblenz: 'My friend Mr Murray of Albemarle Street, London, the most eminent publisher that we have, is about to establish a daily journal of the first importance. With his great influence and connections there is no doubt that he will succeed in his endeavour to make it the focus of the information of the whole world. The most celebrated men in Europe have promised their assistance to Mr Murray in his great project. I wish to know whether you can point out any one to him who will occasionally write a letter to him from your city . . . You yourself would make a most admirable correspondent . . .' (*Benjamin Disraeli Letters*, 25 October 1825, i, 31).

Murray was obliged to give up his houses in Whitehall Place and Wimbledon and to move his family into rooms above his office in Albemarle Street, where he received a cross letter from Disraeli's mother defending her son from suggestions that *The Representative* had been ruined 'through his mismanagement' and 'bad conduct'. 'It would not be believed', she wrote, 'that the experienced publisher of Albemarle Street could be deceived by the plans of a boy of twenty whom you had known from his cradle and whose resources you must have as well known as his Father, and had you condescended to consult that Father the folly might not have been committed.'[18]

In the financial crash which followed the collapse of *The Representative*, Disraeli also suffered. He lost the very little money which he possessed and was left so deeply in debt that for years thereafter this increasing indebtedness hung hauntingly over him, and his reputation, such as it was, suffered from attacks like those launched upon him in the pages of the *Literary Magnet* where he was described as being 'deposed amidst the scoffs and jeers of the whole Metropolitan Literary World' after 'a display of puppyism, ignorance, impudence and mendacity which [had] seldom been exhibited under similar circumstances'.

Unable to pay his debts and reluctant to approach his father for help in settling them, Disraeli now decided to make some money in writing about the circumstances in which they had been incurred.

Disraeli began writing *Vivian Grey*, his satirical 'society' novel, with enthusiasm and energy, letting sheet after completed sheet fall to the floor; and when he had written enough for the book to be judged, he looked for a publisher, the one he knew being no longer approachable. *Tremaine, or the Man of Refinement*, 'a novel of fashionable life', had recently been published anonymously with some success. Its author was Robert Plumer Ward and its publisher the busy, chatty, energetic Henry Colburn.

Plumer Ward's rather dull and staid solicitor was Benjamin Austen, whose clever, attractive and lively young wife presided over a kind of literary and artistic salon at their house in Guildford Street, near to the D'Israelis' in Bloomsbury Square. Acting as Ward's agent, Sara Austen asked Isaac D'Israeli to review *Tremaine* and, in this way, Benjamin learned of Mrs Austen's activities.

He sent her what he had so far written of *Vivian Grey*, a novel in conscious imitation of Plumer Ward's *Tremaine*.

Mrs Austen expressed herself 'quite delighted'. 'I have gone through it twice,' she wrote, 'and the more I read it the better I am pleased.' She entered into 'the *spirit* of the book entirely'. She was 'in a state of complete excitation on the subject,' she wrote later. She was also attracted by its author. 'Remember', she wrote to him, sending the letter by a servant as though from her husband, 'that you have the entrée *whenever you like to come – at all hours* – in the morn[ing] I am generally alone.'

Disraeli immediately settled down to finish the book – which he dedicated to his father, 'the best and greatest of men' – sending it, chapter by chapter, to Mrs Austen who, editing it as she went along, copied it out in her own hand to protect the anonymity of the author who was supposed to be a gentleman well qualified to reveal the foibles and eccentricities of the beau monde. When enough had been written for her to approach a publisher, Sarah Disraeli sent the manuscript to Henry Colburn who, offering £300 for the copyright, made much of the supposed identity of the author. 'By the by,' Colburn said one day to the editor of a magazine in which he hoped the novel would be reviewed, 'I have a capital book out – *Vivian Grey*. The authorship is a great secret – a man of high fashion – very high – keeps the first society. I can assure you it is a most piquant and spirited work, quite sparkling.'[19]

The story is to a considerable extent autobiographical: Vivian Grey is the son of a literary man with a huge private income; he leaves school to read in his father's library; he sets out to impress the politically influential and treacherous Marquess of Carabas, whose resemblance, in certain respects, to John Murray, the publisher himself found insupportable and, in the end, unforgivable.

The first part of *Vivian Grey* was published on 22 April 1826 and reviewed at length by William Jerdan in the *Literary Gazette*, a magazine of which he was editor. The book sold well and was, in general, favourably reviewed, although Jerdan maintained that the anonymous author knew too little about society to have had much experience of it himself and too much about the literary world about which the 'mere man of fashion knows little and cares less'.

Everyone was talking about the book, Plumer Ward told Sara

Austen. 'Its wit, raciness and boldness are admired'; and it became a kind of literary game to identify the models on which various characters were based. Lord Brougham, George Canning, Lord Eldon, Lady Caroline Lamb, John Murray's German sister-in-law Mrs William Elliot, Harriot Mellon, the actress, wife of the banker Thomas Coutts, the playwright Theodore Hook, and J.G. Lockhart were all identified as being represented or caricatured in the book – as well, of course, as John Murray, the Marquess of Carabas, whose loquacity in his cups is clearly based on Murray's:

> Here the bottle passed, and the Marquess took a bumper. 'My Lords and Gentlemen, when I take into consideration the nature of the various interests, of which the body politic of this great empire is regulated; (Lord Courtown, the bottle stops with you) when I observe, I repeat, this, I naturally ask myself what right, what claims, what, what, what – I repeat what right, these governing interests have to the influence which they possess? (Vivian, my boy, you'll find the Champagne on the waiter behind you.) Yes, gentlemen, it is in this temper (the corkscrew's by Sir Berdmore), it is, I repeat, in this temper, and actuated by these views, that we meet together this day.'[20]

Murray threatened to go to law and might well have done so had not his friend, the solicitor Sharon Turner, advised against it. 'If the author were to swear to me that he meant the Marquess for you,' Turner assured Murray, 'I could not believe him. It is in all points so entirely unlike.' But Murray was unconvinced. He never invited Isaac D'Israeli to 50 Albemarle Street again; and never published another of his books. He turned his back on him and Mrs D'Israeli when he came across them in the street.

When the authorship of *Vivian Grey* became generally known, comment about it was far more wounding than it had been when Henry Colburn first published it. Instead of the well-informed authority which readers had been led to believe its author was, he was now revealed to be, in the words of *Blackwood's Magazine*, 'an obscure person, for whom nobody cares a straw'. He was, in fact, 'a swindler' in the words of the *Literary Magnet*, 'a swindler – a scoundrel – a liar . . . who, having heard that several horsewhips were preparing for him . . . had the meanness to call upon various persons who have been introduced in *Vivian Grey*, and deny, *upon his honour as a gentleman*, that he was the author of the book'.

Disraeli was particularly upset by the review in *Blackwood's*, and in a later novel he described his feelings upon reading it: 'With what horror, with what blank despair, with what supreme appalling astonishment did I find myself for the first time in my life the subject of the most reckless, the most malignant and the most adroit ridicule ... The criticism fell from my hand ... I felt that sickness of heart that we experience in our first scrape. I was ridiculous. It was time to die.'[21]

In the face of such attacks as that in *Blackwood's*, Disraeli fell ill. '*What is the matter?*', Sara Austen, who was by now half in love with him, wrote anxiously. 'My shaking hand will tell you that I am nervous with the shock of your illness ... For God's sake take care of yourself. I dare not say for my sake do so ... If without risk you can come out tomorrow, let me see you at twelve or at any hour which will suit you better. I shall not leave the house till I see you. I shall be miserably anxious till I do. My spirits are gone till you bring a renewal of them.'[22] When his doctor advised him against going out, Mrs Austen suggested that he went abroad for a time with her husband and herself.

Affecting to make light of the attacks on him and his book, Disraeli wrote to Austen's husband facetiously suggesting that, although he had left his last place 'on account of the disappearance of the silver spoons', he defied anyone to declare that he was not sober and honest, except when entrusted with the key of the wine cellar, when he had candidly to confess that he had 'an ugly habit of stealing the Claret, getting drunk and kissing the maids'.[23]

Despite the frivolous tone of this letter, Disraeli was deeply upset by the attacks to which he was subjected, not so much those upon his book as those upon him personally. He affected to be little concerned now or later about these attacks and allowed a new edition of the book, edited by his sister, to appear in 1853, maintaining most improbably that the characters in it were not drawn from life. Yet in the summer of 1826 he fell into an even deeper depression. He spent much of each day in his bedroom in Bloomsbury Square with the blinds drawn. On the verge of a nervous breakdown such as his father had once suffered, he welcomed the Austens' suggestion that they travel abroad together.

3

A CONTINENTAL HOLIDAY

'I feel now that it is not prejudice when I declare
that England with all her imperfections
is worth all the world together.'

HAVING READILY ACCEPTED the Austens' suggestion of a Continental holiday, Disraeli was equally ready to borrow the money to pay for it and, having made arrangements to do so, he wrote the first of his reports describing his journey to his father on 9 August:

> My dear Father,
> We reached Paris Sunday afternoon and are now in the Rue de Rivoli, the best situation here . . . Paris is delightful. I never was so much struck with anything in the whole course of my life . . . I expected another London but there are no points of resemblance. I did not expect in so short a distance to have met such a contrariety of manners and life . . .* I am going to the Louvre this morning and to the Opera this evening . . . I have not kept my journal, but of course shall . . . God bless you.
> Yours most affectionately,
> B. Disraeli.[1]

A fortnight or so later, on 21 August from Geneva, he wrote again, assuring his father that the 'unparalleled heat of the season' did not affect him in the least, and that he had not had 'a day's nor an hour's illness' since he had left England: he felt 'ten thousand times better' than he had done for the past three years. He would, no doubt, have

---

* Of the two cities, however, he preferred London, which was 'a mystery which could never be preconceived and which can never be exhausted'.

enjoyed the trip more had Austen been a more entertaining companion and had not Sara been so coyly flirtatious, so ready to speak French even more quickly than she did English, and had she not kept so critical an eye on the amount of Burgundy he drank while affecting to be amused by it.[2]

From Geneva, Disraeli wrote again to his father:

I take a row now every night with Maurice, Lord Byron's celebrated boatman [who] is very handsome and very vain, but has been made so by the English, of whom he is a regular pet . . . He talks of nothing but Lord Byron . . . He told me that in the night of the famous storm described in the third Canto of C[hilde] H[arold], had they been out five minutes more the boat must have been wrecked. He told Lord Byron of the danger of such a night voyage, and the only answer which B. made was stripping quite naked and folding round him a great *robe de chambre* so that in case of wreck he was ready prepared to swim immediately . . .

One day Byron sent for him and, sitting down in the boat, he put a pistol on each side (which was his invariable practice) and then gave him 300 napoleons, ordering him to row to Chillon. He then had two torches lighted in the dungeon and wrote for two hours and a half. On coming out, the *gendarme* who guarded the castle humbly asked for *quelque-chose à boire*. 'Give him a napoleon,' said his Lordship. '*De trop, milor,*' said Maurice, who being but recently installed in his stewardship was somewhat mindful of his master's interest. 'Do you know who I am?' rejoined the master, 'Give it to him and tell him that the donor is Lord Byron!' This wonderful piece of information must have produced a great effect on the poor miserable tippling *gendarme*. But in the slightest thing was Byron, by Maurice's account, most ludicrously ostentatious. He gave him one day five napoleons for a swimming race across the lake. At the sight of the club foot Maurice thought he was sure to win, but his Lordship gained by five minutes.

Byron, he says, was not a quick swimmer, but he was never exhausted, by which means he generally won when the distance was great. One morning Maurice called for him very early to swim. Byron brought to the boat his breakfast, consisting of cold duck, &c., and three or four bottles of wine, and then amused himself, while they were sailing to the appointed place, by throwing the provisions gradually into the water. Upon this, honest Maurice gently hinted that he had not himself breakfasted, and that he should swim much better if he had some portion of his

Lordship's superfluity. 'Friend Maurice,' said B., 'it ill becomes true Christians to think of themselves; I shall give you none. You see I eat no breakfast myself; do you refrain also for the sake of the fishes.' He then continued his donations to the pikes (which here are beautiful) and would not bestow a single crumb on his companion. 'This is all very well,' says Maurice, 'but his Lordship forgot one little circumstance. He had no appetite; I had.' He says that he never saw a man eat so little as B. in all his life, but that he would drink three or four bottles of the richest wines for his breakfast.[3]

According to Sara Austen, Disraeli also refused to stint himself with wine. 'He seems to enjoy everything,' she told his sister, 'and has just said High Mass for a *third* bottle of Burgundy.'[4]

'Mrs A[usten] is very well,' Disraeli reported in turn to his father. 'I hope to God my mother is better. Love to all.'

A fortnight or so later, Disraeli gave a further report to his father from Milan, describing the 'painfully sublime' scenery of the Alps which had also deeply impressed so many travellers from the north in the earlier days of the Grand Tour when one such tourist 'started with affright' as he obtained the first glimpse of their 'awful and tremendous amphitheatre'.

'We gazed till our eyes ached, and yet dared not withdraw them from the passing wonders,' Disraeli told his father, having driven across the Simplon Pass which had been created on Napoleon's orders some twenty-five years before. 'Nothing could be more awful than the first part of our passage; the sublimity of the scenery was increased by the partial mists and the gusts of rain. Nothing is more terrific than the near roar of a cataract which is covered by a mist. It is horrible.'[5]

The journey through the Alps was interrupted by an excursion to the Great St Bernard, so Disraeli recalled years later, and 'the brotherhood, on hearing that a young Englishman was in the hospice, expressed an anxious desire to see me, and I waited on the Superior. I found that all the anxiety arose from a desire to hear how the Thames Tunnel [work upon which had begun some years before and was not completed until 1843] had succeeded. I had to confess that I had never seen it, and I afterwards reflected that one must travel to learn what really is to be seen in one's own country, and resolved at once on my return to supply the omission. But, do you know, I have never seen it yet.'[6]

When we arrived at the summit of the road the weather cleared [Disraeli continued his account in his letter to his father] and we found ourselves surrounded by snow. The scenery here and for a mile or two before was perfect desolation, cataracts coursing down crumbled avalanches whose horrible surface was only varied by the presence of one or two blasted firs. Here in this dreary and desolate scene burst forth a small streak of blue sky, the harbinger of the Italian heaven. The contrast on descending into Italy is wonderfully striking . . . the purple mountains, the glittering lakes, the cupola'd convents, the many-windowed villas crowning luxuriant-wooded hills, the undulation of shore, the projecting headland, the receding bay, the roadside uninclosed, yet bounded with walnut and vine and fig and acacia and almond trees bending down under the load of their fruit, the wonderful effect of light and shade, the trunks of every tree looking black as ebony . . . the thousand villages each with a tall, thin tower, the large melons trailing over walls, and, above all, the extended prospect, are so striking after the gloom of alpine passes.[7]

By way of Lake Maggiore, Disraeli and his friends came upon Lake Como, 'a gem', the shore of which was 'covered with glittering palaces', one of which was the Villa d'Este, the residence of the late Queen Caroline, the detested, lubricious German wife of King George IV, whose antics with her major-domo and others of her entourage had led to her conduct being examined by the House of Lords.

'The Villa's apartments are left in exactly the same state' as she had left them to return to England to claim her rights as Queen five or so years before. 'There is the theatre in which she acted Columbine, and the celebrated statues of Adam and Eve carved with the yet more celebrated fig leaves. It is a villa of the first grade, and splendidly adorned, but the ornaments are, without an exception, so universally indelicate that it was painful to view them in the presence of a lady . . . Here, if they possessed any interest, might you obtain thousands of stories of her late Majesty, but the time is passed, thank God, for them. Our riots in her favour are the laughing stock of Italy.'[8]

Having examined everything worth seeing in Milan, and admired the dress of his fellow dandy Count Gicogna – 'the leader of the *ton* at Milan, a dandy of genius worthy of Brummell'[9] – Disraeli and his friends moved on to Brescia, then to Verona, which was, so he said, 'full of pictures which have never been painted', then on to Vicenza, where the 'famous Palladian palaces' were 'in decay' and disgustingly smelly. 'They are built of brick,' he wrote, 'sometimes plastered, occasionally *white-washed*; the red material is constantly appearing and vies in hideous colour with the ever offensive roof. It is a miserable thing that a man worthy of Athens or Rome should have worked with such materials.' The Villa Rotunda, which had served as a model for the Earl of Burlington's Chiswick House, was in an advanced state of dilapidation.

From Vicenza Disraeli and his friends set out for Padua and, following the course of the Brenta, arrived in Venice on 8 September as the sun was setting 'on a grand fête day'.

They took a gondola to their hotel, which was, so Disraeli told his father,

> once the proud residence of the Bernadinis, a family which has given more than one Doge to the old Republic;* the floors of our rooms were of marble, the hangings of satin, the ceilings, painted by Tintoretto and his scholars, full of Turkish triumphs and trophies, the chairs of satin and the gilding, though of two hundred years' duration, as brightly burnished as the new mosaic invention. After a hasty dinner we rushed to the mighty Place of St Mark. It was crowded. Two Greek and one Turkish ship of war were from accidental circumstances in port and their crews mingled with the other spectators ... Tired with travelling we left the gay scene but the moon was so bright that a juggler was conjuring in a circle under our window, and an itinerant Italian opera performing by our bridge. Serenades were constant during the whole night; indeed music is never silent in Venice. I wish I could give you an idea of the moonlight there, but that is impossible. Venice by moonlight is an enchanted city; the floods of silver light upon the moresco architecture, the perfect absence of all harsh sounds of carts and carriages, the never-ceasing music on the waters produced an effect on the mind which cannot be experienced, I am sure, in any other city in the world.[10]

The next five days were spent in sightseeing and, in a later letter to his father, Disraeli described his impressions of the Doges' Palace – in which 'in every room you are reminded of the glory and the triumphs of the republic' – and of St Mark's, that 'Christian mosque', 'a pile of

---

* Disraeli was misinformed about this: there are no Bernadinis in the list of Venetian Doges.

precious stones', outside which the four 'brazen horses' – not long since returned from Paris, having been looted on Napoleon's orders – '*amble, not prance as some have described them*'.

Napoleon had also given orders for the gates of the Ghetto to be pulled down and for the Jews to live where they liked. Many Jews had chosen to remain, however, and Disraeli's great-aunt was still living there. If he knew of her presence, he made no effort to seek her out; nor did he try to see his Basevi cousins in Verona; nor yet did he go to Cento where his grandfather had been born.

'According to common opinion,' however, Disraeli 'saw all that ought to be seen but never felt less inclined to quit a place' than he felt on leaving Venice for Bologna. On his way there he made an excursion to the tomb of Petrarch at Arqua and from Ferrara he went to Tasso's cell. 'The door posts of this gloomy dungeon are covered with the names of its visitors,' he wrote. 'Here scratched with a great nail on the brick wall I saw scrawled "Byron" and immediately beneath it, in a neat banker's hand was written "Sam Rogers".'*[11]

Reluctant as he had been to leave Bologna also, Disraeli found Florence 'a most delightful city' and astonishingly cheap; 'an English family of the highest respectability may live in Florence with every convenience and keep a handsome carriage, horses, liveries etc. for five hundred a year', that was to say in present-day terms about £17,000 a year.

'You may live in a palace built by Michael Angelo,' he continued, 'keep a villa two miles from the city in a most beautiful situation, with vineyards, fruit and pleasure gardens, keep *two* carriages, have your opera box, and live in every way as the first Florentine nobility, go to Court, have your own night for receiving company on less than a thousand a year.'[12]

'There are some clever artists and sculptors in Florence,' Disraeli told his father:

Among the latter since the death of Canova, Bertolini [Bartolini] is reckoned the most eminent in Italy.† He is a man of genius. I

---

* Samuel Rogers had been in Italy four years before. He was not overburdened with the business of the family bank in Cornhill.
† Bartolini's reputation has not outlived him.

had the honour of a long conversation with him . . . He is a friend of Chantrey but the god of his idolatry, and indeed of all Italians, is Flaxman.

    In one of my speculations I have been disappointed. In the Pitti Palace there is the most beautiful portrait of Charles I by Vandyke, the most pleasing and noble likeness that I have seen. It is a picture highly esteemed. I engaged a miniature painter here to make me an exquisite copy of this picture with which I intended to surprise you. After a week's work he has brought it today, but has missed the likeness! And yet he was the Court painter, Signor Carloni. I have refused to take the work and am embroiled in a row but in this country firmness is alone necessary and the Italians let you do what you like, so I've no fear as to the result. My mortification and disappointment, however, are extreme.[13]

This letter was written on 29 September 1826. The next was written in Turin on 10 October and in it, having given his impressions of Pisa – 'where the Cathedral and its more wonderful Baptistry, the leaning tower and the Campo Santo rivetted [his] attention' – he said that he expected to be at Dover on the 24th, having, according to Austen's calculations, travelled over two thousand miles, and his share of the expenses, including £20 for prints and other purchases, being no more than £150.[14] On 15 October he wrote to his sister from Lyons:

Nothing can have been more prosperous than our whole journey. Not a single *contretemps* and my *compagnons de voyage* uniformly agreeable. Everything that I wished has been realized. I have got all the kind of knowledge that I desired . . . I had a great row about the portrait of Charles 1st, but was quite successful. The consequence is that I have got a new miniature in which the likeness is exactly hit and at a cheaper rate . . . I am glad that I at last get some account of my mother – my best love to her; we must meet soon. My father says that he has been very idle and I fear from his tone that I am to believe him. I have been just the reverse, but I would throw all my papers into the Channel only to hear that he had written fifty pages.[15]

Mrs Austen, in a letter to Sarah D'Israeli, confirmed that the journey had passed without the least disagreement. 'Your brother is so easily pleased, so accommodating, so amusing, and so actively kind, that I shall always reflect upon the domestic part of our journey with the greatest pleasure.' Indeed, Benjamin, so Sara Austen said, had behaved 'excellently, except when there is a button, or rather buttons, to be put on his shirt; then he is violently bad, and this happens almost daily. I said once "They cannot have been good at first"; and now he always threatens to "tell my Mother you have abused my linen".'[16]

Travelling homewards through France, Disraeli and his friends left the main road to go to see the Layard family. Austen Henry Layard, the future excavator of Nineveh, was then nine years old. In later life he retained 'a vivid recollection' of Disraeli's appearance, 'his black curly hair, his affected manner and his somewhat fantastic dress'.[17]

His holiday was almost over now; and, as he approached the Channel, Disraeli congratulated himself upon having seen five capitals and twelve great cities, and, although he might well see more cities, he could not hope to see more 'varieties of European nature'. 'I feel now,' he added, 'that it is not prejudice when I declare that England with all her imperfections is worth all the world together, and I hope it is not misanthropy when I feel that I love lakes and mountains better than courts and cities, and trees better than men.'[18]

4

MENTAL BREAKDOWN

'I was bled, blistered, boiled, poisoned, electrified, galvanised;
and, at the end of the year, found myself with exactly
the same oppression on my brain.'

AFTER HIS RETURN TO LONDON, Disraeli continued to see much
of Sara Austen, with whom he went for walks in Bloomsbury and by
whom he was frequently invited to dinner at the Austens' house in
Guildford Street. He was working hard on the second part of *Vivian
Grey*, which, as with the first part, Mrs Austen copied out for him from
the hastily written sheets of paper on which the author's handwriting
was often so difficult to decipher that she had to make her own sense
of it.

When part two of the book was published in February 1827, it
did not arouse much enthusiasm. William Gladstone expressed a fairly
common opinion when he called 'the first quarter (*me jud.*) extremely
clever, the rest trash'.[1] Henry Crabb Robinson, the journalist, could not
bring himself to finish it and resolved not to try to read anything else
by the same author. The author himself conceded that it did not make
very satisfactory reading, and that in parts it was actually unintelligible
and, in general, fragmentary and formless. It did, however, contain
occasionally amusing remarks as, for instance, 'Like all great travellers,
I have seen more than I remember and remember more than I have
seen.'[2] Disraeli had grown tired of the character of Vivian Grey and in
part two he had created a new hero, Beckendorf, whom most readers
did not find convincing.

However, he received £500 from the publisher, Henry Colburn, for this sequel to the book, and was consequently able to settle an outstanding bill for £140 which he had owed John Murray. But he could not pay his other debts: he and Thomas Evans, his fellow clerk at Frederick's Place, still owed Robert Messer well over £1,000 which had been incurred by their South American speculations.

Soon after the publication of the disappointing second part of *Vivian Grey*, Disraeli fell ill again and, as in the case of a manic depressive, his previous high spirits suddenly collapsed, and from excited gaiety he sank into a trough of gloomy despair. The onset of the illness was heralded by an alarming ticking noise in his ears such as that endured by those suffering from tinnitus. 'From the tick of a watch,' Disraeli wrote, 'it assumed the loud confused moaning of a bell tolling in a storm . . . It was impossible to think. I walked about the room. It became louder and louder. It seemed to be absolutely deafening. I could compare it to nothing but the continuous roar of a cataract.' At the same time he felt confused and weak; in the morning he fainted while dressing; the noise in his head he 'could only describe as the rushing of blood into his brain'. In his conscious state he was 'not always assured' of his own identity, 'or even existence'. He would shout aloud to be sure that he was, indeed, alive; and he would take down one of his books to look at the title page to be sure that he was not just a character in a nightmare.[3]

He could not write; he could not bring himself to look into his legal textbooks. In 1827, he told Benjamin Austen that he was just as ill as ever; he felt that he was in the situation of those 'jackanapes at school who wrote home to their parents every week to tell them that they have nothing to say'; and when, in the following month, he went with the Austens to stay in a house in Essex which his father had taken for the autumn, he became more ill than ever.[4]

He was still 'quite idle', so he told Sharon Turner in March 1828, still 'decidedly an invalid', and 'profoundly depressed', undergoing treatment by a succession of doctors who prescribed various and often contradictory treatments for a condition diagnosed as 'a chronic inflammation of the membranes of the brain'. 'I was bled,' he said, 'blistered, boiled, poisoned, electrified, galvanised; and, at the end of the year, found myself with exactly the same oppression on my brain.'

One of the doctors who treated him was Buckley Bolton, a young physician with a fashionable practice, who prescribed large doses of digitalis, a tincture derived from the leaf of the wild foxglove, intended to strengthen the involuntary muscular contraction of the muscle fibres in the heart. It is a depressant and was, no doubt, responsible for the moods of despair into which Disraeli sank. But Bolton had an attractive wife, Clara, whom Disraeli was to invite to stay at Bradenham, the house to which his father and family were soon to move, and with whom he was to have an affair.

At the same time he began to resent or conceive dislike for various friends or relations, even, for a time, for his father, who makes a recognizable appearance in *Vivian Grey*, not only as Vivian's father, but also as the tiresome, pedantic Mr Sherborne, a man who disapproves of most of his contemporaries and even more of those 'puppies' who think 'every man's a fool who's older than themselves'.

Disraeli himself believed that his mental breakdown was caused by frustration at his inability to achieve the reputation he felt he deserved. 'Whether or not I shall ever do anything which may mark me out from the crowd I know not,' he told Sharon Turner. 'I am one of those to whom moderate reputation can give no pleasure and who, in all probability, am incapable of achieving a great one.'[5] He was also, he might well have added, incapable of throwing off the anti-semitic prejudices which he believed lay in the way of his achieving a great reputation in a gentile world.

It has also been suggested that 'sexual frustration deepened his depression'. Certainly Sara Austen played an elaborate, teasing game with 'My dear Ben', keeping secrets from his family (when out of London, she wrote to him at her own address in Guildford Street) and especially from his sister, Sarah, who was determined not to be replaced as the most important woman in her brother's life. 'They [his family] need not know that I have written to you *first*,' Mrs Austen wrote from Lichfield in April 1828, 'and I will so manage my letter to Sarah that she shall seem to have the preference.'[6]

Enjoying her role as trusted amanuensis, Sara Austen encouraged Disraeli in his work; and when the idea of a satire on the Utilitarians, which was at the same time to ridicule the novel of fashionable life, came into his mind, she greeted it with her usual enthusiasm. 'Mind you write Pop,' [*The Voyage of Captain Popanilla*] she wrote to him while she was still in Lichfield. 'I shall want to work when I get home.'[7]

He settled down to work with an enthusiasm which had seemed to have deserted him, writing with his former speed and energy, composing a fantasy about an island named Fantasie, the inhabitants of which, in naked innocence, spend much of their time making love, just as Vivian Grey would, no doubt, have liked to do with the beautiful Violet Fane, a character in the earlier book in which – at a significant picnic in a passage excised in later editions – a 'facile knife' sinks 'without effort into a bird's plump breast, discharging a cargo of rich stuffed balls of the most fascinating flavour'.

Popanilla, dedicated to Robert Plumer Ward – who told its author that it was equal to Swift's *Tale of a Tub* – was published by Henry Colburn in June 1828, and was greeted with even less éclat than the second part of *Vivian Grey*, receiving but two reviews, both of them short. Cast down by this reception, Disraeli fell ill again and felt no better when his parents took him to Lyme Regis for the benefit of the sea air. Sarah D'Israeli did not know 'what to say to comfort' him; nor did William Meredith, his sister's fiancé; nor yet did Isaac D'Israeli, who wrote:

> My son's life within the last year and a half with a very slight exception, has been a blank in his existence. His complaint is one of those perplexing cases which remain uncertain and obscure till they are finally got rid of. Meanwhile patience and resignation must be his lot.[8]

Concerned about the 'precarious health' of Benjamin and other members of his family, so he told Robert Southey, Isaac D'Israeli decided to 'quit London with all its hourly seductions' and to take a house in the country. In the summer of 1829, therefore, the D'Israelis gave up the house in Bloomsbury and moved to Bradenham, a handsome Queen Anne house with over 1,300 acres at the foot of the Chiltern Hills in Buckinghamshire, a few miles from High Wycombe, which was itself some three hours' coach journey from London.

> In the front of the hall [Disraeli was to write of this property] huge gates of iron, highly wrought, and bearing an ancient date as well as the shield of a noble house opened on a village green round which were clustered the cottages of the parish with only one exception, and that was the vicarage house, a modern building, not without taste, surrounded by a small but brilliant

garden ... Behind the hall the country was common land but picturesque ... It had once been a beech forest.[9]

Isaac D'Israeli settled down to country life with surprising speed and contentment; so did his daughter Sarah, who was often to be seen in the little village taking food and presents to the poor and sick and giving orders to – and taking advice from – the gardeners. Her younger brothers, Ralph, now aged twenty, and James, sixteen, were also happy at Bradenham.

Benjamin, too, liked Bradenham, and he spoke fondly of its trees, its beeches and junipers and its wild cherries.

He told Benjamin Austen in October 1829 that he was 'desperately ill'. But, even so, he 'hoped to be in town in a day or two – *incog*, of course, because of the duns eager to nab [him]'. He would then find his way to Austen's chambers and shake his 'honest hand.'

He had begun another book, *The Young Duke*, which, so he told William Meredith, was 'a series of scenes, every one of which would make the fortune of a fashionable novel. I am confident of its success, and that it will complete the corruption of the public taste.'[10]

Indeed, he was sufficiently confident to approach John Murray, suggesting an interview and assuring the publisher that it had always been his intention, should it ever be his 'fate to write anything calculated to arrest public attention', that the house of Murray 'should be the organ of introducing it to public notice'.

Not surprisingly, Murray declined the offer of an interview but 'assured Mr Disraeli that, if he cared to submit the manuscript, the proposal would be entertained with the strictest honour and impartiality'.

This was scarcely more encouraging than the comment that Isaac D'Israeli was quoted as having made when informed that the title of his son's new book was to be *The Young Duke*. 'Young Duke! What does Ben know of dukes?'[11]

Nor were others, to whom the manuscript was shown, as enthusiastic as its author had hoped they would be. Colburn's reader, who was asked for an opinion in March 1830, had reservations; so, too, had Edward Lytton Bulwer, whose *Pelham* had been published with great success two years before and whose opinion and friendship Disraeli valued. He was much cast down by these criticisms; but Colburn gave him £500 for the book and, when it was published, the critics were kind and some were enthusiastic.

The *Westminster Review* told its readers that 'to parasites, sycophants, toad-eaters, and humble companions', the book would be 'full of comfort and instruction in their callings'. But this verdict was exceptional. As his sister told him, without overdue flattery, most of the weekly and Sunday papers 'reviewed it with excessive praise'. She herself thought it was 'most excellent'. 'There is not a dull half page . . . One reading has repaid me for months of suspense, and that is saying everything if you knew how much my heart is wrapt up in your fame.'

As for Disraeli himself, he protested that he did not care a jot about *The Young Duke*. 'I never staked any fame on it.' It was, he said later, the only one of his books not written from his own feelings and experience. It is the fantastical story of a young coxcomb, George Augustus Frederick, Duke of St James's, a sprig of one of the richest families in Europe, who is corrupted by society, but redeemed when he abandons rebellion for conformity and accepts the responsibilities of his inheritance.

Disraeli was much more interested in a project which he had been considering for some time, a tour in the East. He went up to London occasionally to discuss his plans with Meredith, who was to accompany him, travelling incognito, as he put it, for fear he might be seen and dunned by the various people to whom he owed money. He was careful, in fact, not to let his plans become public knowledge and thus alert his creditors to his intention of going abroad again and giving them good reason for demanding the settlement of his debts before he went.

'Keep this letter to yourself *without exception*,' he wrote to Benjamin Austen on 8 December 1829, having persuaded him to give him a letter of credit for £500, addressed to various bankers, to help finance his proposed journey to Constantinople. 'Though generally accused of uncommunicativeness, I like a gentle chat with a friend provided it is strictly confidential and he be a tried and trusty one like yourself,' he told Austen. 'Women are delightful creatures, particularly if they be pretty, which they always are; but then they chatter – they can't help it – and I have no ambition – in case my dearest project fails – to be pointed out as the young gentleman who *was* going to Constantinople . . . By the bye, I advise you to take care of my letters, for, if I become half as famous as I intend to be, you may sell them for ten guineas apiece to the *Keepsake*.'[12]

To Austen's wife – of whose possessive devotion he had long since grown tired – he wrote three months later, acknowledging her 'repeated kind messages', complaining that his health could not be worse and that, of all places, London was the one to which he was least suited.

> My plans about leaving England are more unsettled than ever [he continued]. I anticipate no benefit from it, nor from any-thing else, but I am desirous [of leading] an even more reclu-sive life than I do at present ... I grieve to say that my hair grows very badly, and I think more grey, which I can unfeignedly declare occasions me more anguish than even the prospect of death.[13]

Despite the gloomy remarks about London and his health which he made in his letter to Sara Austen, Disraeli was in town again three weeks later, 'in excellent spirits,' according to Meredith, who had invited him to dinner. He was 'full of schemes for the projected journey to Stamboul and Jerusalem; full, as usual, also of capital stories, but he could make a story out of nothing'.

> He came up Regent Street, when it was crowded [Meredith wrote in his diary], wearing his blue surtout, a pair of military light blue trousers, black stockings with red stripes, and shoes! 'The people', he said, 'quite made way for me as I passed. It was like the opening of the Red Sea, which I now perfectly believe from experience. Even well dressed people stopped to look at me.' I should think so![14]

That same month Disraeli also had dinner with Edward Lytton Bulwer at his house in Hertford Street, together with four men who were, respectively, to become a Secretary of State, Ambassador at Con-staninople, a Cabinet Minister and Lord Chief Justice; and, once again, Disraeli was remarkable for the colourful eccentricity of his dress and the wit and fluency of his conversation.

> He wore green velvet trousers [his host remembered], a canary-coloured waistcoat, low shoes, silver buckles, lace at his wrists and his hair in ringlets ... If on leaving the table and asked which

was the cleverest of the party, we should have been obliged to say, 'the man in the green velvet trousers'.*

Shortly after this dinner party at Bulwer's, Disraeli was staying at the Union Hotel in Cockspur Street when he wrote to T. M. Evans, his former fellow clerk, to whom he owed money, and to whom he addressed a long and devious letter, apologizing for having been 'too long silent', explaining that it was because, for the last three years, life had not afforded him a moment's ease, and now 'after having lived in perfect solitude for nearly eighteen months', he was about to be shipped off 'for the last resource of a warmer climate'.

He protested that to leave England in such a state as his, without finally arranging his 'distracted affairs', cost him 'a pang which [was] indeed bitter'. And he said that it would be a great consolation to him to know before his departure that 'dear Evans' was 'prospering in the world'.

He went on to acknowledge Evans's 'generous and manly soul'; to say that the first step he would take when he had the power to do so would be in Evans's favour; and that he hoped 'some day or other, we may look back to these early adventures, rather as a matter of philosophical speculation than individual sorrow'. He hoped to see Evans, on his return from his travels, at Bradenham House but at present he was 'only the inmate of an unsocial hotel'.[15]

On the day he wrote to Evans from the Union Hotel, Cockspur Street, he wrote also to Austen to say that he had passed 'the last week, nearly in a *trance* from digitalis'. 'I sleep', he had told him, 'literally sixteen out of the twenty-four hours and am quite dozy now.' He could but hope that his forthcoming travels would 'effect a cure'.[16]

---

* 'I never wore green velvet trousers,' Disraeli protested when this description of his attire was published in *The Encyclopaedia Britannica*, 'nor do I believe that anybody ever did; [and] I never wore buckles in my shoes except at Court.' However, the description remained in the eleventh edition of the *Encyclopaedia* in 1911.

5

TRAVELS AND ADVENTURES

'We ate; we drank; we ate with our fingers,
we drank in a manner I never recollect – the wine was not bad
but had it been poison . . .
it was such a compliment for a Moslemin
that I must quaff it all . . . we quaffed it in rivers.
The Bey called for the Brandy . . . we drank it all –
the room turned round.'

'THIS ROCK', wrote Disraeli of Gibraltar, 'is a wonderful place with a population infinitely diversified – Moors with costumes radiant as a rainbow or an eastern melodrama . . . Jews with gaberdines and skull-caps, Genoese, Highlanders [of the garrison] and Spaniards.'[1]

'In the Garrison Library', he told his father, 'are all your books', adding archly, 'it also possesses a copy of another book, supposed to be written by a member of our family, and which is looked upon at Gibraltar as one of the masterpieces of the nineteenth century. You may feel their intellectual pulse from this. At first I apologised and talked of youthful blunders and all that, really being ashamed; but finding them, to my astonishment, sincere, and fearing they were stupid enough to adopt my last opinion, I shifted my position just in time, looked very grand, and passed myself off as a child of the sun, like the Spaniard in Peru.'[2]

He had arrived at Gibraltar with William Meredith in the middle of June 1830 and had soon been presented to General Sir George Don, the acting governor of the fortress in the absence of its official governor, the Duke of Kent.

Don was 'a very fine old gentleman almost regal in his manner,' so Disraeli wrote. 'He possesses a large private fortune, all of which he here disburses, and has ornamented Gibraltar, as a lover does his mistress.'[3]

So often drawn to women older than himself, Disraeli was much taken with Lady Don, who was 'without exception one of the most agreeable personages [he] had ever met, excessively acute and *piquante* . . . To listen to her you would think you were charming away the hour with a blooming beauty in Mayfair; and, though excessively infirm, her eye is so brilliant and so full of *moquerie* that you quite forget her wrinkles. All in all,' he added with characteristic hyperbole, she was 'the cleverest and most charming woman [he] had ever met'.[4]

As well as Government House, a former convent, where he introduced his visitors to his favourite drink, champagne and lemonade, Sir George enjoyed the use of 'a delightful Pavillion . . . at the extreme point of the Rock' as well as a villa at San Roque. He suggested that, having enjoyed his hospitality at these places, his guests should make an excursion into Spain, a venture which foreign tourists seldom undertook since the few *posadas* offered little apart from a roof for the night and plenty of bugs. But the scenery was 'most beautiful' and, although the terrain was infested with robbers and smugglers, these miscreants, so Disraeli was assured, 'commit no personal violence but lay you on the ground and clean out your pockets. If you have less than sixteen dollars they shoot you. That is the tariff and is a loss worth risking.' In the event, Disraeli and Meredith were not troubled by these bandits; but on their return to Griffith's Hotel in Gibraltar they encountered two Englishmen who had been robbed of all their possessions in a village through which they also had passed a day or two earlier with their French guide and man-servant, an excellent cook and 'celeberated shot' who, so Disraeli said, 'could speak all languages except English of which he [made] a sad affair'.

> He is fifty but light as a butterfly . . . He did everything, remedied every inconvenience, and found an expedient for every difficulty. Never did I live so well as among these wild mountains of Andalusia, so exquisite is his cookery . . .
>
> You will wonder how we managed to extract pleasure from a life which afforded us hourly peril for our purses and perhaps for our lives, which induced fatigue greater than I ever experienced, for there are no roads and we were never less than eight hours a day on . . . two little Andalusian mountain horses.[5]

Disraeli ended his long letter to Bradenham by sending his fondest regards to his 'beloved Sa' and 'a thousand kisses' to his 'dearest mother'.

'Tell Ralph I have not forgotten his promise of an occasional letter . . . And tell [Washington] Irving [whose *Legends of Alhambra* was to be published shortly] that he has left a golden name in Spain.'

Disraeli and Meredith were themselves so taken with Spain that they stayed there for two months, far longer than they had originally intended. In the middle of July, they went to Cadiz where 'Figaro [was] in every street, and Rosina in every balcony'.[6] And, towards the end of the month, they were in Seville, where Disraeli wrote to his father to tell him that, while his health had improved and the 'fearful heat' of Seville suited him, the improvement was 'very slight' and his recovery would, at best, be 'a long affair'. He was even more pessimistic in a letter from Granada to his mother, to whom he complained about the palpitations in his heart and head which were followed by 'an indescribable feeling of idiocy' and 'for hours' he was 'plunged into a state of the darkest despair'.

He was worried also by what he took to be incipient baldness: 'I am sorry to say my hair is coming off, just at the moment it had attained the highest perfection, and was universally mistaken for a wig, so that I was obliged to let the women pull it to satisfy their curiosity. Let me know what my mother thinks. There are no wigs here that I cd wear. Pomade and all that is quite a delusion. Somebody recommends me cocoa-nut oil, which I cd get here, but suppose it turns it grey or blue or green?'

In her reply, Sarah told him that 'Mamma advises him to try Coca-Nut or anything'. She was sure that she could arrange for him to be sent a wig.[7]

In a letter to his mother, he said that if he were a Roman Catholic he would enter a convent, 'But as I am a member of a family to which I am devotedly attached and a good Protestant I shall return to them and to my country, and to a solitary room which I will never leave. I shall see no one and speak with no one. I am serious. Prepare yourself for this.'

The tone of the rest of his letter, however, belied this gloomy prognostication. Although, as he said, 'rather an admirer of the blonde', he wrote enthusiastically of Spanish ladies, 'their glossy black hair and black mantillas, their gleaming eyes and dignified grace'. He wrote also of the delicious fruits of the Peninsula, of *paella*, 'the most delicious dish in the world', and of tomato sauce for which he provided a recipe – and, having done so, he added a note for his mother: 'I need not tell the mistress [of] so experienced a cuisine as you to add a small quantity of onion in frying the tomatas.'[8]

> I travelled through the whole of Andalusia on horseback [he reported with pride to Benjamin Austen]. I was never less than twelve hours on my steed, and more than once saw the sun set and rise without quitting my saddle, which few men can say, and I never wish to say again. I visited Cadiz, Seville, Cordova and Granada . . . I sailed upon the Guadalquivir, I cheered at bullfights; I lived for a week among brigands and wandered in the fantastic halls of the delicate Alhambra [a building which stood comparison, he thought, with the Parthenon and York Minster].
>
> I entered Spain a sceptic with regard to their robbers, and listened to all their romances with a smile. I lived to change my opinion. I at length found a country where adventure is the common course of existence.[9]

'Run, my dear fellow, to Seville,' he told Austen in another letter, 'and for the first time in your life know what a great artist is – Murillo, Murillo, Murillo!'[10]

On his way to Córdoba, riding by moonlight, his party's guide suddenly informed them that 'he heard a trampling of horses in the distance', and Disraeli gave an entertaining description of his alarm in a letter to his sister:

> Ave Maria! A cold perspiration came over me. Decidedly they approached, but rather an uproarious crew. We drew up out of pure fear, and I had my purse ready. The band turned out to be a company of actors travelling to Cordova. There they were, dresses and decorations, scenery and machinery, all on mules and donkeys. The singers rehearsing an opera; the principal tragedian riding on an ass; and the buffo, most serious, looking as grave as night, with a cigar, and in greater agitation than them all. Then there were women in side-saddles, and whole panniers of children . . . All irresistibly reminded me of Cervantes. We proceed and meet a caravan of armed merchants, who challenged us, and I nearly got shot for not answering in time. Then come two travelling friars who give us their blessing and then we lose our way. We wander about all night, dawn breaks, and we stumble on some peasants sleeping in the field amid their harvest. We learn

that we cannot regain our road, and, utterly wearied, we finally sink to sound sleep with our pack-saddles for our pillows.[11]

The occasional complaints about his health in his letters are at odds with passages of cheerfully facetious self-congratulation:

> I maintain my reputation of being a great judge of costume to the admiration and envy of many subalterns [he had written from Gibraltar]. I have also the fame of being the first who ever passed the Straits with two canes, a morning and an evening cane. I change my cane as the gun fires ... It is wonderful the effect these magical wands produce.[12]

He later added a fan to his accoutrements, which made the canes 'extremely jealous'.

At the Alhambra in Granada, so Meredith said, the elderly guide was convinced that Disraeli 'was a Moor, many of whom come to visit this palace, which, they say, will be theirs yet again. His southern aspect, the style in which he paced the gorgeous apartments and sat himself in the seat of the Abencerrajes [a prominent family in the Nasrid Kingdom of Granada in the fifteenth century], his parting speech, "*Es mi casa*", "This is my palace", all quite deceived the guide.'

'Oh! Wonderful Spain!' Disraeli wrote enthusiastically to his sister on 14 August. 'Think of this romantic land covered with Moorish ruins and full of Murillo! ... I thought that enthusiasm was dead within me and that nothing could be new. I have hit perhaps upon the only country which could have upset my theory, a country of which I have read little, and thought nothing, a country of which, indeed, nothing has been written and which few visit.' 'I dare to say', he added, 'that I am better.'

He was occasionally homesick, though. 'Write to me about Braden-ham,' he told Sarah, 'about dogs and horses, gardens, who calls, who my father sees in London, what is said. That is what I want. Never mind public news ... Keep on writing but don't *bore* yourself. A thousand, thousand loves to all. Adieu, my beloved. We shall soon meet. There is no place like Bradenham, and each moment I feel better I want to come back.'[13]

A few days after this letter was written, Disraeli and Meredith sailed for Malta, where they were incarcerated for a week in the Lazaretto before being allowed out to take rooms at Beverley's, a much better hotel than the 'horrid' Griffith's Hotel in Gibraltar.

Valetta, the capital of Malta, was a place of which he expected nothing and found much, Disraeli wrote in a letter to Benjamin Austen. Indeed, he said, 'it surprises me as one of the most beautiful cities I have ever visited, something between Venice and Cadiz . . . It has not a single tree but the city is truly magnificent, full of palaces worthy of Palladio.'[14]

Here they met a handsome and dissipated young man, a most energetic womanizer, James Clay, who had been at Oxford with Meredith. He was the son of a rich merchant and a nephew of Sir William Clay, Secretary to the Board of Control in Lord Melbourne's ministry. He had chartered an impressive fifty-five-ton yacht with a crew of seven, and was attended by an equally impressive-looking manservant with mustachios which, in Disraeli's words, 'touch the earth. Withal mild as a lamb, tho' daggers always about his person.' This was Giovanni Battista Falcieri, Byron's former manservant.[15]

> The presence of Clay [observed Robert Blake in his excellent account of Disraeli's tour] removed whatever restraining influence Meredith may have had on Disraeli. He now behaved with a flamboyance, conceit and affectation which did him no good, though he seems to have been wholly unaware of this in his letters.[16]

'Affectation tells here even better than wit,' Disraeli wrote from Malta. 'Yesterday at the racket court [as I was] sitting in the gallery among strangers, the ball entered, slightly struck me, and fell at my feet. I picked it up and, observing a young rifleman excessively stiff, I humbly requested him to forward its passage into the court, as I really had never thrown a ball in my life. This incident has been the general subject of conversation at all the messes today.'[17]

It is most doubtful that this kind of affectation created such 'a good impression' as Disraeli thought it did; or that his collection of pipes – his 'Turkish pipe six feet long with an amber mouth piece', his Meerschaum, and his 'most splendid Dresden green china pipe' – helped him to become the 'greatest smoker in Malta'. Nor can his flamboyant clothes have elicited the admiration he liked to suppose, consisting, as one outfit did, of 'the costume of a Greek pirate, a blood-red shirt with silver studs as big as shillings, an immense scarf or girdle full of pistols and daggers, a red cap, red slippers, blue broad-striped jacket and trousers . . . Excessively wicked.'[18] This ensemble, so James Clay assured him, helped him to achieve a 'complete and unrivalled triumph', a description more suited to Disraeli's own opinion of his success than to Clay's. Indeed, Clay, who later became an authority on whist and Member of Parliament for Hull, gave Sir William Gregory, an Irish Member, the impression that Disraeli on Malta had been an object of derision and distaste rather than admiration.

'It would not have been possible to have found a more agreeable, unaffected companion when they were by themselves,' Gregory wrote. 'But when they got into society, his coxcombry was intolerable . . . He made himself so hateful to the officers' mess that, while they welcomed Clay, they ceased to invite "that damned bumptious Jew boy" who, when he had been invited, turned up in Andalusian dress.'[19]

William Meredith said that when Disraeli 'paid a round of visits', he would do so in his 'white trousers, and a sash of all the colours in the rainbow. In this wonderful costume he paraded all round Valetta, followed by one-half of the population, and, as he himself said, putting a complete stop to all business. He, of course, included the Governor [Sir Frederick Ponsonby] and Lady Emily in his round to their no small astonishment.'

> Yesterday I called on Ponsonby [Disraeli told his father]. I flatter myself that he passed through the most extraordinary quarter of an hour of his existence. I gave him no quarter and at last made our nonchalant Governor roll on the sofa, from his risible convulsions. Then I jumped up, remembered that I must be sadly breaking into his morning, and was off, making it a rule always to leave with a good impression. He pressed me not to go. I told him I had so much to do! I walked down the Strada Reale, which is nearly as good as Regent Street, and got five invitations to dinner (literally a fact). When I arrived home I found an invitation for Tuesday.[20]

At the beginning of October 1830, Clay and his friends sailed for Cyprus, a 'most lovely island', in a chartered yacht, the *Susan*, a name which, so Disraeli said, was a 'bore, but, as we can't alter it, we have painted it out'; and from there they sailed for Prevesa, now in Greece, at that time part of the Turkish empire.

They then travelled overland to Arta, where Disraeli was deeply moved by the muezzin call from the minaret. Here the Albanian governor provided the travellers with an escort to take them on to Yanina, where they were presented to the Grand Vizier before whom Disraeli 'bowed with all the nonchalance of St James's'.

The Grand Vizier was 'a little, ferocious-looking, shrivelled, care-worn man, placidly dressed with a brow covered with wrinkles, and with a countenance clouded with anxiety and thought'.

The English travellers, who had been shown into his divan 'ahead of a crowd of patient supplicants in the ante-chamber', were then taken to the Grand Vizier's son, who was the very reverse of his father – 'incapable of affairs, refined in his manners, plunged in debauchery and magnificent in dress. Covered with gold and diamonds, he bowed to us with the ease of a Duke of Devonshire and said the English were the most polished of nations.'

> I can give you no idea in a letter of all the Pashas and all the Agas that I have visited [Disraeli told Benjamin Austen]; all the pipes I smoked, all the coffee I sipped, all the sweetmeats I devoured ... For a week I was in a scene equal to anything in the *Arabian Nights* – such processions, such dresses, such cortèges of horsemen, such caravans of camels, then the delight of being made much of by a man who was daily decapitating half the Province. Every evening we paid visits, attended reviews, and crammed ourselves with sweetmeats; every evening dancers and singers were sent to our quarters by the Vizier or some Pasha.[21]

Meredith gave a description of his friend's costume on such occasions: 'Figure to yourself a shirt entirely red with silver studs ... green pantaloons with a velvet stripe down the sides, and a silk Albanian shawl with a long fringe of divers colours round his waist, red Turkish slippers and, to complete all, his Spanish jacket covered with embroidery and ribbons. Was this costume English or fancy dress? asked a little Greek Physician. He was told *"Inglese e fantastico"*.'[22]

In an exceptionally long letter to his father, Disraeli gave an amusing description of a drunken evening during 'this wondrous week in Albania':

We ate; we drank; we ate with our fingers, we drank in a manner
I never recollect – the wine was not bad but had it been poison
the forbidden juice was such a compliment from a Moslemin that
I must quaff it all . . . we quaffed it in rivers. The Bey called for
the Brandy – unfortunately there was another bottle – we drank
it all – the room turned round; the wild attendants who sat at
our feet seemed dancing in strange and fantastic whirls; the Bey
shook hands with me . . . he roared; I smacked him on the back.
I remember no more. In the middle of the night I woke. I found
myself sleeping on the divan, rolled up in its sacred carpet; the
Bey had wisely reeled to the fire.[23]

'We sailed from Prevesa through the remaining Ionian islands,'
Disraeli continued his account of his travels. 'A cloudless sky, a summer
atmosphere, and sunsets like the neck of a dove, completed all the
enjoyment which I anticipated from roving in a Grecian sea. We were
obliged, however, to keep a sharp lookout for Pirates, who are all about
again – we exercised the crew every day with muskets, and their increasing prowess, and our own pistol exercise, kept up our courage.'[24]

I am quite a Turk [he wrote to Benjamin Austen], wear a turban,
smoke a pipe six feet long and squat on a divan . . . I find the
habits of this calm and luxurious people entirely agree with my
own preconceived opinions of propriety, and I detest the Greeks
more than ever. I do not find mere travelling on the whole very
expensive, but I am ruined by my wardrobe . . . When I was
presented to the Grand Vizier I made up such a costume from
my heterogeneous wardrobe that the Turks who are mad on the
subject of dress were utterly astounded.

In Athens, Disraeli and his companions were, so he claimed, the
first Englishmen to visit the Acropolis, which had been shut up for nine
years. 'Athens is still in the power of the Turks,' he wrote, 'but the ancient
remains have been respected. The Parthenon and the other temples
which are in the Acropolis, have necessarily suffered during the siege,
but the injury is only in the detail; the general effect is not marred . . .
The temple of Theseus looks, at a short distance, as if it were just
finished by Pericles.' 'Of all that I have visited,' he added, 'nothing has
more completely realized all that I imagined and all that I could have
wished than Athens.'[25]

All the houses in the city were, however, roofless and there were 'hundreds of shells and cannon balls lying among the ruins'; while the surrounding country was desolate.

> Happy are we to get a shed for nightly shelter [Disraeli told his father, having made an excursion to Marathon] and never have been fortunate enough to find one not swarming with vermin. My sufferings in this way are great. And the want of sleep from these vermin, and literally I did not sleep a wink the whole time I was out, is very bad, as it unfits you for daily exertion . . . We found a wild boar just killed at a little village and purchased half of it – but it is not as good as Bradenham pork.[26]

He was thankful when the wind changed and the *Susan* was able to set sail for Constantinople, of which he caught sight just as the sun was setting on 10 December 1830. 'It baffled all description,' he wrote of that first sight of it: 'an immense mass of buildings, cupolas, cypress groves and minarets'. He felt an excitement which, so he said, he thought was dead.[27]

In Constantinople they found the British Ambassador, Sir Robert Gordon, welcoming, hospitable and – Disraeli was pleased to discover – as hostile to the Greeks as he was himself. A cousin of Byron and a future ambassador extraordinary in Vienna, Gordon was clearly delighted to have Disraeli and his friends as his guests and was much put out when they left after a visit lasting six weeks, pressing them to stay longer, offering them rooms in the embassy and, so Disraeli said, most reluctantly taking leave of them 'in a pet'.

He made the most of them, however, while they were there:

> Tell Ralph we are very gay here [Disraeli reported to his father], nothing but masquerade balls and diplomatic dinners. The Ambassador has introduced us everywhere. We had the most rollicking week at the Palace [the embassy] with romping of the most horrible description and things called 'games of forfeits'. Gordon, out of the purest malice, made me tumble over head and heels!

Since descriptions were 'an acknowledged bore', he said that he would leave Constantinople to his father's imagination. But he did describe it, all the same. He wrote of the bazaar, 'perhaps a square mile of arcades intersecting each other in all directions and full of every product of the empire from diamonds to dates'.

Here in Constantinople [he went on, ready as always to describe an exotic wardrobe] every people have a characteristic costume. Turks, Greeks, Jews and Armenians are the staple population . . . The Armenians wear round and very unbecoming black caps and robes, the Jews a black hat wreathed with a white handkerchief, the Greeks black turbans. The Turks indulge in all manner of costume. The meanest merchant in the Bazaar looks like a sultan in an Eastern fairy tale. This is mainly to be ascribed to the marvellous brilliancy of their dyes . . . The Sultan [Mahmoud II] dresses like a European and all the young men have adopted the fashion. You see the young Turks in uniforms which would not disgrace one of our crack cavalry regiments, and lounging with all the bitterness of Royal illegitimates.[28]

What he called his 'Turkish prejudices' were 'very much confirmed' by his visit to Turkey. The life of the people greatly accorded with his taste, which was naturally 'somewhat indolent and melancholy', he told his friend, the novelist, Edward Lytton Bulwer. 'To repose on voluptuous ottomans and smoke superb pipes, daily to indulge in the luxury of a bath which requires half a dozen attendants for its perfection; to court the air in a carved caique, by shores which are a perpetual scene; this is, I think, a far more sensible life than all the bustle of clubs, all the boring of drawing-rooms, and all the coarse vulgarity of our political controversies . . . I mend slowly but I mend.'[29]

In letters to his father, he was more specific about his health which, he said, continued improving. 'In fact,' he wrote, 'I hope the early spring will return me to Bradenham in a very different plight to that in which I left it. I can assure you that I sigh to return altho' in very agreeable company; but I have seen and done enough in this way.'

Prevented by contrary winds from landing on Rhodes, the *Susan* sailed on to Cyprus, where Disraeli and Clay spent a day, Meredith having now left them to go to Egypt. From Cyprus they went on to Jaffa and thence made the tiring and potentially hazardous journey on horseback to Jerusalem, where, since there were no hotels or inns in the Holy City, Disraeli and his party had to stay in the monastery of St Salvador, where they were 'admitted into a court with all [their] horses and camels . . . and warmly welcomed by the most corpulent friars' Disraeli had ever seen waddling around them.[30]

On their second night, one of the 'best houses in Jerusalem' was allotted to the visitors by these fat and jolly Franciscan friars who sent them provisions every day.

'I could write half a dozen sheets on this week, the most delightful in all our travels,' Disraeli recorded. 'We dined every day on the roof of our house by moonlight and of course visited the Holy Sepulchre ... an ingenious imposture of a comparatively recent date.'

> Surprised at the number of remains in Jerusalem – tho' some more ancient than Herod [Disraeli noted briefly]. The tombs of the Kings very fine. Weather delicious – mild summer heat ... received visits from the Vicar General of the Pope, the Spanish Prior etc. Never more delighted in my life.

Disraeli also climbed the Mount of Olives and, so he said, 'endeavoured to enter [the Mosque of Omar] at the hazard of my life. I was detected and surrounded by a horde of turbaned fanatics, and escaped with difficulty ... I caught a glorious glimpse of splendid courts and light airy gates of Saracenic triumph, flights of noble steps, long arcades, and interior gardens, where silver fountains spouted their tall streams amid the taller cypresses.'[31]

> It is impossible to say when I will be home [Disraeli wrote to his sister after his arrival in Egypt from Palestine], but I should think in three months. From Alexandria ... I crossed the desert to Rosetta. It was a twelve hours job, and the whole way we were surrounded by a mirage of the most complete kind. I was perpetually deceived and always thought I was going to ride into the sea. At Rosetta I first saw the mighty Nile with its banks richly covered with palm groves.

In Egypt he met Mehemit Ali, the Pasha, who discussed with him the idea of introducing parliamentary democracy into the country. 'I will have as many Parliaments as the King of England himself,' the Pasha said to him. 'But I have made up my mind, to prevent inconvenience, to elect them myself.'[32]

From Rosetta, Disraeli sailed up the Nile to Cairo and then on towards Thebes. And one day, as he wandered away from the moored boat, the sky darkened as columns of sand suddenly appeared and came rapidly towards him.

I rushed to the boat with full speed [he wrote] but barely quick enough. I cannot describe the horror and confusion. It was a Simoom [a hot, dry, suffocating sand-wind]. It was the most awful sound I ever heard. Five columns of sand taller than the Monument [the column, 202 feet high, built in 'perpetual remembrance' of the Great Fire of London] emptied themselves on our party.

Every sail was rent to pieces, men buried in the earth. Three boats sailing along overturned ... the wind, the screaming, the shouting, the driving of the sand were enough to make you mad. We shut all the windows of the cabin, and jumped into bed, but the sand came in like fire.[33]

Having returned to Cairo, Disraeli and Clay remained there, waiting for Meredith to come back from a trip he had made on his own to Thebes, which Disraeli described in irritation as 'the unseen relics of some unheard-of cock-and-bull city'; and, in Cairo, soon after his return to them, Meredith fell gravely ill with smallpox and died on 19 July 1831.

Disraeli reported the death in a distracted letter to his father: 'I would willingly have given up my life for his.'

Oh! my father, why do we live? The anguish of my soul is great. Our innocent lamb [Sarah, Meredith's fiancée] is stricken. Save her, save her. I will come home directly ... I wish to live only for my sister ... I think of her day and night ... My dear father, I do not know whether I have done all that is necessary. I have sent a courier to Clay [who had gone on to Alexandria to make arrangements for their homeward journey]. Mr Botta [Paul Emile Botta, the son of the historian, a physician, the inspiration for the character of Count Marigny in Disraeli's 'Psychological Romance', *Contarini Fleming* of 1832, and 'the most philosophical mind' that Disraeli had ever come across] has been very kind to me as I could not sleep and dared not be alone and my anguish was overwhelming ... It was some satisfaction that I was with our friend to the last. Oh! my father, I trust a great deal to you and to my dear mother.[34]

'Oh, my sister, in this hour of overwhelming affliction my thoughts are only for you,' he wrote to his 'own Sa'. 'Alas! my beloved, if you are lost to me where am I to fly for refuge? I have no wife, I have no betrothed ... Live then, my heart's desire, for one who has ever loved you, and who would have cheerfully yielded his own existence to have saved you the bitterness of this letter.'*[35]

'If I cannot be to you all of our best friend,' he added, 'at least we will feel that life can never be a blank while illumined by the pure & perfect Love of a Sister and a Brother.'[36]

Sarah did, thereafter, live for her brother and the family, and, in return, Disraeli's affection for her remained deep and constant.

'I believe he never entirely got over his sense of suffering at the crushing disappointment of her early hopes,' his friend Sir Philip Rose, said; 'and, amid the many stirring incidents of his eventful life, the death-bed scene at Cairo was not seldom recalled. He rarely spoke either of his sister or of Meredith, but that was his habit where his feelings were deeply concerned . . . On the first occasion of his becoming Prime Minister I remember saying to him, "If only your sister had been alive now to witness your triumph, what happiness it would have given her", and he replied, "Ah, poor Sa, poor Sa! We've lost our audience. We've lost our audience."'[37]

Leaving Clay to finish their planned tour, Disraeli sailed for Malta, where he intended to take the earliest possible boat to England after enduring a month's quarantine on the island. Clay was also obliged to spend a tedious quarantine in the Lazaretto in Venice, where he wrote a characteristically breezy letter to Disraeli:

> Many returns of this day [21 December 1831, Disraeli's twenty-seventh birthday] . . . Between us we have contrived to stumble on all the thorns with which (as Mr Dickens, the Winchester Porter, was wont poetically to observe) Venus guards her roses; for while you were cursing the greater evils [of some venereal disease] I contrived to secure the minor viz. a gleet [a form of gonorrhoea] from over-exertion and crabs [*pediculus pubis*, crab-lice]. The former I richly earned and it wore itself out, the latter was quickly cured and I am in high cue for a real debauch in Venice.

---

* Disraeli's grief was no doubt exacerbated by his consciousness of having upset Meredith by the closeness of his friendship with Clay, from which Meredith felt excluded. Sarah had chided her brother about this: 'You and William are both equally uncommunicative respecting each other; if you have not *separated* do occasionally condescend to acknowledge each other's existence' (Donald Sultana, *Benjamin Disraeli in Spain, Malta and Albania*, 1976; 47).

Yesterday being *my* birthday I drank our very good health . . .
After dinner a capital batch of letters (yours included) arrived
. . . I drank and drank again and read and re-read my letters
until it became impossible to distinguish one correspondent from
another. On reading what I thought was your hand-writing I
found an exhortation to marry and settle, and when I took up,
as I believed, a letter from my mother, I read that 'Mercury
[hydrargyrum, salts of mercury then prescribed for the treatment
of syphilis] had succeeded to Venus' – a most extraordinary communication from an elderly gentlewoman.[38]

While Disraeli's family naturally and strongly disapproved of James Clay,
they were also concerned when he took up with another young man of
equally dubious reputation, Henry Stanley, brother of Edward Stanley,
the future fourteenth Earl of Derby and Conservative Prime Minister.

Having become friendly on the voyage home from Malta to Fal-
mouth, Disraeli and Henry Stanley travelled by coach together from
Cornwall to London, where they parted. Disraeli spent two or three
nights at the Union Hotel, where he commonly stayed when in London.
Stanley, so it was supposed, went home to Knowsley Hall. But he did
not arrive there, and his family became worried. It was known that
he had gone to London with Disraeli, who was asked to help find
him; and he was eventually discovered in a gambling house kept by one
Effie Bond.

Disraeli owed Bond money; and it was suspected by Henry Stanley's
elder brother, Edward, that, while pretending to look for Henry, Disraeli
was, in fact, working with the unscrupulous Effie Bond to part the
impressionable young man from his money.

Edward Stanley consequently conceived 'a strong prejudice against
Disraeli', wrote Sir Philip Rose, 'and it was not until the force of public
and political affairs [when Edward Stanley had succeeded his father as
Earl of Derby] induced them to become associates that his hostility
disappeared. It is probable that his feeling was rather the resentment of
a proud man at a stranger having become mixed up in his family secrets,
and cognizance of a brother's misconduct, than any real distrust or belief
that his brother had been led into difficulties by Disraeli . . . The letters
from Lord Stanley and Colonel Long, his brother-in-law, conclusively
show that *they* had no complaint against Disraeli, and not only acquitted

him of all blame, but were grateful for his interference and aid, and the Hon. Henry's own letters show that Disraeli had given him the best and most disinterested advice.'[39]

Having returned to Bradenham, Disraeli settled down to work 'like a Tiger'. He had to undergo another 'six weeks' course of Mercury' for his venereal complaint, as he told Benjamin Austen, and this had 'pulled [him] down'. But his head was 'all right'; and he felt quite well again.[40] Indeed, despite the 'overwhelming catastrophe' of Meredith's death, he was, he said, in 'famous condition – better indeed than [he] had ever been in [his life] and full of hope and courage'.

His journey, as his biographer, W.F. Monypenny, commented:

> proved a capital event in his life and had marked effects on his whole subsequent career, both literary and political. It not only enlarged his experience beyond that of most young Englishmen of his day, but, what was even more important to one of his peculiar temperament, it helped to give definite purpose and significance to that Oriental tendency in his nature which, vaguely present before, was henceforth to dominate his imagination and show itself in nearly all his achievements. We can see the influence of the Eastern journey in *Contarini Fleming*, in *Alroy*, in *Tancred*, and in *Lothair*; but we can see it not less clearly in the bold stroke of policy which laid the foundations of English ascendancy in Egypt, in the act which gave explicit form to the conception of an Indian Empire with the sovereign of Great Britain at its head, and in the settlement imposed on Europe at the Berlin Congress [of 1878].[41]

6

'THE JEW *D'ESPRIT*'

'Now tell me, what do you
want to be?'

SOON AFTER HIS RETURN to Bradenham in 1832, Disraeli's book, *Contarini Fleming*, was with its publishers and *The Wondrous Tale of Alroy* was shortly to follow it.

John Murray was at first in two minds as to whether or not to accept *Contarini Fleming*. Sir Walter Scott's biographer, J. G. Lockhart, expressed doubts about it, and suggested that it be sent for an opinion to Henry Hart Milman, the poet and historian, who had few reservations. It might well be 'much abused' and was 'very extraordinary', Milman said, but it was also 'very powerful and 'very poetical'. William Beckford, to whom Disraeli sent a copy, was also enthusiastic. 'How wildly original!' he wrote in reply. 'How full of intense thought! How awakening! How delightful!' It was 'a truly wonderful tale'.[1]

'As far as I can learn,' Disraeli wrote to his sister on 28 May 1832, 'it has met with decided success. Among others Tom Campbell [the poet and editor of the *New Monthly Magazine*], who as he says, never reads any books but his own, is delighted with it. "I shall review it myself," he exclaims.'[2]

'*Contarini* is universally liked, but moves slowly,' Disraeli continued in another letter to Sarah a few weeks later. 'The staunchest admirer I have in London, and the most discerning appreciator [of the book] is old Madame d'Arblay [the former Fanny Burney]. I have a long letter which I will show you – capital.'[3]

Heinrich Heine was even more enthusiastic. 'Modern English letters have given us no equal to *Contarini Fleming*,' Heine wrote. 'Cast in our Teutonic mould, it is nevertheless one of the most original works ever written; profound, poignant, pathetic.'

This was a view the author himself was inclined to share. 'I shall always consider [*Contarini Fleming*] as the perfection of English prose,' he wrote with characteristic immodesty, 'and a chef d'ouvre [sic].' But the sales of the book remained sluggish; and the author and publisher received no more than £36 between them.[4]

'Don't be nervous about the sale, that's nothing,' Tom Campbell tried to comfort Disraeli. 'This will *last*. It's a philosophical work, Sir.'

Disheartened by the poor sales of *Contarini Fleming*, Murray returned the manuscript of Disraeli's next book, *The Wondrous Tale of Alroy*, when it was offered to him the following year. Published instead by Henry Colburn, it was even less successful than its predecessor; and, while its author had had 'no doubt of its success', it aroused derision rather than the 'golden opinions' which, so he told Sarah, he was expecting.

'Oh reader, dear! Do pray look here,' one critic wrote in a parody of its style, 'and you will spy the curly hair and forehead fair, and nose so high and gleaming eye of Benjamin Dis-ra-e-li, the wondrous boy who wrote *Alroy* in rhyme and prose, only to show, how long ago, victorious Judah's lion-banner rose.'*[5]

Having withdrawn his name from the books of Lincoln's Inn, Disraeli now began seriously to consider the political career which he had been vaguely contemplating for some time past. While abroad, he had become an assiduous reader of that 'excellent publication', *Galignani's Messenger*, and on his return he declared that, 'in the event of a new election', he intended to offer himself as a parliamentary candidate for High Wycombe, the constituency in which Bradenham was situated. In the

---

* Disraeli sent a pre-publication copy of *Alroy* to his sister without telling her that he had dedicated the book to her. 'My darling brother, what can I say for all the beautiful expressions of love you have poured out to me,' she wrote when thanking him. 'I who am nothing, so utterly unworthy of belonging to you. Yet I am indeed proud of your love and tenderness, for which all mine is but a poor return – but they are all I have to give. I had grown so impatient for Alroy that had he not appeared last night I am sure I should have gone quite mad, and then to come with such an introduction, how kind you are, how much too good' (*Benjamin Disraeli Letters*, i, 339).

meantime, with Edward Lytton Bulwer's help, he determined to make himself better known in London society.

In letters to Sarah he charted his success in this respect. At Bulwer's house in Hertford Street, so he told her, he met Lord Strangford and Lord Mulgrave, later Marquess of Normanby, with whom he also had 'a great deal of conversation', and Lord Eliot, later Earl of St Germans, who invited him to a male dinner party where he sat next to John Charles Herries, the former Chancellor of the Exchequer, 'old, grey-haired, financial', who turned out to be 'quite a literary man – so false are one's impressions'.

At one 'very brilliant party' at Bulwer's he met Charles Pelham Villiers, the Earl of Clarendon's younger brother, Member of Parliament for Wolverhampton, as well as Colonel Webster, 'who married Bodding-ton's daughter', a man who 'talked to [him] very much' and 'turned out to be Lord William Lennox', 'Colonel and Captain A'Court, brothers of Lord Heytesbury', and Captain Yorke, later fourth Earl of Hardwicke.

Disraeli's provenance was not such as to gain him entry yet into the greatest houses, but less particular hostesses, encouraged by Bulwer, welcomed his company and enjoyed his sprightly, witty, fertile conver-sation. He was entertained by Lady Cork, Lady Dudley Stuart and Lady Charleville; he became a regular guest at Lady Blessington's house, and a close friend of Lady Blessington's lover, the attractive, egotistical, inor-dinately extravagant Count D'Orsay, the husband of her stepdaughter and the acknowledged arbiter of dandiacal fashion.

At Lady Blessington's Disraeli was introduced to Lord Durham; at the opera he met William Beckford; at Lord Eliot's he sat next to the awkward and reserved Sir Robert Peel, the former Home Secretary and future Prime Minister, who – so he confidently assured his sister in letters which boasted outrageously of his social success – was 'most gracious'. 'He is a very great man, indeed,' he told Sarah, 'and they all seem afraid of him. By-the-bye, I observed that he attacked his turbot most entirely with his knife ... I can easily conceive that he could be very disagreeable, but yesterday [at Eliot's] he was in a most condescend-ing mood and unbent with becoming haughtiness. I reminded him by my dignified familiarity both that he was an ex-Minister and I a present Radical.'[6]

Disraeli's reception by Peel seems, however, not to have been so obliging as he claimed. 'Probably from nervousness, Disraeli did not recommend himself to Sir Robert Peel,' according to Lord St Germans. He asked him to lend him some papers. But 'Peel buried his face in his neckcloth and did not speak a word to Disraeli during the rest of the meal ... From his appearance or manner Sir Robert Peel seemed to take an intuitive dislike to him.'[7]

Peel was far from being the only person whom Disraeli offended. He himself continued to assure his sister that he was the greatest social success both in London and in the country. Certainly, there were those who were overwhelmed by his brilliance. Yet there were many others who were exasperated by him; by his habit of pontificating with his thumbs tucked into the armholes of his waistcoat; by his irritating practice of prefacing his remarks with an incantation, picked up in the Near East, 'Allah is great'; by his elaborate affectation of weary boredom on being asked to meet someone whom he had no wish to know.

'The world calls me "*conceited*",' he wrote in what has become known as the 'Mutilated Diary' of 1833, because large sections have been excised from it. 'The world is in error. I trace all the blunders of my life to sacrificing my own opinion to that of others.'[8]

At Bulwer's, as well as dandies and literati and up and coming politicians there was also 'a large sprinkling' of bluestockings, among them Lady Morgan, the Irish novelist, Caroline Norton, R. B. Sheridan's grand-daughter, the Whig hostess, and Letitia Landon, the poet, with whom her host was believed to be having an affair. She looked, so Disraeli said, 'the very personification of Brompton – pink satin dress and white satin shoes, red cheeks, snub nose, and her hair a la Sappho'. At a later soirée, Disraeli met her again; but this time she 'was perfectly *à la française* and really looked pretty'.[9]

The prolific novelist and dramatist, Catherine Gore – whose *Manners of the Day* had been praised by King George IV as 'the best and most amusing novel published in his remembrance' – was also there, and so was another bluestocking who, so Bulwer said, was particularly anxious to meet him. 'Oh! My dear fellow,' Disraeli said, 'I cannot really – the power of repartee has deserted me.'[10] But his host insisted. 'I have pledged myself – you must come,' he said, and Disraeli was accordingly intro-duced to a very sumptuous personage looking like 'a full rich blown rose'. 'I never', Disraeli commented, 'rec'd so cordial a reception in my life.'[11]

On another occasion, Bulwer's wife asked him to take a lady, considerably older than himself, into dinner. 'Oh! Anything rather than that insufferable woman,' he said before walking languidly towards her.

'In the course of an evening at Bulwer's,' Disraeli told Sarah, 'I stumbled over Tom Moore, to whom I introduced myself ... "I have heard of you, as everybody has," he said. "Did we not meet at Murray's once?"'[12]

He went on to talk about London's gentlemen's clubs, membership of which Disraeli was finding it difficult to acquire. He would have liked to join White's which, founded at White's Chocolate House in 1693 on the site of what is now Boodle's, was the oldest and grandest of the St James's gentlemen's clubs; but its members were most unlikely to support the candidature of a prospective member of Disraeli's background, appearance, race and manner, not to mention his authorship of *Vivian Grey*. Much the same objections would be raised by the members of Boodle's, a large proportion of whom were country gentlemen of decidedly conservative views, and of Brooks's, membership of which was described in 1822 by John Campbell, later Lord Chancellor, as a 'feather in [his] cap' since it consisted of 'the first men of rank and talent in England'.

Disraeli then thought of the Travellers' Club, founded in 1819 for gentlemen who had travelled abroad for at least five hundred miles from London in a straight line; and, since he had travelled further than most, he was qualified on that score. But its members did not want him; most particularly the Whig Lord Auckland, whose influence with other members of the committee was paramount, did not want him, and so he was blackballed. This was no disgrace, he assured Sarah. 'These things happen every night and to the first people.'

He would, he decided, join instead the Athenaeum, of which his father had been a founding member. This, the most intellectually élite of London's clubs, had been founded as recently as 1824 for artists, writers and scientists, almost singlehandedly by John Wilson Croker, the Irish politician and essayist whom Lord Macaulay detested 'more than cold boiled veal'. Membership of this club was more likely for Disraeli to achieve than that of the Travellers', although its members did not take kindly to the young man when they heard that he had ignored the club's rules by walking upstairs to talk to his father in the library. However, his friend, Edward Lytton Bulwer, undertook to support his candidature. Disraeli had grown very attached to Bulwer, his one close friend in the literary and publishing world and, so he said, one of the few men with whom his intellect came 'into collision with benefit'. He invited him to stay at Bradenham, telling Sarah that he was to do there 'just what he liked'; and he went with Bulwer for a short holiday to Bath where they arrived late one evening at a public ball in all their extravagant finery and, as he was delighted to record, 'got quite mobbed'.

Bulwer thought it as well to warn him, however, that he might well be blackballed at the Athenaeum, as its members would have reason to fear that he would 'clap them into a Book . . . These quiet fellows have a great horror of us Novel writers,' Bulwer explained. 'For my part, if I had not got into all my Clubs (at least the respectable ones) before I had taken to Authoring I should certainly be out of them all at this time.'[13]

While waiting for his election to the Athenaeum, Disraeli was advised to try for membership of the recently founded Conservative Club; but he thought it unwise to join a club so obviously associated with the Tories; and it was not until 1836 that he joined a club with a less identifying name, the Carlton.

By this time the committee of the Athenaeum had made up their mind; and Disraeli was blackballed as he had been by the Travellers'. His family believed that John Wilson Croker was to blame; and in his novel, *Coningsby*, Disraeli was to caricature Croker as Rigby, a man 'destitute of all imagination and noble sentiments . . . blessed with a vigorous, mendacious fancy, fitful in small expedients, and never happier than when devising shifts for great men's scruples'.*

Denied membership of both the Athenaeum and the Travellers', Disraeli joined a less prestigious club, the Albion, which few had heard

---

* In fact, it seems more likely that Croker was not responsible for Disraeli's failure to become a member of the Athenaeum, but that it was to his reputation and 'outlandish behaviour' that the members objected (M. F. Brightfield, *Life of J. W. Croker*, 1940, 234–40). He was later elected to the Farmers' Club; but the secretary of this club was 'directed to inform Mr Disraeli that his resignation would be accepted on payment of the arrears due from him' (Charles Graves, *Leather Armchairs*, 1903, 71).

of and which did not long survive.* However, it turned out to be 'a very capital club', so he was to say. 'Few in number, but not at all the set I anticipated – a great number of M.P.s and tho' not fashionable, distinguished. The grub and wines the best in London, and all on a finished scale.'[14]

Those who saw Disraeli for the first time in the reception rooms of private houses were not surprised by the difficulties he encountered in finding a gentlemen's club which would have him as a member, since the young man with the lustrous black curls would stride about in clothes which seemed almost to excite ridicule, suits of satin-lined black velvet with embroidered waistcoats, rings on his gloved fingers, gold chains round his neck. 'He wore waistcoats of the most gorgeous colours and the most fantastic patterns with much gold embroidery, velvet pantaloons and shoes adorned with red rosettes,' wrote one observer. 'His black hair pomaded and elaborately curled and his person redolent with perfume.'[15]

The beautiful, eccentric and quarrelsome Irishwoman, Rosina Bulwer – for whose extravagances her husband had to pay by his writings – did not at all care for him. One day in her house, wearing his exotic green velvet trousers, he rose from a cane chair to stalk about the room with his coat-tails over his arms, revealing the marks of the chair imprinted on his seat. Who is that? asked Samuel Rogers. Rosina, violently anti-semitic, answered, 'Oh! Young Disraeli, the Jew.' 'Rather the Wandering Jew,' said Rogers, 'with the mark of Cane upon him.'[16]

A pretentious woman, who appeared at her husband's parties in a 'blaze of jewels' and carrying about with her a tiny dog named Fairy, with which she seemed besotted, Rosina Bulwer did not trouble to conceal her dislike of Disraeli, of whom she was to draw an unpleasant portrait in her novel, *Very Successful* (1856), in which he appears as Jericho Jabber, the 'Jew d'Esprit' who marches about the room, 'ostentati-

---

* Disraeli seems to have made another attempt to become a member of the Athenaeum in 1843. He was unsuccessful (Humphrey Ward, *History of the Athenaeum, 1824–1925*, 1926; *Benjamin Disraeli Letters*, iv, 87). He did not become a member until 1866. He also had to wait until 1840 for election to Crockford's, the gambling club in St James's Street, for which Lord Ossulston offered to put him up in 1834 (A.L. Humphreys, *Crockford's or The Goddess of Chance in St James's Street, 1828–44*, 1955, 105).

ously admiring the ceiling'. Nor, indeed, did she get on well with her husband, who appears as the villain in her novel, *Chevely, or the Man of Honour*, which was published soon after she had consented to a legal separation. Nor did Disraeli try to hide his dislike of Rosina Bulwer and of the Irish generally: 'I never see her', he said, 'without thinking of a hod of mortar and a potato. Nature certainly intended that she should console her sorrows in Potheen.'*[17]

Unsuccessful in obtaining membership of a good London club, Disraeli was also initially unsuccessful in his attempt to get into Parliament. He had publicly announced his desire to do so at a party given by Caroline Norton, in whose house he met Lord Melbourne. 'Well, now, tell me, what do you want to be?' Melbourne asked him after they had been talking together for some time. 'I want', the young man replied, 'to be Prime Minister.' 'Melbourne gave a long sigh.'[18]

It was, perhaps, on this occasion at Mrs Norton's that Disraeli threw across the table to Melbourne a letter from Paul Emile Botta, the Italian doctor and archaeologist, describing Arab sexual practices. The painter, Benjamin Robert Haydon, was of the company and was shocked. Talking 'much of the East', Disraeli seemed to Haydon 'to be tinged with a disposition to palliate its infamous vices. I meant to ask him if he preferred Aegypt, where sodomy was *preferment* to England where it very properly was Death.' Referring later to Disraeli's behaviour, Haydon commented, 'I think no man would go on in that odd manner, wear green velvet trousers and ruffles, without having odd feelings. He ought to be kicked. I hate the look of the fellow.'[19]

Although he had already decided to offer himself as a candidate at High Wycombe, he had not yet made up his mind which party to commit himself to. He had an instinctive dislike of the Whigs, but had not yet otherwise developed any strong political inclinations. In any case, he felt drawn to Westminster not, it seems, by any sense of public service, but by ambition and vanity, the desire for fame, the need to make himself remarkable. Realizing that it might prove fatal to attach himself

---

* Rosina Bulwer was quite as rude about Disraeli, claiming that he had committed sodomy with her husband and that 'this was the reason why he had been offered a Cabinet post' (Leslie Mitchell, *Bulwer Lytton: The Rise and Fall of a Victorian Man of Letters*, 2003, 62).

to a falling star, he shied away from the Tories, whose influence was rapidly waning; and he made up his mind to present himself as a Radical. 'Toryism is worn out,' he told Benjamin Austen, 'and I cannot condescend to be a Whig . . . I start in the high Radical interest.'[20]

7

THE CANDIDATE

'All the women are on my side
and wear my colours.'

AT THE BEGINNING OF JUNE 1832, Disraeli went down from London
to High Wycombe to begin his canvass of the constituency. The sitting
members were Sir Thomas Baring, the financier, and the Hon. Robert
John Smith, Lord Carrington's son and heir who lived at Wycombe
Abbey on the outskirts of the town, in which he had much influence,
and who later became known as 'glass-bottom Carrington' because of
his *idée fixe* that 'an honourable part of his person was made of glass,
so that he was afraid to sit thereon, and during the whole of his uneventful life, he persistently refused to sit whenever it was possible by any
exercise of ingenuity to stand up or lie down'.[1]

Having declared himself a Radical, Disraeli told Benjamin Austen
that he took with him 'strong recommendatory epistles' from those
stalwarts on the left, Daniel O'Connell, Joseph Hume and Francis Burdett. A few days later he wrote again to Austen, dating his letter from
the Red Lion, the inn, now demolished, that stood in the High Street
with a statute of a red lion on the portico: 'I write you a hurried
note after a day's hard canvass. Whigs, Tories and Radicals, Quakers,
Evangelicals, Abolition of Slavery, Reform, Conservatism, Corn Laws –
here is hard work for one who is to please all parties. I make an excellent
canvasser.'[2]

> We are hard at it [he added in a letter to Mrs Austen]. Sir Thomas
> [Baring] you know has resigned [in order to contest a seat in
> Hampshire]. His son was talked of; I have frightened him off . . .

Yesterday Colonel [Charles] Grey [son of the Prime Minister] came down with a hired mob and a band. Never was such a failure. After parading the town with his paid voices, he made a stammering speech of ten minutes from his phaeton. All Wycombe was assembled. Feeling it was the crisis, I jumped up on the portico of the Red Lion and gave it to them for an hour and ¼. I can give you no idea of the effect. I made them all mad. A great many absolutely *cried*. I never made so many friends in my life or converted as many enemies. All the women are on my side and wear my colours, pink and white. The Colonel returned to town in the evening absolutely astounded out of his presence of mind; *on dit* never to appear again . . . If he comes I am prepared for him.[3]

Prone as Disraeli was to hyperbole, there seems no doubt that his speech, so much more fluent and dramatic than Grey's, was well received, and that he was loudly cheered when, pointing to the head of the red lion on the inn's portico, he said that when the poll was declared he would be there, and pointing to the tail, that his opponent would be there. He did not, however, convert a majority of those few men who were entitled to vote, since, although the Reform Bill had just become law, voting in this election was still confined to the names on the old register. When the result of the poll was announced, he had gathered but twelve votes; his opponent had twenty-three.[4]

Defiant in defeat, he made another long speech which almost resulted in a duel with Lord Nugent, a local magnate and convinced Whig, who considered himself insulted by him. More temperate and carefully reasoned was the address he issued on 3 December as an opening blast in his campaign in the election of the following year and in which he declared that he came forward once again, this time 'wearing the badge of no party and the livery of no faction'.

In a speech made after a dinner given for him by his supporters, he declared, 'I care not for party. I stand here without party. I plead the cause of the people.' He was 'a Conservative to preserve all that is good in our constitution, a Radical to remove all that is bad'.[5]

So confident was he of victory this time that he ordered a chair to be made in his electioneering colours so that he could be carried in triumph through the streets of the town by his jubilant supporters. But the electorate did not choose to have it so;* and once again he was to be disappointed: on this second occasion Robert John Smith gained 179 votes, Colonel Grey 140 and Disraeli 119.

He did not accept his defeat gracefully: he declared that had 'he let money fly', he 'would have come in'. 'The election or rather contest did not cost me £80 . . . and Grey not short of £800.'[6]

On 7 February, the disappointed candidate 'went to the House of Commons to hear Bulwer [Radical Member for St Ives] adjourn the House'. 'I was there yesterday, during the whole debate,' he told Sara Austen. 'Bulwer spoke, but he is physically disqualified as an orator; and, in spite of all his exertions, never can succeed . . . Between ourselves, I could floor them all. This *entre nous*; I was never more confident of anything than that I could carry everything before me in that House. The time will come . . . Grey spoke highly of my oratorical powers. Bulwer said he never heard "finer command of words".'[7]

Disappointed but not cast down by his first forays into the political world, Disraeli plunged once more into the social world of London. He remained, of course, an apparently conceited dandy; but his underlying seriousness and his conversational gifts now became more widely recognized. He was a 'very handsome young man', in the opinion of Henry Layard, Sara Austen's nephew, 'with a countenance in which beauty of feature and intellectual expression were strikingly combined'.[8] He was also, Layard might have added, still excessively self-regarding. His letters to his sister continued to assure her of his social success:

> Yesterday I dined with the Nortons [the Hon. George and his wife, Caroline Norton]. It was her eldest brother's birthday, who, she says, is the only respectable one of the family, and that is because he has a liver complaint. There were there the other brother Charles and the old Charles Sheridan, the uncle, and others. The only lady beside Mrs Norton, her sister Mrs Blackwood [later Lady Dufferin], also very handsome and very Sheridanic. She told me she was nothing. 'You see Georgy's the beauty, and Carry's the wit, and I ought to be the good one but then I

---

* 'People tried all they could to understand him,' wrote an early biographer. 'But they were completely puzzled by this Oriental apparition' (George Henry Francis, *The Rt. Hon. Benjamin Disraeli, M.P. A Critical Biography*, 1852, 23).

am not.' I must say I liked her exceedingly; besides she knows all my works by heart and spouts whole pages . . .[9]

In the evening came Lady St Maur, and anything so splendid I never gazed upon. Even the handsomest family in the world, which I think the Sheridans are, all looked dull . . .

Mrs Norton sang and acted, and did everything that was delightful. Ossulston [son of the Earl of Tankerville] came in – a very fine singer, unaffected and good-looking. Old Mrs Sheridan – who, by the bye, is young and pretty, and authoress of *Carwell* – is my great admirer; in fact, the whole family have a very proper idea of my merits! and I like them all.[10]

Disraeli was at his most splendid. He was wearing a 'black velvet coat lined with satin, purple trousers with a gold band running down the outside seam,' Lady Dufferin recalled, insisting that there was no exaggeration in the description, 'a scarlet waistcoat, long lace ruffles, falling down to the tips of his fingers, white gloves with several brilliant rings outside them, and long black ringlets rippling down upon his shoulders'.[11]

Lady Dufferin also recalled Disraeli's riposte to a remark of her 'insufferable' brother-in-law, the dissolute and pretentious barrister, the Hon. George Norton, who asked his guest to drink a particular kind of wine, saying he had never tasted anything so good before. Disraeli agreed that the wine was very good. 'Well,' said Norton, 'I have got wine twenty times as good in my cellar.' 'No doubt, no doubt,' said Disraeli, 'but, my dear fellow, this is quite good enough for such *canaille* as you have got here today.'[12]

Three or four months after this dinner at the Nortons', at the end of June 1833, Disraeli again wrote to his sister to assure her that his social life was as busy as ever: his table was 'literally covered with invitations', some from people he did not even know. He dined one day with the St Maurs, where he spoke to Lady Westmorland ('very clever') and decided that Lord St Maur had 'great talent', which developed itself in a domestic circle though otherwise he was 'shy-mannered'. In the evening there was a good soirée at Lady Charleville's, where he met Lady Aldborough, who was deaf; and he could not 'bear deaf people', who never could repeat what he had said 'even to Princes'.

There was a prince that evening at Lady Charleville's, the Prince of Canino, born Luciano Buonaparte. He met another Buonaparte at Mrs

Wyndham's, Joseph Buonaparte, Luciano's eldest brother, with 'his beautiful daughter'; and afterwards he went to the Caledonian Ball 'in a dress from my Oriental collection'.[13]

'London is emptying fast but gay,' he wrote three weeks later, on 30 July. 'Lady Cork [the eighty-seven-year-old widow of the seventh Earl of Cork] had two routs. All my best people, no blues [bluestockings]. At a concert at Mrs Mitford's I was introduced to Malibran [Maria-Félicita Malibran, the operatic contralto] who is to be the heroine of my opera. She is a very interesting person.' 'My letters are shorter than Napoleon's,' he added in his letter to Sarah, 'but I love you more than he did Josephine. I shall be down tomorrow.'

When he did get down to Bradenham that summer, he began writing an account of himself, at once a self-examination and a self-congratulation, in parts contradictory, in his 'Mutilated Diary'.

'I have passed the whole of this year in uninterrupted lounging and pleasure,' he wrote. 'My life has not been a happy one. Nature has given me an awful ambition with fiery passions. My life has been a struggle, with moments of rapture.'

> My disposition is now indolent [he continued]. I wish to be idle and enjoy myself . . . [Yet] my career will probably be more energetic than ever, and the world will wonder at my ambition. Alas, I struggle from Pride. Yes! It is Pride that now prompts me, not Ambition. They shall not say I have failed.
>
> I have not gained much in conversation with men. Bulwer is one of the few with whom my intellect comes into collision . . . Lockhart is good for *tête-à-têtes* . . . But he is overrated . . . The man from whom I have gained most in conversation is [Paul Emile] Botta . . . If I add to these my father, the list comprises the few men from whose conversation I have gained wisdom . . .
>
> I make it a rule now never to throw myself open to men. I do not grudge them the knowledge I could impart . . . but, as I never get anything in return, I do not think the exertion necessary.
>
> As a lively companion, of ceaseless entertainment and fun, no one, perhaps, equals Charles Mathews, the son of the comedian, but far exceeding his father, who is, I understand, jealous of him . . .
>
> I can read characters at a glance; few men can deceive me.

> My mind is a continental mind. It is a revolutionary mind. I am
> only truly great in action. If ever I am placed in a truly eminent
> position I shall prove this. I could rule the House of Commons
> although there would be a great prejudice against me at first.[14]

But now at Bradenham it was to poetry that he devoted many, if
not most, of the waking hours of his life.

'I live here like a hermit, and have scarcely seen my family,' he told
Sara Austen. 'I rise at seven, and my day passes in study and composition.'
For a time he left Bradenham for Southend and there also, 'living on
snipes and riding a good deal', he passed his days 'in constant composition'.[15]

He had first conceived the idea for this great work of poetry, to be
called the *Revolutionary Epick*, during his tour of the Middle East. 'Standing upon Asia,' he said, 'and gazing upon Europe, with the broad Helles-
pont alone between us, and the shadow of night descending on the
mountains, these mighty continents appeared to me, as it were, the rival
principles of government that, at present, contend for the mastery of
the world. "What!" I exclaimed, "Is the revolution of France a less
important event than the siege of Troy? Is Napoleon a less interesting
character than Achilles?"'[16]

After weeks of hard work he told Sara Austen that he had already
written four thousand lines of verse and was ready to print them. 'The
whole of it is matured in my mind,' he said, 'though probably it could
not be completed under thirty thousand lines.' He sought her help in
finishing it: 'Are you sure a Creole is dark?' he asked her about the
Empress Josephine. 'No matter, I will make her brunette. And what
exactly is a sou-wester?' He was 'perfectly ignorant of the geography of
the wind' and had no atlas to which he could refer.[17]

In the third week of January 1834, the first canto having been
finished, he offered to bore the Austens with a recitation of it one
evening when they were on their own. Undeterred upon arrival at their
house to find a party assembled for dinner, he took the floor to perform,
in his own words, 'the part of the importunate author'.

Henry Layard was among the guests and provided an account of
that evening:

There was something irresistibly comic in the young man dressed in the fantastic, coxcombical costume that he then affected – velvet coat of an original cut thrown wide open . . . and ruffles to its sleeves. Shirt collars turned down in Byronic fashion, an elaborately embroidered waistcoat whence issued voluminous folds of frill, and shoes adorned with red rosettes – black hair pomatumed and elaborately curled, and his person redolent with perfume – announcing himself as the Homer or Dante of the age.[18]

In 'pretentious tones' he read the whole of the first canto, making dramatic gestures which presented one of those in his audience, his fellow author, Samuel Warren, with an irresistible opportunity to ridicule him. Warren did so with such accurate mimicry that the audience burst into laughter.[19]

Derision as much as bewilderment and disappointment greeted the work when it was published in two parts in March and June 1834. Disraeli had expected a far different response.

'I have executed the work to my satisfaction, and, what is more, to the satisfaction of my father, a critic difficult to please,' he told Benjamin Austen. 'I await the result with composure, although I am not sanguine of pleasing the million. I feel that I have now done enough for my reputation and that I am at length justified in merely looking to my purse.'[20]

Concealing as best he could the disappointment he felt at the reception of the heroic verses of the *Revolutionary Epick* – the dedication of which the Duke of Wellington had been offered and had declined, on the grounds that he never did accept such offers because of the necessity of perusing every work presented to him for this purpose[21] – Disraeli once more became an unmistakable sight in London drawing-rooms in the season of 1834.

Back in London in May, he dined with the widowed Lady Blessington. 'Also there were Lords Castlereagh, Elphinstone and Allen . . . Lord Wilton was the absent guest, having to dine with the King, but he came in the evening.' 'Hope's ball on Monday was the finest thing in the year,' he continued his account, 'supped off gold and danced in the sculpture gallery. Today is the Drawing-room . . . I dine with O'Connell on Saturday . . . I was at Lady Dudley Stuart's on Sunday – a pleasant circle – and made the acquaintance of Lord Hertford [Lord Monmouth in Disraeli's *Coningsby* and Lord Steyne in Thackeray's *Vanity Fair*].

I dine with Lady Cork today to meet the Mulgraves, Tavistocks and Lincolns ... I made [William] Beckford's acquaintance at the opera on Thursday. Conversation of three hours ... I dined [again] yesterday with Lady Blessington and Durham [the Lord Privy Seal in Earl Grey's cabinet] and he talked to me nearly the whole evening; and afterwards at Lady Salisbury's.'

An American journalist, N.P. Willis, known as 'Namby Pamby' Willis, was among the guests at Lady Blessington's and described in the *New York Mirror* how Count D'Orsay, 'in splendid defiance of others' dullness', sparkled throughout the first half-hour of dinner which would otherwise 'have passed off with the usual English fashion of earnest silence ... Bulwer and Disraeli were silent altogether.'

He would have 'foreboded a dull dinner,' this guest continued, had he not 'read the promise of change in the expression' of the 'open brow, clear sunny eye and unembarrassed repose of the beautiful and expressive mouth of Lady Blessington'. The change 'came presently'.

> She gathered up the cobweb threads of conversation going on at different parts of the table and ... flung them into Disraeli's fingers. It was an appeal to his opinion on a subject he well understood, and he burst at once, without preface, into that fiery vein of eloquence which, hearing many times after, and always with new delight, has stamped Disraeli in my mind as the most wonderful talker I have ever had the fortune to meet. He is anything but a declaimer. You would never think him on stilts. If he catches himself in a rhetorical sentence, he mocks at it in the next breath. He is satirical, contemptuous, pathetic, humorous, everything in a moment. Add to this that Disraeli's is the most intellectual face in England – pale, regular, and overshadowed with the most luxuriant masses of raven-black hair – and you will scarce wonder that meeting him for the first time Lord Durham was impressed ... Without meaning any disrespect to Disraeli, whom I admire as much as any man in England, I remarked to my neighbour, a celebrated artist, that it would make a glorious drawing of Satan tempting an archangel to rebel.[22]

'I have had great success in society this year in every respect,' Disraeli told his sister with accustomed self-congratulation in June 1834.

> I make my way easily in the highest set ... I am also right in politics as well as society, being now backed by a very powerful

party, and I think the winning one . . . I was at the Duchess of St Albans on Monday, but rather too late for the fun. It was a most brilliant *fête*. The breakfast a real banquet but I missed the Morris dancers . . . In the evening at Lady Essex where the coterie consisted of the new Postmaster-General and his lady, the Chesterfields, the George Ansons, the Albert Conynghams and Castlereagh. Tuesday after the Opera I supped with Castlereagh who gave a very recherché party . . . Tonight after paying my respects to their Majestys [King William IV and Queen Adelaide] at the Opera, I am going to the Duchess of Hamilton's . . . Yesterday Lord Durham called upon me . . . A good story [told him by Lady Cork]:

Lady Cork: Do you know young Disraeli?

Lord Carrington: Hem! Why? Eh?

Lady Cork: Why, he is your neighbour, isn't he, eh?

Lord Carrington: His father is.

Lady Cork: I know that. His father is one of my dearest friends. I dote on the Disraelis.

Lord Carrington: This young man is a very extraordinary sort of person. The father I like; he is very quiet and respectable.

Lady C.: Why do you think the young man extraordinary? I should not think that *you* could taste him.

Lord C.: He is a great agitator. Not that he troubles us much *now*. He is never amongst us now. I believe he has gone abroad again.

Lady C., *literatim*: You old fool! Why, he sent me this book this morning. You need not look at it; you can't understand it. It is the finest book ever written. Gone abroad, indeed! Why, he is the best *ton* in London! There is not a party that goes down without him. The Duchess of Hamilton says there is nothing like him. Lady Lonsdale would give her head and shoulders for him. He would not dine at your house if you were to ask him. He does not care for people because they are lords; he must have fashion, or beauty, or wit, or something: and you are a very good sort of person, but you are nothing more.

The old Lord took it very good-humouredly, and laughed. Lady Cork has read every line of the new book. I don't doubt the sincerity of her admiration, for she has laid out 17s. in crimson velvet, and her maid is binding it . . .[23]

Soon after this letter was written Disraeli joined 'a water party . . . almost the only party of pleasure that ever turned out to be pleasant . . . The day was beautiful . . . We sailed up to Greenwich . . . We had a magnificent banquet on deck, and had nothing from shore except white-bait piping hot . . . I never knew a more agreeable day, and never drank so much champagne in my life.'

A few weeks later Disraeli was back at Bradenham and soon picked up his pen to continue the notes which he did not choose to describe as a diary: 'What a vast number of extraordinary characters have passed before me or with whom I have become acquainted. Interviews with O'Connell, Beckford and Lord Durham . . . I have become very popular with the dandies. D'Orsay took a fancy to me, and they take their tone from him. Lady Blessington is their muse and she declared violently in my favour . . . I am as popular with first-rate men as I am hated by the second-rate.'[24] He could scarcely include the Duke of Wellington among the first-rate men with whom he was popular, but he did meet him, so he said, at Lady Cork's 'wearing his blue ribbon [as a Knight of the Order of Garter] on the eve of the day Lord Grey resigned [8 July 1834]. "He always wears his blue ribbon when mischief is going on," whispered Ossulston to me.'

As for enemies in his account of second-rate men, Disraeli mentions only one – Samuel Rogers: 'Considering his age I endeavour to conciliate him, but it is impossible. I think I will give him cause to hate me.'[25]

Among the first-rate men with whom he was popular, he did not mention Bulwer, whose place in his affection had been taken by D'Orsay, who, so he told Lady Blessington, would be very welcome if he cared to come down to Bradenham for a few days. 'I suppose it is vain to hope to see my dear D'Orsay here,' he wrote to her. 'I wish indeed he would come. Here is a cook by no means contemptible. He can bring his horses if he likes, but I can mount him. Adieu, Lady Blessington, some day I will try to write you a more amusing letter; at present I am in truth ill and sad.'

Later that year he told Benjamin Austen that, for 'exactly two months', since 24 August, he had been suffering from a 'strange illness' that kept him to his sofa – 'great pain in the legs and extraordinary languor'.

'It came upon me suddenly,' he reported. 'I struggled against it for some time, but mounting my horse one day, I had a slight determination of blood to my head and was obliged to throw myself to the ground. This frightened me, remembering old sufferings, and I laid up. Quiet, diet and plenteous doses of ammonia (heavenly maid) not only restored me, but I felt better and more hearty this last fortnight than I long remember.'[26]

8

AFFAIRS

'I may commit many follies in life, but
I never intend to marry for "love".'

EARLIER THAT YEAR, IN FEBRUARY 1834, while staying at The
Grange, Southend, Disraeli had made one of his rare excursions into
the hunting field.

'I hunted the other day with Sir Henry Smythe's hounds,' he told his
sister with characteristic and not altogether mocking self-congratulation,
'and although not in scarlet was the best mounted man in the field . . .
I stopped at nothing. I gained great *kudos*, having nearly killed an
Arabian mare in a run of 30 miles.'*1

This Arabian mare belonged to Henrietta, Lady Sykes, with whom
he had been much taken when he had met her in a box at the opera
on 18 May 1833. Also in the box was Lady Charlotte Bertie, the twenty-
one-year-old daughter of the Earl of Lindsay, who noted in her diary
that Disraeli was 'wild, enthusiastic and very poetical . . . The brilliance of my companion affected me and we ran on about poetry and
Venice and Baghdad and Damascus and my eye lit up and my cheek
burned.'2

Disraeli was clearly attracted to this young woman and, a few days
later, asked his sister if she would like her as a sister-in-law. She was,
he said, 'very clever, [had] £25,000, and [was] domestic. As for "love"

---

* He was not exaggerating. The diary of the Master of the East Essex Hunt shows that on
that day there was, indeed, a record run of thirty miles (*Victorian History of the Counties
of England . . . Essex*, ii, 576, quoted by Jane Ridley, *The Young Disraeli*, 144).

and beauty all my friends who married for love and beauty either beat their wives or live apart from them. This is literally the case. I may commit many follies in life, but I never intend to marry for "love", which I am sure is a guarantee of infidelity.'[3]

Sarah did not like the idea of Lady Charlotte as a sister-in-law and thought it unlikely that she had as much money as her brother supposed. She suggested that he should make another proposal to William Meredith's sister, Ellen, whom he had already asked and by whom he had been refused.

For the moment, however, while looking about for a suitable wife, Disraeli was content to have a married woman as a mistress; and his family supposed that he had found such a mistress in Clara Bolton, the wife of his doctor, George Buckley Bolton.

Mrs Bolton was another woman whom Sarah did not care for. Nor did other women who knew her, for she was considered socially pretentious, conceited, devious and unprincipled, though by no means stupid, while her husband, the doctor, was ill-bred, cocky and, it was supposed, as a *mari complaisant*, not above accepting money from his wife's admirers. These admirers, so Clara Bolton was anxious to assure Disraeli, were many and diverse, not a 'formal set', she told him, listing their names. 'I give them nothing to do,' she said, '& nothing to eat and yet they come.' Disraeli often went. 'We all agree,' he said, 'it's better than a club.'

The other woman, Henrietta Sykes, who was in the box at the theatre with Lady Charlotte Bertie, was the wife of Sir Francis Sykes, the third baronet, owner of Basildon Park in Berkshire as well as a town house in Upper Grosvenor Street. His grandfather had become extremely rich in the service of the East India Company; his father, a Member of Parliament, had married a daughter of the first Lord Henniker. His wife was the daughter of Henry Villebois of Martham Hall, Norfolk, also a rich man, a partner in the brewery firm of Truman and Hanbury. Lady Sykes herself, according to her friend, Lady Charlotte Bertie, was 'a fine woman and very pleasant and good-natured'. She was also extremely pretty, wilful, impetuous, sensual and susceptible. She had four young children.

The prospect of meeting this woman, with whom her brother had

soon fallen in love, elicited a worried letter from Sarah Disraeli when
her brother proposed bringing her down to Bradenham:

> I am so afraid it will rain & then Lady Sykes will die of ennui,
> for how can we amuse her of an evening as it is, & then the long
> mornings too. She will hate us. Let us know as well as you can
> what *établissement* travels with her . . .
>
> Send the claret directly as we want that at any rate & it will
> not be good if it have not time to settle . . . I write in the greatest
> haste[4] . . . I am somewhat nervous at the idea of entertaining our
> visitors whose tastes I cannot even guess at.[5]

The next day Disraeli replied:

> I received yours this morning. We come on Saturday but at what
> hour very doubtful. I sho[uld] think about 3. Lady Sykes will
> venture to bring her only daughter [Eva] aged three. But no
> nurserymaid. I assured her my mother wo[uld] not disapprove
> of a pretty child. For the rest her page and soubrette, [Isabella
> Margaret] Munro . . . I shall send my groom with my horse in
> Munro's gig. Be not alarmed about amusement; our guests are
> indolent and loungy.[6]

Sarah need not have been so worried. Apparently the visit was not
such a strain as she had feared it might be; and, when Lady Sykes and
her lover returned to London, they were evidently more deeply in love
than ever. She wrote him a series of passionate letters assuring him of
her devotion, telling him how much she missed him when he left her,
how she could not restrain her tears. 'If you knew how desolate this
house is – your white stick on the sopha, a ghost of departed joy . . .'

> It is the night Dearest the night that we used to pass so happily
> together . . . I cannot sleep. I love you . . . I love you indeed I do
> . . . The dear head, is it better? That it were pillowed on my bosom
> for ever. I would be such an affectionate old Nurse to my child
> and kiss and soothe every pain . . . Good Angels guard my dearest.
> A thousand and a thousand kisses – Good night. Sleep and dream
> of – your Mother.[7]

> *Love me*, my Soul, love me and be assured that the measure of
> my idolatry for you is full to the brim [she wrote in another
> letter]. Every breath I draw is yours, even *now* your kisses live on
> my lips and face and I feel the passion of your embrace . . . Best
> beloved, do you love me? Do you indeed? How often have I asked

you that question, how often been soothed by your assurance of
devotion to me. I do not doubt you, oh no, I dare not – it would
drive me mad.[8]

When Sir Francis heard of his wife's affair with Disraeli – being told
of it, Lady Sykes supposed, by Mrs Bolton, with whom Sir Francis
himself was by now having an affair – he forbade his wife ever to see
Disraeli again.

Lady Sykes had no doubt as to how to deal with her husband and
the woman she called 'Madame'. She stormed round to Mrs Bolton's
house, where she found her husband's carriage waiting in the street
outside. 'I walked in [she told Disraeli] *sans* knocking and up to the
drawing room *sans* being announced. Fancy their consternation. I really
thought Francis would have fainted.'

'We are victorious,' she closed her version of this encounter.
'Madame cried and wrung her hands. F[rancis] cried and begged me
to be merciful. I did *not* cry and had apologies from both.'

Mrs Bolton, who had once, so she said, received letters from Disraeli,
protesting 'undying, unspeakable, obligation', now told Lady Sykes that
she had heard on excellent authority that no one would visit her any
more and that Disraeli himself would leave her. 'Indeed, he has left you
already,' she said, 'I know him well. He is everywhere despised.'

Ignoring such outbursts from Mrs Bolton, Henrietta Sykes agreed
to go for a few days with her husband to France, whence she wrote to
Disraeli: 'Think of the happy ten minutes on the sopha . . . and how
delicious would be . . . the happiness of returning to the peaceful cot
and reposing in each other's arms. It would be bliss, bliss beyond compare, and hope whispers it will be realized – most idolized, I love you,
I adore you, I worship you with fond idolatry.'[9]

On her return from the Continent, Disraeli left Bradenham almost
immediately to see Henrietta again; and one day in London her father
saw them together in the street and walked past, ignoring them: a slight
which, in their absorption with each other, they did not notice. Mr
Villebois, however, instructed one of Henrietta's sisters to let her know
that he would continue to ignore them until their intimacy ceased. His
heart was 'almost broken' by the scandal, he said; and he trusted that
she would end the disgraceful relationship.

'I wrote back', Henrietta told her lover, 'to say . . . I was *agonized* by his displeasure but so long as Francis allowed me your society I should enjoy it.'[10]

The scandal which so distressed Mr Villebois was exacerbated when Disraeli accepted an invitation to stay with the Sykeses at Southend – where they had taken a house, Poulter's Grange – Sir Francis having invited him on the implied condition that the Boltons were to stay there too. 'I think ... you will like the quiet of this place,' Henrietta wrote. 'The greatest drawback will be the *damnable* Boltons. They poison love, my greatest scource of enjoyment.'[11]

Disraeli did not tell his sister where he was going and, when she found out, she was much distressed. 'My dearest, why have you forgotten me?' she wrote to him, care of the post office at Southend. 'Will you come back next Saturday?' 'My dearest love,' she wrote again the following day, 'No letter again this morning. After you left me so unhappy I was sure you would not have failed to have kept your promise of writing to me if there was not something amiss. Pray send me a single line. We are so dull here.' The next day Disraeli did reply to her letters, giving the excuse for not having been in touch with her before that he had been writing hard.

He certainly had need to earn money from his writing, to create, as he put it, 'something great & lasting' which would be profitable and, although he had by now dropped Benjamin Austen in his pursuit of more rewarding, distinguished and entertaining friends, he wrote to him asking for a further loan so that he could avoid 'the cruelty' of having his 'power of creation marred at such a moment'.

Austen's patience had worn too thin for this. 'I am sorry to say, my dear Disraeli,' he replied huffily, refusing the request, 'that you have tried me too often.' He relented, however, after having received an ingratiating letter from Disraeli, who assured him that there was 'not a person in the world' who would more readily hazard everything he valued to serve Austen and his wife. 'I was so circumstanced last year that my acquaintance I utterly rejected ... [My] relations I never went near, and I disregarded an entrance which offered itself to me to the most brilliant society of the metropolis.' His debts, he added falsely, were '*entirely* and *altogether* electioneering debts'. Friends, he continued, were 'not made every day ... It is in youth only that these connections are formed, and yours was my last. Had the friend [William Meredith] who in his gloomier hours never found me wanting, been spared to me, I should not have been forced to write this humiliating letter! Farewell!'[12]

Mollified by this abject and misleading letter, Austen lent Disraeli £1,200 at 2½ per cent. This, however, did not go far to alleviate his problems; and his financial affairs grew ever more complicated as his solicitor, Philip Rose, endeavoured to satisfy or, at the least, to quieten his numerous creditors by all manner of financial expedients. Loans were borrowed from such generous friends as D'Orsay, with whom he fell out when they were not repaid, while money was, so it seems, extracted from Sir Francis Sykes, whose mental state was becoming increasingly confused.

Struggling to finish *Venetia*, a novel based on the life of Byron, Disraeli told William Pyne, a rich solicitor, that he 'found it difficult to command the Muse amidst all these vexations'. But he did contrive to command it, to finish *Henrietta Temple*, a novel inspired by his affair with Lady Sykes, which was published by Henry Colburn in 1837, the same year as *Venetia*. He also managed to survive all threats to have him incarcerated in a debtors' prison, though coming close to arrest on more than one occasion and once at High Wycombe being driven to hide in a well to evade the sheriff's officer.[13]

'I am hourly, nay, every minute, annoyed by the coarse vulgarity of the one and the hypocrisy, the low cunning of the other,' Henrietta Sykes wrote to Disraeli of the Boltons following his return to Bradenham, after he had spent a month at Southend. 'I went into your room today, arranged your wardrobe, *kissed* the Bed, swallowed my tears and behaved as a heroine . . . Today's letter was the kindest, dearest – write me many such.'[14]

It was not long before he had no need to do so, as Sir Francis went abroad for over two years; and Disraeli, by then on the best of terms with him, went with him to Harwich to see him off. They were now agreed about the perfidy of the Boltons: he was, in Sir Francis's words, a 'dreadful' person; she filled him with 'disgust'. Fortunately, she went to live alone in Rotterdam where she was, Sarah D'Israeli heard, the 'object of much scandal'.

So, indeed, was Disraeli, who now spent much of his time, nights as well as days, in the Sykes's house. He wrote in his diary, 'What a happy or rather amusing society H[enrietta] and myself commanded this year. What Delicious little suppers after the Opera.'[15]

By now, however, Disraeli's passion for Lady Sykes had begun to cool. He had grown tired of her cloying possessiveness, of receiving such letters as:

> I swear I suffer the torments of the damned when you are away and although there is nothing I would not sacrifice to give you a moment's enjoyment I cannot bear that your amusement should spring from any other source than myself . . . Are you angry, love, at my selfishness? You never answer questions and I sometimes think I bore you by writing . . . It appears an age since we parted and I would that we were never separated for a moment. Is it vain to suppose you would love me better and better the longer we were together? . . . I love you even to madness.

The affair lingered on, and continued to be the subject of scandalous stories, not only about Disraeli and Lady Sykes, but also about Henrietta and Lord Lyndhurst, the good-natured, indiscreet, gossiping and, to women, extremely attractive American-born former and future Lord Chancellor, with whom Disraeli – who described him as looking like 'a high-bred falcon' – was on the most friendly terms. Indeed, it was suggested that, as a means of forwarding his political career, Disraeli encouraged Lady Sykes to have an affair with Lyndhurst who, though contentedly married to a Jewish wife, had not the least objection. Nor, indeed, had Lady Sykes, who told Disraeli that she could make Lyndhurst do as she liked, 'so whatever arrangement you think best tell me & and I will perform it'.

> I can well remember the scandal in the country at this connexion [wrote Sir Philip Rose], and especially at the visit of Lady Sykes to Bradenham accompanied by Lord L[yndhurst] and the indignation aroused in the neighbourhood at D. having introduced his reputed mistress and her Paramour to his *Home* and made them the associates of his *Sister* as well as of his father and mother. It did him much harm at the time and to show how unfavourable impressions linger long afterwards I have had it thrown in my teeth by influential county people within very recent years [the late 1870s and early 1880s] that this was an act which would never

be forgotten and which all D's subsequent career could never obliterate.*[16]

In the summer of 1834, Lady Sykes received what she called a 'disagreeable' letter from her sister warning her that she would be socially ostracised if her relationship with Disraeli continued. She advised her to go to Norfolk to stay with their father at Martham Hall. Lady Sykes declined to do this; but at last she did agree to go abroad with Lyndhurst and some members of his family. She 'liked L. very much,' she told Disraeli. 'He is very good natured' but 'only thought of driving away care'. He was also 'a perfect fool where women are concerned'.[17]

Disraeli was asked to go abroad with them but he declined the invitation.

It was not long before Lady Sykes had found another lover in the attractive, good-looking, gregarious Irish painter, Charles Dickens's friend, Daniel Maclise. But when she and Maclise were discovered in bed together, Sir Francis threatened proceedings for what was known as 'criminal conversation' and inserted a paragraph in the *Morning Chronicle* giving notice that 'HENRIETTA SYKES the wife of me SIR FRANCIS SYKES Baronet hath committed ADULTERY with DANIEL MACLISE ... Portrait and Picture Painter (with whom she was found in bed at my house)...'[18] Proceedings were not pursued, however, because of the other scandalous matters which would inevitably have come to light, including a story that £2,000, which had been paid to Lady Sykes in excess of her allowance, had somehow 'found its way into Disraeli's pocket'.[19]

Lady Sykes was disgraced and no longer seen in polite society in London. Disraeli, loyal to past friends, wrote her a letter of sympathy, to which she replied: 'I regret that I should have awakened feelings of bygone years ... Whatever may be my present sufferings I have brought

---

* 'Rose goes on to add, however,' Robert Blake commented, 'that the letters suggest that the pressure for the invitation came from the D'Israeli family rather than from Benjamin himself, and that it might have been embarrassing for him to refuse. Examination of these papers and others which Sir Philip Rose probably had not seen enables us to clear up some points. It was Henrietta who first introduced Disraeli to Lyndhurst, and whatever the circumstances in which she first met the latter, it was not the result of any initiative on Disraeli's part. He therefore can be acquitted on that charge' (Robert Blake, *Disraeli*, 117).

them on myself & no one can judge more harshly of my conduct for the last 2 months than I . . . I thank God no one can reproach me of anything but romantic folly . . . I cannot think for I am distracted & feel as if there were no resting place on earth for me.'

Her life in society was over, and in May 1846 the death of the widow of Sir Francis Sykes was only briefly noticed in the newspapers.

What is apparently the last letter she wrote to Disraeli was very different from those she had written in the torridity of their affair:

> What can I say sufficient to convey to you my deep admiration of your book [*Henrietta Temple: A Love Story*] and the extreme pleasure I felt in reading it. You know I am not very eloquent in expressing my feelings, therefore I must fail to convey to you a tythe part of the extreme gratification I have in your brilliant success . . . It is possible that I may go abroad with Francis – he is perfectly recovered and *tolerably* kind to me.[20]

9

THE REFORMING TORY

'I am considered a great
popular orator'

THROUGHOUT THE TIME of his affair with Lady Sykes, Disraeli had lost no opportunity of seeking the approval of men of political standing and influence, such as the friendly Lord Lyndhurst.*

> I dined on Saturday *en famille* with Lyndhurst [he told his sister on 4 November 1834]. A more amiable and agreeable family I never met. The eldest daughter is just like her mother and, although only thirteen, rules everything and everybody – a most astounding little woman ... I saw Chandos [Lord Chandos, eldest son of the Duke of Buckingham] today, and had a long conversation with him on politics. He has no head, but I flatter myself I opened his mind a little ... D'Orsay has taken my portrait.[1]

As well as with Lyndhurst and Chandos, Disraeli was closely in touch and in correspondence with Lord Durham, whom he asked to use his influence to persuade 'young Hobhouse [Sir John Hobhouse, later Lord Broughton]' to resign from the political contest in his favour. 'My dear Lord,' he wrote, 'my affairs are black; therefore, remember me and serve me if you can. My principles you are acquainted with; as for my other qualifications, I am considered a great popular orator.'[2]

---

* Disraeli's manner of speaking at this time seemed sometimes to have been modelled on Lyndhurst's. Having met Disraeli for the first time at the Londonderrys', Frances Mary Gascoyne-Cecil wrote in her diary: 'He bears the mark of the Jew strongly, and at times his way of speaking reminded me so much of Lord Lyndhurst, I could almost have thought him in the room. He is evidently very clever, but superlatively vulgar' (Carola Oman, *The Gascoyne Heiress: The Life and Diaries of Frances Mary Gascoyne-Cecil*, 248).

Lord Durham, however, replied that he was not in a position to help: he did not know Hobhouse well enough to intervene. But these were times which required the 'presence in Parliament of every true and honest politician' and he trusted and hoped, therefore, that Disraeli would find his way there yet. 'If an occasion offers when I can forward your views,' he added, 'I shall not fail to do so.'[3]

These were certainly times of great political excitement; and, as Bulwer told Isaac D'Israeli, his son, Benjamin, was 'restless and ambitious as usual', but 'such dispositions always carve out their way'.

> It was a lively season that winter of 1834! [Disraeli wrote in his novel, *Coningsby*] What hopes, what fears and what bets! ... People sprang up like mushrooms; town suddenly became full. Everybody who had been in office and everybody who wished to be in office ... were alike visible. All of course by mere accident; one might meet the same men every day for a month, who were only 'passing through town' ... The town, through November, was in a state of excitement; clubs crowded, not only morning rooms but halls and staircases swarming with members eager to give and to receive rumours equally vain; streets lined with cabs and chariots, grooms and horses ...
>
> But, after all, who were to form the government, and what was the government to be? Was it to be a Tory government, or an Enlightenment-Spirit-of-the-Age ... Liberal-Moderate-Reform government? ...
>
> Great questions these, but unfortunately there was nobody to answer them. They tried the Duke [of Wellington]; but nothing could be pumped out of him. All that he knew, which he told in his curt, husky manner, was, that he had to carry on the King's government ... 'This can't go on much longer,' said Taper to Tadpole [typical party wire-pullers] ... At last he [Sir Robert Peel] came; the great man in a great position, summoned from Rome [where he had been on holiday] to govern England. The very day that he arrived he had his audience with the King.

In the subsequent election campaign of 1835, Disraeli decided to stand once more for High Wycombe and to do so as a Radical-leaning Tory, sworn enemy of the Whigs. 'It is not enough to say of Mr Disraeli', ran a letter in the *Bucks Gazette*, 'that he delivered himself with his usual ability [on the day of nomination]. The difficulties that he had to encounter were most ably met and judiciously avoided; to steer between the shoals of Toryism on the one hand and the quicksands of Radicalism on the other (for he was supported by the two parties) required the utmost skill and well did he acquit himself.'

'I stand astonishingly well at Wycombe,' Disraeli himself assured Benjamin Austen, 'and may beat the Colonel [Charles Grey] yet. Had I the money, I might canter over the County, for my popularity is irresistible.'[4] It was, however, not irresistible enough: he received 128 votes as against 147 for Charles Grey and 289 for the Hon. Robert J. Smith.

'I am not at all disheartened,' Disraeli protested. 'I do not in any way feel like a defeated man. Perhaps it is because I am used to it. I will say of myself like the famous Italian general, who, being asked in his old age why he was always victorious, replied, it was because he had always been beaten in his youth.'[5]

> I have fought our battle and have lost it; by a majority of fourteen, [he wrote to the Duke of Wellington in a less jaunty, even servile mood]. Had I been supported as I wished, the result was certain as I anticipated. Had Lord Carrington exerted himself in the slightest degree in my favour, I must have been returned. But he certainly maintained a *neutrality*, a neutrality so strict that it amounted to a blockade ... It is some consolation to me, even at this moment, that I have at least struggled to support your Grace. I am now a cipher; but if the devotion of my energies to your cause, *in* and *out*, can ever avail you, your Grace may count upon me, who seeks no greater satisfaction than that of serving a really great man.[6]

In writing in such terms to the arch-Tory Duke of Wellington, Disraeli was, at least, sincere in his conversion to the Conservative cause and his rejection of the radicalism with which he had endeavoured in the past to modify it. He now nailed his colours to the mast, so to speak, by asking Lord Strangford to propose him, and Lord Chandos to second him, as an applicant for membership of the Carlton Club, which had been founded in 1832 after a general election in which only 179 Tories were returned out of a total membership of the House of Commons of 658, the intention being to form a social club which could serve as a meeting-place for Conservatives anxious to restore the fortunes of their party.

* * *

'They have opened a subscription for me at the Carlton [Club],' Disraeli told Sarah on 27 April 1835. 'Tomorrow is nomination day.' He wrote from Taunton, for which he was now standing as a Tory candidate. 'Not that I can win this time,' he warned her, for Henry Labouchere (afterwards Lord Taunton) would surely do so, having been returned at the head of the poll in the general election of 1830 and having represented the borough ever since. 'But come in at the general election I must,' Disraeli continued, 'for I have promises of two-thirds of the electors. I live in a rage of enthusiasm; even my opponents promise to vote for me *next time*. The fatigue is awful. Two long speeches today, and nine hours canvass on foot in a blaze of repartee. I am quite exhausted, and can scarcely see to write! I believe in point of energy, eloquence and effect I have far exceeded all my former efforts. Had I arrived twenty hours sooner the result might have been in my favour.'

In Taunton, as elsewhere, his exotic appearance was as much remarked upon as the remarkable fluency of his speeches. One of those who heard him speak was astonished by the figure he cut:

> Never in my life had I been so struck by a face as I was by that of Disraeli. It was lividly pale, and from beneath two finely arched eyebrows blazed out a pair of intensely black eyes. I never have seen such orbs in mortal sockets, either before or since. His physiognomy was strictly Jewish. Over a broad, high forehead were ringlets of coal-black, glossy hair, which, combed away from his right temple, fell in luxuriant clusters or bunches over his left cheek and ear, which it entirely concealed from view. There was a sort of half-smile, playing about his beautifully formed mouth, the upper lip of which was curved as we see it in the portraits of Lord Byron . . . He was very showily attired in a dark bottle-green frock-coat, a waistcoat of the most extravagant pattern, the front of which was almost covered with glittering chains, and in fancy-pattern pantaloons. He wore a plain black stock, but no collar was visible. Altogether he was the most intellectual-looking exquisite I had ever seen.[7]

He did his best to dispel the reputation for inconsistency of which his enemies made great play. It was 'absolutely essential' for him to do so, Bulwer advised him: he must explain to the voters that 'although a Tory you are a reforming one; because it is generally understood that you committed yourself in some degree with the other party'.[8]

Disraeli endeavoured to do so, and in a long speech on nomination day, attacking the Whigs as an 'anti-national party' and elaborating their 'incapacity', he declared that it was his 'duty to oppose them, to ensure their discomfiture and, if possible, their destruction'.

Tireless and persuasive as he was on the hustings, however, Disraeli's time as a parliamentarian had not yet come: he received 282 votes against Labouchere's 452. By general consent, however, his eloquence and wit in presenting his version of democratic Toryism were widely admired and even among those who were initially irritated by the extravagance of his clothes and gestures there were many who were won over in the end by his apparent sincerity and the astonishing fluency of his utterance. One of those who attended a banquet given for him by the Conservatives of Taunton provided this account of his manner and eloquence:

> He commenced in a lisping, lackadaisical tone of voice . . . He minced his phrases in apparently the most affected manner, and, whilst he was speaking, placed his hands in all imaginable positions; not because he felt awkward and did not know, like a booby in a drawing-room, where to put them, but apparently for the purpose of exhibiting to the best advantage the glittering rings which decked his white and taper fingers. Now he would place his thumbs in the armholes of his waistcoat, and spread out his fingers on its flashing surface; then one set of digits would be released and he would lean affectedly on the table, supporting himself with his right hand; anon he would push aside the curls from his forehead . . . But as he proceeded all traces of this dandyism and affectation were lost. With a rapidity of utterance perfectly astonishing he referred to past events and indulged in anticipations of the future. The Whigs were, of course, the objects of his unsparing satire, and his eloquent denunciations of them were applauded to the echo. In all he said he proved himself to be the finished orator – every period was rounded with the utmost elegance, and in his most daring flights, when one trembled lest he should fall from the giddy height to which he had attained, he so gracefully descended that every hearer was wrapt in admiring surprise . . . His voice, at first so finical, gradually became full, musical, and sonorous, and with every varying sentiment was beautifully modulated . . . The dandy was transformed into a practised orator.[9]

*   *   *

The sequel to this election in Taunton was a virulent quarrel with Daniel O'Connell, Member of Parliament for Dublin, who had angrily responded to reports which appeared in the press of Disraeli's having insulted him as an incendiary and a traitor. O'Connell replied to this 'blackguardism' in terms equally insulting: the 'annals of ruffianism' did not furnish anything like the behaviour of this 'reptile' Disraeli.

> He is an author, I believe, of a couple of novels [O'Connell wrote], and that was all I knew about him until 1831 or 1832, when he wrote to me, being about to stand for High Wycombe, requesting a letter from me to the electors. He took the letter with him, got it printed and placarded all over the place. The next I heard of him was his being a candidate for Marylebone; in this he was also unsuccessful. He got tired of being a radical any longer after these two defeats and was determined to try his chance as a Tory. He stood the other day at Taunton, and by way of recommending himself to his electors he called me an incendiary and a traitor. Now, my answer to this piece of gratuitous impertinence is, that he is an egregious liar ... What! Shall such a vile creature be tolerated in England?

He was a 'living liar', O'Connell continued in ever-increasing anger. The British Empire was degraded by tolerating a 'miscreant of his abominable description'. He possessed 'all the necessary requisites of perfidy, selfishness, depravity, want of principle etc. which would qualify him for the change from Radical to Conservative. His name shows that he is of Jewish origin. I do not use it as a term of reproach; there are many most respectable Jews. But there are, as in every other people, some of the lowest and most disgusting grade of moral turpitude; and of those I look upon Mr Disraeli as the worst.'[10]

These insults, Disraeli considered, could not go unchallenged; and he must, he felt, demand satisfaction.[11] Having killed a man in a duel, O'Connell had taken a vow never to fight another; so Disraeli challenged O'Connell's son, Morgan O'Connell, who replied that he was not responsible for his father's remarks. Thereupon Disraeli wrote to Daniel O'Connell in terms of outrage no less virulent than those in which O'Connell had addressed him:

> If it had been possible for you to act like a gentleman, you would have hesitated before you made your foul and insolent comments

upon a hasty and garbled report of a speech which scarcely contains a sentence or an expression as they emanated from my mouth ... Although you have long placed yourself out of the pale of civilisation, still I am one who will not be insulted, even by a Yahoo.

When Disraeli's long letter appeared in the press, he wrote again to O'Connell's son:

I deduce from your communication that you do not consider yourself responsible for any insults offered by your father, but only bound to resent the insults he may receive. Now, Sir, it is my hope that I *have* insulted him; assuredly it was my intention to do so. I wished to express the utter scorn in which I hold his character and the disgust with which his conduct inspires me ... I shall take every opportunity of holding your father's name up to public contempt. And I fervently pray that you, or someone of his blood, may attempt to avenge the unextinguishable hatred with which I shall pursue his existence.[12]

There were those in his party and within his family who thought that Disraeli had gone too far. But he himself vehemently protested that his conduct was as praiseworthy as he chose to depict it. 'It is very easy for you to criticise,' he told his sister, 'but I do not regret the letter: the expressions were well weighed ... Others think [it] perfect ... worthy of Swift ... The general effect is the thing, and that is, that all men agree I have shown pluck ... There is one opinion among *all* parties – viz: that I have *squabashed* them.' In his diary he later wrote: 'Row with O'Connell in which I greatly distinguish myself.'[13]

Years later he told Reginald Brett (the future Lord Esher) that he never forgave an injury. When a man injured him he wrote his name down on a piece of paper and put it in a drawer and afterwards 'something usually happened to him'.

10

DEBTS AND DUNS

'I trust there is no danger of
my being nabbed.'

TOWARDS THE END OF JUNE 1835, Disraeli sent his sister a long
description of a fancy-dress ball which 'exceeded in splendour anything
ever known in London'. His own dress he described as 'admirable'.

> Lady Chesterfield was a Sultana, and Mrs Anson a Greek, with
> her own hair lower than the calf of her leg. She was the most
> brilliant in the room . . . Lady Londonderry as Cleopatra was in
> a dress literally embroidered with emeralds and diamonds from
> top to toe. It looked like armor and she a Rhinoceros . . .
>   The finest thing is that at half past 2 Lyndhurst gave a supper
> in George Street to eighty of the supremest *ton* and beauty.
> You can conceive nothing more brilliant than his house illu-
> minated with a banquet to a company so fancifully dressed . . .
> Lyndhurst looked like a French Marshal, Wilton was Philip 4th,
> and the Duke [of Wellington] lent him his Golden Fleece set in
> diamonds for the evening. The D of W spoke to me at the ball
> and said he did not know I was in London. He asked after my
> father.[1]

Such entertainments as this supper given by Lord Lyndhurst in
George Street did not prevent Disraeli from keeping 'tolerably busy', as
he described himself in one of his arch and faintly flirtatious letters to
the 'fair and agreeable' Lady Blessington, in October 1835.

In the summer, he had been writing articles anonymously for the
Morning Post, vituperatively admonishing such personalities as the
Attorney-General, John Campbell, that 'base-born Scotchman, a son of

the manse, that coarse Pict', that 'booing, fawning, jobbing progeny of haggis and cockaleekie' who was to become the first Baron Campbell.

> I have sent you the *Morning Post* every day, which is the only paper now read [Disraeli wrote to Sarah], and in whose columns some great unknown has suddenly risen, whose exploits form almost the sole staple of political conversation ... The back numbers for the past week cannot be obtained for love or money, and the sale has increased nearly one third. All attempts at discovering the writer have been baffled, and the mystery adds to the keen interest which the articles excite.[2]

He had also been working on a book of two hundred pages which was to be published under the title *A Vindication of the English Constitution in a Letter to a Noble and Learned Lord* [Lord Lyndhurst] by 'Disraeli the Younger'.

This book elicited from D'Israeli the Elder a characteristic letter to the author:

> Your vulgar birthday [his thirty-first] was, it seems, last Monday, but your nobler political birthday has occurred this week, and truly, like the fable of old, you have issued into existence armed to the full panoply of the highest wisdom. You have now a positive *name* and a being in the great political world which you had not ten days ago. It is for you to preserve the wide reputation which I am positive is now secured. I never doubted your powers ... You never wanted for genius, but it was apt in its fullness to run over. You have now acquired what many a great genius never could – a *perfect style* ... All that now remains for you to do is to register 'a vow from Heaven' that you will never write anything inferior to what you have now written, and never write but on a subject which may call forth all your energies ... Take care of your health – that is the only weak part which I fear about you.[3]

Disraeli the Younger told his sister that he sent a copy of the book to Sir Robert Peel even though he was 'convinced that he would never notice, or even confess to having heard of it, being as you well know, by reputation the most jealous, frigid and haughty of men'. But, on the contrary, in his letter of acknowledgement, Peel wrote to say that, having been attracted by the name of the author as well as by some extracts which had appeared in 'the public papers', he had taken 'the first opportunity of procuring a copy and had been gratified and surprised to find that a familiar and apparently exhausted topic could be treated with so much of original force of argument and novelty of illustration'.[4]

Disraeli showed the letter to Lord Lyndhurst, who told him that the praise was 'much, considering the writer'. He himself considered the work 'a masterly union of learning, skill, and eloquence'.

Such was not likely to be the opinion of the Whigs, whom Disraeli had so roundly condemned in his book; and the review of it in the Whig paper, the *Globe*, was as abusive as Disraeli was in his attack on that 'obscure animal', that 'miserable poltroon', that 'craven dullard', that 'literary scarecrow', that 'mere thing stuffed with straw and rubbish' which was the *Globe*'s editor.

Having attacked the Whigs in the *Morning Post*, Disraeli, writing under the pseudonym, *Runnymede*, now attacked the Whig government of Lord Melbourne in the pages of *The Times* with the warm approval and support of its editor, Thomas Barnes, who was, in Lord Lyndhurst's opinion, 'the most powerful man in the country'.

> The *Letters of Runnymede* are the only things talked of in London [their author told Sarah D'Israeli with typical self-congratulation in January 1836]. The author is unknown and will probably so remain. One or two papers have foolishly ascribed them to me. There is certainly some imitation of my style and the writer is familiar with my works ... The *Letters of Runnymede* are still making a great sensation [he continued a week or two later]. They are considered as rising regularly in power, and the two last, the characters of Lord J[ohn] R[ussell] [the Home Secretary] and O'C[onnell], are generally esteemed the most powerful.[5]

The virulence of the attack on O'Connell was typical of the whole. O'Connell was 'a systematic liar and a beggarly cheat'. His public and private life were 'equally profligate'. He had 'committed every crime that does not require courage'. Lord John Russell was 'a feeble Catiline [traitor] ... an individual, who, on the principle that good vinegar is the corruption of bad wine, has been metamorphosed from an incapable author into an eminent politician'. Lord Palmerston, the Foreign Secretary, was the 'Lord Fanny of diplomacy' who combined the 'smartness of an attorney's clerk with the intrigue of a Greek of the lower Empire'; while the Prime Minister, Lord Melbourne himself, was guilty of 'sauntering over the destinies of a nation, and lounging away the glory of an Empire'.[6]

Even by the standards of the 1830s, these virulent assaults were considered strong meat; and some of the fiercer and more libellous phrases were softened by the editor's pencil. But Disraeli, while pretending not to know the identity of 'Runnymede', was well satisfied with the effect which the letters produced. 'Establish my character as a great political writer by the "Letters of Runnymede,"' he noted in his diary, making a résumé of his progress that year. 'My influence greatly increases from the perfect confidence of L[yndhurst] and my success as a political writer.'[7]

The letters to members of the Tory Opposition were as fulsome as those to members of the Government were vitriolic. 'In your chivalry alone is our hope,' ran the letter to Peel. 'Clad in the panoply of your splendid talents and your spotless character we feel assured that you will conquer.' 'In a Peel, a Stanley, a Wellington and a Lyndhurst,' another letter concluded, 'the people of England recognize their fitting leaders.'[8]

In the spring of 1836, Disraeli had gone down to Lewes to speak in favour of a friend who was a candidate for the borough. His speech there was as effective as his writings had been in the past year; and when he sat down, according to *The Times* – which described him as 'already well known for his literary talents and his opposition to the O'Connell influence in the Government' – 'the most deafening applause prevailed for the space of several minutes'.[9]

Despite this success, a subsequent energetic canvassing in support of the Conservative candidate in a by-election caused by the death of one of the members for Buckinghamshire, and a fine and witty speech delivered at a Conservative banquet in Aylesbury – which, reported in *The Times*, led Sarah to write, 'You have succeeded in doing that which you so much desired, viz., to make a speech that would be talked of all over England' – Disraeli was less concerned with politics in the late 1830s than with the problems occasioned by his debts.

These debts had now risen to over £20,000 (the equivalent in today's money of about £600,000); and there seemed no way of settling them. There had been a time when he could always borrow from Benjamin Austen, but Austen had come to feel that Disraeli was no longer much interested in him now that he had found other more influential friends in smarter circles. When Disraeli asked for a loan of £1,200 in return for an assignment of his copyrights, Austen replied that, as Disraeli already owed him £300 – which he would not ask to be repaid for the moment – he did not feel able to lend him a further £1,200. Austen's wife eventually persuaded her husband to change his mind; but when the time came to repay the money and Disraeli could not do so, Austen again, understandably, became extremely cross. Tired of receiving such letters as a characteristic one in which Disraeli expressed himself 'mortified' by being unable to redeem his pledge but he was 'really TOO ILL',[10] Austen threatened to go to law, and so at length Disraeli was forced to appeal to his father. The debt was repaid. The friendship with the Austens, however, was irrevocably broken, and they were left suffering under what Sir Philip Rose described as 'a morbid feeling of slight and neglect'.

Although the debts to Austen were settled at last, this was far from being the end of Disraeli's financial distress. For a time he was helped by the solicitor, William Pyne, who performed 'singular good services'. But by February 1836, the situation had once more become desperate. His creditors were now so clamorous that he was again reluctantly compelled to appeal to his father, to whom he did not care to reveal the full amount of his indebtedness – of which, in any case, he could hazard no more than a rough guess. In a painful interview at Bradenham he 'ventured to say £2,000 might be required'. But this did not go far. He had to return for more. He was given more. Yet, even so, only the more importunate of the creditors were paid. Other debts still loomed and mounted. He found money, however, to bribe the sheriff's officer.[11]

Further debts were blithely contemplated. 'On Saturday,' he had written to Pyne in May 1836, 'the "*Carlton Chronicle*", a new weekly journal, will be started. I have been offered & have provisionally accepted *half the proprietorship* which . . . will require £500. This speculation may turn out & quickly *a considerable property* . . . I think I could scrape enough tog[eth]er. The object is CONSIDERABLE.'[12]

His debts apparently did not cause Disraeli any excessive worry. It was as though he accepted these as part of the necessary accoutrements of a man of fashion. A character in one of his novels expresses himself as being actually 'fond of his debts', one of 'the two greatest stimulants in the world', the other being youth. What would he be without them?

There was, of course, the danger of being 'nabbed', as he put it, by some such creditor as Thomas Mash, a moneylender. He was, for instance, due to speak in December 1836 at a county Conservative dinner 'attended by the Lord Lieutenant, the High Sheriff, four peers, two Privy Councillors, eight baronets and fifty magistrates', he himself now being a magistrate, thanks to the influence of Lords Lyndhurst and Chandos. 'I trust there is no danger of my being nabbed by Mash,' he told Pyne, 'as this would be a fatal contretemps, inasmuch, in all probability, I [shall be] addressing my future constituents.'

Disraeli's ever mounting debts did not, however, interfere with his writing; he spent much of his time in the mid to late 1830s at Bradenham, working on two novels after contributing a series of allegorical articles to *The Times*, as well as a political satire, 'An Heroic Epistle to Lord Viscount Mel—e' which also appeared in *The Times* in March 1837.

The novels were more profitable than such political writings. 'I have agreed to let Colburn have a novel ... for a greater sum than I have ever yet received,' he told his father, whom the news did not please. 'How will the fictionist assort with the politician?' Isaac D'Israeli wanted to know. 'Most deeply am I regretting that you find it necessary to drink of the old waters.'[13]

But even now Disraeli had not allowed his father to know how desperately pressing his debts were, how constantly they were increasing because of his extravagance, and how he was dogged by debt collectors whose activities led him to be wary of appearing in public. To Pyne, who did what he could to help him in his difficulties, he once wrote, 'Peel has asked me to dine with a party today of the late Government at the Carlton. Is it safe? I fear not.'[14]

Benjamin Austen had suggested that he should again ask his father to help him but Disraeli had replied, 'I do not wish by extraordinary money applications to one who is always very generous to me, to revive a most painful subject.' An approach was made instead to Count D'Orsay, who replied:

> I swear before God that I have not sixpence at my banker now, having lost the night before last £325. You may judge how disappointed I am not to be able to assist you, but if you find that

I could be of use to you in the way of security I will do for you
what I would not for any other.[15]

In spite of his parlous financial condition, Disraeli, in his sanguine,
improvident way, continued to live well beyond the means at his disposal
and went so far as to consider the purchase of the estate of Chequers
Court. 'I should suppose,' he told Pyne, as if such sums were a mere
bagatelle, '[that the price will be] not under £40,000, perhaps £10,000
more as there is timber; but at any rate I should like to leave half the
purchase money on mortgage if practicable; if not, we must manage
some way . . . Be of good cheer, the Spring is coming, and will bring
us all good fortune . . . I enclose the *blasted bills*.'[16]

At the same time, he was 'in treaty for Lord Althorp's rooms' in
Albany, bachelor apartments in the large house in Piccadilly which, built
for the first Viscount Melbourne in the 1770s, had subsequently been
acquired by Frederick, Duke of York and Albany. 'The rooms were once
Byron's,' Disraeli wrote to Pyne. 'I shall be lodged in a way that suits
me; gloomy and spacious, with room to stroll and smoke, and able to
spout occasionally without being overheard by any damned fellow who
steals all your jokes and sublimities.'[17]

For the time being, when in London, he stayed with D'Orsay, who
lived in Kensington in a house adjoining Lady Blessington's Gore House,
which was 'a magnificent mansion' on the site of the present Royal
Albert Hall and previously occupied first by Admiral Lord Rodney, then
by William Wilberforce.

Periods of 'carefree insouciance and sublime serenity' alternated
with occasional days of anxiety both in London and at Bradenham,
where he wrote to Pyne, 'Of all things preserve me from a Sheriff's
officer'. One of these duns was reported to have been making inquiries
about him at Wycombe and he feared it might no longer be possible to
prevent 'a disgraceful catastrophe'. 'Every possible claim that could be
made upon me has poured in during the last two months,' he lamented
in a rare moment of deep anxiety. 'I never have been so distressed.' He
was now paying interest on some of his debts at 40 per cent.

He did not neglect his work, however; and *Henrietta Temple*, begun
in 1834 and resumed in 1836, was published in 1837 and was followed a
few months later by *Venetia, or The Poet's Daughter*, a book the last

chapters of which were were written in the shadows, so to speak, of increasingly threatening duns and creditors. 'I find it difficult to command the Muse amid all these vexations,' he told Pyne. 'The form of Davis or the unknown visage of Green [two creditors] mix themselves up, by some damnable process, with the radiant countenance of my heroine, and tho' visions of spunging houses and K[ing's] Bench, [a debtors' prison] might have been in keeping with the last vol. of *Henrietta Temple*, they do not accord quite so well with the more etherial scenes of the fair Venetia. I hope my inspir[ati]on has not been much diluted by these distractions, but I am a little nervous.'*[18]

Soon after the publication of *Henrietta Temple*, Disraeli wrote to his sister to tell her that he had heard from Lord Strangford, who had been staying with the Duke of Wellington at Stratfieldsaye, that another guest, Lady Wilton, had cried so much on reading the book that she 'had excited all their curiosity'.

'Colburn [the publisher] is in high spirits about H.T.,' Disraeli continued. 'He says he shall not be content unless he works it up like [Bulwer's] *Pelham*. There were many reviews yesterday. You have, of course, seen the *Athenaeum*', which described the work as 'vexatious', 'high-flown' and 'foolish' but also as 'clever'.

Neither Bulwer nor Lady Blessington thought highly of the book. But at least it sold more copies than any of his previous novels, and enabled him to pay a handsome compliment to his friend Bulwer, who appeared unmistakably in the book as Count Alcibiades de Mirabel:

> There was something in Count Mirabel's very presence which put everybody in good spirits. His lightheartedness was caught by all. Melancholy was a farce in the presence of his smile; and there was no possible combination of scrapes that could withstand his kind and brilliant raillery.

In *Venetia*, which followed *Henrietta Temple*, there is a less flattering version of some aspects of Lord Byron in the character of Lord Cadurcis and of the poet's excitable mother – who once bit a lump out of a saucer

---

* A week later Disraeli wrote again to Pyne: 'There is one question to which I beg your kind and immediate attention. *Can I remain here* [at Bradenham] *for one week with safety and propriety?*' (*Benjamin Disraeli Letters*, 603, 25 April 1837).

– in Mrs Cadurcis. In this book, described by its author as 'very good indeed', there are also recognizable aspects of Lady Caroline Lamb in Lady Monteagle and of Shelley in Marmion Herbert.

Henry Colburn would have welcomed more of what he called 'these originals', on the lines of Lady Bellair, whom he took to be based on the author's friend, the eccentric Lady Cork. They were, he said, good selling points. Others, however, lamented their instrusion. The critic of the *Edinburgh Review*, for example, took Disraeli to task for his bad taste in 'intruding into the domestic life of a poet and his relations and extracting the materials of fiction out of events so recent and so melancholy'. He also regretted the introduction of Lady Caroline Lamb into the novel as Lady Monteagle since, although she had died in 1828, her husband, Lord Melbourne, was still alive.

Venetia was not so successful commercially as *Henrietta Temple*; but Disraeli could reassure himself with the reflection that it had, in general, enjoyed a more favourable critical reception. He was by now, in any event, not so much concerned by his standing as a novelist as by his future as a politician.

THE MEMBER
FOR MAIDSTONE

'The clouds have at last dispelled
and my prospects seem as bright as day.'

'DISTINGUISHED MYSELF VERY MUCH' in the election of [Sir Francis] Burdett for Westminster; the success mainly attributable to myself,' Disraeli wrote with characteristic immodesty in his diary, recalling the 'very great fun' of his energetic canvassing in the London streets in May 1837.[1]

Sir Francis was 'the father of the House, though it was difficult to believe that from his appearance'. Disraeli wrote of Sir Franceys Scrope, the character based on Burdett in his last novel, *Endymion*, which was to appear in 1880: 'He was tall, and had kept his distinguished figure, a handsome man with a musical voice, and a countenance now benignant, though very bright, and once haughty.' Sir Francis's daughter, the extremely rich Angela Burdett-Coutts, also appears in *Endymion* – as Adriana, 'the greatest heiress in England': and it seems that, for a time, Disraeli considered the possibility of asking her to be his wife, as Endymion does Adriana; but Adriana, who has the 'sweetest temper in the world', carries about with her 'a doleful look' and an 'air of pensive resignation'. 'Her books interested her . . . and she liked to be alone or with her mother.' She was, indeed, as Disraeli found Miss Burdett-Coutts, a 'quiet, unpretending person'.*[2]

---

* 'Angela and Hannah [her companion, Hannah Meredith] had a technique for dealing with [unwanted] suitors,' Edna Healey wrote in her history of Coutts Bank. Hannah would

Soon after Disraeli had helped in the election of Miss Burdett-Coutts's father as Member for Westminster, King William IV died at Windsor Castle on 29 June 1837, and his niece, the eighteen-year-old Princess Victoria, succeeded him.

Lord Lyndhurst told Disraeli about the scene in Kensington Palace where 'the peers and privy councillors and chief personages of the realm pledged their fealty to the new sovereign'. Lyndhurst was 'greatly affected by the unusual scene: a youthful maiden receiving the homage of her subjects, most of them illustrious, with a sweet and natural dignity'. He 'kissed the young Queen's hand, which all agreed was remarkably sweet and soft. She read her address well and was perfectly composed, though alone in the council chamber and attended by no women.'[3]

The death of the sovereign then requiring the dissolution of Parliament, a general election had to be called; and Disraeli, by now recognized as one of the brightest of the young Conservatives, was offered the opportunity of standing for a remarkable number of seats: not only for Marylebone and Taunton, for which he had stood before, but also for Derby, Chichester, Dartmouth, Ashburton, Barnstaple and Maidstone. He settled for Maidstone, which was then represented by a Liberal, and a Conservative, Wyndham Lewis, feeling confident that he could defeat the Liberal candidate and might well receive more votes than the Conservative also.

'The clouds have at last dispelled,' he told his sister, 'and my prospects seem as bright as day.'[4] On the evening of 30 June 1837, he drove down to Maidstone where he began his campaign with an effective opening speech, pledging his loyalty to the Crown, to the national Church and religious toleration, and ending, 'Resident in an agricultural County, and deeply interested in the Land, I will on all occasions watch with vigilant solicitude over the Fortunes of the British Farmer, because I sincerely believe that his welfare is the surest and most permanent basis of general Prosperity.[5] I assure you that you will at all times find me a sedulous Guardian and energetic Champion of your local interests.'[6]

'Last night there was a full meeting,' Disraeli reported to Sarah on

---

wait in the next room while they proposed: then Angela would cough, which was the signal that she had refused, and that Hannah could make her entrance ... Disraeli at his most perfumed and exotic ... in his gorgeous gilded waistcoats had little charm for the modest Angela' (Edna Healey, *Coutts & Co., the Portrait of a Private Bank* 1992, 287).

4 July, 'and I think I made the best speech I ever made yet ... More than an hour in length.'

Four days later he was back in London, as confident as ever. 'I have just returned having completed a most TRIUMPHANT CANVASS,' he told his sister. 'I doubt whe[the]r there will be a contest.'

Wyndham Lewis was deeply impressed. 'Disraeli was on his legs more than an hour,' he told his wife; 'he is a splendid orator and impressed the people.'[7] Equally impressed by his opponent's skill and following, the Liberal candidate withdrew from the contest. He was replaced by a Radical, Colonel Perronet Thompson, editor of the *Westminster Review*, who affected not to be sure how to pronounce Disraeli's name.

Some observers did not rate Disraeli's chances as highly as he did himself. 'He was not popular with the mob,' wrote one of them, John Hollams. 'They offered him bacon, ham, etc. and repeatedly suggested that he was a Jew; but he was very ready in replying to them. Taking up the slur directly, Disraeli did not dally long in his remarks before he referred to Colonel Perronet Thompson, "I hope I pronounce his name aright ..."'[8]

'Disraeli's appearance was very remarkable,' Hollams continued, 'long black hair in curls – and he was dressed in an extraordinary way, the extreme, it may be supposed, of fashion. Nothing like it had ever been seen in Maidstone before.'[9]

Dating his letter 'Maidstone, July 27, 1837. 11 o'clock', Disraeli wrote to Sarah: 'Dearest, Lewis 707, Disraeli 616, Colonel Thompson 412. The constituency nearly exhausted. In haste, Dizzy.' So Disraeli was at last elected to Parliament as one of the Conservative Members for Maidstone, helped in his defeat of the Radical candidate by the capacious pockets of the other Conservative candidate, Wyndham Lewis.

Mrs Wyndham Lewis was delighted. She told her brother that Mr Disraeli, her husband's friend, was 'one of the greatest writers & finest orators of the day – age about 30 [he was thirty-two] ... His being so fine a speaker, joined to *my humble worth*, carried everything before us ... Can you fancy me driving about the town – encouraging our friends and playing the Amiable to a pitch of distraction ... [Some of] the women clasp'd Wyndham in their arms and kissed him again and again in spite of his struggles – which set Mr Disraeli and [me] in screams of laughter.'[10]

A few days after his election, Disraeli wrote to Sarah again: 'The Government talks of breaking up! . . . The Whigs now confess that they are beaten to pieces . . . In short, the Government is done, and I doubt whether they will meet Parliament . . . The Whigs are more than low spirited; they are *in extremis*; they give the affair up. Peel says he can carry on the Government with the present Parliament, not the slightest doubt, so I hope we are sitting for seven years. What fun! . . . I am very well and begin to enjoy my new career. I find that it makes a sensible difference in the opinion of one's friends. I can scarcely keep my countenance . . .'[11]

Before taking his seat in the House of Commons, Disraeli had a short holiday. He stayed a week with Lord Chandos at Wotton, a few days with Sir Gore Ouseley, and a few days at Newport Pagnell, 'where there was a great Conservative dinner'. He also went to Woolbeding, near Midhurst, 'a house rather old-fashioned but very convenient and com- pact, covered with ivy and the church adjoining it,' he told his sister. 'The place is used by [James] Maxse as a shooting box. His principal residence is in the West of England and he only lives here in the sporting season . . .* It rains today [24 October 1837] without ceasing. Here at present are nothing but shooting dandies . . . not much in my way . . . We dine at half past six and there is a constant breakfast . . . There is no end of horses, guns and dogs and a very large company of London servants . . . Lady Caroline is very amiable [but] I will not stay here longer than I can help.'[12]

Two days later, Lady Caroline drove him to Cowdray, 'one of the most magnificent demesnes in England'. The carriage in which they travelled was 'one of the most brilliant equipages [he] ever witnessed'. The 'poneys, for such they are styled though they are 15 hands high, are thoroughbred and worthy of George the Fourth, as well as her carriage which is of cane on a frame of a brilliant and rich green; she has two

---

* In a letter to his sister, he described Maxe (sic) as 'a truly worthy fellow and very rich'. His wife, Lady Caroline, daughter of the fifth Earl of Berkeley, was 'amiable and cleverish, tho' with no personal charm'. 'They have long sought my acquaintance, and asked me very earnestly to visit them in Sussex' (*Benjamin Disraeli Letters*, 582, 28).

outriders, and the moment there is the slightest elevation the poneys break into a gallop of their own accord to the fear and astonishment of all passengers ... I doubt whether I shall stay [at Woolbeding] beyond Saturday; but I find it difficult to get away, being very popular with the women, who are charmed I do not shoot. I like my friends; they are very good, warm, hearty people indeed. I am going today to Petersfield to see the Jolliffes [William Jolliffe, Conservative Member for Petersfield, later Conservative Whip].'[13]

'Tomorrow I leave Bradenham to take my seat in Parliament,' he wrote after his return home. 'My health is wonderfully renovated. Were it not for the anxiety the state of my affairs occasionally causes me, I should laugh at illness ... I am now leaving a secure haven for an unknown sea.'

Three days later, he took his seat in the House of Commons and 'found it very full, the Members standing in groups and chatting. About three o'clock there was a cry of "order, order" ... Shaw-Lefevre [later Viscount Eversley, Member for North Hampshire] proposed, and Strutt of Derby [Edward Strutt, later Baron Belper] seconded Abercromby [James Abercromby, the Speaker, later first Baron Dunfermline]. Both were brief, the first commonplace, the other commonplace and coarse; all was tame. Peel said very little, very well. Then Abercromby, who looked like an old laundress, mumbled and moaned some dullness, and was then carried to the chair, and said a little more amid a faint dull cheer. To me of course the scene was exciting enough ...'[14]

'Peel came to the Carlton yesterday,' he continued his account to Sarah, 'and was there a great deal. He welcomed me very warmly; but all indeed noticed his cordial demeanour; he looks very well and shook hands with me in the House.'

A week later Disraeli returned to the House of Commons to be summoned to the Lords for the Queen's Speech. 'The rush was terrific,' he told Sarah. 'Abercromby himself nearly thrown down and trampled upon, and his mace-bearer banging the Members' heads with his gorgeous weapon, and cracking skulls with impunity.'[15]

The House of Lords presented 'a magnificent spectacle', while the Queen 'looked admirably, no feathers but a diamond tiara'. The speech which she was given to read was 'intentionally vague, that no division might possibly occur', and Disraeli and his friend, Lord Mahon (later fifth Earl Stanhope), were thankful to get back to the Carlton unscathed, with their hats crushed and covered with mud, so thick and rowdy were the crowds surrounding Parliament.

On his return to the Commons, Disraeli was obliged to listen to a succession of indifferent speeches, ranging from the 'flippant' to the 'odious', until Peel made one of the 'finest speeches' he had ever heard, 'most powerful and even brilliant'. 'He broke the centre of the Government party for ever. The Radicals were mad . . .'

So, after all, 'there was a division on the Address in Queen Victoria's first Parliament – 509 to 20,' Disraeli told Sarah. 'I left the House at ten o'clock, none of us having dined. The tumult and excitement great. I dined or rather supped at the Carlton with a large party off oysters, Guinness and broiled bones and got to bed at half-past twelve o'clock. Thus ended the most remarkable day hitherto of my life.'[16]

A fortnight later Disraeli rose from his seat behind Peel to make his maiden speech, a speech on an ill-chosen subject – the validity of various Irish elections – which was certain to arouse the anger of the Irish Members. It was a disaster. He had not been expected to make it; O'Connell was speaking when he decided to do so. Lord Stanley had been prepared to answer O'Connell, but Disraeli approached him to ask if he might speak instead. Stanley agreed.

At first Disraeli, the dandiacal, odd-looking Member for Maidstone, was heard patiently enough, even though the florid, self-assured manner in which he began was not calculated to endear him to a House where a certain modest, respectful reticence was traditionally expected of the newly elected. His sallies were occasionally greeted with laughter; but the further he proceeded, the less patient grew the House, the Irish Members in particular hissing, groaning, hooting, catcalling, drumming their feet, talking loudly to each other and imitating animals. William Charles Macready, the actor-manager, who had gone into the gallery to listen to the speech, described it as a 'farcical failure'.[17]

'I wish I could induce the House to give me five minutes more,' Disraeli pleaded above the uproar which he himself later said was 'indescribable'. He persisted manfully, his words all but lost in loud laughter and cries of derision; and then, shouting above the clamour, he declared, 'I sit down now. But the time will come when you will hear me.'[18]

'D'Israeli made his first exhibition this night,' the diarist, Charles Greville, commented, 'beginning with florid assurance, speedily degenerating into ludicrous absurdity, and being at last put down with inextinguishable shouts of laughter.'[19]

The next day Disraeli wrote to Sarah to 'state at once' that his 'début was a failure'. But the failure, he explained, was not occasioned by his breaking down or 'any incompetency' on his part, but from the 'physical powers' of his opponents. 'I can give you no idea how bitter, how factious, how unfair they were . . . I fought through all with undaunted pluck and unruffled temper,' he added with that self-congratulation which came so naturally to him in his letters to his sister and which, on this occasion, was largely justified. 'I made occasionally good isolated hits when there was silence and finished with spirit . . . My party backed me well, and no one with more zeal and kindness than Peel, cheering me repeatedly, which is not his custom.'[20]

When Chandos came up to congratulate him, he replied that there was surely no cause for congratulation and 'muttered "Failure". "No such thing!" said Chandos; "You are quite wrong. I have just seen Peel, and I said to him, 'Now tell me exactly what you think of D.' Peel replied, 'Some of my party were disappointed and talk of failure. I say *just the reverse*. He did all that he could do under the circumstances. I say anything but failure; he must make his way.'"'[21]

This, too, was the opinion of Lord Lyndhurst, who wrote a kind letter:

> My dear Disraeli,
>
> Why have you not called upon me? The scamps of Radicals were determined that you should not speak. I am sure you have the courage to have at them again. You are sure to succeed in spite of their bullying.
>
> Ever yours, Lyndhurst.[22]

Similar encouragement was offered by the Attorney General, John Campbell, whom Disraeli, in an anonymous article in the *Morning Chronicle*, had castigated so rudely two years before. 'Now, Mr Disraeli,' Campbell asked him in the Lobby. 'Could you tell me how you finished one sentence in your speech . . . "In one hand the keys of St Peter and in the other—"?', 'In the other, the cap of Liberty,' Disraeli told him.

'A good picture,' said Campbell affably. Then, after dissociating himself from the row made by Disraeli's detractors, 'You have nothing to be afraid of.'[23]

Disraeli also received welcome encouragement from the dramatist, Richard Lalor Sheil, the Irish Member for county Tipperary whose maiden speech, 'artificial to the last degree', had also been a failure. Bulwer told Disraeli that he had come across Sheil at the Athenaeum where, having just recovered from an attack of gout, he was 'lounging in an easy chair reading a newspaper'. Around him was 'a knot of Low Radicals' abusing Disraeli and 'exulting in his discomfiture in the House'.

> Probably they thought they pleased Sheil . . . Suddenly Sheil threw down the paper and said in his shrill voice, 'Now, gentlemen, I have heard all you have to say, and, what is more, I heard this same speech of Mr Disraeli, and I tell you this: if ever the spirit of oratory was in a man, it is in that man. Nothing can prevent him from being one of the first speakers in the House of Commons! I know something about that place, I think, and I tell you what besides, that if there had not been this interruption, Mr Disraeli might have made a failure; I don't call this a failure, it is a crush. My *début* was a failure, because I was heard, but my reception was supercilious, his malignant. A *début* should be dull. The House will not allow a man to be a wit and an orator, unless they have the credit of finding it out. There it is.' The crowd dispersed, but Bulwer drew near, and said to Sheil: 'D. dines with me today; would you like to meet him?' 'In spite of my gout,' said Sheil, 'I long to know him; I long to tell him what I think.'
>
> So we met; Sheil was most charming. He insisted continually on his position that the clamorous reception was fortunate, 'for', said he, 'if you had been listened to, what would have been the result? You would have done what I did; you would have made the best speech that you ever would have made: it would have been received frigidly, and you would have despaired of yourself. I did. As it is, you have shown to the House that you have unlimited command of language, that you have courage, temper and readiness. Now get rid of your genius for a session. Speak often, for you must not show yourself cowed, but speak shortly. Be very quiet, try to be dull, only argue and reason imperfectly, for if you reason with precision, they will think you are trying to be witty. Astonish them by speaking on subjects of detail. Quote

figures, dates, calculations. And in a short time the House will sigh for the wit and eloquence, which they all know are in you; they will encourage you to pour them forth, and then you will have the ear of the House and be a favourite.'

I think that altogether this is as interesting a *rencontre* as I have ever experienced.[24]

'MOST BRILLIANT AND TRIUMPHANT SPEECHES'

'I was heard with the greatest attention
and sat down amid loud cheers.'

DISRAELI HAD LEARNED HIS LESSON; and, when he spoke again, having waited ten days to do so, he was careful to avoid what his father called those 'theatrical graces' which did 'not do for the English Commons'. He spoke, he said, with 'complete success'; his voice was 'in perfect condition'; his words, listened to 'with the utmost curiosity and attention', were accompanied by 'continued "hear, hears"'; and he 'sat down with a general cheer'.[1]

'Everybody congratulated me,' Disraeli continued his letter to Sarah. 'Colonel Lygon [Henry Lygon, later fourth Earl Beauchamp] said, "Well, you have got into your saddle again, and now you may ride away." Even Granville Somerset [second son of the sixth Duke of Beaufort, M.P. for Monmouthshire] said, "I never heard a few sentences so admirably delivered. You will allow me to say so, after having been twenty-five years in Parliament." But all agree that I managed in a few minutes by my voice and manner to please everyone in the House. I don't care about the meagre report for I spoke to the House and not to the public.'[2]

He was equally pleased with himself for having made a 'successful speech' at the 'largest meeting on record at Maidstone'; and it was his 'firm opinion' that the next time he rose in the House of Commons, which would be very soon, he would sit down 'amid loud cheers'. 'Next to undoubted success,' he concluded his report to Bradenham, 'the best thing is to make a great noise and the many articles that are daily written to announce my failure only prove that I have not failed. One thing is curious, that the opinion of the Mass is immensely affected by that of their leaders. I know a hundred little instances daily which show me that what Peel and Sheil, and other leading men, have said, has already greatly influenced those who are unable to form opinions for themselves – Love to all, D.'[3]

Satisfied as he was by his growing parliamentary reputation, Disraeli was also much gratified by his ever burgeoning social success. He regaled Sarah with descriptions of the receptions, balls, dinners and theatrical performances he had attended or been invited to attend. He went 'to see the young [son of Edmund Kean] Charles John Kean on 19 January 1838 and the theatre was full in spite of the frost . . . One word describes all – mediocrity.' His companions on this occasion were the witty Horace Twiss, Mrs Siddons's nephew, the former Member for Bridport, and his wife, Annie; and they sat in Lord Chesterfield's box which had 'a capital fire, [their] own tea, and it was all really very amusing'. A few evenings later he went to 'a most recherché concert at Parnther's [Robert Parnther's house in Grafton Street]' where he 'found all the élite of the town, and where the season commenced, as all agreed, very brilliantly. The Duke [of Wellington] was there, looking very well in his Garter riband, and the golden fleece.'[4]

'I can scarcely tell you who was not there,' he wrote to Sarah, mentioning a number of the most distinguished guests, including the Duke of Beaufort, the Lansdownes, Lord Salisbury, and Baroness de Rothschild, who was 'universally admired, tall, graceful, dark and pictur-esquely dressed in a robe of yellow silk, a hat and feathers, with a sort of Sévigné beneath magnificent pearls, quite a Murillo'.[5]

Soon after this the Twisses gave 'a queer but amusing party' with another distinguished cast, including the guest of honour, Thomas Barnes, and his wife, who looked, so a fellow-guest, Henry Baring, said, 'like a lady in a pantomime, very funny, surrounded by sons of Dukes and Privy Councillors'.[6]

This party was followed by a 'most brilliant' one at Salisbury House where the assembly was 'most select' and included Georgiana, Lord Lyndhurst's recently married second wife who, so Disraeli said, made a favourable impression. 'I was, of course, presented to her ... Lyndhurst is in high spirits, but if he have not a son, I think he will sink under the disappointment. He talks of nothing else.'

> Lady Salisbury, to whom I had never been introduced, received me with great cordiality [Disraeli continued], and talked to me a great deal. I find I owe the invitation to Lady Londonderry ... I knew almost every man there ... On Saturday I dined with George Wombwell [founder of the famous menageries, said to be the original of Mr Cassillis in *Coningsby*] and met De L'Isle, Adolphus Fitzclarence, Auriol and Hope. I drank a great deal too much wine, but a great deal less than my host and his *fidus* Adolphus. I got away to the Salisburys where there was a most agreeable assembly. [Soon after this] I dined with the Powers-courts. Lady Powerscourt is, without exception, the most beautiful woman in London ... [Among the guests were] Roderick Murchison, a stiff geological prig and his wife silent ... the second Lord Redesdale [who was to be raised to an earldom on Disraeli's recommendation] ... and Mary Somerville [the distinguished writer whose name was to be commemorated in the foundation of the Oxford college]. A lady grown very old [no more than fifty-eight, in fact] and not very easy.[7]

A few days later there was another party at the Salisburys', where there were 'many beautiful women, among them the Princess of Capua'. Lady Aldborough was also there, 'looking as fresh as ever and very witty and amusing; and Lady Stanhope and her daughter, Lady Wilhelmine, and the very quiet and unpretending' Miss Angela Burdett-Coutts. He 'almost forgot to mention the Prince of Capua, a savage, dull-looking fellow covered with moustache and stars. He is entirely ruled by his wife.'[8]

When next Disraeli spoke in the House of Commons, it was on 15 March 1838, in defence of the Corn Laws; and on this occasion there could be no doubt as to his success. He wrote Sarah a long letter to assure her that this was so:

> You will hear with delight that last night very unexpectedly, for I had given up all thought of speaking ... I rose and made a most successful speech. Indeed, it was not merely a very good speech, but it was by far, and by all sides agreed, the very best

speech of the evening, which is always a great thing to achieve, as then nobody else is talked of . . .

I went to our front bench which was clear of all the great guns, who had gone to dinner, except Chandos who recommended me to rise where I was, and boldly speak from the floor. Even here I could not catch the Speaker's eye, and time flew on, and the great guns one by one returned . . . and I was obliged to shift my plan and place . . . But just as I rose to quit my seat the Speaker, imagining I was going to rise to speak, called my name.

I was in for it, put my hat down, advanced to the table, and dashed along. I got the House still in a minute. I was heard with the greatest attention and good humour immediately, succeeded in all my points, and sat down amid loud cheers . . . No one cheered more vehemently than [John Cam] Hobhouse [Byron's friend, Member for Nottingham] who was a little drunk . . . Cutlar Fergusson [the Judge Advocate General] who cheered me very much also, came up to me in the lobby, and spoke as warmly as you possibly can imagine . . . [He said] 'all our people agree it was one of the best speeches ever made on the subject'.

Lord John [Russell] said nothing but sat with his arms folded, and watched me very attentively. I thought he looked malignant . . . but I did him an injustice, for I walked home with [Lord] Ossulston and he said to me, 'I understand you have made a most brilliant speech tonight . . . Johnny says it was the best thing he had heard for a long time; a great thing for one so scant of laudation' . . . As for all the other congratulations I received, it is impossible to enumerate them. In the lobby, all the squires came up to shake hands with me, and thank me for the good service. They were so grateful, and well they might be, for certainly they had nothing to say for themselves . . . At the Carlton I received great congratulations from everybody . . . except Sir W[illiam] Y[oung], one of the Members for Buckinghamshire who grinned the same ghastly smile as he would at Aylesbury . . . In fact, I think I have become very popular in the house.[9]

'We were very grateful for your long despatch,' his 'dearest' Sarah wrote to congratulate him. 'Jem describes the rush into the House as prodigious when you began to speak and then the profound silence, and then all the cheers. He heard many people speak of you, rejoicing in your speech and your reception; and once, before you spoke, Castlereagh rushed in, saying, "Has Disraeli been up?" It seemed by Jem's account of all the sensation that you were quite as great a man at Westminster as at Aylesbury ... God bless you, dearest.'

A few weeks later, Disraeli had further cause to congratulate himself:

> I made a most brilliant and triumphant speech last night – unquestionably and agreed upon by all hands the crack speech of the night, and every one who spoke after me, either for or against, addressed himself to me ... The whole day [25 April 1838] has been passed in receiving compliments on my speech ...[10]

Meanwhile, Disraeli's social life was as busy as ever.

> Town is very agreeable [he wrote on 5 May], the weather soft and warm ... Yesterday I dined with the Londonderrys *en famille* and only met Lord and Lady Hardwicke; but it was most agreeable, for Lady Hardwicke is without exception the most dramatic singer I ever listened to ... She actually sang without stopping for so long a time that it was near one when our *petite comité* broke up. I never met persons who seemed to enjoy life more, or who seemed fonder of each other than the Hardwickes. I have known Lord H. for some time and met him first at Smyrna when he was only Captain Yorke, and always liked him. He is so frank and gay. They asked me to dine with them tomorrow, but [I] am engaged to the Salisburys.
>
> All the world is talking of the grand festival, which is to be given in Merchant Taylors' Hall by the Conservative Members of Parliament to Sir Robert Peel. I am, of course, one of the hosts. It is to be one of the most magnificent and important gatherings ever witnessed ...
>
> > The Chesterfields [he continued] had the audacity to ask 5,000 guineas for the loan of their house to the Russian Ambassador Extra-or[dinar]y for the forthcoming coronation of Queen Victoria and absolutely expected to get it. Lady Jersey asked 2,000. Lady Londonderry thought all this house-letting *infra dig.*, and had the spirit to write to the Empress, who had been most hospitable to herself and Lord L. when in Russia, and offered Holdernesse House and the whole establishment to the Grand Duke, who is coming over; intending themselves to go into a hired house. The offer was declined by the Empress in a letter in English beautifully and correctly written ...
> >
> > On the 19th Lord Chandos gives a grand banquet to the Duke of Wellington, Lord Lyndhurst, Lord and Lady

Londonderry, Lord and Lady Jersey, Sir Robert and Lady Peel, Sir James and Lady Graham, and Lord Stanley. You will be rather surprised I think – at least I was – that I should be invited to it; but Chandos is a good friend and greatly triumphs in my success in the House.

I must cease at present all this gossip . . .'[11]

'London is very gay,' he told Sarah in a letter describing the preparations made for the coronation, a ceremony after his own heart and one to which he was looking forward with the keenest anticipation.

London teems with foreigners. There are full 200 (*on dit*) of distinction, attached to the different embassies, and lodged in every possible hotel from Mivart's [established in Brook Street in 1812 and acquired by William Claridge in 1855] to Sablonière [one of several foreign hotels in Leicester Square]. Lord F[rancis] Egerton told me this morning that he had been paying a visit to a brace of Italian princes in the last-named crib on a third floor, and never in the dirtiest locanda of the Levant, Smyrna, or Alexandria, had he visited a more filthy and offensive scene; but they seemed to enjoy it, and are visible every night, with their brilliant uniforms and sparkling stars, as if their carriage at break of dawn were not changed into a pumpkin . . .

We had a very agreeable party at D'Orsay's yesterday. [Among the guests were] the Duke of Ossuna . . . a young man, but a Grandee of the highest grade . . . He is a great dandy and looks like Philip the 2nd, but though the only living descendant of the Borgias he has the reputation of being very amiable . . . Then there was the real Prince Poniatowsky, also young and with a most brilliant star. Then came Kissiloffs and Strogonoffs, 'and other offs and ons' . . .

I must give up going to the coronation, as we go in state, and all the M.P.s *must be* in court dresses or uniforms. As I have withstood making a costume of this kind for other purposes, I will not make one now, and console myself by the conviction that to get up very early (8 o'ck), to sit dressed like a flunky in the Abbey for seven or eight hours, and to listen to a sermon by the Bp of London, can be no great enjoyment . . .

D.

I went to the coronation after all [he continued in a letter to Sarah]. I did not get a dress till 2.30 in the morning of the ceremony, but it fitted me very well. It turned out that I had a very fine leg, which I never knew before! The pageant within the Abbey was without exception the most splendid, various, and interesting affair at which I ever was present. To describe is of course useless. I had one of the best seats in the Abbey, indeed our House had the best of everything. I am very glad indeed that Ralph persuaded me to go, for it far exceeded my expectations. The Queen looked very well, and performed her part with great grace and completeness, which cannot in general be said of the other performers; they were always in doubt as to what came next, and you saw the want of rehearsal. The Duke [of Wellington] was loudly cheered when he made his homage. Melbourne looked very awkward and uncouth, with his coronet cocked over his nose, his robes under his feet, and holding the great sword of state like a butcher ... The Duchess of Sutherland [Mistress of the Robes] walked, or rather stalked, up the Abbey like Juno; she was full of her situation. Lady Jersey [Sarah, eldest daughter of the tenth Earl of Westmorland by his wife, the heiress of Robert Child, the banker] and Lady Londonderry blazed among the peeresses ...

The Queen behaved with great grace and feeling about Lord Rolle [a large and ancient peer who tripped and fell down the steps to the throne and lay at the bottom 'coiled up in his robes']. Nothing could be more effective. She seemed for an instant to pause, wondering whether etiquette would allow her to rise from her throne, and then did so and held out her hand with infinite dignity and yet delicate sentiment.

Lyndhurst, as I think I told you, paid his homage with singular dignity, but committed the *faux pas* of not backing from the presence.

O'Connell was in court dress and looked very well, and was deeply interested in everything, but was hooted greatly, *on dit*, by the mob. Hume [Joseph Hume, the Radical Member of Parliament for Kilkenny], who would not put on Court attire, was prevented from sitting in our gallery, but was in the Abbey.

The Londonderrys after the review gave the most magnificent banquet at Holdernesse House conceivable. Nothing could be more *recherché*. There were only 150 asked, and all sat down. Fanny [Lady Londonderry] was faithful and asked me, and I figure in the *Morning Post* accordingly. It was the finest thing of the season. Londonderry's regiment being reviewed, we had the band of the 10th playing on the staircase: the whole of the said staircase (a double one) being crowded with the most splendid orange-trees and Cape jessamines; The Duke of Nemours [second son of King

Louis Philippe], Soult [Marshal Soult, Duke of Dalmatia], all the 'illustrious strangers', the Duke [of Wellington] and the very flower of fashion being assembled. The banquet was in the gallery of sculpture; it was so magnificent that everybody lost their presence of mind. Sir James Graham said to me that he had never in his life seen anything so gorgeous. 'This is the grand *seigneur* indeed,' he added. I think it was the kindest thing possible of Fanny asking me, as it was not to be expected in any way.[12]

13

'A PRETTY LITTLE WOMAN,
A FLIRT AND A RATTLE'

'Mark what I prophesy: Mr Disraeli will in a very few years
be one of the greatest men of his day.'

AT THE TIME OF THIS 'MAGNIFICENT BANQUET' at Holdernesse
House, Disraeli had become increasingly attached to the wife of his
fellow candidate at Maidstone, Wyndham Lewis. He had not, at first,
much liked this woman to whom he had been introduced at a 'really
brilliant' *soirée* at Bulwer's in April 1832 and had then described her in
a letter to Sarah as a 'pretty little woman, a flirt and a rattle . . . gifted
with a volubility I should think unequalled'.

Born in Devon in November 1792, Mary Anne Lewis came from a
family whose members had been farmers for generations. Her father,
John Evans, however, had joined the Royal Navy as a captain's servant
at the age of eleven and, ten years later, he had risen to the rank of
lieutenant. In 1788, the year before the storming of the Bastille in Paris
at the outset of the French Revolution, he married the daughter of a
well-to-do parson and died in the West Indies five years later.

Despite her father's early death, Mary Anne Evans, or 'Little Whizzy'
as she was known in the family, was a cheerful, high-spirited child who
grew up to speak with a pronounced Devonian accent and to write in
a hasty, scrawling hand of which a cousin said that if there were any
merit in writing illegibly she would shine at it.

When she was fifteen years old, her grandparents died and her
mother took Mary Anne and Mary Anne's brother, John, soon to be an

officer in the 29th (Worcestershire) Regiment, to live in Gloucester in a substantial house near the cathedral.

Not long after the family's arrival in Gloucester, Mary Anne's mother married again and the family moved to a house in Bristol; and it was at a ball in 1815, given to celebrate the victory over France at Waterloo, that Mary Anne, then twenty-three, met Wyndham Lewis, a wealthy gentleman fourteen years older than herself, the son of a Welsh squire in holy orders. He was a rather staid man of melancholy mien who had been called to the Bar but had never practised, having no need to do so, as his family owned a large share in a highly profitable iron works.

He seems to have been attracted to Mary Anne immediately. Unlike him, as Disraeli was to discover, she was eccentric, volatile and unpredictable, and was to take ingenuous pleasure in her position as a hostess able to give large parties for guests of far higher social standing than herself. Extremely talkative, arch and capricious, she was much given to making remarks of guileless absurdity which from other lips might have been considered as ironic. On first acquaintance, she could appear stupid and tiresome, and certainly she was not well educated; Disraeli was to say that she could never remember who came first, the Greeks or the Romans. But those who knew her well were aware of her astuteness. She was capable of great affection.

She accepted Wyndham Lewis's proposal of marriage not long after meeting him without apparent hesitation.

Her brother, by then a major, wrote to congratulate her in a letter whose style, pompous and pedagogic, was so unlike her own:

> I must congratulate you on your approaching nuptials to a gentle-
> man you seem to have a particular regard for, as he is the finest
> out of so many admirers you have at last fixed on as your husband,
> and I am sure Mr Lewis must be very superior, having engaged
> a heart as *particular* as yours, and I assure you it gives me no
> small satisfaction to hear you express yourself in such warm and
> affectionate terms of him ... Your very timely description of
> Mr Lewis has pleased me beyond measure because I know your
> discrimination is so great ...
>
> You are now, my dear sister, about to enter an entirely new
> state in this life, where you will be obliged in many things to be
> responsible. The charge of a house and perhaps a family conducted
> in a proper manner require the utmost exertions ... I need not

tell you to be always uncommonly regular in your devotion to God, as from Him all blessings flow; but it is your duty also to impress upon your servants [the obligation] of regular attendance at church or chapel . . . I am sure in this respect the example you have had from our excellent mother is engrafted on your mind.[1]

The letters which Mary Anne wrote to him were far less sententious. In one she told him, 'I am gratified in finding by yr last letter that your heart is not quite as susceptible as formerly, and hope that whenever you marry it will be to some fair Damsel in England, who has a little money in her pocket . . . I am happy in the marriage state and I pray to the Almighty . . . [that you will] never marry an Irish woman – not that I have the smallest fear that you would connect your fate with that unprincipled nation.'[2]

In another letter she wrote: 'I have only just found out that I have a *very fine voice*. Is it not extraordinary that none of my family ever told me I had a fine voice?'

Wyndham Lewis's letters to Mary Anne, his 'dear, dearest Darling', were uniformly affectionate: 'You cannot think how I miss my little darling . . . I really begin to think that absence increases love, for a man does not know the value of such a prize till he has been without her society, and then he sees the loss he sustained in its true colours.'

She herself seems to have borne their separations with equanimity:

> Throughout her youth and middle age she had an outstanding repu-
> tation as a flirt, a tremendous pride in her femininity, and an un-
> appeasable appetite for admiration [her biographer, Mollie Hard-
> wick, wrote]. When [her husband] was away, she may well have
> been unable to resist the temptation to lead her admirers to the
> point when 'liberties' would inevitably be taken, and to have en-
> joyed the liberties without crossing the barrier into actual adultery.[3]

She was certainly extremely flirtatious. At a ball, she once encoun-
tered Prince Poniatowski and bet him a ring that she could make him fall in love with her. She preserved a letter from a 'Gentleman who had long deeply admired her' and who asked her to 'walk for a moment in Portman Square at half past six or seven so that he might have an opportunity of addressing her'. She kept another letter from a Spaniard who wished her 'happiness, notwithstanding [her] cruelty'. She was seen from time to time with the dissolute Lord Worcester, and with George

Beauclerk, a descendant of King Charles II and Nell Gwyn, and with the profligate Augustus Fitzharding Berkeley.

By 1838, she was also to be seen, unaccompanied by her husband, with Benjamin Disraeli, who attended dinner parties at her house which he did not much enjoy: one, for instance, was described as 'very dull', though Mrs Wyndham Lewis did all she could to make it less so.

In time, Disraeli began to think more highly of the woman he had at first described as 'insufferable'; and he told his sister of a 'fine dinner at the W[yndham] L[ewise]s' where the Clarendons and Prince and Princess Poniatowski were his fellow guests. The dinner was 'well cooked with gorgeous service', and his host and hostess 'very friendly, more friendly every day'. 'Certainly', he added, 'W.L. is one of the oddest men that ever lived but I like him very much.'[4]

While Disraeli had been at first disinclined to take Mrs Wyndham Lewis too seriously, she had no such reservations about him. 'Mark what I say,' she told her brother, 'mark what I prophesy: Mr Disraeli will in a very few years be one of the greatest men of his day. His great talents, backed by his friends, Lord Lyndhurst and Lord Chandos, will ensure his success. They call him my Parliamentary protégé.'

After Wyndham Lewis had been chosen to stand as parliamentary candidate at Maidstone with Disraeli, the friendship between the two had deepened; and, on 30 July 1837, Disraeli wrote to invite him and his wife to Bradenham: 'We all here wish very much that Mr Wyndham and yourself would come and pay us a visit among our beechen groves. We have nothing to offer you but simple pleasures, a sylvan scene and an affectionate hearth.'[5]

The visit was a notable success. Mary Anne and Sarah took to each other immediately, while Mr D'Israeli was charmed by his guest. He sent her some verses of his own composition after she had gone; and she responded with characteristic hyperbole: 'Accept my delighted thanks for the most perfect lines ever penned by mortal man . . . How gratified and charm'd must I feel for so much wit and kindness all mine.'*

---

* Also at Bradenham now was the Venetian, Giovanni Battista Falcieri, Byron's gondolier and servant, who had been with his master at Missolonghi and, after Byron's death, had fought for the Greek cause in command of a band of Albanians. Disraeli was later instrumental in obtaining a post for him as messenger at the Board of Control and later at the India Office. When 'Tita' died at the age of seventy-six in 1874, Disraeli wrote to Queen Victoria recommending that his widow, who had been housekeeper at Bradenham, should be granted a pension of £50 (Monypenny and Buckle, i, Appendix A).

Following this visit to Bradenham, Disraeli wrote to Mrs Wyndham Lewis again: 'After you went, everything and everybody were most dull and *triste*. The truth is the visit was too short . . . Here everything remains the same, save that it is now the memorable first of September and the boys are out shooting . . . We must ask you for news: you cannot expect it from us in this sylvan solitude . . . All unite in love and affection and compliments to you and Wyndham: I send my quota. Dis.'[6]

> ﹒I have been paying a visit to Mr Disraeli's family [Mrs Wyndham Lewis reported to her brother]. They reside near High Wycombe – a large family house, most of the rooms 30 and 40 feet long, and plenty of servants, horses, dogs, and a library full of the rarest books. But how shall I describe his father, the most lovable, perfect old gentleman I ever met with? A sort of modern Dominie Sampson [the 'poor, modest, humble scholar' in Walter Scott's *Guy Mannering*] – and his manners are so high-bred and natural. Miss Disraeli is handsome and talented, and two brothers. Our political pet, the eldest, commonly called Dizzy, you will see a great deal of; you know Wyndham brought him in for Maidstone with himself.[7]

As the months passed, the friendship between Disraeli and Mrs Wyndham Lewis grew ever more fond. On 5 January, he wrote to her to say:

> I was very sorry not to see you this morning, but very imprudently I sat up writing, which never does for me. Slept little, and only towards morn, and woke very wretchedly shattered. I hope you have had not a very disagreeable journey to town and found Wyndham well.
>
> We all miss you here very much; everything seems flat and everybody dull and dispirited as you think me.[8]

Two months or so after this letter was written, Disraeli heard of Wyndham Lewis's sudden death. 'I have seen Mrs Wyndham,' he told his sister. 'She is, of course, at present, extremely overwhelmed. She was sitting in the room with him when he died.'

Disraeli's initial reaction was concern for the large amount of outstanding debts which had been incurred in the campaign at Maidstone and for which he would now be held responsible.

In his letter of sympathy Disraeli was no less sincere in urging the widow 'not to brood over the past':

The future [he said] may yet be full of happiness and hope. You are too young [she was forty-five, twelve years older than himself] to feel that life has not yet a fresh spring of felicity in store. And I can assure you that you have in my family friends . . . who have from their first acquaintance with you loved and appreciated you. As for myself . . . as you well know I am one of those persons who feel much more deeply than I ever express [but your] talent, firmness and sweet temper will always make me your faithful friend.[9]

He was already hoping to be more than a friend; and the possibility of marriage to the widow began to occupy his thoughts.

His friends naturally assumed that when he considered marriage to Mary Anne Lewis he was thinking mainly of her money; and, no doubt, had she been poor he would not have contemplated her at all. Indeed, he confessed to her himself that when he first made advances to her he 'was influenced by no romantic feelings'. Yet it is clear from the letters he wrote to her, and the poetry he composed for her, that these feelings did come later. When he discovered that she had no more than a life interest in part of her husband's fortune, worth about £5,000 a year (some £150,000 a year in present-day terms), and that the share in the ironworks had gone to her brother, Disraeli nevertheless continued to press his suit. As Mary Anne herself was to say, 'Dizzy married me for my money. But, if he had the chance again, he would marry me for love.'

By the end of July, within four months of the death of her husband, Disraeli was making it quite clear that he loved Mrs Wyndham Lewis. He had been a frequent visitor at her fine house, No. 1 Grosvenor Gate (now 29 Park Lane), where he had watched the 'splendid Review' in Hyde Park after the Queen's coronation, being assigned the balcony on the drawing-room floor as a companion for Lord Rolle, who sat with a footman on either side of him, as was his wont, while the other guests were kept out of sight lest there should be the 'appearance of a party' so soon after Wyndham Lewis's death.[10]

On his way to Maidstone on 26 July, Disraeli wrote 'a scrawl' from a 'wretched pot-house' at Rochester to say that, for the whole of that day, there had not been a moment when Mary Anne had been absent from his thoughts; and the following day, from Maidstone, he wrote again:

> I arrived here just a quarter of an hour before the meeting. Under the inspiration of a glass of brandy and water at Rochester, and the racket of the post-chaise, I contrived to collect some nonsense which turned into a capital speech; but what I shall say at the dinner party I can't devise . . . Let me avail myself of this moment, which I seize in a room full of bustle and chatter, to tell you how much I love you.[11]

A TROUBLED COURTSHIP

'My love can be of no value
to you, dear Dizzy'

AFTER WYNDHAM LEWIS'S DEATH, his widow, deeply distressed by the loss of a husband so kind and affectionate, went through the letters she had received from him, endorsing one of them: 'The last letter I ever received from dear Wyndham.' 'God bless you, my affection-ate kind dear,' it ended, 'and believe me your own devoted and faithful husband.' 'How I miss Whm,' she herself wrote. 'I feel like a body without a soul now that he has gone.'

Explaining that his work in his constituency kept him away from London, Disraeli sent her kind, commiserating notes and letters, the first ending 'God bless you, dearest'. She herself wrote to her 'dear kind friend Dizzy' from Wales, where she had gone to deal with Wyndham's estate. 'I do not know where to turn for love,' she said. Her brother, to whom she had had to refuse the loan of large sums of money which she knew would never be repaid, did not love her as he had done in the past. She told dear Dizzy to spend as much time as he could with his friend, Lady Londonderry, 'because the more you go there or to any other married lady, the less likely you are to marry yourself . . . I hate married men . . . I would much sooner you were dead . . . Selfish? Yes I am . . . but most sincere (& kind)'.

> The future for you may yet be full of happiness and hope [he wrote to comfort her in her distress]. As for myself, I can truly say, that the severe affliction which you have undergone and the excellent, and to me unexpected qualities with which you have

met them, the latent firmness and sweet temper, will always make me your faithful friend.[1]

To alleviate her unhappiness, he later wrote more cheerful letters, telling her, for instance, of a forthcoming splendid banquet to be given by Lord Chandos, at which the Duke of Wellington and Sir Robert Peel were to be fellow guests. By way of reply, she sent him a set of gold chains, of which he was so fond, to wear on this occasion. It was 'an exquisite offering', he told her. He wore the chains, which had belonged to Wyndham Lewis, with 'unaffected delight', quite undeterred by a comment made on an earlier occasion when he had indulged his passion for such accoutrements by a lady whom he was taking in to dinner. 'What *is* the meaning, Ben, of all these chains? Are you practising for Lord Mayor, or what?'

He returned the compliment of Mary Anne's generous gift by presenting her with the gold medal which, as a Member of Parliament, he had been given to commemorate the Queen's coronation.

Contented days at Bradenham were succeeded for Disraeli by days of intermittent misery in London. He had, for some reason, suddenly conceived a wild jealousy. 'I cannot reconcile Love and Separation,' he told Mary Anne. 'I wish to be with you, to live with you, never to be away from you.' He developed an intemperate jealousy of men whom she had known in the past, of Beverly and Beauclerk, and Augustus Stapleton. He also, so he told her, more strongly than ever disliked Mary Anne's friend, Rosina Bulwer (Edward Bulwer's Irish wife), 'that woman' who was 'thoroughly vulgar' and 'quite heartless, typically a daughter of Erin.'[2]

He was, however, soon on more intimate terms than ever with Mary Anne; and it seems that, by the end of 1838, they might have become lovers. Certainly he was concerned that he had left 'his chain and seal as well as his watch' in her house in Grosvenor Street; and certainly by then they were exchanging extremely fond letters and bits of verse. 'Little Dove' told 'Eagle' that she loved him 'so much'. 'Believe me, dearest, I am yours faithfully now and for ever.' 'Dear, dear Dizzy, how I love to think of you and all your tenderness and forbearance . . . Dizzy, I deserve your love so give me all you possess. Me and only me mind.'[3]

'I have been obliged to betake myself to bed again,' he responded when suffering from influenza. 'I wish you were with me there.'

> Would I were that flea
> That is biting your knee . . .
> Or at least a young fly
> That is near your bright eye.
> Or were I a dove
> This I tell you, my love,
> That I should make my nest
> In that exquisite breast . . .
> But I am poor Dis,
> With a secondrate Phiz,
> And all I can do
> Is to love you most true.
> My Mary Anne.[4]

'Till I embrace you I shall not know what calmness is [he wrote to her when she was about to come with her mother to spend the Christmas of 1838 at Bradenham]. I write this to beg you to have your hand *ungloved*, when you arrive, so that you may stand by me, & I may clasp & feel your soft delicious hand as I help your mother out of the carriage; now mind this, or I shall be the more insane with disappointment . . . a thousand and 1000 kisses more, more, come, come, come . . .'[5]

'Dearest dearest Dizzy,' she responded when she had returned to London. 'A few hours after you have received this I shall be clasped to your ever faithful heart. Keep yourself warm and well and do not go out in the cold except to take some delightful walks with your devoted Mary Anne.'

She told him that she had felt compelled to write to him before she wrote to anyone in that new year of 1839; while he wrote message after message declaring his passionate love: 'Sweetheart and soul of my existence . . . my dove and darling . . . my sweet Mary Anne I love you, if possible, each day more truly and more tenderly. All my hopes of happiness in life are centred in your sweet affections, and I wish only to be the solace and glory of your life. A thousand and a thousand embraces. Your devoted Dizzy . . . Soul of my existence. I only write to bless you . . . Bless you, my sweet little dove. I long to embrace you . . . I write every day because it allows me daily to say I am Your dear child Dis . . .'[6]

But, at the beginning of February, having heard rumours of other men in her life, as well as suggestions that – still deep in debt – he was after her money, he was exasperated by her disinclination to settle on a date for the marriage he had proposed and went to 'have it out with her'. There was a 'terrible row'; she lost her temper, called him a 'selfish bully', and ordered him out of her house; he stormed off; and, having returned to his rooms, he wrote her a long letter, by turns self-pitying, angry, rhetorical and self-defending:

> Every hour of my life I hear of an approaching union from all lips except your own ... There was a period ... when allusions to the future ... were frequent from your lips; as if you thought some daily hint of the impending result was necessary to stimulate or secure my affection ...
>
> As a woman of the world, which you are thoroughly, you cannot be unacquainted with the difference that exists between our relative positions. The continuance of the present state of affairs cd only render you disreputable; me it wd render infamous. There is only one construction which Society, & justly, puts upon a connection between a woman who is supposed to be rich & a man whom she avowedly loves & does not marry. In England especially there is no stigma more damning ...
>
> This reputation impends over me ... I must inevitably chuse between being ridiculous or being contemptible; I must be recognised as being jilted, or I must at once sink into what your friend Lady Morgan has already styled me, 'Mrs Wyndham Lewis's De Novo.'
>
> This leads me to the most delicate of subjects, but in justice to us both I will write with the utmost candor. I avow, when I first made my advances to you I was influenced by no romantic feelings. My father had long wished me to marry; my settling in life was the implied, tho' not stipulated, condition of a disposition of his property ... I found you in sorrow, & my heart was touched. I found you, as I thought, aimiable, tender, & yet acute and gifted with no ordinary mind ...
>
> Now for your fortune: I write the sheer truth. That fortune proved to be much less than I, or the world, imagined. It was in fact, as far as I was concerned, a fortune which cd not benefit me in the slightest degree; it was merely a jointure not greater than your station required ... To eat & to sleep in that house & nominally to call it mine – these cd be only objects for a penniless adventurer ...

Had we married, not one shilling of your income shd ever have been seen by me; neither indirectly nor directly wd I have interfered in the management of your affairs.

By heavens as far as worldly interests are concerned, your alliance cd not benefit me. All that society can offer is at my command . . . My nature demands that my life shall be perpetual love.

Upon your general conduct to me I make no comment. It is now useless. I will not upbraid you. I will only blame myself. All warned me; public and private – all were eager to save me from the perdition into which I have fallen. Coxcomb to suppose that you wd conduct yourself to me in a manner different to that in which you have behaved to fifty others!

And yet I thought I had touched your heart! Wretched Idiot! . . . *Nature never intended me for a toy & dupe.* But you have struck deep. You have done that which my enemies have yet failed to do; you have broken my spirit. From the highest to the humblest scene of my life, from the brilliant world of fame to my own domestic hearth, you have poisoned all. I have no place of refuge; home is odious, the world oppressive . . .

Farewell. I will not affect to wish you happiness for it is not in your nature to obtain it. For a few years you may flutter in some frivolous circle. But the time will come when you will sigh for any heart that could be fond and despair of one that can be faithful. Then will be the penal hour of retribution; then you will recall to your memory the passionate heart that you have forfeited, and the genius you have betrayed.[7]

D.

'For God's sake come to me,' Mary Anne replied after waiting a day or two to do so. 'I am ill and almost distracted. I will answer all you wish. I never desird [sic] you to leave the house, or implied or thought a word about money.'[8]

My darling [she wrote the next day], my love can be of no value to you dear Dizzy after all the harsh thoughts you have expressed and, of course, feel towards me . . . I beg you to be explicit and answer this, also my letter of yesterday. In the meantime I will believe all that's kind and fond of you whatever your feelings may be towards your poor Mary Anne.

In a rare mood of contrition, Disraeli replied: 'My darling and my life, I will come to you *immediately* I am dressed.'[9]

She welcomed him warmly and was immediately forgiven; and a date for their marriage was set. His family were delighted: his father, in his characteristically studied style, wrote to his 'dear Daughter', fondly responding 'to the endearing title' she had invested him with, to say that he had learned of her 'approaching union with [his] son with great pleasure and satisfaction', in which everyone at Bradenham participated.

> You have both been so long intimately acquainted with each other's habits and tastes [he continued], that your Papa may confidently augur every domestic enjoyment . . .
>
> You make me quite in love with you, when your truthful language so deeply appreciated the susceptibility of my son's character – at least you know him! and it is delightful to me that he will be united to one who can respond to his feelings . . .
>
> My wife and myself are anxiously awaiting the pleasure of seeing you here . . .[10]

The engagement had not yet been publicly announced and, when it was, many were surprised that Disraeli had chosen to marry an undoubtedly unusual woman so much older than himself; but then he had always been attracted to women older than himself.

Among those to express surprise at his becoming engaged to a woman of her years were the two granddaughters of Henrietta Montefiore who attended a party at their grandmother's house at which Disraeli and Mrs Wyndham Lewis were also present. These young ladies could not but notice the 'little nods and smiles' which were exchanged between the two other guests, and the way they drank to one another's health as they raised their wine glasses to their lips.

> To these young girls Mr Disraeli had been a joyous, fantastic, captivating acquaintance, whilst to them Mrs Wyndham Lewis looked and seemed very much older than the man whom she was about [to marry], quite elderly, in fact, and quite unfit for the post she was about to fill. They thought they were witnessing an amusing flirtation. When they were told of the engagement their surprise was boundless. Can we not hear them saying 'What! an old woman and our brilliant friend? Impossible!'[11]

A HAPPY MARRIAGE

'She was the most cheerful and the
most courageous woman I ever knew.'

IN THE SUMMER OF 1838 Mrs Wyndham Lewis had left London for
a long visit to Bradenham, where Disraeli had written notes to his
'darling', his 'little dove', in such terms as those he had once written to
Lady Sykes, with tears in his eyes as he thought of her, asking her when
she would come to his room to see 'her child'; and, after she had gone
home again, Disraeli wrote to her to say how 'stupefied' he was by her
departure. All was 'dull, silent, spiritless', he had told her in letters almost
facetious in their extravagant regret: 'the charm is broken, the magic is
fled . . . I have not been out of the house since you left it . . . being in
a state of apathy, a dull trance.'[1]

He was working on a play in verse, *The Tragedy of Count Alarcos*,
which was based on a Spanish ballad and set in thirteenth-century
Burgos. It relates in florid blank verse the violent and, in places, horrify-
ing story of the evil *Alarcos* who murders his gentle wife. Disraeli had
high hopes of this indifferent work, the composition of which suited
his present mood. He had, he claimed, never written anything which
was 'more talked of in society', even though it was 'never noticed by the
scribbling critics'. However, Lord Powerscourt, so he told Sarah, raved
about it and 'literally' knew it by heart, while Richard Monckton Milnes,
the poet, was 'astonished' that he did not give it to W.C. Macready, the
actor-manager, as it 'would have made his fortune'. In fact, Macready
was shown it and declined to appear in it, noting in his diary that it
would 'never come to any good'.[2]

Certainly, when a version of it was produced for the first and last time in 1868, the manager of the theatre where it was performed suffered a heavy loss when the production was closed after a run of only five weeks.

Disraeli's disappointment had been reflected in the letters to Mrs Wyndham Lewis which he had written at this time. The pages of his play, he told her, teemed with passages which she would not be able to read without emotion, since they came from his heart and commemorated his misery. 'Your name was before me,' he had assured her, 'the name [which was my] inspiration, [my] hope, perhaps [my] despair'.

There was 'no hell on earth like separated love'; 'love swalloweth up all things'; he longed to be with his 'sweet love', never to be away from her, 'in heaven or on earth, or in the waters under the earth'. 'What future joy and prosperity, what fortune, even what fame [could] compensate for this anguish?'

In his distraction, he fell ill. 'I am entirely overwhelmed,' he told her shortly before Christmas 1838, when there had been some sort of disagreement between them. 'Indeed it has been one of the most miserable weeks that I have ever passed ... I have written to put off all my engagements, and am lying on my sofa so utterly wretched that I cannot convey to you even a faint idea of my frustration. And it is doubly painful, for I cannot bear to complain, as I should have the house full of doctors and, alas! they cannot minister to a mind diseased.'[3]

He wrote to Lord Chandos to 'excuse [his] attendance at the Bucks dinner and [his] visit to Stowe'. D'Orsay came one day to shoot and he never anticipated his arrival 'with so much reluctance or saw him depart with so much satisfaction and yet he [was] really a friend. But what are friends, and what is all the goodness and kindness in the world, if there is a cloud between you and the being you adore? ... I am sure you never wish to show your power over me ... you are above all that. But, indeed, this week is something too terrible to think of.'[4]

Having recovered from his debilitating illness and an attack of influenza, Disraeli resumed his social and political life with an energy that helped him overcome the frustrations of his pursuit of Mrs Wyndham Lewis, who had insisted that there could be no sort of official engagement between them until at least six months had passed since her husband's death.

He told his sister of a dinner party at Sir Robert Peel's house where, arriving late, he found 'some 25 gentlemen grubbing in solemn silence'. 'I threw a shot over the table,' he wrote, 'and set them going, and in time they became even noisy. Peel, I think, was quite pleased that I broke the awful stillness, as he talked to me a good deal, though we were far removed; he sitting in the middle of the table. I had Sir Robert Inglis [Tory Member for Oxford University] on my right hand, whose mind I somewhat opened.'

> The dinner was curiously sumptuous. There was really 'every delicacy of the season'; and the second course of dried salmon, olives, caviare, woodcock pie, foie gras, and every combination of cured herring, &c., was really remarkable. The drawing room and picture gallery were lit up, and the effect was truly fine.*[5]

Soon after this, he dined 'en famille with the Duke of Buckingham, to eat vension; a regular Bucks party'. Then there was the marriage of the Duke of Wellington's son, the Marquess of Douro, to Lady Elizabeth Hay, daughter of the Marquess of Tweeddale. 'There was much cheering in the streets and [there] would have been in the church also, had not the Dean of Carlisle with apostolic naïveté previously warned the audience. The church crowded; 3 or 4 ladies in pulpit; pews engaged weeks before. I have not seen the lady, but, according to Douro, she weighs 11 stone 5 lbs ... They were married at twelve, and at four he was riding in the park.'[6]

Then there was a dinner at the house of William Scrope, Mary Anne's cousin, where Lord Sudely was among the guests: 'the house magnificent'. This was followed by another 'sumptuous banquet' at Greenwich with the Duke of Buckingham; and then Disraeli 'went down to Rosebank to a petit bal given by the Londonderrys, after a dinner for the Duchess of Cambridge [née Princess Augusta of Hesse-Cassel] on her birthday'; and here he met 'a great many' of his friends; 'the brilliant moon, the lamplit gardens, the terraces, the river, the music, the sylvan

---

* On a later occasion at Peel's house, the dinner was equally good but the male company just as tedious: 'The party at Peel's was, like all such male gatherings, dull enough ... That chatterbox Milnes would sit next to me, and I had not even the consolation of a silent stuff' (Benjamin Disraeli Letters, 22 March 1841). He often found the male company at the Carlton Club quite as boring. 'This Club is a tombeau vivant,' he told Sarah on one occasion, 'and the few men lingering about it really corpses' (Benjamin Disraeli Letters, iii, 327).

ball-room and the bright revellers, made a scene like a fiesta in one of George Sand's novels'.

Not long after this, he dined at Sir Francis Burdett's: 'dinner at seven o'clock precisely; everything stately and old-fashioned, but agreeable'.

Despite all these and other festive engagements, Disraeli thought that 'social London [was] rather dull in contradistinction to political London'. For Lord Melbourne, the Whig Prime Minister, resigned in May 1839 over a disagreement about the political affiliations of the ladies of the Queen's household which became known as 'the bedchamber crisis'. But Melbourne resumed office when Sir Robert Peel failed to form a Conservative government.

These were also years of social unrest, of widespread dissatisfaction with the new Poor Law – which, instead of offering relief to paupers, by giving them sufficient money to survive in their own homes, forced them into workhouses – and with the Reform Act which, while welcomed by the propertied middle classes, was a profound disappointment to Radicals and the militant working class. This general discontent continued throughout the 1830s and helped to increase support for the movement known as Chartism, which took its name from a People's Charter drawn up in 1838 by a group of Radicals who demanded of the Government universal male suffrage and vote by secret ballot, equal electoral districts, annual parliaments, an end to property qualifications for Members of Parliament, and the introduction of salaries for them.

Support for these six demands was loudly voiced at meetings held both day and night all over the country. In 1839, there was the threat of a general strike, and later on that year, when seven thousand men marched through the streets of Newport, Monmouthshire, demanding the release of a Chartist orator from the local gaol, soldiers opened fire on them and over twenty were killed.

There were riots, too, in renewed protests against the Corn Laws, which regulated the import and export of corn to guarantee farmers' incomes and which were bitterly resented by the working classes since they kept the price of bread high. They were also resented by manufacturers, who contended that little money was left in people's pockets for the purchase of manufactured goods. The effects of the Corn Laws were exacerbated by a series of poor harvests; and in 1839, an Anti-Corn Law

League was founded to denounce the Laws as benefiting landowners at the expense of workers.

So there was no lack of contentious subjects upon which the ambitious politician could display his oratorical skills. Disraeli made the most of his opportunity, and in letters home he congratulated himself upon his performances in the House and his championship of 'the Conservative Cause', by which he meant 'the splendour of the Crown, the lustre of the peerage, the privileges of the Commons, the rights of the poor'. 'I mean in short,' he had declared at Maidstone, 'that harmonious union, that magnificent concord of all interests, of all classes, on which our national greatness and prosperity depends.'

Now in Parliament he had occasion to write home of his repeated successes with characteristic pride in his performances. His speech on Talfourd's Copyright Bill, for example, a measure which proposed extending an author's copyright in his work from the existing twenty-eight years, or the duration of the author's life, to sixty years from the date of the author's death, he describes in a letter to Sarah as 'a most brilliant and triumphant speech – unquestionably, and agreed upon by all hands the crack speech of the night, and everyone who spoke after me, either for or against, addressed himself to me; but this you cannot judge by reports'.

The next day, Mrs Wyndham Lewis was told that 'every paper in London, Radical, Whig or Tory, has spoken of my speech in the highest terms of panegyric, except that wretched *Standard*, which under the influence of that scoundrel [the journalist, William] Maginn, always attacked me before I was in Parliament and now always passes over my name in silence ... Mrs Dawson [Robert Peel's sister] stopped the carriage in the street yesterday to congratulate me.'

Some time later, so he told Sarah, he 'rose with several men at the same time; but the House called for me, and I spoke with great effect and amid loud cheering and laughter'. A week later, he made another speech on the question of the reform of municipal corporations in Ireland, advancing views in opposition both to the Government and to the Conservative leaders. His speech on this occasion was, he said, 'very successful' and the 'best *coup*' he had ever made; and it was 'no easy task', for he spoke 'against the Government, a great mass of the Conservative party, and even took a different view from the small minority itself'. 'I was listened to in silence and the utmost attention,' he wrote. 'Peel especially complimented me, sore as he was at the Conservative schism, and said, "Disraeli, you took the only proper line of opposition to the bill."'

Shortly after this, he made what was generally considered 'the best speech on our side'. Having done so, he told Sarah he went to the Carlton where 'two old foes, Lord Lincoln and Lord Ashley tendered me their congratulations with extended hands.'

The next month he made another 'most capital speech', this time on Chartism. 'The *Morning Herald*', he added, 'has taken up the speech and written a leader on it, and calls it "a speech of very considerable talent".'[7]

'The complete command of the House I now have is remarkable,' he assured Sarah on 16 August 1839, 'and nothing can describe to you the mute silence which immediately ensued as I rose, broken only by Members hurrying to their places to listen.'

Highly gratified by his repeated successes in the House of Commons, Disraeli was also now content that the differences with Mary Anne, which had led to his being 'entirely overwhelmed', had been resolved, and he had subsequently told her that he was 'mad with love. My passion is frenzy.' 'Lose not a moment in coming. I cannot wait . . . I can scarcely believe in the joy of our immediate meeting. Will the time ever pass until that rapturous moment?' He wrote to her as his 'dear sweet wife', his 'dear little wife', his 'own sweet life'.[8] And that summer, on 28 August 1839 – having delivered what he described as a 'most capital speech on Chartism' the month before[9] – Disraeli and Mary Anne Lewis were indeed married at last at St George's, Hanover Square, Lord Lyndhurst being best man, and William Scrope giving the bride away.[10] Bride and bridegroom drove to Tunbridge Wells for the first part of their honeymoon, leaving London in a carriage presented by her father-in-law to the bride, who was wearing what her husband praised as 'a travelling dress of exotic brilliance'.

Mary Anne reported to her father-in-law: 'I wish you could see your happy children . . . Dizzy is so lost in astonishment at finding himself a husband that the first time he had to introduce me to some friends he called me Mrs Wyndham Lewis! . . . And at the ceremony he was going to put the ring on the wrong finger! Is not his conduct most atrocious, considering we all know him to be so great a character, that naughty man!'

The weather in Tunbridge Wells was dreadful and they rarely left their rooms except for drives to Lord Camden's Bayham Abbey and to Penshurst, where they found that Lord De L'Isle had gone out shooting but his children were 'quite charming'. One day on the Pantiles they met Lord Monteagle of Brandon (the former Chancellor of the Exchequer, Thomas Spring-Rice), but otherwise there was, as Disraeli put it, 'scarcely anybody here' that they knew 'or cared to know'.

By 19 September they were in Baden-Baden, 'a most picturesque, agreeable, lounging sort of place' in Disraeli's opinion, but, in his wife's, 'not much better than Cheltenham – public dinners, balls, promenades, pumps, music and gambling'.

From there they drove through the Black Forest to Stuttgart, where they 'fell upon great *fêtes* which pleased [them] much. The King [of Württemberg] surrounded by a brilliant court, sat in a pavilion in the midst of a beautiful mead and distributed prizes to the Württemberg peasants for oxen, horses, etc. More than 20,000 persons present . . . the peasantry in rich and bright dresses, dark velvets with many large silver buttons, vivid vests and three-cornered cocked hats . . . The whole scene was very patrician. Her Majesty came in half-a-dozen blue carriages with scarlet liveries.'

> We visited the studio of [Johann Heinrich von] Dannecker, [Disraeli told Sarah] and I insisted on seeing the artist, whom I found a hale old man, more than eighty, but with a disorder in his throat which prevents him from speaking. He was much affected by our wishing to see him, and when we drove off opened the window of his room, and managed to say, 'Viva, viva!' . . .
>
> I have read enough of Hallam [Henry Hallam, author of *An Introduction to the Literature of Europe*] to make me thirst for literary history in detail . . . I don't think English literature his strongest point.[11]

From Stuttgart they drove to Munich, where they stayed for over a fortnight, much impressed by how much the King of Bavaria, Ludwig I, had done for the arts – 'galleries of painting and sculpture, Grecian temples, Gothic and Byzantine churches, obelisks of bronze, equestrian statues of brass, theatres and arcades in fresco'. They saw the King several times, 'tall, meagre, and German – a poet, which accounts for Munich, for a poet on a throne can realise his dreams'.

From Munich they drove to Frankfurt, then on to Ratisbon and thence to Paris, disappointed only by the Danube, 'an uncouth stream which presented a shallow, shoaly look with vast patches of sand and shingle in the midst of its course'.

In Paris they stayed at the Hôtel de l'Europe in the rue de Rivoli and, so Disraeli said, were 'very gay', being entertained by Lord Canterbury, a former Speaker of the House of Commons. They were also invited to the Embassy by Henry Bulwer, Edward Bulwer's brother, the *chargé d'affaires* and, so Disraeli said, 'now a great man'.[12]

'Mary Anne is particularly well,' Disraeli wrote home, 'and in her new costume looks like Madame de Pompadour, who is at present the model of Paris, at least in dress.'[13]

When they got home it was clear, to nearly everyone's surprise, that they were perfectly happy. She adored him; he treated her with devoted courtesy. 'There was no care which she could not mitigate,' her husband said of her fondly, 'and no difficulty which she could not face. She was the most cheerful and the most courageous woman I ever knew.' As the years went by, her unconventional taste, dress and manners became increasingly eccentric, not to say bizarre. But Disraeli pretended not to notice that there was anything about her that was not both attractive and admirable; and if anyone spoke of her slightingly he came at once to her defence. She responded by giving up her whole life to his. Although he was always reluctant to reveal to her – as he had been to reveal to his father – the full burden of his debts, she settled many for him without complaint. If she were ill or tired, she pretended not to be for his sake. Shortly before she died she told a friend that her life had been one long 'scene of happiness, owing to his love and kindness'.

THE BRILLIANT ORATOR

'From Sir Robert Peel downwards there is but
one opinion of my great success.'

EARLY IN THE NEW YEAR OF 1840, on his return to London, Disraeli delivered a speech in the House which, so he congratulated himself, outshone all his previous efforts. 'I never spoke better,' he said. 'I have never heard more continuous cheering . . . the house very full . . . and every man of distinction there . . . It is in vain to give you any account of all the compliments, all the congratulations, the shaking of hands etc. which occurred in the lobby . . . From Sir Robert Peel downwards there is but one opinion of my great success.'[1]

Content with his progress in the Commons, Disraeli was also content in his social life, in his marriage, and in the house at Grosvenor Gate which his wife had brought to their marriage. It was rather a pretentious house. 'Snobbish visitors sniffed at the decoration, which was thoroughly conventional, the kind of effect an upholsterer might have contrived,' Jane Ridley wrote in her *The Young Disraeli*. 'The large downstairs dining room was painted a dull brown, and hung with conventional paintings – the statutory Dead Game, and a bad copy of a Murillo . . . Upstairs the huge L-shaped drawing room was a blaze of splendour, crimson Wilton carpets, gold silk damask curtains and heavy gilt-framed mirrors . . . To the Victorian eye, Grosvenor Gate was distinctly old-fashioned and a touch vulgar . . . but to this Disraeli, short-sighted and almost devoid of taste, was oblivious. Nor did he object to Mary Anne's bright-brown servants' livery, though the coats were badly made and brown was a colour unknown to heraldry.'[2]

As well as a coachman, there were as many as eight indoor servants (who were dismissed with 'distressing frequency'). 'Even when Mary Anne was away, [her husband] rarely spoke to them and they never spoke to him.'[3] When the master and mistress went on holiday together, they were left on board wages and provided with twelve pieces of soap and seven pounds of candles.[4]

At Grosvenor Gate, the Disraelis could give dinner parties for up to sixty guests, the meals provided by a caterer for a cost to their host of a guinea each.*

'Yesterday, I gave my first male dinner party,' he wrote on 19 January. 'Lyndhurst, Powerscourt, Ossulston and D'Orsay were amongst the guests and everything went off capitally ... I have been introduced formally to the Duke of Wellington,' he added contentedly. 'He accorded me a most gracious and friendly reception, and looked right hearty.'[5]

'I have asked nearly sixty M.P.s to dine with me,' he wrote a few days later. 'There is scarcely anyone of station in the House of Commons or society that I have not paid this attention to, which was most politic.' For such parties at Grosvenor Gate extra servants were hired and were clothed in the appropriate livery, prompting *The Satirist* to ask, 'Was there ever such an impudent, insolent, Hebrew varlet as this fellow D'Israeli?'

After this large party for Members of Parliament, Disraeli, so he said, 'rested on his oars' by going with Mary Anne for a week or so to Brighton where he ate 'a great many shrimps' and found several other 'birds of passage' there, including Charles Shaw-Lefevre, later Viscount Eversley, 'the most amiable of men, fresh as a child and enjoying his holidays'.[6]

Later on that year, Disraeli spent a few days with James and Caroline Maxse in Sussex at Woolbeding, which was looking 'very beautiful, a paradise of flowers and conservatories, fountains and vases, in the greenest valley with the prettiest river in the world. This was a former temple of Whiggery. Charles James Fox's statue and portrait may be seen in every nook and every chamber, a sort of rural Brooks's Club.'[7]

---

* According to Lady Dorothy Nevill, it was Disraeli who set the fashion of employing a caterer to provide such dinners at a fixed price (G.M. Young, ed., *Early Victorian England*, i, 115).

The house was 'rather old fashioned', but the grounds were 'remarkable for their beautiful forms with the river winding all about,' he told Sarah. 'The place is only used by Maxse as a shooting-box . . . He either possesses or rents nearly twenty-two thousand of the finest covers in the world. He has six principal keepers and thirty-two watchers out.'[8]

The following month, Disraeli enjoyed a 'delightful visit' to The Deepdene, near Dorking in Surrey, where, in the midst of romantic gardens and a picturesque park, the millionaire amateur architect, Thomas Hope, had built 'a perfect Italianate palace, full of balconies adorned with busts'. Among the other guests were the Revd William Harness, Lord Byron's friend, 'now grown an oldish gentleman but still juvenile in spirits, and ever ready to act charades and spout poetry, and Mr and Mrs Adrian Hope, Mrs Hope being a French lady, a child of nature' who had never heard of Sir Robert Peel.[9]

The Disraelis returned for Christmas to The Deepdene, where there was a 'very merry and agreeable party'. 'We have had many Christmas gambols, charades and ghosts,' Disraeli reported to Bradenham; 'and our princely host made all the ladies a Christmas box; [and gave] to Mary Anne two beautiful specimens of Dresden china.'[10]

Early the next year, the Disraelis went to stay with Sir Baldwin Leighton at Loton Park, Salop, 'one of the most charming old English halls, and filled with a family in their way as perfect. A complete old English gentleman, whom I first met at Stamboul, a most agreeable wife, the finest amateur artist I know, and children lovelier than the dawn.'[11]

The Disraelis could not afford to entertain as lavishly as most of those with whom they stayed, but it was generally agreed by their guests that the meals at Grosvenor Gate were excellent. One day the Lyndhursts and Tankervilles, General Cecil (Cis) Forester and Henry Cope came to dinner, and they had what their host called a perfect 'Spanish pudding'. Tankerville said that his French chef had been trying to make it, but his attempts were a fiasco. 'He says he finds a French cook can never execute out of his school. Cis wants the recipe for the mess, but Mary Anne won't give it.'[12]

*   *   *

Disraeli had by now lost his seat at Maidstone and had been returned as one of the two Conservative candidates at Shrewsbury, where his wife had been most active in his support and had won him many votes. 'My dear Mary Anne,' he told his mother, 'has greatly contributed, if not effected the result and one thing she alone did; namely to make me from a somewhat unpopular, to one of the most popular candidates in her Majesty's dominions.[13]

It had, however, been an acrimonious contest. When Disraeli's crest, the Castle of Castille with the motto *Forti nihil difficile* (nothing is difficult for the brave), was emblazoned on a banner, a local paper suggested that the motto should be translated: 'The impudence of some men sticks at nothing.' But this was relatively harmless compared with copies of a broadsheet about Disraeli which, addressed to the 'Honest Electors of Shrewsbury', contained lists of debts to 'Tailors, Hosiers, Upholsterers, Jew money lenders (for this child of Israel was not satisfied with merely spoiling the Egyptians), Sponging House Keepers and, in short, persons of every denomination who were foolish enough to trust him.' The electors were warned against a man 'seeking a place in Parliament merely for the purpose of avoiding the necessity of a Prison'.

Pieces of paper were held up in his face; and a man drew a cart towards the platform, upon which Disraeli was making a speech, declaring that he had come to take him back to Jerusalem. Such insults were combined with repeated charges that his debts amounted to £20,000, his wife having failed to rescue him from his financial difficulties.[14]

He had never put himself forward as an astute man of business. At this time, indeed, he was borrowing money at over 40 per cent and was still reluctant to reveal to his father the true state of his finances. He also continued to conceal from his wife the sad plight of these, which he seems not to have fully appreciated himself; and when a writ was delivered to his wife when he was out, there was what he described to the solicitor, William Pyne, as a 'terrible domestic crisis'.[15] To the electors of Shrewsbury he had declared: 'I should not have solicited your suffrages had I not been in possession of that ample independence which renders the attainment of any office in the state, except as the recognition of public services, to me a matter of complete indifference.' This was a delusive claim. Soon after having made it, he was writing to Pyne: 'I am really badly distressed for *argent* (*pocket money*). Can you get me five hundred at once?'*[16]

Demands and writs for money continued to be received at both Bradenham and Grosvenor Gate; debts mounted; and recourse was had to more moneylenders, who charged interest equally exorbitant as that charged by those to whom he was already in debt.

His father, now losing his sight, having received a demand made upon him for the settlement of a large, long-standing debt, 'learned with surprise and sorrow that anyone should have entered into pecuniary matters with any son of mine at a period of life when he was not only legally but I should think morally incompetent to regulate himself'.

His son dismissed the matter as an affair of not the slightest importance. For him what mattered was that, having been 'only five days out of Parliament', he was elected as the new Member for Shrewsbury and, as a Member, he was safe from arrest for debt.

The Tories having been returned at the election of 1841 with a large majority, the Queen, distressed at the thought of having to part with her 'kind and excellent' Whig Prime Minister, Lord Melbourne, wrote to her uncle King Leopold of the Belgians:

> You don't say you sympathise with me in my present heavy trial, the heaviest I have ever had to endure, and which will be a sad heart-breaking to me ... I feel very sad and, God knows, very wretched at times, for myself and country, that such a change must take place ... But my dearest Angel [Prince Albert of Saxe-Coburg-Gotha, whom she had married in February 1840] is indeed a great comfort to me.[17]

Thanks to Prince Albert's help and influence, the Queen did not find her first interview with her new Prime Minister as much of an ordeal as she had expected, though she confided in George Anson, her husband's private secretary, that she felt she could never 'get over Peel's awkward manner'.

'He made many protestations of his sorrow, at what must give the

---

* His financial straits still did not upset him unduly. A day or two after complaining to Pyne of his being 'really badly distressed', he told his sister, 'I spoke with great effect last night in the house – the best speech on our side ... It even drew applause and words of praise from Peel' (*BDL*, 1156, 15 May 1841, iii, 334).

Queen pain (as she said to him it did),' she told Melbourne, 'but of course Peel accepted the task. The Duke of Wellington's health [being] too uncertain . . . to admit of his taking office . . . but to be in the cabinet, which the Queen expressed her wish he should.'

Other places in the cabinet were found for Lord Lyndhurst as Lord Chancellor, Lord Wharncliffe as Lord President of the Council, the Duke of Buckingham as Lord Privy Seal, Henry Goulburn, Chancellor of the Exchequer, Sir James Graham, Home Secretary, the Earl of Aberdeen, Foreign Secretary and Viscount Stanley as Secretary for War and the Colonies. Other appointments followed day by day, but Disraeli waited in vain for the summons he was expecting. When no summons had come by 5 September, he would wait no longer and wrote to Sir Robert:

> I have shrunk from obtruding myself upon you at this moment, and should have continued to do so if there were anyone on whom I could rely to express my feelings.
>
> I am not going to trouble you with claims similar to those with which you must be wearied. I will not say that I have fought since 1834 four contests for your party, that I have expended great sums, have exerted my intelligence to the utmost for the propagation of your policy, and have that position in life which can command a costly seat . . .
>
> I confess to be unrecognised at this moment by you appears to me to be overwhelming, and I appeal to your own heart . . . to save me from an intolerable humiliation.[18]

Mrs Disraeli, the close friend of Peel's sister, without telling her husband, so she said, also wrote to Sir Robert:

> I beg you not to be angry with me for my intrusion, but I am overwhelmed with anxiety. My husband's political career is for ever crushed, if you do not appreciate him.
>
> Mr Disraeli's exertions are not unknown to you, but there is much he has done that you cannot be aware of, though they have had no other aim but to do you honour, no wish for recompense but your approbation.
>
> He has gone farther than most to make your opponents his personal enemies. He has stood four most expensive elections since 1834, and gained seats from Whigs in two, and I pledge myself as far as one seat, that it shall always be at your command.
>
> Literature he has abandoned for politics. Do not destroy all his hopes, and make him feel his life has been a mistake.

May I venture to name my own humble but enthusiastic exertions in times gone by for the party, or rather for your own splendid self? They will tell you at Maidstone that more than £40,000 was spent through my influence only.

Be pleased not to answer this, as I do not wish any human being to know I have written to you this humble petition.

I am now, as ever, dear Sir Robert,
Your most faithful servant,

Mary Anne Disraeli[19]

'My dear Sir,' Peel wrote to Disraeli, 'Your letter is one of the many I receive which too forcibly impress upon me how painful and invidious is the duty which I have been compelled to undertake. I am only supported in it by the consciousness that my desire has been to do justice ... I trust that, when candidates for Parliamentary office calmly reflect on my position ... they will then understand how perfectly insufficient are the means at my disposal to meet the wishes that are conveyed to me by men whose co-operation I should be proud to have, and whose qualifications and pretensions for office I do not contest.'[20]

It seems, however, that Peel, who had in the past seemed to regard Disraeli in a favourable light and had been prepared to overlook his occasional divergences from the party line, had denied him office on the insistence of Lord Stanley who – still disposed to condemn him for his supposed part in the affair of Henry Stanley and the notorious Effie Bond – declared, 'If that scoundrel [were] taken in [he] would not remain [himself].'[21]

The Disraelis' bitter disappointment was plain to all their friends and family. Disraeli's sister tried to comfort Mary Anne. 'I suffer much for your and dear D's disappointment,' she wrote to her, 'but we must not despair. After all, it is not half so bad as losing an election. Our *Examiner* has missed this morning, so we do not know the latest appointments; but up to the latest, except Gladstone [who was appointed Vice-President of the Board of Trade] there is not one single untitled or unaristocratic individual.'[22]

Despite his disappointment and his annoyance with Peel, Disraeli gave his support to the Government for the time being and, after a short holiday at Caen, concentrated upon enhancing his reputation as one of the most gifted speakers on the government benches. He found an opportunity to do so by putting down a motion on the unlikely subject of a proposed merger of the consular and diplomatic services.

'I went through my whole speech this morning, without a reference to a single paper, so completely am I master of all its details,' he told his wife. 'It took me three hours ... I am full of confidence as to its effect on the House, but I am very doubtful as to the opportunity being speedily offered.'

The opportunity came on the late afternoon of 8 March 1842 and he seized it with confidence. In a long letter he reported his success to his wife:

> The affair last night realised all my hopes; the success was complete and brilliant. I rose at five o'clock to one of the most disagreeable audiences that ever welcomed a speaker. Everybody seemed to affect not to be aware of my existence, and there was a general buzz and chatter. Nevertheless, not losing my head, I proceeded without hesitation for ten minutes [and then] affairs began to mend; when a quarter of an hour had elapsed there was generally an attentive audience; and from that time until near half-past seven, when I sat down, having been up about two hours and twenty minutes, I can say without the slightest exaggeration, that not only might you have heard a pin fall in the House, but there was not an individual, with[ou]t a single exception, who did not listen to every sentence with the most marked interest, and even excitement. The moment I finished, Peel, giving me a cheer, got up and went to dinner upstairs ... Lord John Manners & several others came in turn and sat by me to give me the general impression of the House, that it was not only, by a thousand degrees, the best speech I had ever made, but the best one that was ever made. The enthusiasm of young Smythe was extraordinary; he and several others particularly mentioned my manner, perfectly changed and different to what it used to be – 'Exactly as you talk at the Carlton or at your own table,' he said, 'particularly my voice, not the least stilted, but the elocution distinct, the manner easy, a little nonchalant, and always tinged with sarcasm.' ... And what think you of the mighty *Mister Cobden* [Richard Cobden, the Member for Stockport] coming up to me to offer me his thanks for the great public service I had done, &c.?[23]

At supper at Crockford's later, he was also congratulated by Horace Twiss, the hospitable and amusing Vice-Chancellor of the Duchy of

Lancaster. 'Between mighty mouthfuls', the bon vivant Twiss, the favourite nephew of the actress, Mrs Siddons, assured him that he could be compared to Lord Palmerston.

His wife was more proud of him than ever, even more solicitous. While she was looking after her ailing mother at Bradenham, she wrote to him in London, telling him to take care of his hair and to instruct his hairdresser how to dress it as she did, not just to cut it but 'to DRESS IT and, if he dresses it too formal', to 'pull it about a little'. 'I am now and ever your devoted Wife,' she told him, 'your own little slave your darling yr friend sweetheart companion & bedfellow – your own property.'

YOUNG ENGLAND

'The puppets are moved by Disraeli
who is the ablest man amongst them.'

'WHAT I THINK YOU OUGHT TO DO,' Lady Montfort tells Endymion, in Disraeli's 1880 novel of that name, 'is to take advantage of this interval before the meeting of Parliament and go to Paris. Paris is now the capital of diplomacy.'

In October 1842, Disraeli and his wife were themselves in Paris, staying once again at the Hôtel de l'Europe in the rue de Rivoli in rooms overlooking the gardens of the Tuileries; and in letters to his 'dear Sa', Disraeli recounted their doings and described the bewildering variety of people whom they met and by whom they were entertained.

> We have found agreeable acquaintance in the de Gramont family [he told her on 14 October in the manner of a columnist in a society magazine]. The Duchess is Count D'Orsay's sister and like him in petticoats . . . She receives three times a week in her little house in the Faubourg St Honoré crammed with pretty furniture, old cabinets, and pictures of the de Gramonts . . . The Duc as well as his spouse extremely good-looking and brother of Lady Tankerville, who we also find here . . . staying with Marshal Sebastiani who married her sister . . .[1]

There follows a list of English visitors and French politicians, descriptions of meals and entertainments to which they were invited, and descriptions of such Parisian notabilities as Eugène Sul, the novelist and dandy – 'the only *littérateur* admitted into fashionable society here; the rest are savages' – and the statesman and historian, Louis Adolphe

Thiers, a 'very little man . . . with a face full of intelligence and an eye full of fire . . . He looked and chatted like a little journalist; a monkey, but wonderfully sharp and clever . . .'

'Thiers receiving every evening, Mary Anne and myself paid our respects to him a few nights after. We met there [the historian, François] Mignet and Count Walewski [the future Minister of Foreign Affairs, Napoleon's son by his mistress, the Polish Countess Walewska] . . . Thiers paid Mary Anne the greatest courtesy and attended her to her carriage.'

Lady Lyndhurst's father, Lewis Goldsmith, gave the Disraelis 'a good banquet, attended by numerous diplomatists who all talked at the same time, shouted and gesticulated, the noise Neapolitan, and the *salle à manger* being very small . . . the effect was overwhelming'.

> We have dined also with [the Duke of Wellington's brother] Lord Cowley [the British Ambassador in Paris], a very pleasant dinner . . . The Ambassador is very like the Duke but much taller . . . We have passed an evening at Madame Baudrand's, the wife of the General and Aide-de-Camp to the King. She is an Englishwoman and young enough to be his daughter . . . Many Frenchmen have English wives – Madame Lamartine, Odilon-Barrot and De Tocqueville . . .[2]

Tireless in his excursions, Disraeli 'made a visit, or rather a pilgrimage' one day to the historian, Augustin Thierry, who had been blind since the age of thirty-five but continued to work with the help of secretaries. After this, he 'called for M.A. and made a visit together to Madame Thiers', then made his 'début at the Comtesse de Castellane' and, on the following Tuesday, he 'dined with the Minister for Foreign Affairs', a dinner 'given only to the great personages', including various ambassadors, the German explorer, Alexander von Humboldt, General Sebastiani, Military Governor of Paris, and Baron Regnier, the Chancellor of France. François Guizot, their host, he described as 'a man of no charm . . . not exactly pedantic but hard, dogmatic, arrogant'.

> All was sumptuous, servants in rich liveries and guests with every ribbon of the rainbow. Sat between Sebastiani and Rothschild, whom I found a happy mixture of the French dandy and the orange-boy. He spoke to me without ceremony, with 'I believe you know my nephew?' On Wednesday, after making a preliminary visit to Madame Castellane to present Mary Anne, we went

to a grand rout at the British Embassy, where we saw every diplomatic character in Paris, including the fat Nuncio of the Pope, and the Greek Minister, Odelli, in native costume, many of the high French and shoals of the low English . . .

One day [Disraeli continued his account], I went to the Sorbonne where I paid a visit to the celebrated [Victor] Cousin, late Minister of Information and now Dean of the University . . . He delivered me a lecture which lasted an hour and a half . . . I also made a visit to the prince of journalists, M. Bertin de Vaux, an ox who lives in a fat pasture manured by others. He lives in a fine hotel, and lives like a noble . . .

Yesterday [Disraeli wrote on 21 November 1842] was my most distinguished visit; like a skilful general, I kept my great gun to the last.

This was a private audience with King Louis Philippe.

I was with his Majesty nearly two hours alone, the conversation solely political, but of the most unreserved and interesting kind. He was frank, courteous, and kind. In taking my leave, which of course I could not do until he arose, he said he hoped my visit to St. Cloud had made as favourable an impression on me as mine had on him; that he hoped to see me in the evenings at the palace, when he should have the pleasure of presenting me to the Queen . . . we hear that the poor Queen is still dreadfully depressed [her eldest son having been killed in a carriage accident in July] . . . I ought to tell you that while, previous to the audience, I was sitting in the chamber of the aide-de-camp, one of the courtiers brought me from the King, by his Majesty's express order, a despatch just received, and which he had not himself read, containing the news of the conquest of Cabul and the release of the prisoners.* His Maj[est]y sd aft[erwar]ds he was happy that our meeting took place on a day wh: had brought such good news for England.[3]

Returning to his hotel one evening towards the end of the month, Disraeli 'found a note from General Baudrand, saying that at St Cloud in the morning the King had said, "Mr Disraeli has never been at St Cloud in the evening. I wish to present him to the Queen."'

I passed for the first time in my life an evening in the domesticity of a Court. When I arrived the Royal family were still in the

---

* British forces had capitulated at Kabul in the Second Afghan War in January. The war ended with the proclamation of victory on 10 October 1842.

apartments of the Duchess of Orleans . . . In about a quarter of an hour the Court was announced, and his Majesty entered with the Queen. The Queen and the ladies, all in deep mourning, seated themselves around a large round table, working. Ices were handed round and the King commenced speaking a few words to each [person present].

He was extremely gracious when he observed me, and, after saying a few words expressing his pleasure that I had arrived, called a courtier to present me to the Queen. Her Majesty is tall and sad, with white hair; a dignified and graceful phantom. In the course of the evening the King conversed with me a considerable time. I am a favourite with him.

Soon after this, Disraeli received a command to dine at the Tuileries on the following Monday at six o'clock.

I was ushered through a suite of about twenty illuminated rooms, to the chamber of reception, where I formed one of the circle, and where I found seated the Queen of Sardinia, at present a guest, and her ladies. Soon after the Court entered and went round the grand circle. I was the only stranger, though there were sixty guests. Dinner was immediately announced, the King leading out the Queen of Sardinia, and there were so many ladies that an Italian princess, duchess or countess fell to my share . . . In the evening the King showed the Tuileries to the Queen of Sardinia, and the first lady in waiting invited me, and so did the King, to join the party, *only eight*. It is rare to make the tour of a palace with a King for the cicerone. In the evening there was a reception of a few individuals, but I should have withdrawn had not the King addressed me and maintained a conversation with me of great length. He walked into an adjoining room, and motioned me to seat myself on the same sofa. While we conversed the chamberlain occasionally entered and announced guests . . . 'J'arrive,' responded his Majesty very impatiently, but he never moved. At last even his Majesty was obliged to move, but he signified his wish that I should attend the palace in the evenings . . .

You must understand that I am the *only* stranger who has been received at Court. It causes a great sensation here. The King speaks of me to many with great *kudos*.

Years later, Disraeli made some notes, elaborating upon his impressions of the King. His audience with him, he wrote, was long and not formal.

Few foreigners have enjoyed a greater intimacy with that sovereign than myself. I have been in the habit of remaining after the evening receptions at the Tuileries, and sitting with him in his cabinet until a very late hour, he himself dismissing me by a private way, as all the royal household had retired ... Sometimes he would speak only of his early life, his strange adventures, escapes, hardships, and necessities. The last time I was alone with him in 1846 he had indulged in this vein, and in reply to an observation which I had made I remember well his saying: 'Ah, Mr Disraeli, mine has been a life of great vicissitude!' He would always speak English with me. He had a complete command of our language, even of its slang ... His English was a little American.*.

In the King's time there never was a dinner given at the Tuileries without a huge smoking ham being placed, at a certain time, before the King. Upon this he operated like a conjurer. The rapidity and precision with which he carved it was a marvellous feat: the slices were vast, but wafer-thin. It was his great delight to carve this ham, and indeed it was a wonderful performance. He told me one day that he had learnt the trick from a waiter at Bucklerbury, where he used to dine at an eating house for 9d. per head.

One day he called out to an honest Englishman that he was going to send him a slice of ham, and the honest Englishman – some consul, if I recollect right, who had been kind to the King in America in the days of his adversity – not used to Courts, replied that he would rather not take any. The King drew up and said: 'I did not ask you whether you would take any; I said I would send you some.'

Our life goes on the same, only more bustling [Disraeli told Sarah on 16 January 1843]. I have been a great deal at Court; had the honour of drinking tea with the Queen. I am in personal as well as political favour ... We have been to a concert given by the Duchesse Decazes and we were the only English there.

One of our most amusing parties was a strictly French dinner, to which we were invited by the Odilon-Barrots [the deputy for Eure, a leading member of the Opposition, and his wife] ... In the evening a *soirée*, in which all the Opposition figured. By-the-bye, the Turkish Ambassador dined at Barrot's; I happened to praise some dish which I remember eating in Turkey; and on Sunday his cook brought one as an offering to Mary Anne. Raschid

* The King had lived in America for over two years during the French Revolution.

Pasha is his name, a great celebrity. I went by invitation one evening to talk Eastern politics and smoke a chibouque, which he offered me, brilliant with diamonds.

Another day we went to an assembly at the Hôtel de Ville, given by the wife of the Prefect of the Seine – costly beyond description, in the style of the Renaissance; and after it, where do you think we went at half-past twelve at night? To the masked ball at the Opera. They had an admirable box, the scene indescribable ... the *salle* of the Grand Opera formed into one immense Belshazzar's hall with a hundred streaming lustres. The grand galoppe, five hundred figures whirling like a witches' sabbath, truly infernal. The contrast, too, between the bright fantastic scene below and the boxes filled with ladies in black dominoes and masks, very striking.

'Our latter days at Paris were some of our most brilliant,' Disraeli wrote to Sarah from the Carlton soon after his return to London, 'the principal features, the ball at the English Embassy; 1,000 folks and orange trees springing from the supper table; my farewell audience with his majesty; a grand dinner at Molé's [Louis-Mathieu Molé, a former prime minister]. I sat between Humboldt and [Alexis] Tocqueville [the political scientist and historian] and was surrounded by celebrities [including] Victor Hugo. But above all spectacles was the ball at Baron Solomon de Rothschild – an hotel in decoration surpassing all the palaces of Munich; a greater retinue of servants and liveries more gorgeous than the Tuileries, and pineapples plentiful as blackberries.'[4]

In July 1843, Disraeli resumed his energetic social round in a 'most animated' London season. There were 'grand *fêtes* every day seemingly interminable'. An 'extremely brilliant' assembly following a banquet, held by the Duchess of Buckingham and attended by no fewer than six dukes and King George IV's brother, the King of Hanover, was followed by a 'select reception' and 'royal dinner' given by Lord Lyndhurst. 'We formed a royal circle and the King went round,' Disraeli told his sister. 'I was presented by the Lord Chancellor in a flowery harangue and received gracious compliments from His Majesty. He even shook hands with me. The second King who has shaken hands with me in six months!'[5]

A 'most delightful fête', attended by 'all the world of grandeur', was held at Gunnersbury Park on 29 July by Hannah Rothschild. Then the Disraelis went to stay again at The Deepdene with Henry Hope, and in Mary Anne's words, 'remained there all September'. It was a house in which they enjoyed staying. 'One of our greatest amusements,' Mary Anne reported to Bradenham, 'were two honey bears, tolerably tame, who I often went to play with; fancy my fright when these horrific-looking pets came howling after me the first time I went to take a composing draught. Sometimes they are chained but oftener have their liberty, and use it by frightening the maids and running round the fine galleries – you never heard such a noise. I never kept company with them without witnesses, feeling they might in their fondness hug me to death.'

The Disraelis were also to be seen this summer at Bearwood, near Wokingham, Berkshire, the house of John Walter, the proprietor of *The Times*, where Walter's daughter, Catherine, thought Mr Disraeli was the 'oddest being' she ever saw, and Mrs Disraeli 'the greatest curiosity [she] ever met'.

On their return 'they went to Manchester, Liverpool and Chester, Mary Anne continued. 'At the former place we were much fêted. There was a grand literary meeting at the Free Trade Hall . . . Dis made a fine speech – all said by far the finest – literary not political.'

He shared a platform on this occasion with two more of the best speakers of the day, Richard Cobden and Charles Dickens, who conceived 'a lifelong aversion' to Disraeli. 'I little thought', Dickens was later to say after Peel had been driven from office, 'that I should ever live to praise Peel. But d'Israeli and that Dunghill Lord [John Manners] have so disgusted me, that I feel inclined to champion him . . . It must come, as Cobden told them in the House, to a coalition between Peel and Lord John [Russell].' This would make a strong government, Dickens thought, and, 'as governments go, a pretty good one'.[6]

Upon his arrival in Paris in 1842, Disraeli had encountered, among those English people already there, two young men who had both been at Eton and Cambridge. One of these was Alexander Baillie-Cochrane, later Lord Lamington, Conservative Member for Bridport, 'who delighted in the society of men of letters'. The other was George Sydney Smythe, Lord Strangford's brilliant, extravagant and profligate son, Member for

Canterbury, and the model for Buckhurst in Disraeli's novel *Coningsby* and for Waldershare in *Endymion*. Also at Eton and Cambridge with Cochrane and Smythe was Lord John Manners, the extremely handsome, earnest and good-natured Conservative Member for Newark.

These young men were associated in what became known as Young England, the parliamentary group which advocated a closer trust and respect between the territorial aristocracy and the labouring classes, and the extinction of the predominance of the middle-class bourgeoisie. As well as in Disraeli's *Coningsby* – which was published in 1844 and which explored the nature of aristocratic party politics – the social and political ideas of the times in which Young England flourished were also discussed in both his novels: *Sybil, or The Two Nations* (1845) and *Tancred*, which appeared in 1847.

Disraeli, instinctively predisposed to like brilliant, profligate and extravagant young men, was welcomed by Young England as an important addition to the group's cause. Smythe, in his light-hearted way, said that the coterie should now be known as the 'Diz-Union'.

Not all its members liked or trusted Disraeli. Lord John Manners, for instance, wondered whether the man really believed everything he said so fluently and, on occasions, glibly, and whether, indeed, the views he so elegantly expressed were altogether sincerely held. Manners's father, the Duke of Rutland, considered Disraeli a 'designing person'. Alexander Baillie-Cochrane, while admiring his great gifts, occasionally questioned the sincerity of some of his utterances and was never quite sure what thoughts were passing through the devious mind behind that enigmatic face, what true feelings were concealed beneath that ironic yet extravagant manner.

Beresford Hope, brother of the millionaire Henry Hope, when approached by Lord John Manners, replied, 'The co-operation of such men as D'Israeli, though he may be clever, will not be of permanent good to anyone, as he has not the character to support it.'

If some members of Young England had reservations about Disraeli, there were those in Peel's administration who were fully convinced of his unreliability. Sir James Graham, for example, the rather pompous Home Secretary, wrote to his friend, the Irish essayist, John Wilson Croker:

> With respect to Young England, the puppets are moved by Disraeli who is the ablest man among them: I consider him unprincipled and disappointed, and in despair he has tried the effect of bullying. I think with you that they will return to the crib after prancing, capering and snorting; but a crack or two of the whip well applied may hasten and ensure their return. Disraeli alone is mischievous; and with him I have no desire to keep terms. It would be better for the party if he were driven into the ranks of our open enemies.[7]

For two sessions, with the exception of one occasion when he voted in a minority mainly Radical, Disraeli had generally supported Peel's government; but he was now growing increasingly disapproving of various aspects of its policies, more outspoken in his attacks, and, as he made clear in *Coningsby*, highly critical of the Conservatives' recent past. So, when he wrote to Sir James Graham soliciting a government post for his younger brother, James, the request was dismissed by Graham as 'impudent' considering his 'conduct and language in the House of Commons'.

> I am very glad that Mr Disraeli has asked for an office for his brother [Peel told Graham]. It is a good thing when such a man puts his shabbiness on record. He asked me for office himself, and I was not surprised that, being refused, he became independent and a patriot. But to ask favours after his conduct last session is too bad. However, it is a bridle in his mouth.[8]

In a long letter to Peel, Disraeli conceded that he might indeed have made some remarks 'deficient in that hearty good-will' which ought to be his 'spontaneous sentiment' to his 'political chief', and which he had generally accorded him in 'no niggard spirit'. But, 'with frankness and great respect', he continued, 'you might have found some reason for this, if you had cared to do so, in the want of courtesy in debate which I have had the frequent mortification of experiencing from you since your accession to power . . . I am bound to say I look upon the fact of not having received your summons, coupled with the ostentatious manner in which it has been bruited about, as a painful personal procedure, which the past by no means authorised.'[9]

In a letter almost as long, dated 6 February 1844, Peel replied that he was unconscious of having on any occasion treated Disraeli with the want of that respect and courtesy which he readily admitted was his due. If he had done so, it was 'wholly unintentional on [his] part'.[10]

While retaining doubts about the sincerity of Peel's guarded reply to his letter, Disraeli was as yet no more prepared for an open breach with Peel than Peel was with him; and, after the long debate on the Government's Irish administration which soon followed, Disraeli, together with his three friends in Young England, Smythe, Cochrane and Manners, voted with the Government.

His subsequent speech on the Irish question was so widely admired – even by Peel who described it as 'very able' – that his wife asked him to note down what had been said of it. He willingly obliged her: Ralph Bernal Osborne, Member for Chipping Wycombe and a future Secretary of the Admiralty, evidently told Smythe that he thought it the 'greatest thing' he 'ever heard'. Lord John Manners said that at a breakfast party at the house of Richard Monckton Milnes, 'nothing was spoken of except Disraeli's speech'. Francis Stack Murphy, the Irish lawyer and Member for County Cork, agreed with Bernal Osborne that 'it was the most brilliant speech he had ever heard'.

Earl Stanhope, the historian, so Disraeli went on, 'followed me into a corner with outstretched hand to congratulate me on a speech . . . which was unquestionably one of the ablest ever delivered. His panegyric was unqualified.'[11]

Even Charles Greville was impressed. 'D'Israeli made a very clever speech,' he wrote in his diary, 'not *saying* so much, but implying it, and under the guise of compliment making an amusing attack on Peel . . . [He was] very clear and original, full of finesse, in some respects the most striking speech of all.'

'Dis must, I think now, be *quite satisfied*,' Sarah D'Israeli wrote to Mary Anne. 'It was the best speech he has made and, what is more, the most applauded, and in his own original vein. Are not Young England proud of their leader? . . . I went yesterday to Turville [to Lord Lyndhurst's house near Henley-on-Thames] . . . We did not see much of him, as he was full of work and not dressed; but when he did appear he said a great deal in a little time. Almost his first enquiry was after Dis . . . I am told he is not exactly one of Young England but their mentor and guide. The speech about Ireland was mentioned – "And a very good speech it was," he added; whereupon I said, "So it pleased Sir Robert Peel to say."'[12]

18

CONINGSBY AND SYBIL

'Papa says the man who has made
the finest speech of the session has written
the best book that ever was written.'

'I GET ON TO MY SATISFACTION: but authors are not the best critics of their productions,' Disraeli had written to Lord John Manners from Bradenham on 29 November 1843, when he was busy writing the novel which had been 'conceived and partly executed amid the galleries of *The Deepdene*' and dedicated to Henry Hope. This was *Coningsby, or The New Generation*, the 'main purpose of which', so its author wrote, 'was to vindicate the just claims of the Tory party to be the popular political confederation of the country'.

While finishing work on the book he sent his wife a series of notes which she carefully preserved, as she did all the communications he sent to her:

1. My darling,
   I feel a great desire for a cigar, but will not smoke one unless you approve. I have one here.*

2. M[y] d[arlin]g,
   I propose to go out now; I have written 9 pages, & will return and write again.
   Thine D

---

* Disraeli was a heavy smoker; and it was this which made William Beckford, who could not abide tobacco smoke, reluctant to meet him, though he greatly admired his work (Timothy Mowl, 'Disraeli's Novels and the Beckford Connection', HL, 32).

3. Darling,
I wish you wo[ul]d come up & talk a little over a point, if you
are not particularly engaged.
D

4. My dearest,
I have finished the vol: & am inclined for a stroll. Are you?
D

5. My dearest,
It is impossible to get on better. I have already written ten
pages, & have never stopped. Send me ½ a glass of wine & a
crust of bread.
Thine own

6. My darling,
I must tell you that I am very well, & writing to my heart's
content.
D[1]

Published by Colburn in May 1844, *Coningsby* was an immediate success,
the first edition being sold within a fortnight. Its success owed much
to the author's by now well-known practice of introducing into the
novel various living characters in public life and others which readers
chose to identify as such.

As with his recent speech on the Irish question, Disraeli was
delighted by the book's reception. He told his wife that Henry Hope
was 'enchanted' by it and Hope himself later wrote to tell the author
how much he admired the 'story, the style, the terrible power of wit
and sarcasm ... [This was] merely to repeat what the newspapers say,
but there is besides a spirit of daring and chivalry in attacking people
who have always been deemed bugbears ... which much delights and
refreshes me.' Baillie-Cochrane was described as 'raving' over the book;
Manners as 'full of wild rapture', Smythe 'tipsy with admiration, the
most passionate and wild', Sarah D'Israeli and her father were 'fascinated
and delighted beyond expression'.[2] 'Papa says', Sarah added, 'the man
who has made the finest speech of the session has written the best book
that ever was written'. Lord Lyndhurst found it 'full of wit and talent'.
'Even you and Dis's family', Lady Blessington told Mrs Disraeli, 'take
not a livelier pleasure or a greater pride than I in the brilliant success
of *Coningsby*.'[3]

Sydney Smith, the witty, kindly Canon of St Paul's, was so taken with the book that he asked to meet the author, which he did at a dinner given by Baring Wall in the 'most beautiful house [designed by William Kent] [Disraeli] had ever entered'. Smith was placed next to Disraeli, who found him 'delightful'. Also there was Charles Greville, the diarist and Clerk to the Privy Council, Henry Labouchere, soon to be reappointed President of the Board of Trade, and Lord Melbourne. Disraeli said that he did 'not remember a more agreeable party'.

'*Coningsby* keeps moving,' he added in the letter describing this 'most exquisite dinner with the most charming society' in this 'most refined and sumptuous house. Our dinner was worthy of the "veritable Amphitryon" and served off a set of Dresden china of the most marvellous beauty ... Even the salt cellars and handles of knives and forks were china.'

Coningsby was selling 'about 40 copies a day on average,' Disraeli told Sarah. 'We are preparing for a third edition having [on 13 June 1844] only 400 or so on hand of the second, and the demand being steady.'[4]

In the book, Henry Coningsby was identified as George Smythe; the monstrous Lord Monmouth as the Marquess of Hertford; the unpleasant Nicholas Rigby more uncertainly as John Wilson Croker; Lord Henry Sidney as Lord John Manners; Lord Backhurst as Alexander Baillie-Cochrane; Millbank as W.E. Gladstone. Sidonia, the greatest banker in Europe, was based partly and loosely on Lionel de Rothschild and partly and even more loosely on the author himself, though the heartlessness of Sidonia was not a trait shared by either Rothschild or Disraeli.

Some of the houses in which these fictional people lived were similarly identified as real residences – the Duke of Rutland's Belvoir Castle, for example, as Lord Monmouth's and the Marchioness of Londonderry's Rosebank as the Thamesside house of Lady Everingham.

As with Dickens's women and, in particular, with Dickens's Little Nell, most of Disraeli's female characters are less well drawn, less memorable than the men, though there are two, both intended as portraits of women in London society, who are well delineated and convincing. One is the Marchioness of Londonderry, as represented by the Marchioness of Deloraine, who 'would have been extremely agreeable if she had not restlessly aspired to wit', and the other, Sarah, Countess of Jersey, as represented by Lady St Julians, who suggests that 'people who get into Parliament ... soon find that they have no more talent than other people, and, if they had, they learn that power, patronage and pay are reserved for us and our friends'.

Peel, 'a gentleman of Downing Street', lurks in the background of the book as a humbug who instructs Mr Hoaxem on how to conceal his own mind while confusing the minds of others.

Just as Disraeli's attacks on Peel and his policies were to be more out-spoken in *Sybil, or The Two Nations* than they had been in *Coningsby*, published in 1844, the year before, so did his phillippics in the House of Commons grow increasingly bitter. While acknowledging his 'many admirable' qualities, he came to the conclusion that Peel was 'without imagination', and 'for a very clever man, deficient in the knowledge of human nature ... He had a bad manner of which he was sensible; he was by nature very shy. But, forced early in life into eminent positions, he had formed an artificial manner, haughtily stiff or exuberantly bland, of which, generally speaking, he could not divest himself ... He was never at his ease, and never very content except in the House of Com-mons ... He had no wit but he had a keen sense of the ridiculous ... Notwithstanding his artificial reserve, he had a hearty and a merry laugh; and sometimes his mirth was uncontrollable ... Nor, notwithstanding his consummate Parliamentary tactics, can he be described as the greatest party leader that ever flourished among us, for he contrived to destroy the most compact, powerful and devoted party that ever followed a British statesman.'

In his speeches in the House of Commons Disraeli took advantage of Peel's sensitivity to ridicule and provoked him into making undignified defences of his manner and behaviour. After an attack which, so Disraeli told Sarah, created 'a great scene in the Commons from which that respectable assembly [has] not yet recovered', Peel was 'stunned and stupefied, lost his head, and vacillating between silence and spleen, spoke much and weakly ... Never was a greater failure.'

A subsequent attack on Peel, according to a report in *Hansard*, was greeted with 'great cheering' and 'great laughter'; but 'no written report', in the words of a journalist writing in the *Weekly Chronicle*, could 'give an idea of the effect produced in the House of Commons. Disraeli's manner of delivery, the perfect intonation of the voice, the peculiar looks of the speaker – all contributed to a [remarkable] success ... No man within our recollection has wielded a similar power over the sympathies and passions of his hearers.'

His whole manner as an orator is peculiar to himself [wrote another observer in *Fraser's Magazine*]. It would scarcely be tolerated in another; he seems so careless, supercilious, indifferent to the trouble of pleasing ... His action, where he has any, is ungraceful; nay, what is worse, it is studiously careless – even offensively so. With his supercilious expression of countenance, slightly dashed with pomposity, and a dilettante affectation, he stands with his hands on his hips, or his thumbs in the armholes of his waistcoat, while there is a slight, a very slight, gyratory movement of the upper part of his body, such as you will see ballroom exquisites adopt. And then, with voice low-toned and slightly drawling, without emphasis, except when he strings himself up for his points, his words are not so much delivered as that they flow from the mouth, as if it were really too much trouble for so clever, so intellectual – in a word, so literary a man to speak at all ...

So much for his ordinary level speaking. When he makes his points, the case is totally different. Then his manner changes. He becomes more animated, though still less so than any other speaker of equal power over the House. You can then detect the nicest and most delicate inflexions in the tones of his voice; and they are managed, with exquisite art, to give effect to the irony or sarcasm of the moment ... In conveying an innuendo, an ironical sneer, or a suggestion of contempt, which courtesy forbids him to translate into words – in conveying such masked enmities by means of a glance, a shrug, an altered tone of voice, or a transient expression of face, he is unrivalled. And all the while you are startled by his extreme coolness and impassivity ... You might suppose him wholly unconscious of the effect he is producing; for he never seems to laugh or to chuckle, however slightly, at his own hits. While all around him are convulsed with merriment or excitement at some of his finely-wrought sarcasms, he holds himself, seemingly, in total suspension ... and the moment the shouts and confusion have subsided, the same calm, low, monotonous, but yet distinct and searching voice is still pouring forth his ideas.[5]

*   *   *

'*Sybil* was finished yesterday,' Disraeli told his sister on May Day 1845. 'I thought it never would be ... I have never been through such a four months, and hope never again. What with the House of Commons, which was itself quite enough for a man, and writing 600 pages, I thought sometimes my head must turn. I have never had a day, until this, that I have felt, as it were, home for the holidays.'[6]

The idea of this book, *Sybil, or The Two Nations* (the second novel of a proposed trilogy of which *Coningsby* was the first), a novel dealing with the social conditions of the people – the rich and poor of the two nations of the subtitle – had been simmering in his mind since the autumn of 1843; and in that year and the next he had travelled north to see for himself the lives led in the industrial centres of Yorkshire and Lancashire, maintaining in the 1870 preface to his novels that he had 'visited and observed with care all the localities introduced' in them but not mentioning published authorities such as the official reports known as Blue Books or those issued by such bodies as the Children's Commission.

In pursuit of his material he had been to stay with Lord Francis Egerton at Worsley Hall near Manchester, with Richard Monckton Milnes at Fryston, and with the Ferrands at St Ives, and at Bingley in the West Riding of Yorkshire. He had not always created a good impression in northern country houses. At Fryston, for example, he met Gathorne Gathorne-Hardy, then a thirty-year-old lawyer, who thought his conversation 'far from striking', being too studiedly epigrammatic. His judgements of men's characters were admittedly perceptive and just; but his vanity and self-esteem were 'most displeasing'.

While *Sybil* provoked less eager discussion as to the personalities upon which its characters were based, its accounts of working-class industrial life, and its rays of grim humour, received as much praise from critics as anything in the earlier book:

> The denizens of mining districts, boys and girls scarcely distinguishable from each other, work on hands and feet in mines for up to sixteen hours a day, clad in canvas trousers and fastened to a belt of leather running between their legs, pushing tubs of coal up subterranean roads and railways. They knew little or nothing of the world beyond the mine or of the world of the past, believing at the best in our Lord and Saviour Pontius Pilate,

who was crucified to save our lives, and in Moses and Goliath and the rest of the Apostles.

Disraeli rightly identified as one of the worst and most resented abuses the masters' habit of forcing the workers either to accept part of their wages in food or to buy their food and other necessities at shops known as tommy shops – owned by the masters or by the masters' relations or friends – where prices were inflated. In *Sybil*, Disraeli recorded a conversation between a group of black-faced miners in the Rising Sun who complain bitterly of the butties or middlemen who contract to supply a certain amount of coal for an agreed sum and who pay the wages of the colliers under contract to them in goods:

'The question is,' said Nixon, looking round with a magisterial air, 'what *is* wages? I say 't'aint tea, 't'aint bacon. I don't think 'tis candles. But of this I be sure, 't'aint waistcoats . . . Comrades, you know what has happened; you know as how Juggins applied for his balance after his tommy-book was paid up, and that incarnate nigger Diggs [a butty and owner of a tommy shop] has made him take two waistcoats. Now the question arises, what is a collier to do with waistcoats? Pawn 'em, I s'pose, to Diggs' son-in-law, next door to his father's shop, and sell the tickets for sixpence . . . The fact is we are tommied to death . . .'

'And I have been obliged to pay the doctor for my poor wife in tommy,' said another, '"Doctor," I said, says I, "I blush to do it, but all I have got is tommy, and what shall it be, bacon or cheese?" "Cheese at tenpence a pound," says he, "which I buy for my servants at sixpence! Never mind," says he, for he is a thorough Christian, "I'll take the tommy as I find it."' . . .

'Juggins has got his rent to pay, and is afeard of the bums [bailiffs, men employed in arrests],' said Nixon; 'and he has got two waistcoats!'

'Besides,' said another, 'Diggs's tommy is only open once a-week, and if you're not there in time, you go over for another seven days. And it's such a distance, and he keeps a body there such a time; it's always a day's work for my poor woman; she can't do nothing after it, what with the waiting, and the standing, and the cussing of Master Joseph Diggs; for he do swear at the women.'

'This Diggs seems to be an oppressor of the people,' said a voice from a distant corner of the room.

Master Nixon looked around, smoked, puffed, and then said,

'I should think he wor; as bloody-a-hearted butty as ever jingled [got drunk]'.[7]

The lives of these colliers is contrasted in the book with those of Alfred Mountchesney, a rich young member of Crockford's, who 'rather likes bad wine because one gets so bored with good', of the hero of the book, Charles Egremont, and of Egremont's brother, the 'cynical, arrogant' Earl of Marney who describes his poor, downtrodden tenants in their ramshackle hovels as being particularly well off:

> I wish the people were as well off in every part of the country as they are on my estate. They get here their eight shillings a week, always at least seven, and every hand is at this moment in employ, except a parcel of scoundrels who prefer wood-stealing and poaching, and who would prefer wood-stealing and poaching if you gave them double the wages. Every man at Marney may be sure of his seven shillings a week for at least nine months in the year; and for the other three, they can go to the House [workhouse], and a very proper place for them; it is heated with hot air, and has every comfort . . . The poor are well off, at least the agricultural poor, very well off indeed. They have no cares, no anxieties; they always have a resource, they always have the House. People without cares do not require so much food as those whose life entails anxieties.[8]

19

DAMNING ATTACKS

'Had I been him, I would have rushed
out and murdered you, or run home
and hanged myself.'

WHEN DISRAELI SAT DOWN after his latest and most damaging attack upon Peel – and upon Peel's decision, at a time of famine in Ireland, to repeal the protective duties on foreign imported grain known as the Corn Laws – it was some time before Sir James Graham, who stood up to follow him, could make himself heard above the hubbub to express his pleasure that the Member for Shrewsbury had now abandoned his undeclared mutiny for outright rebellion. Peel – who was described as twitching nervously, changing colour and trying but failing to look indifferent as he pulled his hat down over his eyes – was said, in Gladstone's words, to 'have failed utterly' in his reply.

By now the increasingly vituperative attacks on Peel by Disraeli – who was as unrelenting in his enmities as he was steady in his friendships – had become so bitter as to shock some Members. 'D'Israeli must have taken a vow of hatred to Sir R. Peel,' wrote Lord Ashley. 'No ordinary condition of mind wd. lead to such ferocity.'

'He positively tortured his victim,' wrote Charles Greville, 'after another of his diatribes.' Disraeli 'hacked and mangled Peel with the most unsparing severity.'

Highly satisfied with his recent parliamentary performances, Disraeli was nevertheless deeply concerned about the state of his wife, who seemed to be suffering from some sort of mental breakdown. 'She is

very low & shattered,' he told his sister, 'not slept for the past week &
must have change of air & scene immediately, so I hope we shall contrive
to get off on Monday afternoon . . . I am quite worn out . . . I need not
tell you how many pangs it costs me to leave London with[ou]t seeing
you all – but there is no alternative. I can keep MA here no longer.
1000 loves, D.'[1]

Two days later he wrote to Sarah again: 'My dearest Sa. We had
intended to go off this afternoon but MA is so unwell, that I have
postponed it till tomorrow – when I hope we may escape as change of
scene is badly wanted, I assure you.'[2]

Before they left, so Baroness de Rothschild related, Mary Anne
dashed round to the Baroness's house in Piccadilly Terrace, pulled vigor-
ously on the bell-pull and, entering the house, fell into her 'reluctant
arms' and announced:

> 'I am quite out of breath, my dear, I have been running so fast,
> we have no horses, no carriage, no servants, we are going abroad;
> I have been so busy correcting proof-sheets [of *Alroy* and *Contarini
> Fleming*], the publishers are so tiresome, we ought to have been
> gone a month ago; I should have called upon you long ere now,
> I have been so nervous, so excited, so agitated, poor Dis has been
> sitting up the whole night writing; I want to speak to you on
> business, pray send the darling children away' &c., &c., for it
> would, without any exaggeration, take more than ten pages to
> put down conscientiously all the lady's words, not noting excla-
> mations and gestures and tears. You know that I am easily terrified
> and almost speechless. I have never seen her in such a state of
> excitement before, and all I could do was to gasp out – 'Has
> anything happened?'
>
> Mrs Disraeli heaved a deep sigh and said: 'This is a farewell
> visit, I may never see you again – life is so uncertain . . . Disi and
> I may be blown up on the railroad or in the steamer, there is not
> a human body that loves me in this world, and besides my adored
> husband I care for no one on earth, but I love your glorious race,
> I am rich, I am prosperous, I think it right to entertain serious
> thought, to look calmly upon one's end' &c., &c.
>
> Mrs Disraeli's conversation is not exactly remarkable for
> clearness of thought, precision of language, or for a proper concat-
> enation of images, ideas and phrases, nevertheless, I had always
> been able to comprehend and to reply, but on that memorable
> Friday, I was quite at a loss to understand her meaning. *Je vous*

fais grâce de mes réponses, as they are not particularly interesting. I tried to calm and quiet my visitor who, after having enumerated her goods and chattels to me, took a paper out of her pocket saying: 'This is my Will and you must read it, show it to the dear Baron, and take care of it for me.' I answered that she must be aware of my feelings, that I should ever be truly grateful for such a proof of confidence, but could not accept such a great responsibility, 'But you must listen,' replied the inexorable lady: she opened the paper and read aloud:

'In the event of my beloved Husband preceding me to the grave, I leave and bequeathe to Evelina de Rothschild [the Baroness's daughter, aged six] all my personal property.'

I leave you to picture to yourself my amazement and embarrassment. Mrs Disraeli rose and would hear no answer, no objection.

'I love the Jews – I have attached myself to your children and she is my favourite' . . .

Away rushed the testatrix, leaving the testament in my unworthy hands . . . The next morning I breakfasted in a hurry, walked in a hurry to the abode of genius and his wife, to show I returned the Will. There was a scene, a very disagreeable one, and then all was over . . .'[3]

By the middle of September 1845, the Disraelis were at Cassel in French Flanders, 'without having had', so Disraeli told his sister, 'the slightest intention' of going there. 'But hearing that the place had beauty & seclusion & that we might be saved the expense of a journey, we mutually were of opinion that we shd. pitch our tent here if we could find any sort of accommodation.'

'That was difficult [he continued] as it is an extremely savage place. Few of the inhabitants, and none of the humbler classes, talk French [their language was Flemish]. There is no library, bookseller's shop, nor newspaper of any sort . . . We have taken a house for a month [they stayed over two months]. We are to pay 16 shillings per week, furnished and [we] have hired a Flemish cook, who, Mary Anne desires me to tell my mother, stews pigeons in the most delicious way: eggs, cloves, & onions, ending in a red-brown sauce . . . Fruit and poultry plentiful and cheap. Six fowls for 5 francs, meat 6d pr lb.' At Boulogne, he added by way of postscript, they found '*Sybil* affiched in a large placard, "Disraeli's new novel", in every window'.

'I get up at half past five, and don't find it difficult, going to bed by nine,' Disraeli continued. 'We do not know & have not interchanged a word with a single person of even average intelligence on any subject. The names of the Duke of W[ellington] and Sir Robert Peel & all those sorts of people are equally unknown here ... We have a pretty garden which gives us mignonette and Alpine strawberries which MA picks for me and often wishes she could do the same for my father* ... MA cannot leave her young pigeons, who live in the house and breakfast with us.' At the bottom of the letter Mary Anne added a postscript: 'Good Night, my dears, Kiss the dear Papa for me real French fashion & tell Mama with my love I will learn their fashion of cooking veal & pigeons – I know not what James would say to the wine here, a little spice & brandy makes it drinkable. Yr. affectionate Mary Anne & Dis.'

'This place seems to agree with both of us,' Disraeli added a few days later. 'Our villa looks upon a charming landscape [over which] our promenades are in general very extensive, for the place abounds in paths ... MA is looking exremely well, quite recovered ... and scales styles and even leaps ditches ... MA is anxious that my father shd partake of a new dish we are very fond of, so, my dear mother, this part of the letter is addressed to your tender care. Potatoes, after boiling & bread crumbs mixed with chopped parsley, pepper and salt, then rolled in egg yolk & flour & fried served up in the shape of sausages. This is the delicate meagre dish of a Nunnery: we think it delicious ... MA is now as plump as a partridge.'[4]

Disraeli spent his days thinking about and writing parts of his new novel, *Tancred, or The New Crusade*, and reading *Galignani's Messenger* and English newspapers sent on from London.

From their retreat, 'on the top of a mountain', where Mary Anne, so she calculated, walked three hundred miles in two months – of which she was 'very proud' – the Disraelis went on to Paris where they stayed once again at the Hôtel de l'Europe in the rue de Rivoli.

---

* 'Though not in any way a gourmet, there were two things of which [Disraeli] was especially fond,' – one venison, the other strawberries – Lady Dorothy Nevill wrote in her *Reminiscences*. 'During their season I used to constantly send him baskets of his favourite fruit.' 'You have made me not only the most graceful but the most magnificent of presents,' he wrote in a characteristic letter thanking her for one basketful. 'I have never feasted on my favourite fruit in entirety before. They were not only plenteous but really without precedent superb' (Nevill, *Reminiscences*, 208–9).

From here Disraeli wrote to Lord John Manners on 17 December 1845 to ask, 'What is going to happen?' Peel had resigned and Lord John Russell was trying to form a government; but whether or not he would be able to do so was most uncertain.

'Conjecture', Disraeli wrote, 'is quite baffled here in high places. In lower ones there is a general opinion that Peel will return in triumph; but this appears to me a superficial conclusion and I cannot but believe it highly improbable.'[5]

He said as much to Lord Palmerston, to whom he wrote on 14 December after a conversation with King Louis Philippe, who, until recently, had 'seemed confident as to Peel's triumph', but now 'repeated more than once that Guizot [the French Foreign Minister] was disabused of his idea that Peel would return'. 'The King,' Disraeli added, 'assuming that there would be a Whig Government, spoke to me very much of your Lordship's accession to office ... The conversation lasted about half an hour, when the King, rising, said; "We must not lose all the music." There was a concert. "There are persons here to whom I must give a word, but do not go, as I wish to speak to you again" ... [Upon his return], the moment we were seated, he said, "What you have said of Lord Palmerston [becoming Foreign Secretary in Russell's adminis-tration] has given me much pleasure. I have been thinking of it. I feel also persuaded that Peel cannot be brought back in triumph; and if he were to return, he is no longer the same man."[6]

As it happened Peel did return but not for long; and, in the mean-time, Disraeli narrowly avoided fighting a duel with Peel's brother, Colonel Jonathan Peel, who had accused Disraeli of lying in the House. Disraeli, expecting he would have to accept Colonel Peel's challenge, called upon Lord George Bentinck to represent him. Sir Robert Peel was himself, so Disraeli was to tell his friend Lord Rowton, a 'very "fightable" man' who had wanted on more than one occasion in the past to fight Disraeli, but had been 'restrained by Lord Granby and others'. His brother, the Colonel, approached his friend Captain Henry John Rous, the future Admiral and Conservative Member for Westminster, to rep-resent him. A conference between the two seconds took place at White's Club and a settlement was reached.[7]

Soon after his return to London, Disraeli stood up in the Commons to make the most effective and damning attack on Peel which he had yet delivered. His oratory had now become so greatly admired in the House, by his opponents as well as by his supporters, that Members had taken to hurrying into the chamber to take their seats to hear him.

When he resumed his seat after making one particularly effective speech in May 1846, the House rang with 'cheers which, for duration and vehemence', so it was said, 'are seldom heard within the walls of Parliament'.

> I heard your speech [Lord Ponsonby, the diplomatist, shortly to be appointed Ambassador at Vienna, wrote to Disraeli]. It lasted, they say, three hours, and when it was over I wished it to last three hours more. I thought your argument admirably managed, and perfectly sound in essence, and I doubt if any classic orator of Rome or England ever did anything so well as you crucified Peel. Had I been him, I would have rushed at and murdered you, or run home and hanged myself.
>
> John Russell tired me in a quarter of an hour, and I left the House dissatisfied.
>
> I never in my life heard any speech so much cheered as yours was; I never saw so much effect produced by one.[8]

'His conclusion for a good twenty minutes was a steady philippic against Peel, which was very powerful indeed, and produced a great effect on all parts of the House,' confirmed Byron's friend, John Cam Hobhouse. 'Peel looked miserable, and his brother, Jonathan, more wretched still, and bursting with mortification. Even Macaulay [the historian] told me he thought the effect very powerful, and the speech the best Disraeli ever made. Russell, who followed, was unable to go on for some time on account of the prolonged cheering!'[9] Charles Greville was quite as impressed by Disraeli's speech as were Ponsonby and Hobhouse. 'His fluency is wonderful,' Greville wrote.

> He hacked and mangled Peel with the utmost unsparing severity. It was a miserable and degrading spectacle. He was cheered with vociferous delight, making the roof ring again, and when Peel spoke they screamed and hooted at him in the most brutal manner. When he vindicated himself, and talked of honour and conscience, they assailed him with shouts of derision and gestures of contempt. Such treatment in a House of Commons where for years he had been an object of deference and respect, nearly overcame him. The Speaker told me that for a minute or more

he was obliged to stop and for the first time in his life, probably, he lost his self-possession; and the Speaker thought he would have been obliged to sit down, and expected him to burst into tears. They hunt him like a fox, and they are eager to run him down and kill him, and they are full of exultation at thinking they have nearly accomplished this object. It is high time such a state of things should finish. To see the Prime Minister and Leader of the H. of Commons thus beaten and degraded, treated with contumely by three-fourths of the party he has been used to lead, is a sorry sight.[10]

Disraeli himself was fully satisfied with his performance. In later years, he referred to his 'great speech in 1846 on the second [actually third] reading of the Bill for the repeal of the Corn Laws which was followed by the loudest and the longest cheer that ever was heard in the House of Commons'.

20

TANCRED

'We may have to listen to the squeak or
the bray of the obscure animals in their
forests whenever a new light breaks into
their dark recesses.'

'I SHOULD HAVE WRITTEN BEFORE,' Disraeli told Lord John
Manners soon after his return to Bradenham, 'but though I left London
in great vigour, I experienced, within a few days of my arrival here, that
periodical languor, and even prostration, which always attends, with me,
a change of life, especially if that change be one to pure air and regular
habits. After a fortnight or so I get seasoned, as I am now, and it seems
impossible that I could ever live anywhere except among the woods and
turfy wildernesses of this dear county.'[1]

As soon as he felt recovered from his languor, he settled down to
continue with the writing of his new novel, *Tancred, or The New Crusade*,
which, so he told Lady Londonderry, was proving 'much more troublesome and unmanageable' than he had anticipated.

This novel, which was to be published in March 1847, the third of
the trilogy of which *Coningsby* and *Sybil* were the two earlier parts, tells
the story of Tancred, son of Lord and Lady Montacute, who bewilders
his parents by abandoning London society and going to the Holy Land to
find a fulfilling faith and philosophy and a resolution of the antagonism
between Christianity and Judaism.

Disraeli sent a copy to a Jewish friend, telling her, 'Notwithstanding it is in the form of a novel, I hope you will read; & read even with
attention, as it is a vindication, &, I hope, a complete one, of the race
from wh. we alike spring.'[2]

Disraeli later declared that he preferred *Tancred* to all his other novels; and his family and friends assured him of its excellence. Lady Blessington wrote to say that it made her 'comprehend the East better than all the books [she] had ever read on it';[3] while his father praised the book with characteristically extravagant enthusiasm: it was 'a work for its originality and execution without a rival; faultless in composition, profound in philosophy and magical in the loveliness of its descriptions'. It was, in fact, 'a wonderful book – in which every succeeding adventure is more original than the preceding'. 'Did the East,' Mr D'Israeli asked, 'ever produce anything so thoroughly completely Eastern?' He was concerned, however, that it might, perhaps, not be so enthusiastically received by the 'unenlightened public'. 'We may have to listen', he wrote, 'to the squeak or the bray of the obscure animals in their forests whenever a new light breaks into their dark recesses.'[4]

Certainly the publisher, Henry Colburn, was disappointed in the sales of the book. He eventually disposed of the 1,500 copies of the first edition and reported to Mrs Disraeli when he had sold a further fifty of the second; but he had to confess that the book was not doing quite as well as he 'could wish'. Eventually, these two editions of 2,250 copies earned the author £775, considerably less than he had hoped and less than either *Coningsby* or *Sybil*.[5]

Much of the popularity of Disraeli's earlier books was owing to the readers identifying various characters in them with living persons. But in *Tancred* there was not the same pleasure to be derived. There were, indeed, but three characters whose living models could be identified with any certainty. One of these was Tancred's mother's friend, the Bishop, who is clearly based upon the energetic and disputatious Bishop of London, Charles James Blomfield, who, in his appearance in *Tancred*, 'combines a great talent for action with very limited powers of thought'. Disraeli's Bishop is, indeed, a 'bustling, energetic' man, 'gifted with an indomitable perseverance, and stimulated by an ambition that knew no repose. He has an inordinate passion for affairs . . . [and can] permit nothing to be done without his interference'. Consequently, he 'was perpetually involved in transactions which were either failures or blunders . . . Enunciating second-hand, with characteristic precipitation, some big principle in vogue, as if he were a discoverer, he invariably shrank from its subsequent application, the moment that he found it might be unpopular or inconvenient.'

The second easily identifiable character is Lord Eskdale, who had already made an appearance in *Coningsby* as a politician with an 'imperturbable countenance and clear sarcastic eye'. He is obviously based on the second Earl of Lonsdale, the immensely rich President of the Board of Trade in Peel's shortlived administration of 1834–5; a keen sportsman whose horse won the Derby in 1831; a generous patron of Italian opera in London; and a connoisseur and discriminating collector of porcelain. As Lord Eskdale in *Tancred*, he is described as 'a man with every ability, except the ability to make his powers useful to mankind'.

The third character whose identity was obvious is Mr Vavasour, 'a social favourite, a poet . . . as well as a member of Parliament . . . sweet tempered, and good hearted, amusing and clever. Vavasour liked to know everybody who was known, and to see everything which ought to be seen. He also was of opinion that everybody who was known ought to know him; and that any spectacle, however splendid or exciting, was not quite perfect without his presence . . . He was everywhere, and at everything; he had gone down in a diving bell and gone up in a balloon . . . His life was a gyration of energetic curiosity; an insatiable whirl of social celebrity . . . His breakfasts were renowned. Whatever your creed, class or country, one might almost add your character, you were welcome at his matutinal meal, provided you were celebrated . . . Individuals met at his hospitable house who had never met before, but who for years had been cherishing in solitude mutual detestation . . . and paid each other in his presence the compliments which veiled their ineffable disgust.'

This immediately recognizable portrait – which Disraeli admitted he had made as attractive as he could, 'consistent with that verisimilitude necessary' – had been prompted by Richard Monckton Milnes, who, piqued not to find himself represented in *Coningsby*, in which other Young England men had been portrayed, had complained of the omission 'with tears in his eyes'.

'He spoke to me on the matter with great earnestness,' Disraeli wrote in a memorandum years later. 'And I at length promised to remember his wish to appear in a sympathetic light in a future novel.' He was, after all, 'a good-natured fellow . . . highly instructed and very clever', even though he was, at the same time, 'always ridiculous, from an insane jealousy'.

His father, Robert Pemberton Milnes, who had been Member of Parliament for Pontefract, had been offered a peerage but had rejected it, possibly, so Disraeli thought, to vex his only son. He was a 'tall, handsome man with a distinguished presence', whereas the son was 'unfortunately short, with a face like a Herculanean masque or a countenance cut out of an orange'.

'The moment' Monckton Milnes 'was on his legs in the House of Commons, he was nervous and took refuge in pomposity. His irresistibly comic face, becoming every moment more serious, produced the effect of some celebrated droll . . . and before he had proceeded five minutes, though he might be descanting on the wrongs of Poland or the rights of Italy, there was sure to be a laugh.'[6]

Like Mr Vavasour's, Monckton Milnes's breakfasts were renowned. Disraeli, however, 'hating breakfasting out', made a habit of refusing them; but, having done so 'a 1000 times', was eventually induced to attend one when 'urgently' pressed to do so because Ibrahim Pasha, the Viceroy of Egypt under Ottoman rule, was to be there.

Disraeli later made an amusing memorandum of what he called this 'strange scene' one day in the 1840s:

Went late [because] kept up at the House . . . All the breakfast eaten . . . Some coffee on a disordered table. M[onckton] M[ilnes] murmured something about a cutlet, not visible . . . Ibrahim not there but Suleiman Pacha and some Egyptian Grandees. They were fighting the battle of Konieh (I think) like Corporal Trim [in *Tristram Shandy*]. '*Voila la cavalrie*,' said Suleiman, and he placed a spoon. '*l'infanterie est là*' and he moved a coffee cup, etc. etc. D'Orsay standing behind him and affecting great interest in order to make the breakfast go off well. A round table; at the fireplace, Milne's father, a Shandean squire, full of humour and affectation, and astonished at the scene, not accustomed to in Yorkshire. Cobden there; a white-faced man whom I did not know, who turned out to be [A.W.] Kinglake, the author of *Eothen*, which I had not read and never have; and other celebrities.

I declined to sit down but watched the battle and was regretting I had come when someone touched me on the back. I looked round and it was Prince Louis Napoleon [later the Emperor Napoleon III, then living in exile in England]. 'Are you very much interested in this', he said. 'Not at all, for I am neither the conqueror nor the conquered.'

'Come here then,' and he invited me to the recess of a window.

'Have you any news from Paris?' he asked me with earnest enquiry – excited.

'None, sir.'

'Then I will tell you the most important. Two thousand Sous-Lieutenants have signed a document that they will not rest until the family of Buonaparte are restored to the throne.'

'That, indeed, sir, is most important,' and I believed I was talking to a madman. I believe it now to have been quite true.[7]

"The author of Vivian Grey," a drawing on paper by Daniel Maclise.

Disraeli in 1828, aged twenty-four, in a watercolor by C. Bone.

Mary Anne Disraeli in 1840 by A. E. Chalon. She was twelve years older than Disraeli; they married in August 1839.

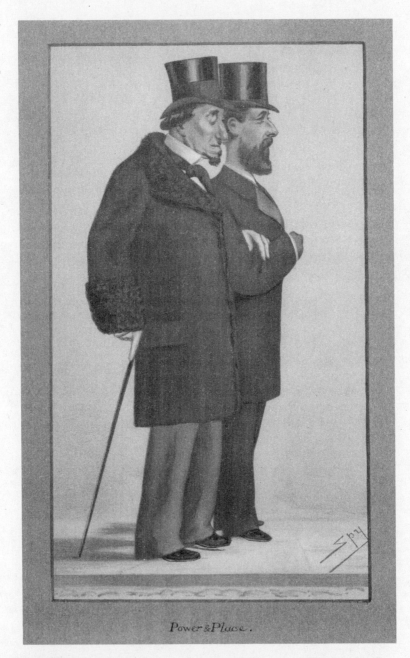

Power & Place.

Disraeli with his secretary, Montagu Corry, later Lord Rowton. A cartoon by "Spy" (Sir Leslie Ward).

In a confidential letter to his private secretary, Montague Corry, Disraeli describes his first audience with Queen Victoria.

Pages from Disraeli's Mutilated Diary. Here he writes, "I am only truly great in action. If ever I am placed in a truly eminent position I shall prove this. I cd. rule the House of Commons, altho' there wd. be a great prejudice against me at first".

Disraeli when Chancellor of the Exchequer, by Sir Francis Grant.

DIZZY.

He lives on the hope of a General Election.

A caricature of "Dizzy" in *The Hornet* of 19 July 1871.

THE QUEEN AT HUGHENDEN.
TEN YEARS AGO.

Queen Victoria visits Disraeli at Hughenden.

The Earl of Beaconsfield in 1877, a portrait after Von Angeli.

Disraeli in the House of Lords with Montagu Corry looking over his shoulder. An engraving after a sketch by Harry Furniss.

PART TWO

1846–81

THE JOCKEY
AND THE JEW

'His eyes gleamed like a wild animal at feeding time,
and his whole deportment was so excited
that no man out of Bedlam ever came near it.'

HAVING FINISHED *TANCRED*, which was to be published in 1847,
Disraeli did not write another novel for over twenty years; and his
colleague, Lord George Bentinck, son of the Duke of Portland, was
relieved to hear that he had 'not quite abjured politics' – as he had
threatened to do at least for the next three months. In December 1846,
soon after Peel's resignation as Prime Minister, Disraeli welcomed
Bentinck to his house to discuss their future programme.

Bentinck had formerly been better known on the turf than he had
been in the House of Commons where, ever since his election as Member
for Lynn in 1828, he had sat in total silence, often wearing, so Disraeli
said, 'a white greatcoat which softened, but did not conceal, the scarlet
hunting-coat'. But, having disposed of his entire racing stud – and lost
his chance of winning the Derby, which was to be won in 1848 by one
of the horses he had sold – he now devoted himself to gambling and
to politics in alliance with Disraeli, with whom he proposed that they
should work in concert.* The 'jockey and the Jew', as their opponents

* In his biography of Lord George Bentinck, Disraeli described how, the morning
after Bentinck's colt, Surplice, won the Derby, he came across him in the library of the
House of Commons reading about sugar tariffs, then a matter of debate: when the Derby
was mentioned, 'he gave a sort of groan: "All my life I have been trying for this, and
for what have I sacrificed it!" he murmured. It was in vain to offer solace. "You do not

called them, were complementary: Bentinck was no orator, but he had other qualities which Disraeli lacked. His manner of speaking, when developed, was in marked contrast to Disraeli's. The Peelite, John Young, described Bentinck's making 'a furious onslaught on the Government'. His voice was 'raised to screaming pitch – his eyes gleamed like a wild animal at feeding time, and his whole deportment was so excited that no man out of Bedlam ever came near it.'

Now that Disraeli sat on the Opposition front bench with other leaders of his party, it was noticed that, unlike Bentinck, he was careful to present a far less flamboyant presence than he had done in the past. His clothes, one observer noticed, were far more sober than they had been. He appeared to have 'doffed the vanity of the coxcomb with the plumage of the peacock'.[1] In winter, he now wore a dark frock coat with a double-breasted plush waistcoat and, in summer, a plain pale blue, tightly buttoned coat, with the outlines of that 'unquestionable pair of stays' still to be seen through it from the back. His speeches were more restrained, less colourfully ungrammatical, his gestures now few and moderated. It was as though he had chosen to play the part of the statesman, with appropriate gravitas, rather than the gadfly.

In a letter to Sarah D'Israeli, B.E. Lindo, her cousin, wrote of the respect in which Disraeli was held at this time:

> I was very charmed with Dizzy's display last Tuesday, and astonished at the command and control of the House which he possesses – the buzz everywhere in the lobbies and the galleries when he rose, and the rush into the House, which filled in no time after he had begun. In every way I was astonished and pleased … Dizzy's figure suits the floor of the House admirably, while his voice is so various, modulated musically at one moment and pouring out its thunder the next, and you hear plainly every whisper. He extracted cheers from a full House of opponents. What would they have been if they had gone with him! He certainly is the wonder of the day, and begins to be universally acknowledged so.[2]

---

know what the Derby is," he groaned. "Yes I do; it is the blue ribbon of the turf." "It is the blue ribbon of the turf," he slowly repeated, and, sitting down at the table, he buried himself in a folio of statistics' (Disraeli, *Lord George Bentinck, A Political Biography,* 539).

A less flattering picture of him at this time appeared in an article in *Fraser's Magazine*, in which the author wrote of Disraeli's self-absorbed air and 'habitual stoop' as he glided along 'noiselessly, without apparently being conscious of externals, and more like the shadow than the substance of a man'. His clothes were 'shaped, apparently, with too much care for effect and his curling black hair [could] hardly be distinguished from the ringlets of a woman ... When he is speaking he shrouds himself in his own intellectual atmosphere' and, if interrupted by a supporter with a suggestion, 'he would either take no notice or dismiss the interruption' with a gesture of impatience. He never laughed when he made an amusing remark but would stand impassively waiting for the laughter of others to cease. 'The moment the shouts and confusion have subsided, the same calm, low, monotonous voice is heard, while he is preparing another sarcasm, hissing hot, into the soul of his victim.'

When others were speaking, he sat 'with his head rigid, his body contracted, his arms closely pinned to his side ... looking like one of those stone figures of ancient Egypt that embody the idea of motionless quiescence for ever.'[3]

Having become less flamboyant in dress, and rather more grave and measured in manner, Disraeli, conscious of being one of the leaders of a 'country' party when he neither owned a country house nor represented a country constituency, now endeavoured to acquire both and to become a Member of Parliament for the county he loved rather than for Shrewsbury where he had of late been feeling less and less at home.

He accordingly delivered a farewell address to the electors of Shrewsbury on 24 May 1847 and, the next day, issued his appeal to those of Buckinghamshire, for which constituency, with two other candidates, he was returned unopposed.

Having changed his constituency, which he was to represent for almost thirty years, Disraeli turned his attention to the acquisition of a large country house.

Hughenden Manor near High Wycombe came on to the market at this time. Its surrounding park and woodland, together with its garden, which Mary Anne was to transform, extended in all to 750 acres and the place was offered for almost £35,000. He had nothing like enough money to pay for it. Nor had Mary Anne, who had already paid off so many of her husband's debts and would have paid for others had she known of them. He could not have contemplated the purchase of Hughenden Manor without help from outside the family. He borrowed £5,000 from his solicitors; obtained an overdraft of £14,000 from his bank; and gratefully accepted a loan of £25,000 generously offered to him by Lord George Bentinck and Bentinck's two rich brothers.

As the prospective occupier of an imposing country house and estate, Disraeli became an increasingly respected figure in the House of Commons. His speeches on the disabilities still imposed upon Jews were admittedly not generally well received, except by his father, who declared with his characteristic hyperbole that one of these speeches was 'the most important ever delivered in the House of Commons'. At least it had to be conceded, as Lord John Russell did concede, that it was admirably brave of Disraeli to express opinions so diametrically opposed to those held by most of the members sitting behind him.

Yet he still aroused feelings of distaste in the House. After Lord George Bentinck's decision to retire, Charles Greville was to record in his diary on 7 January 1848: 'Nobody can think of a successor to Bentinck and, bad as Disraeli is, he seems the best man they have. It seems, however, they detest him, their only man of talent, and in fact they have nobody.'[4]

'There can be no doubt that there is a very strong feeling among Conservatives in the House of Commons against him,' wrote the Earl of Malmesbury of Disraeli a month later. 'They are puzzled and alarmed by his mysterious manner, which has much of the foreigner about it, and are incapable of understanding and appreciating the great abilities which certainly underlie, and, as it were, are concealed by this mask.' 'To get office,' Malmesbury added later, Disraeli 'would do anything and act with anyone.'[5]

Other names were put forward as possible successors to Peel as leader of the Conservative Party, including that of the Marquess of Granby of whom Bentinck had written to Disraeli: 'His high station, noble bearing, mild and conciliatory manners would combine and rally the whole party under his banner, and then you and I, sitting one on each side of him, would easily – when he required help, which I do not think would be often – carry him through.'

Nothing, however, had been decided when Parliament reassembled on 3 February, there being a general hope in the party that Bentinck might change his mind about retiring and there being doubts, soon confirmed, that the modest Granby would agree to undertake the responsibility of leadership.

When Bentinck demonstrated his firm determination to resign the leadership by taking up a position on the bench behind the one he had formerly occupied, it seemed inevitable that Disraeli must succeed him.

> You ask me of Disraeli's manner of speaking and effectiveness in debate [Bentinck wrote to J.W. Croker],* I will answer you by giving you my brother Henry's observations on the various speakers in the House. Henry is rather a cynical critic. He expressed himself greatly disappointed with Sir Robert Peel and Lord John Russell, and concluded by saying that Disraeli was the only man who at all came up to his ideas of an orator. His speeches this session have been first-rate. His last speech . . . was admirable. He cuts [Richard] Cobden to ribbons; and Cobden writhes and quails under him just as Peel did in 1846. And mark my words . . . it will end before two sessions are out in Disraeli being the chosen leader of the party.[6]

Throughout the session, Disraeli continued to make speech after admirable speech on a variety of topics from foreign affairs, the suspension of the Habeas Corpus Act in Ireland, parliamentary reform and female suffrage, to a Sugar Bill, a Public Health Bill, and the Jewish Disabilities Bill.

On the subject of female suffrage, he declared – seventy years before the right to vote in Britain was granted to 8.4 million women – 'In a country governed by a woman, where you allow women to form part of the other estate of the realm – peeresses in their own right, for example – where you allow a woman not only to hold land, but to be a lady of the manor and hold legal courts, where a woman by law may be a churchwarden – I do not see, when she has so much to do with State and Church, on what reason . . . she has not a right to vote.'

---

* Croker has been identified as the model for La Croasse in Lord Brougham's *Albert Lunel, or The Chateau of Languedoc* (1844), as Con Crawley in Lady Morgan's *Florence Macarthy* (1818) – an act of revenge for Croker's review of her *France* in the *Quarterly Review* – as Mr Wenham in Thackeray's *Vanity Fair* (1847–8), as well as the contemptible Mr Rigby in *Coningsby*.

Another highly effective speech delivered on 30 August 1848, attacking ministerial inefficiency, so Disraeli declared years later, 'made me leader'.

> The success [he told his wife] has succeeded our most sanguine expectations and hopes!!! I spoke exactly three hours, omitted scarcely one point of great importance, very few secondary. The attendance on our side was admirable . . . The cheering capital & genuine; not factitious. We had, in fact, a considerable majority over the Government & cd have turned them out, had there been a division . . . All my friends delighted: universally admitted my greatest speech.* Smythe beyond expression. He tells me that in the Peers' Galleries – *especially his father* [Viscount Strangford] – *all the 18th century* say there never was anything like it.
>
> I am now going to Delane. God knows how long and how often I shall be there [at *The Times*], as the speech must be eight columns at least.[7]

He had confessed to Lady Londonderry that he had felt 'exhausted and dispirited' the day before making the speech – 'a sad mood on the eve of a general engagement'; but he could now declare that he had 'won the battle completely'. He sent her a copy of *The Times* with a report of his speech in it, apologizing for being so 'very egotistical and coxcomical'.[8]

Almost everyone agreed that the speech was a triumph. The grumpy Greville wrote of it being 'nothing but a theatrical display'; but even he had to concede that it was 'very sparkling and clever'. Other commentators were unanimous in their praise. Lord Brougham, the former Lord Chancellor, wrote to him to say that he had 'closed the session most magnificently'. Beresford, the Conservative Whip, considered the speech 'very able and powerful'.

Preoccupied though he was with his political career and his duties in the House of Commons, Disraeli did not neglect his wife when she was in London; and the following letter is characteristic of many which he sent to her:

---

* He surpassed himself, so he told his sister the following summer, when he made what he described as 'the most successful speech' he had ever made, his friends being 'really enthusiastic' (*Benjamin Disraeli Letters*, 1954, v, 7 July 1849).

My dearest Love,

As I cannot bear to be away from you the whole day, & as it is now nearly four o'ck, I send this letter by a messenger to beg that you will call for me at the Carlton, where I shall remain until ½ past five, so that we may be together a little. The breakfast [at Monckton Milnes's] was brilliant ... several incidents have occurred since which I must leave for viva voce. I hope you will be able to come as I shall be mournful if I do not see you my dearest Marianna. Yours, Dis.[9]

My dearest love [he wrote in another, similar letter when she was at Hughenden and he in London],

Not a line from you. I am miserable – a single word wd. have made me happy. I am off to B[righton] by an early train: now – the cab is at the door ... I feel sure I shall return this evening as there is an express train ... 1000 loves & embraces my Darling wife, D.[10]

THE COUNTRY GENTLEMAN

'I have a passion for books and trees.'

AS SOON AS HE HEARD of Lord George Bentinck's sudden death of a heart attack on 21 September 1848 while walking from Welbeck Abbey to Lord John Manners's house at Thoresby, Disraeli, who had been staying with the Londonderrys at Wynyard Park, County Durham, made haste to return to London; and on 23 September he wrote from Grosvenor Gate to Lord Henry Bentinck to say that his brother's death was 'the greatest sorrow' he 'had ever experienced': 'I can offer nor receive consolation. All is unutterable woe!' He told Lord John Manners that he was 'oppressed with intolerable gloom'; and Lord Walpole that he was 'overwhelmed by a great calamity'.[1]

It was generally agreed that no one could fill Lord George's place, as leader of the Conservative Party, except Disraeli. 'They pulled together without any difficulty,' Lord Malmesbury wrote in his diary. 'It will leave Disraeli without a rival, and enable him to show the great genius he undoubtedly possesses without any comparison.'[2]

Yet while he had many influential supporters, including Lord Mandeville, Member of Parliament for Bewdley (later seventh Duke of Manchester), Henry Drummond (the banker and Member for West Surrey), Samuel Wilberforce, Bishop of Oxford, and the *Morning Chronicle* among them, there was widespread agreement in the party with Charles Greville's view that Disraeli was a man 'whose character was so disreputable' that he could not be trusted. Charles Newdegate, Member for North Warwickshire, wrote to Lord Stanley to say that he had been 'warned repeatedly not to trust Disraeli. I see nothing in his

public conduct to justify the want of confidence so many seem to feel
... Yet I conclude there is some circumstance of his earlier life, with
which I am not familiar, but have little doubt you are. I can scarcely
help believing there must be some foundation for so general an opinion
as I have alluded to and it makes me very uneasy.'[3]

Lord Stanley, still inclined to have these reservations about Disraeli,
proposed that John Charles Herries might take the lead. But Herries
was reluctant to do so. So, still, was the Marquess of Granby.

Indeed, in a letter written to Lord Stanley from Erlestoke, Westbury,
where he and his wife were staying for Christmas, Disraeli himself
declared that, while he would never have abandoned Lord George
Bentinck – whose biography he undertook to write – he was 'now free
from all personal pursuits' and was 'no longer disposed to sacrifice
health and a happy hearth, for a political career which [could] bring
one little fame, and, even if successful in a vulgar sense, would bear
[him] a reward which [he] now little appreciated'.[4]

To Hobhouse he remarked that the 'summit of Heaven's bliss' was
to be possessed of '£300 a year, and live a retired life amidst books'.[5]

Lord Stanley had other ideas. 'I am doing you bare justice,' he wrote
to Disraeli, 'when I say, as a debater, there is no one of our party who
can pretend to compete with you; and the powers of your mind, your
large general information, and the ability you possess to make yourself
both heard and felt, must at all times give you a commanding position
in the House of Commons.' He had to confess, however, that Disraeli's
assumption of its leadership would not be unopposed by certain sections
of the party.[6]

Disraeli's reluctance, real or assumed, did not long persist. 'With reference to the great question,' he wrote to Lord John Manners on 29 January
1849, 'nothing will induce me to attempt the task unless it is with the general wish and consent of the whole party . . . Sincerely I wish that the duty
had fallen to the lot of another; but if it falls to me, I will attempt to fulfil it to the death . . . I am not a candidate for the Leadership, tho' I am
prepared to undertake the task at the unequivocal desire of the party.'[7]

So it was agreed. On 31 January, Disraeli wrote a note marked 'most
confidential' to his wife: 'a proposition that the party shd be led by
myself, Granby & Herries with equal power; that I shd, or rather must
be the real leader'.[8]

Samuel Philips, the editor of the *Morning Herald*, commented that the proposal was to place the leader of the Conservative Party 'like a sandwich between two pieces of bread (very *stale* bread – Herries and Granby) in order that he might be made fit for squeamish throats to swallow'.[9]

Within a year Disraeli was, indeed, the acknowledged leader of the Opposition in the House of Commons and had taken the first major step towards power.

Towards the end of her life, Mrs Isaac D'Israeli paid a rare tribute to her eldest son; she had never thought so before but she conceded at last 'that Dis was equal to Mr Pitt'. She died soon afterwards on 21 April 1847, and her husband, struggling in his blindness to prepare a new edition of his *Life and Times of Charles I*, did not long survive their 'dear mother', as Disraeli's brother James referred to her. He died on 19 January 1848.

In his will, their father directed that his personal property should be divided into twelve parts, four parts going to Sarah, two each to Ralph and James, the rest, with his real estate, to Benjamin. To his 'beloved daughter-in-law' he left his collection of prints and to his daughter his portrait as 'a mark of his sense of her devotion and [his] entire affection'.

Sarah was now forty-six years old and, since she now had to leave Bradenham, she decided to take a house on the south coast and found one that suited her at Hastings.

Disraeli was in dire need of the money which his father had bequeathed to him. Although his wife had made large sums over to him, and was ready to give more, he was still much in debt; and was even more deeply so now that he was – after a long delay while the financial arrangements were settled – landed proprietor of Hughenden Manor, to which he and his wife moved on 6 December 1848,[10] having spent what he described to Lady Blessington as a terrible time 'seeming to have lived in waggons like a Tatar chief'.[11]

It was a large, imposing, white-washed, three-storeyed house with two bays extending from ground to roof with a door between leading out on to a terrace facing due south. Visitors were surprised that the rooms were redecorated and furnished with so little taste, as they were, indeed, at Grosvenor Gate.

The pictures at Hughenden were nearly all portraits of Disraeli's friends and colleagues, his 'Gallery of Affection'. The *objets d'art* were mostly such mementoes as commemoration plates, alabaster busts and crowded bric à brac.

On the ground floor, as well as the dining-room and drawing-room, which Disraeli called 'the saloon', there was a library necessarily large to accommodate the thousands of books which he had brought with him.* He had inherited twenty-five thousand volumes from his father and had disposed of a large number of them at Sotheby's, his collection at Hughenden being 'limited', so he said, 'to Theology, the Classics and History' and some rare and valuable volumes on the Italian Renaissance. He 'much lamented the loss of a prized copy of the first edition of his father's first work, *Curiosities*, which had belonged to Byron,' so his secretary said. 'It was much marked and noted. It had been sent to Mr I[saac] D['Israeli] by Murray who secured it, it having been seized in the Albany under a writ of execution. Mr I.D. valued it beyond measure. It was abstracted from the Library after 1850 and Mr D. has told me who he conceives appropriated the volume.'

It was in this book-lined room that Disraeli worked when he was at Hughenden; and he also had a study on the floor above from which he could look out contentedly beyond the terrace where his peacocks strutted. 'My dear lady,' he once observed to a guest, 'you cannot have a terrace without peacocks.' Beyond the terrace was the garden and, beyond that, the beech woods through which Disraeli delighted in walk-ing, taking an axe with him so that he could cut the ivy away from the trunks of the trees.

'I have a passion for books and trees,' he wrote. 'I like to look at them. When I come down [to the country] I pass the first week in sauntering about my park and examining all the trees.'†

Sometimes, with his dog for company, he would walk up the hill

---

* 'My library is my weak point,' he once said. 'It is that, of wh: of all material possessions, I am most proud and fond. I inherited, & I enriched it' (*Benjamin Disraeli Letters*, 2572, 21 October 1863, VI, 273).

† 'Bathing in the sea and breakfasting in forests [he once wrote in a letter to Lady Gwendolen Cecil] in my mind [are] the two most beautiful objects in the world. After all, there is no scenery like Sylvan scenery ... No wonder the ancients worshipped trees; for my part I love trees more than pictures. By the bye, the foliage this year [1879] in England is rich beyond memory' (Kenneth Rose, *The Later Cecils*, 1975, 38).

on the other side of the house where his wife had planted cedars and firs, yews and laurels in what became known as the German Forest; Mary Anne often accompanying him in her pony carriage as he walked round the ornamental lake on which swam his two swans, Hero and Leander.

Disraeli found, so he said, great amusement in talking to the people at work in the grounds at Hughenden. 'Their conversation is racy . . . An old but very hale man told me to-day that he was going to be married, and that his bride would be much younger than himself, but he had lodged in her cottage now for more than a year, and he thought she would do for him. He said he was a widower, and he added, speaking of his first wife, "And I can truly say, from the bottom of my heart that for fifty years I never knew what it was to have a happy hour." I told my wife of this and they are to have a wedding dinner.'

> I very much like the society of woodmen [Disraeli continued]. Their conversation is most interesting . . . I don't know any men who are so complete masters of their business, and of the secluded, but delicious world in which they live . . .
> To see Lovett, my head woodman, fell a tree is a work of art. No hustle, no exertion, apparently not the slightest exercise of strength. He tickles it with his axe, and then it falls exactly where he requires it. He can climb a tree like a squirrel, an animal which, both in form and colour and expression he seems to me to resemble.

Like his wife, Disraeli was reluctant to have a tree felled and he took much pleasure in having one planted. Indeed, so many trees were planted at Hughenden to commemorate the visits of friends and colleagues that the grounds, and even the lawns in front of the house, were so choked with them that, after his death, several of those near the house had to be cut down to admit light into the downstairs rooms.

After an exhausting session in London, Disraeli took to going down to Hughenden, to 'recover [his] equilibrium', to enjoy the company of his wife and to seek the comfort of his books and trees. Gradually he enlarged his estate until it extended to 1,400 acres, increasing the amount of his debts which he still seemed to be able to ignore except when they crowded upon him in moments of depression.

Relying upon the efficient Philip Rose to attend to his 'private affairs',

Disraeli could enjoy the life of a country gentleman scarcely troubled by those tangled financial matters which would have driven most men almost to distraction. He did not hunt, nor did he shoot or fish, but he wore the country clothes – sometimes in a rather exaggerated form – of those who did, undertaking the responsibilities of a country squire by performing the duties of a justice of the peace and a deputy-lieutenant, and presiding, as lord of the manor, over such local events as the flower shows which were held in the park.[12]

He was on easy terms with his neighbours, the Carringtons of Wycombe Abbey and Sir Harry Verney of Claydon House, Member of Parliament for Buckingham for over fifty years.

Disraeli did not, however, initially get on well with the local parson, the Revd John Pigott, whose vicarage was close to his house and whose sense of duty impelled him to reprove the Lord of the Manor for having gone up to London after matins on a Sunday in April 1849. It was, Mr Pigott wrote, 'a breach of that commandment which, though not so rigidly enforced as on that people from whom with a natural pride you record your descent, is still not less binding on a Christian'. It was his bounden duty, the vicar went on, to act towards Mr Disraeli as he would act towards his 'poorer and less intellectual neighbours' in the parish, and to reprove him and require a better example in future.

To this impertinent reproof Disraeli replied:

> Dear Sir,
>
>   It is quite true that, in consequence of public circumstances of urgency and importance, I was obliged suddenly to leave Hugh-enden on Sunday to my great personal annoyance and incon-venience. I departed without even a servant.
>
>   Had you made any temperate enquiry you might perhaps have ascertained that it is not my habit to travel on Sunday, and I would venture also to observe that my object in attending Divine Service is not merely or principally to set an example to others.[13]

He ended his letter by suggesting that, while the duties of a spiritual pastor should certainly be undertaken 'without regard of persons', it was desirable that these duties should be performed 'with reflection and not in a hasty and precipitate spirit'.

Mr Pigott replied, 'I freely receive your somewhat severe rebuke. It is the first of the kind bestowed on me during the twenty-six years in which I have been in Holy Orders.' He hoped, however, that they would learn to know each other better. As it happened, their relationship was not long tested: Pigott soon left the parish and Disraeli exercised his right as patron of the living to bestow it upon a man, the Revd C. W. Chubbe, with whom he felt confident he would get on well.[14]

After months of negotiation, the purchase of Hughenden was at last completed; and Disraeli was able to write to his wife: 'It is all done and you are the Lady of Hughenden.'[15]

Not long afterwards, he wrote to her from Grosvenor Gate: 'My darling, you have, I am sure, done at Hughenden what no other woman, or man either, cd do. You have gained a year in our enjoyment of that place, where I trust every year shall be happier & happier . . . I did not like to press you to come to me on Tuesday, tho' I have much wanted you . . . Pussy now comes into my room every morning at breakfast, and jumps on my head and rubs my nose. He seems colossal after our little favourite – and very dirty – I don't think he will ever be clean again. Adieu, my dearest wife. May I soon embrace you. Your ever affec husbd D.'[16]

Mary Anne treasured such letters as these. As she was to tell Lord Rosebery, there were many people who called themselves her friends; but she had no friend like Dizzy.[17]

There were those, of course, who were shocked by the woman's eccentricities and her outlandish remarks, while acknowledging the undoubted warmth of her nature. She was 'great fun,' Sir Stafford Northcote wrote to his wife after meeting Mary Anne in the train on their way to Knowsley. 'We made capital friends, though I could not help occasionally pitying her husband for the startling effect her natural speeches must have upon the ears of his great friends. Still, there is something very warm and good in her manner which makes one forgive a few oddities. She informed me she was born in Bramford Speke, and I told her they must come and see her birthplace some time when they are in Devonshire. What do you say to the idea of asking them to Pynes? It would complete the astonishment of our neighbours.'[18]

Not all her neighbours in Buckinghamshire were as taken with her as Sir Stafford Northcote. Nor were her husband's tenants, whose rents were raised to a level appreciably higher than those charged by the rich and easy-going gentleman who had previously owned the Hughenden estate.

Indeed, the journalist and contributor to *Punch* and the *Observer*, Sir Henry Lucy, said that neither of the Disraelis was well liked in the neighbourhood, Mrs Disraeli, in particular, having given 'mortal offence' by her parsimony. Providing an example of this, Sir Henry wrote that, having ordered a quarter of a cheese, she sent it back because her husband had been called away to London. When she died, he added, 'The smoke room at "The Falcon" was full of substantial traders, people and farmers belonging to High Wycombe and its neighbourhood. The dead lady up at the Manor House was the sole subject of conversation. It was sorrowful to note that there was none to say God bless her.'[19]

From time to time until her death in 1863, Disraeli received letters and presents from an elderly, childless Jewish lady of modest fortune, eccentric, shrewd and observant. The widow of James Brydges Willyams, a colonel in the Cornish militia, she was the daughter of Abraham Mendez da Costa, and, in the words of Philip Rose, she had 'an eccentric pride in the race from which she sprang, this, in fact, being the tie that first attracted her to Mr Disraeli and secured her devoted attachment to him'. This 'female Croesus', Charlotte de Rothschild told her son, Leopold, 'has piercing black eyes, wears a jet-black wig with an enormous top knot; no crinoline, is quite a miser, starves herself into a skeleton ... Keeps neither horses nor carriages, nor men servants – only an enormous watch-dog to protect her and her gold.'[20]

Disraeli entered wholeheartedly into her wish to have her coat of arms approved by the College of Heralds; and he conducted a lengthy correspondence on her behalf with the College, and with the Portuguese and Spanish embassies, in their efforts to trace the connection between her own family of Mendez da Costa and his of the Laras. He did so trace it to his own satisfaction; but he was to baulk at her suggestion that he should adopt the names and arms of both Lara and Mendez da Costa in addition to his own.

Philip Rose well recalled the day on which the name of Mrs Brydges Willyams had first been mentioned to him. Disraeli had brought him a letter, saying that it required 'an immediate answer'.

Rose could not find this letter among Disraeli's papers; but he remembered the gist of it:

> I have often before addressed you in reference to your political speeches and your published works; but I now write to you in a private subject. I am about to make my will; and I have to ask, as a great favour, that you will oblige me by being one of the executors . . . I think it right to add that whoever are my executors will also be my residuary legatees, and that the interest they will take under my will, although not a considerable one, will, at all events, be substantial.[21]

From the day upon which this letter was received until Mrs Brydges Willyams's death in her late eighties, Disraeli maintained a regular correspondence with her, exchanging presents as well as letters, and from time to time going down to Torquay, with his wife, to stay at the Royal Hotel and spending most afternoons and evenings at her house, Mount Braddon, just outside the town.[22]

With one of his earliest letters to her, dated 2 August 1851, Disraeli sent her a copy of *Tancred* – 'a vindication', he told her, 'of the race from which we alike spring' – as well as a copy of the 'last and classical edition' of his father's *Curiosities of Literature*.[23] In her letter of thanks for these 'two most admirable works' she added that she was going up to London for a fortnight to see the Great Exhibition and would be delighted to meet him if he would 'appoint a time and place at the Crystal Palace'.[24]

He did not meet her on this occasion – he had been warned that she was mad – but later instructed Messrs Colnaghi to send her a copy of a portrait of himself which they had recently published. He asked her to 'interpret the arrival of this silent guest as, in a manner, returning [her] visit to London, which [they] should be very glad to hear that [she] thought of repeating this season'.

Three days later he wrote again:

> I, like you, was not bred among my race, and was nurtured in great prejudice against them . . . I beg to assure you that I am not 'unapproachable' to those who tenderly interest me, like yourself. If you come to town this season, I hope to see you, and very often.[25]

After the end of the season that year, Mrs Willyams did not come to London, so Disraeli and his wife went to see her at Torquay where they 'passed a most acceptable week'. 'We have done nothing', he added, 'but talk of you and yours ever since.'

That autumn, writing from Hughenden, he told her that his life was so uneventful that she must take a letter from him 'as a morning call from some insipid country neighbour, who begins by talking about the weather'. 'I won't do that,' he added, 'but I must talk about myself, which is still worse.' He ended this long letter with a protestation of the affection which he was to feel for this elderly, rather odd Jewish lady for the rest of her life:

> How often I wish that next summer may be green and golden, and that you may be under this roof [at Hughenden], and a visitant to many places which I think would interest you! And how often I recall, with charm, and often with consolation, the kindness which you have shown to me, and the mysterious sympathy which now binds us together – Ever Yours, D.[26]

From that time on, he filled his letters with accounts of his life in the country, with the names and descriptions of guests, of Lord Henry Lennox, for instance, and of George Smythe who, 'both as to ability and acquirement [was] perhaps the most brilliant man of the day', and of Baron Rothschild and all his family who stayed two days and were the principal guests at a 'dinner to the neighbourhood'. He wrote also of servants' balls at which there was dancing till past five o'clock in the morning to the music of a fiddle, 'which must surely have been heard at Torquay', and the stamp of the dancing feet of the servants who went to work the next morning 'without ever having retired to rest – what rural rakes!' And he described a fête, which Mrs Disraeli gave for local schools – 'a hundred-strong and a hundred neighbours to meet them ... and they had a most capital band. It really was a sight worthy of Watteau and [he] enjoyed it infinitely more than the fête given by H.R.H. the Duchess d'Aumale at Orléans House, which [he] had the honour to attend a few days before.'

There were harvest homes at which 'all the farmers of the parish unite together and give to their collected labourers a festival in a tent which will hold hundreds, with banners and a band ... and all go in procession to the church which is adorned with flowers and sheaves. The children sing chorales, and everyone has a favour and a stalk of corn in his buttonhole.'

There were fishing parties on the banks of the rippling waters of Hughenden's stream and one day, 'in the first twilight', while attempts were being made to catch a fish for Mrs Willyams, a fine trout, 'a gentleman of 4¼ pounds', was landed and sent off straight away to Torquay in a basket with a brace of grouse which had been despatched to Disraeli from Northumberland.

Presents were constantly being sent and received between Hughenden and Torquay. Books and flowers, violets and roses, lobsters, the neck from a fat buck which the Queen had sent down from Balmoral. Mullets and prawns, soles and turbot came from Devon and, in return, venison, sent to Hughenden by friends in Scotland, was sent on to Torquay. These were followed by 'magnificent blackcocks from Drummond Castle', 'unfortunately robbed of their chief beauty, for such is the demand for their splendid tails – in order to furnish black and green and deep dark blue feathers for young ladies' coquettish hats – that the gamekeepers retain them for their perquisites'.

Disraeli was particularly pleased to receive flowers and, above all, roses from Devon:

> Your beautiful plants duly arrived here, and were immediately installed in a most fitting situation, where we shall cherish them as if they were yourself [he wrote in acknowledgement]. But my delight this year were the roses which you sent Mary Anne, and which she generously transferred to me ... I think I never met with roses so beautiful in form ... Altho' I have not written to you since I was here [at Hughenden] last, you have not been absent from my thoughts – that was, indeed, impossible, since you were represented on my table, every day, in the form of the most beauteous flowers that ever adorned a chamber ... I am sure that Syon or Chatsworth, with all their acres of gigantic conservatories, could never send their lords a tribute more fragrant and lustrous than I am indebted for to your ever-thoughtful kindness.

He professed himself equally delighted with the presents of food which arrived from Devon; and in one characteristic letter wrote, 'Where did you get the lobster which arrived for my déjeuner this morning?

From the caves of Amphitrite [the sea goddess, wife of Poseidon]? It was so fresh! Tasted of the sweetness – not the salt – of the ocean and almost as creamy as your picturesque cheese.'[27]

Gradually Hughenden was being transformed, the exterior brickwork revealed, the ground floor gothicized, the drawing-room redecorated – not very successfully, Lord Ronald Gower thought: 'a terribly gaudy apartment ... very lofty, and the walls all green paper, clothed with *fleur-de-lys* and adorned with large-panelled brown carved wood – or composition – frames, which are the only relief to the green wilderness of wall.' As for the outside of the house, Gower thought it 'a curious bit of nondescript architecture'.[28]

'We have realised a romance we had been many years contemplating,' Disraeli told Mrs Brydges Willyams. 'We have restored the house to what it was before the Civil Wars, and we have made a garden of terraces, in which cavaliers might roam and saunter, with their ladye-loves! The only thing wanting is that you should see it, but I am going to have in due time a competent artist down, who will photograph the house, gardens and the monument' – this being a memorial to his father, which his wife had had erected while he was away from home, a monument fifty feet high, 'and of the Italian style of the Renaissance period ... at the same time rich and graceful. It is [he added] one of the most beautiful things not only in the county of Buckingham but in England.'

He told Mrs Brydges Willyams about the contents of the house as well as its reconstruction – of the two 'splendid jars' which were installed in the 'chief saloon', each on top of a cabinet, and of a stand, specially built, on which 'a number of Gould's Birds [was] always open' and in which the illustrations were really so lifelike that, 'when one enters the room, one is almost tempted to walk on tiptoe, lest one might frighten them away'.

Beyond the windows of the library, Mary Anne supervised the adornment of the terrace 'in the Italian style with a beautiful series of vases, which came from Florence, and which sparkle in the sun, their white and graceful forms well contrasting with the tall geraniums and blue Agapantha lilies which they hold. I think you would admire this terrace very much. It has only one fault – that you never walk on it.'

'All the alterations to the house have prevented our receiving our friends this year, so I have been like a man on a desert island – tho' free from the despair of a Robinson Crusoe or an Alexander Selkirk, for I have a future – at Mount Braddon! ... In making the alterations here, a great number of owls have been disturbed among the yew trees, but they have been religiously cared for ... Their hooting at night is wilder and louder than the south-west wind, which, indeed, is the only accompaniment to their weirdish arias. And they tap the windows with their fell beaks.'

As the years passed more trees appeared and, upon his return to Hughenden in the autumn, he found a 'great difference' in their colour; 'the limes all golden, the beeches ruddy brown, while the oaks and elms and pines [were] still dark and green, and contrast well with the brighter tints'. 'But not a leaf has fallen,' he wrote; 'they want the first whisper of the frost, and then they will go out like lamps when the dawn breaks on a long festival.'

23

THE CHANCELLOR

'I hope you will make as good a Chancellor of
the Exchequer as you have been a husband
for your affectionate MARY ANNE'.

One day in February 1852, Lord Derby, who had succeeded Lord John
Russell, Peel's successor as Prime Minister, called at Disraeli's house in
Grosvenor Gate to talk to him about his becoming Chancellor of the
Exchequer in the new Conservative government. The proposal had
already been made to Disraeli and he had demurred on the grounds
that it was a branch of government of which he had no knowledge. 'You
know as much as Mr Canning did,' Derby commented. 'They give you
the figures.'[1] The Chancellor was also given a highly satisfactory salary
of £5,000 a year. Having made the proposition to Disraeli, however,
Derby seems to have had second thoughts. 'My father', his son, Lord
Stanley, wrote in his diary, 'admired Disraeli's temper, tact and ability
but seemed jealous lest he should aim at the first place and sneered at
his tendency to extremes of alternate excitement and depression.'

Once Disraeli had agreed to accept the post of Chancellor – which
he may have been given because it did not involve much contact with
the Queen – Derby said that Lord Malmesbury was to be Secretary for
Foreign Affairs. Herries, he added, 'must be Colonial Secretary; Henley
should go to the Board of Trade'. [S.H.] Walpole, a recruit of the previous
year, was to be Home Secretary; John Manners was to be in the Cabinet.
Having sketched out this Cabinet, Lord Derby told Disraeli he must now
go home at once. 'He had to write to the Queen, and to all these persons
and many others, and begged me to be with him early on the morrow.'[2]

When I called on the morrow [Disraeli wrote in a memorandum concerning the formation of Derby's Cabinet], I found his house already full of people; men in every room. His servant told me Mr Herries was with his Lord and that he had enquired several times for me, and that my name was to be taken in immediately. A very few minutes elapsed before I was in his presence. It was rather a face of consternation. 'I really think we shall break down,' he said. 'What am I to do for a Colonial Secretary?'

So then it turned out that Herries, evidently disgusted at not being C[hancellor] of the E[xchequer], had peremptorily refused the Secretaryship. I instantly counselled my giving up the Chancellorship, which I didn't want but Lord D[erby] would not hear of it . . .

'I know the man,' I said. 'He will do very well.'
'Who?'
'[Sir John] Pakington [Member for Droitwich].'
'I have just sent for him to be U[nder] S[ecretary] to Walpole. It should be a country gentleman. I thought it was a capital arrangement. He will be here in a few minutes.'

Sir John Pakington was announced. He remained in the waiting-room, while I was convincing Lord Derby that he would make a competent Secretary of State. It was naturally rather hard work. I don't know that Lord Derby had even a personal acquaintance with Pakington at that moment . . .

Pakington was introduced, elated with the impending destiny of becoming an U[nder] S[ecretary]. Lord Derby explained the situation in his happiest manner. Never shall I forget Pakington's countenance, as the exact state of affairs broke upon him; never did I witness such a remarkable mixture of astonishment and self complacency.[3]

Although he endeavoured to maintain an impression of calm urbanity, Disraeli could not disguise his pleasure and excitement at his achievement of high office after over fourteen years in Parliament. Lord Melbourne described him as being 'in a state of delight at the idea of coming into office. He said "he felt just like a young girl going to her first ball", constantly repeating "Now we have got a *status*".[4]

By the time all the appointments to the Cabinet had been made, it was noted that only three of the new Ministers had been in high office before – Derby, Herries (the new President of the Board of Control) and the Earl of Lonsdale (Lord President). And so, as none of the others was even a privy councillor, a large number of men, including the Duke of Northumberland as First Lord of the Admiralty, had, in Disraeli's words, to humble themselves on their knees before the Queen, their 'serene and imperturbable female sovereign', who presented them with their seals of office.

Letter after letter of congratulation was delivered at Grosvenor Gate. One of them, addressed to 'The Right Honourable the Chancellor of the Exchequer' at Number 11 Downing Street, was from Mrs Disraeli: 'Bless you, my darling, your own devoted wife wishes you joy. I hope you will make as good a Chancellor of the Exchequer as you have been a husband to your affectionate MARY ANNE.' Another letter from the misinformed Lord Lyndhurst expressed pleasure that Disraeli had been appointed Foreign Secretary, a post for which he was 'admirably suited'.[5]

The Duke of Wellington, by now very deaf, was even more confused. 'Who? Who?' he kept asking in penetrating tones when the names of the members of what consequently became known as the 'Who? Who? Ministry' were announced. Whenever he did catch a name it was as likely as not to be unknown to him. Upon being told of Sir John Pakington's appointment, he asked 'Who?' in a very loud voice and, when told, announced, 'Never heard of the gentleman.'[6]

The Queen was similarly unimpressed by her new ministry:

> Great and not *very* pleasant events have happened since I last wrote to you [she began a letter to King Leopold of the Belgians on 24 February 1852]. I know you have been informed of Lord Derby's assumption of office, with a very sorry Cabinet. I believe, however, that it is quite necessary they should have a trial, and then have done with it. Provided the country remains quiet, and they are prudent in their foreign policy, I shall take the trial as patiently as I can . . .
>
> Alas! your confidence in our excellent Lord Granville is no longer of any avail, though I hope ere long he will be at the Foreign Office again, [as he was to be in 1870–4 and 1880–5] and I cannot say that his successor [Lord Malmesbury], who has never been in office (as indeed is the case with almost all the new Ministers), inspires me with confidence.[7]

She did, however, like and respect Lord Derby, 'a most talented, capable and courageous Prime Minister . . . Our acquaintance is confined almost entirely to him, but then he is the Government. They do nothing without him. He has all the Departments to look after, and on being asked by somebody if he was not much tired, he said "I am quite well with my babies."[8]

The Queen's relationship with her Chancellor of the Exchequer was, at first, rather wary. 'Mr Disraeli (alias Dizzy)', she told King Leopold, 'writes very curious reports to me of the House of Commons proceedings – much in the style of his books.'[9]

They were 'just like his novels,' she added in her journal, 'highly coloured'.[10]

A long and characteristic report written on 15 March 1852 gave the Queen succinct accounts of the speeches made by Charles Pelham Villiers, Member for Wolverhampton ('terse and elaborate, but not in his happiest style'); of his own reply, of Lord John Russell's speech ('not successful'); and of Spencer Walpole (who spoke 'with great taste and moderation'); all of which was 'most humbly submitted to her Majesty by her Majesty's most dutiful subject and servant, B. Disraeli'.

These long, conscientious and regular reports to the Queen, combined with all the other responsibilities of a demanding office, kept Disraeli so busy that, as he wrote to his sister from the Chancellor of the Exchequer's office in Downing Street, he had 'literally no time to take [his] meals'. 'The Lord President [Lord Lonsdale] however, gives today his first Cabinet dinner,' he continued, 'so business and food may be combined. In the evening Lady Derby gives her reception, which I shall attend, otherwise I do not attempt to go anywhere. Mary Anne, however, is very gay and ubiquitous.'[11]

One of Disraeli's friends who was found a place as a junior Lord of the Treasury in the new administration was Lord Henry Lennox, third son of the Duke of Richmond, an amusing, impetuous, rather frivolous and gossipy young man of no remarkable talent to whom he had become devoted.

'I am so glad you are dull,' Disraeli wrote in one letter characteristic of many. 'I also feel lonely.' In other, similar letters he addressed Lennox as 'my beloved' and in one he wrote, 'It was very kind of you to write to me, and most delightful to me to hear from you ... work absorbs, or should absorb one; nevertheless, I think very often of my young companion, and miss him sadly, for his presence to me is always a charm, and often a consolation.' 'I apprehend my morning will be very much engaged,' other letters ran; 'but I hope we may dine together, alone, at the Conventry [a raffish club in Piccadilly] . . . I am so tired that I can only tell you that I love you.'

'Write to me, dearest D.,' Lennox replied in one of his equally affectionate letters, 'when you have time! a *nice* kind affectionate letter; amusing it *must* be . . . I have read your dear kind letter again and again, & I am so grateful for it. Remember my dearest D., I am, henceforth, your own property, to do what you like with, my hopes & wishes are centred in but one thing; need I add that is your increasing success – only let me be with you & by you . . . Thanks, a thousand thanks for your charming letter . . . I dine at Hatfield tonight but shall be down here tomorrow. Till then farewell, my dearest D! How could you suppose I could *not be dull* without you.'[12]

'The language', as Robert Blake has suggested, 'must be discounted as the hyperbole of the time. But it remains something of a mystery that Disraeli should have been as fond as he was of such an essentially trivial personality.' And to quote the biographer Stanley Weintraub: 'Although he would continue to attract young disciples throughout his career, no other relationship had the flirtatious dimensions of the Henry Lennox affair, nor was conducted with someone so shallow . . . It seems from the evidence [to have been] entirely unphysical if marginally homoerotic.'[13]

Another of Disraeli's perceptive biographers, Sarah Bradford, agrees with this view: 'Biographers of Disraeli have scouted the use of terms such as "I can only say I love you", as quite normal in the context of Victorian male friendships, but Disraeli was not in the habit of using such terminology in his correspondence with men, not even in letters to his dearest friend, d'Orsay. That he should do so to a man seventeen years younger than himself, charming and amusing but certainly not extraordinarily gifted, points to an affection verging on infatuation . . . The latent homosexual element in Disraeli's friendship with younger men cannot be ignored in the case of Lennox, even if the relationship was almost certainly not physical.'[14]

Although 'perennially in search of an heiress', Lennox does not seem to have conducted the pursuit with any urgent enthusiasm. He failed to captivate a Spanish princess; failed also in his pursuit of the daughter of a rich tradesman, then, despite his parents' anti-Semitic prejudices, he pursued with equal lack of success Sir Anthony de Rothschild's eldest daughter. 'It is always the same thing,' he complained to Disraeli in 1863, 'either the lady has too little money or I am too old.' He died a bachelor twenty-three years later.

As Chancellor of the Exchequer, Disraeli was as busy as ever:

> The business is very hard and anxious [he told Sarah in the second week of June]. Up to three o'clock every morning, and in my place in the House again at noon. It cannot, I suppose, last very long – at least, if it do, I shall not.
>
> I go nowhere ... I shall not be at the long series of civic events which are coming, E[ast] I[ndia] Company, M[erchant] Taylors [Company] – being all, and perhaps fortunately, on House of Commons Days ...
>
> On Sunday I was two hours with the Prince [Consort] – a very gracious and interesting audience. He has great abilities and wonderful knowledge – I think the best educated man I ever met ... His intellect is energetic and lively.[15]

A week later he wrote to Sarah again to say that the session was going well:

> The Speaker says he never remembers so much and so hard work ... I think we shall carry every one of our Bills of the slightest importance ... The Court is very gracious; I was with the Prince Consort two hours again on Sunday last.[16]

As the new leader of the Government in the House of Commons, Disraeli deserved and received much praise, not only from those, such as Lord Lyndhurst, predisposed in his favour but also from men who had been harshly critical of him in the past, even from Charles Greville, who had written in March 1852: 'There are great complaints of Diz in the H. of Commons. They say he does not play his part as Leader with tact and propriety, and treats his opponents impudently and uncourteously, which is egregiously foolish and will end by exposing him to some great mortification; the H. of C. will not stand such behaviour from such a man.'[17]

In May, however, Greville praised Disraeli's speech on bringing in his budget as 'a great performance, very able and received with great applause in the House'.[18] And by July, Greville wrote:

> Disraeli has given undoubted proofs of his great ability, and showed how neatly he could handle such a subject as finance, with which he never can have been at all familiar; but having been well taught by his subalterns, and applying a mind naturally clear, ready and acute to the subject, he contrived to make himself fully master of it, and to produce to the H. of Commons a financial statement the excellence of which was universally admitted and gained him great applause.[19]*

His demeanour in the House at this time was described by a journalist in the *Leader*:

> His body is half thrown across the table, one hand resting behind him, flirting with a laced cambric, the other white hand tapping gently on a red box. He is talking to Lord John [Russell] . . . who seems to think the eloquence rather amusing. Mr Disraeli has a most exquisite voice, and he is using only its gentlest modulations. He is quite colloquial, and his tone is friendly and familiar – especially when he comes to a bitter innuendo, when he turns his head to the country gentlemen that they may hear it and laugh . . .
>
> Mr Disraeli is getting near the end of his speech, and is now recapitulating and fastening all the points together as is his wont . . . He approaches the peroration – his forte; and here he raises his head, he throws back his collar, he puts by his cambric, he turns from Lord John and faces the House. He speaks slower; he ceases his affected stammer . . . his articulation is elaborate; and there is dead silence. But he is still unexcited [until he comes to his closing sentences which are] delivered with a louder voice and with more vehement gestures; and, having got the cheer at the right spot, the orator sinks into his seat as nonchalantly as though he had been answering a question about Fahrenheit . . . and turns to ask [his young friend] Lord Henry Lennox whether [Giulia] Grisi [the soprano] was in good voice last night![20]

---

* In presenting his budget later that year Disraeli was on his feet for five hours. A report of the speech occupies fifty-two pages in *Hansard* (*Hansard's Parliamentary Debates*, 3rd series, Vol 121).

Soon after this account of Disraeli's gifts as an orator appeared in the *Leader*, the pages of this and most other newspapers and journals were filled with panegyrics and obituaries of the Duke of Wellington, who had died on 14 September 1852 at the age of eighty-three at Walmer Castle in Kent. As Leader of the House of Commons, Disraeli was required to deliver a suitable eulogy of the great man. He was, as he confessed to Mary Anne, 'a little disturbed' by the responsibility, all the world, as he said, 'expecting a great speech from me and I at least resolved that I will make one without the word "duty" appearing'.

The word 'duty' did not appear; but a part of the speech, which Lord John Russell (who spoke after him) described as most eloquent, was borrowed – almost word for word – from an article on Marshal de Saint-Cyr by Adolphe Thiers which had appeared in 1829 in the French review, *La Revue Trimestre*, and subsequently in an English translation in the *Morning Chronicle* in July 1848. The plagiarism, described by George Earle Buckle as 'perhaps the most striking of the many acts of plagiarism charged against Disraeli', was revealed by the *Globe* which printed the speech and Thiers's article in parallel columns.

'A shout of "stop thief" was raised,' according to *The Times*, 'and a whole pack of jealous *littérateurs* were immediately on the scent of their offending, and perhaps too successful brother.'

Disraeli's friends tried to help him. Bulwer Lytton gave him notes for a speech which Disraeli could make if questions were asked in the House; and George Smythe, who had translated the piece about Marshal de Saint-Cyr in the *Morning Chronicle*, explained that, years before, Disraeli had drawn his attention to the passage in question, while Richard Monckton Milnes wrote to Disraeli to say that, 'though politically opposed, we are literary *collaborateurs*. If you think it worth while to let me know anything of the circumstances of the passages from Thiers that made part of your speech on the Duke, which you would like me to state authoritatively, in the society in which I live, I shall be glad to do so, as a plain matter of justice.'[21]

Disraeli took up the offer with gratitude, telling Milnes that he really thought he had 'the best disposition in the world'. The facts, he said, were these:

A good many years ago I read the passage in question in a defunct French journal . . . I never had heard of M. Thiers, nor had anyone else. We were both of us then equally obscure . . . The passage was engraven on my memory . . . Association of ideas brought it back when, musing for a moment amid the hurry and strife of affairs, over a late solemn occasion, I summoned it from the caverns of my mind . . . Conceive my astonishment – I ought to say my horror – when I read the article in the *Globe*. Instead of cribbing it from the *Morning Chronicle*, the very fact of my having seen it in that journal would, of course, have prevented my using it.[22]

Either Milnes or Disraeli gave this explanation to John Delane, who provided a leading article in *The Times* which asked: 'Why do authors drag down every one of their fraternity who may happen to become a Minister of State? . . . Authors will never have their proper consideration, in the face of dukes, millionaires, squires, and prize cattle, till they are loyal to their own body.'

Despite such protestations, Disraeli had provided his critics with ammunition which they found irresistible and they peppered his reputation with gibes and jokes and drew each other's attention to cartoons in *Punch* which made the most of Disraeli's embarrassment.

Charles Greville, who described Disraeli's funeral oration as 'pompous', said that it exposed him to 'much ridicule and severe criticism', that 'D'I had been unmercifully pelted' over it, and well deserved the pelting for 'such folly and bad taste'. 'His excuse is', Greville continued, 'that he was struck by the passage, wrote it down, and, when he referred to it recently, forgot what it was, and thought it was his own composition. But this poor apology does not save him. Derby spoke very well on the same subject, a few nights after in the H. of Lords, complimenting the authorities, the people and foreign nations, particularly France. It is creditable to Louis Napoleon to have ordered [Count] Walewski [French Ambassador in London] to attend the funeral.'

MARITAL DIFFICULTIES

'I meditate decamping privately.'

DESPITE THE FACT THAT many Members of Parliament were still prejudiced against him – in a letter to Lord Derby, Thomas Babington Macaulay, then Member for Edinburgh, wrote that his eloquence was 'his only respectable quality' – Disraeli was much encouraged by the reception accorded him by the undergraduates at Oxford, where he received an honorary degree in June 1853.

In May that year he had presided over a meeting in London of the Royal Literary Fund, and had been warmly received; but Oxford undergraduates were less predictable and he had been concerned that from them he would not be given so enthusiastic a welcome. He had scarcely been comforted by Lord Derby, the Duke of Wellington's successor as Chancellor of the University, who had recommended him for an honorary degree and who had written to him to say, 'We shall have to run the gauntlet of the public opinion of the undergraduates. I do not think, however, that we have much to apprehend on that score.'[1] Disraeli was not so sure and seemed apprehensive about his reception before a gathering which was to include Gladstone, Macaulay, Samuel Wilberforce, William Aytoun, poet and Professor of Rhetoric in the University of Edinburgh, Samuel Warren, the novelist, and Sir Archibald Alison, the historian.[2]

Disraeli was, however, given a resounding welcome by the assembled undergraduates in the Sheldonian Theatre.[3] As he approached the Chancellor it was noticed that his lips were trembling slightly in his otherwise impassive face. But when, in response to the question, '*Placet-ne vobis,*

Domini?' the undergraduates filled the theatre with shouts of '*Maxime placet! Immense placet!*', his relief was apparent. He returned to his seat, took out his eyeglass, scanned the faces in the ladies' gallery and, with a gesture that disconcerted some of the staider members of the audience, kissed his hand to his wife.[4]

After this ceremony he attended a dinner at Christ Church and here again he was welcomed enthusiastically by a crowd of undergraduates assembled in Tom quadrangle who stood in the rain to watch him pass by. 'Gentlemen,' he said to them, 'within these classic walls I dare not presume to thank you. But believe this: never will I forget your generous kindness.'[5]

A week or so later, a Russian army marched across the river Pruth and the sequence of events, which were to lead to a British army landing in the Crimea, had begun.

Lord Aberdeen, who had replaced the Earl of Derby as Prime Minister in December 1852, was not a man to lead a country at war.

> Lord Aberdeen seemed paralysed with the responsibility of action [Disraeli wrote in the weekly journal, the *Press*]. The curse of 'antiquated imbecility' has fallen in all its fulness on [him]. His temper, naturally morose, has become licentiously peevish. Crossed in his Cabinet, he insults the House of Lords, and plagues the most eminent of his colleagues with the crabbed malice of a maundering witch![6]
>
> We are on the eve of great events; and it is just as well that the people of this country should be prepared for their occurrence ... A single blunder in the conduct of our foreign affairs may cost us as much as a series of bad harvests ... The designs of Russia are to be resisted by a vigilant and skilful diplomacy ... The time has come when grave pomposity can no longer pass for wisdom, or moroseness for courage ... Lord Aberdeen has precipitated the convulsion, and is, at the same time, alike unfit and unprepared to control the storm ... He will betray the honour and the interests of our country – it is the law of his nature and the destiny of his life.[7]

Eventually, following the calamities of the war in the Crimea, it fell to John Arthur Roebuck, the Radical Member for Sheffield, to move a resolution 'that a Select Committee be appointed to enquire into the condition of our Army before Sebastapol and into the conduct of those Departments of the Government whose duty it has been to minister to the wants of that Army'.[8] The motion was carried by a two-thirds majority. The next day Lord Aberdeen resigned.

The Government had fallen with 'such a whack', as Gladstone put it, that 'they could hear their heads thump as they struck the ground'.[9]

Although he was over seventy, Palmerston was the obvious choice as Lord Aberdeen's successor. But the Queen, who did not like him, and who considered his unpunctuality and his patronizing, not to say domineering, manners a conscious affront to her dignity, was determined not to have the rude old man she called 'Pilgerstein' as her Prime Minister if she could help it. She sent for Lord Derby, but he declined to take office. She even sent for Lord John Russell, whose resignation from the Government as soon as he had heard of Roebuck's motion had recently filled her with 'indignation and disgust'. So the Queen was obliged to send for 'Pilgerstein'.

He was 'really an imposter,' Disraeli said of him, 'utterly exhausted and at the best only ginger beer and not champagne, an old painted pantaloon, very deaf and short-sighted, with dyed hair and false teeth which would fall out of his mouth when speaking if he did not hesitate and halt so much in his talk'.[10]* But he still had much life and vigour and sound sense in him. And he knew a good deal about the Army. He had been Secretary-at-War when he was twenty-four and he had worked hard and well in this appointment for nearly twenty years, earning the dislike of George IV, of practically all his colleagues and of everyone connected with the Horse Guards. 'It is quite extraordinary,' the Duke of Wellington's friend, Mrs Arbuthnot, said, 'how he was detested.'[11]

The virulence of Disraeli's strictures on Lord Aberdeen had been exacerbated by concern for Mary Anne, who was, in his own words, 'greatly

---

* It was not so long before Disraeli himself had trouble with his false teeth. 'Would you like to know what happened the other night in the House?' a Radical Member said to Lord John Manners one day in 1871. 'Well, in the best part of his speech and in the middle of a sentence his teeth fell out. He caught them up with extraordinary rapidity in his right hand, turned round apparently to ask a question of his neighbour, put them in and resumed his speech at the exact word where he had left it off.'

suffering from a state of nervous debility'. 'As she is the soul of my house, managing all my domestic affairs, it is, irrespective of all other considerations, a complete revolution in my life. Everything seems to me to be anarchy.'

His marriage had been going through a difficult time. Mary Anne had been jealous when her husband had, for the sake of his political career, gone to stay in country houses without her and had taken unattached and, no doubt, as she supposed, attractive ladies in to dinner. More than once he had retreated from her anger to the Carlton Club; and, upon his return home, he had discovered the locks on his desk had been forced. The papers in the drawers were not the love letters which Mary Anne had expected to find. There were, however, scenes and 'violent temper'.

He gave a report to his sister:

> My dear Sa,
>
> The storm wh: has, more or less, been brewing in my sky for the last 12 months, burst rather suddenly yesterday, & at present I am residing at an hotel, leaving Grosvenor Gate to its mistress. An accés of jealousy brought affairs to a crisis, & I found all my private locks forced – but instead of love letters, there were only lawyers' bills & pecuniary documents. Had I not been taken unawares, I shd have secured these papers, wh: may produce some mischief – but I hope may not.
>
> My case is very clear, tho' between ourselves, it might have been otherwise. There is only one point in wh: I felt a little embarrassed, & used yr. name to carry me thro'.
>
> I said that I was going out of town last Thursday to Bucks Assizes – but I did not, & Meyer Rothschild unintentionally let the cat out of the bag.
>
> I have replied that I went out of town to see you – & that after the last rows, I was resolved that yr. name shd. never be mentioned by me to her again – and that the 'deceit', as she calls it, is the necessary consequence of her violent temper & *scenes*, wh: I will bear no more. So remember this – LAST THURSDAY.
>
> I don't know how all will end: I shall not give up a jot, whatever tides. I am rather confused & shaky of course, having had a bad night, in a strange bed, without my usual conveniences, so pardon this rough epistle, & believe me,
>
> yr affec brother D.[12]

That same day, 18 July 1849, Disraeli wrote also to Philip Rose: 'I called on you yesterday to consult you on a domestic ... point ... If Madame consults you upon it, or, rather, wishes to do so, you will confer with me before you see her.'[13]

Mary Anne had had some reason to suspect that there might be love letters in the house, since her husband had been telling her on occasions that he was visiting his sister when, in fact, he was not, and was either seeing a mistress, possibly Lady Londonderry, or making some financial arrangements which he wanted to keep hidden from his wife.

It seems that she thought it as well to give up opening his letters; but, even so, he asked Sarah to write to him at the Carlton Club whenever she had something to say that it might be as well that his wife did not know about and, when writing to him at Hughenden, to say nothing that might arouse Mary Anne's suspicions. 'In these cursed days of progress,' he told his sister, 'Wyc. [ombe] has two posts & your letters arrive in the middle of the day sometimes ... As long as letters come only in the morning, all must be right – but when mid-day arrives ...'

She could not thank him enough for his letters to her. She did not have words to 'convey the value they were' to her. Living alone, she missed him terribly. She longed to be in his 'atmosphere' again; and, before long, she moved from Hastings to Twickenham so as to be nearer to him when it became possible for them to meet. As for Disraeli himself, he doubted, so he told her on 25 August, that he 'could bear this life much longer'. 'I suppose something will turn up, only visiting country houses seems to me even something worse: constantly dressing and indigestion. I suppose I must find refuge in Blue Books [official reports of Parliament and the Privy Council]. I have piles already.'[14]

He was feeling quite as depressed three months later. 'I am not physically ill,' he told Sarah, 'but hipped and dispirited beyond expression. Indeed, I find this life quite intolerable – & wish some earthquake wd. happen.'[15]

By the middle of November, however, Mary Anne was once more his 'dearest wife', and he was soon signing himself 'your affec husband', and writing from Burghley, Lord Exeter's house, telling her that he was 'anxious to return' to their 'tête a tête dinners'.[16]

As well as concern for his lonely sister, Disraeli was bothered by complaints and demands from his brother, James. Their other brother, the amiable and contented Ralph, five years younger than Benjamin, gave him little trouble. But Jem, as he was known in the family, was a demanding and difficult young man who was frequently a trial to Benjamin, to whom he wrote occasional and 'offensive' letters, complaining that his elder brother had acted 'sneakenly' towards him: 'I don't mind the abuse,' Benjamin commented, 'but I do the spelling.'*

Despite Jem's petulance, Benjamin did his best to help him, not only by attempting to have him made a magistrate, but also asking other favours for him from 'Ld. Stanley, Sir Jas, Graham, Ld. John Russell & the Ld. Lt., always unsuccessfully', and using his influence to obtain for him a County Court Treasurership and a Commissionership of Excise, scarcely qualified though he was for either position.

To make matters worse, for long periods Jem and Mary Anne were not speaking to each other; and Disraeli found family life scarcely tolerable, all the less tolerable when Mary Anne was suffering from what he supposed was gout which, he said, 'completely knocks up her principal resources, & terribly taxes me. The pony chair is now indispensable.'[17]

Towards the end of 1849, he had gone away for a few days. His hosts and hostesses were 'dreadful bores'; but 'anything [was] better than Hughenden,' he told his sister. 'I meditate decamping privately on Monday to town,' he confided in her; and he wrote to Philip Rose, asking him to send a letter telling him that he was wanted in London 'on business'. It was not until November 1851 that the quarrels were made up and Disraeli was able to write to his sister: 'You will be glad to hear that James and M[ary] A[nne] have at last, after having cost me much disquietude, made up their affairs very well – & now the talk is of a great family party at Christmas.'[18] The date upon which this letter was written was Mary Anne's fifty-ninth birthday. Her husband, to commemorate the day, presented her with this verse:

* The squabbles with Jem continued intermittently for months. 'I shall be very glad to see Ralph & I hope we shall manage that Jem shall accompany him & put an end to these absurd misunderstandings, wh: greatly vex me, & prevent my working,' Disraeli told Sarah on 17 October 1851. 'She [Mary Anne] noticed him at Wycomb the other day, but instead of going up to her, & settling the affair he passed on. I have endless rows on this infernal subject. J[em], as if there were not sufficient cause for complaint, has discovered another: that I might at least have obtained position, if not fortune, for getting him made a magistrate, wh: he says I cd, have done' (Benjamin Disraeli Letters, 2185, v477).

This is an offering to a perfect Wife –
Long may this day illumine my happy life.
Long may the sun upon this bright day shine –
And long may I, this day, call thee Love, mine.[19]

In 1868 Jem died suddenly, and Benjamin found himself appointed his executor, 'without having had the slightest hint of such an office devolving on [him] & having to give orders about everything which [he] least understood and most disliked'. This duty he found all the more disagreeable when he became responsible for paying off Jem's mistress for a figure eventually settled at £6,000. As residuary legatee, however, he did eventually receive the most welcome sum of £5,300.[20]

Some years before his brother's death, Disraeli had, in 1859, suffered a far more poignant loss in the death of his beloved fifty-seven-year old sister, the 'ever faithful friend' in whom he confided with a trust and openness he could not bring himself to show to anyone else. She had not had a happy life since leaving Bradenham; and went so far as to tell her brother, Benjamin, that his successful career was 'the only thing in [her] life that [had] never disappointed [her]'. The death of her fiancé, William Meredith, had been followed by the death of another man whom she had had hopes of marrying.

'I have had a sleepless night,' Disraeli wrote to his brother, Ralph, after watching over their sister as she died. 'Language cannot describe what this sudden, & by me never contemplated, catastrophe has produced on me. She was the harbor of refuge in all the storms of my life & I had hoped she would have closed my eyes.'[21]

Disraeli continued to go to country houses on his own when his wife's ill health kept her at home. He went to stay with Lord Exeter at Burghley House, with the Carringtons at Missenden Abbey and with the Duke and Duchess of Rutland at Belvoir Castle where he was 'received by six servants bowing in rows'. He had by now, as Robert Blake observed, 'convinced himself that he belonged to the aristocratic order as much as any of those whom he met in the grand world of Tory politics. He had a fundamentally patrician outlook. To stay at the great country houses, the castles and palaces of the English nobility, gratified him not as the social triumph of an adventurer but as the belated recognition of an equal.'[22]

Yet even so he was likely to decline invitations to houses where his presence was required for purely social reasons and where political matters were unlikely to be discussed.

'I have been forced to give up every country house but my own,' he wrote, not altogether truthfully, to Lady Londonderry, declining an invitation to Wynyard. 'And I have been too much engaged to ask anyone here.' 'I am surrounded by piles of Blue Books, and two posts a day bear me reams of despatches, so that my recess of relaxation has combined the plodding of a notary with the anxiety of a house steward.'

He might also have complained that as owner of the estate at Hughenden, he was expected to play his part as a country squire, to discuss country matters with his fellow squires, to get to know the local farmers, and to keep an eye on the cases which came before the quarter sessions.

He was so busy, in fact, so occupied with the affairs of Buckinghamshire and Westminster, so tied to his desk, that he had no time to take any exercise apart from an occasional walk beneath his beloved trees, on one occasion at least shocking the Whip, William Beresford, by wearing not only a moustache but also a Tyrolean hat. 'Now this is very sad,' Beresford wrote to Lord John Manners. 'For he is not the person who ought to attract attention by outré dress and appearance, but by his talents. I hope this style is only assumed while he is rusticating.'[23] On a later occasion, Sir Stafford Northcote, Member for Dudley, had cause to complain of Disraeli having 'set up a small peaked beard'.[24]

Disraeli's health, never robust, began to suffer. He was worried by bleeding gums for the relief of which he even tried leeches, without success. In the autumn of 1854, he complained of 'a sort of equinoctial attack – a great sluggishness and disability'. He had to get up at seven o'clock to work because he could not concentrate once the sun had set.

Later he had more than one attack of influenza, and suffered from what he described as 'the horrors of a torpid liver'. He was beginning to look decidedly older than his years. The barrister and occasional journalist, Edward Kenealy, described him at this time as 'wearing out'. 'He had grown less Jewish than when I last saw him,' Kenealy continued, 'and the impression which he leaves is one of pain rather than pleasure ... I was sorry to see him so careworn and restless, and wondered why he bothers himself about such miserable cheats as the rewards of political battle.'[25]

The American author, Nathaniel Hawthorne, having caught sight of him, then aged fifty-two, in the vestibule of the House of Commons, wrote:

> By and bye came a slender person in a black frock[coat], buttoned up and black pantaloons, taking long steps, but I thought rather feebly or listlessly. His shoulders were round; or else he had a perpetual stoop in them. He had a prominent nose, a thin face and a sallow, very sallow complexion, and was a very unwhole-some-looking person; and had I seen him in America, I should have taken him for a hard-worked editor of a newspaper, weary and worn with night-work and want of exercise; shrivelled and withered before his time. It was Disraeli and I never saw any other Englishman look in the least like him.[26]

Despite his sallow, unwholesome appearance, and his uncertain health, Disraeli was still possessed of a remarkable stamina. Although sessions in the Commons were then often prolonged into the early hours of the morning, because many Members had to earn their living at a time when they received no pay, Disraeli was rarely absent from his place and was capable of delivering speeches of extraordinary length: on more than one occasion he spoke for three hours, and in December 1852, for no fewer than five hours in a session not concluded until a quarter to four in the morning.*[27]

When she was a little better, he took his wife on a visit to Merstham in Surrey to stay with the Joliffes, to Wimpole to stay with the Hardwickes, then to the Malmesburys at Heron Court, Christchurch; and on 9 December, with Malmesbury and Hardwicke, he went for three days to Knowsley Park in Lancashire where he found Lord Derby recovering from an extremely painful attack of gout and disinclined to turn his attention to politics from his blank-verse translation of the *Iliad* on which he had been occupied for some time and which he was anxious to finish.

---

* This was not one of Disraeli's best performances, provoking ribald comments and rude gestures from certain Whig Members. 'I could', Macaulay maintained, 'have said [the whole of Disraeli's inordinately long speech] as clearly, or more clearly in two hours.'

From Knowsley he wrote to his wife:

> This place is remarkable: a wretched house yet very vast: an irregular pile of many ages: half of it is like St James's Palace, low, red, with turrets: the other like the Dutch façade of Hampton Court ... Behind the house is a park almost as large as Windsor, and with great beauty. I think it is a circumference of ten or twelve miles, with red deer as well as fallow deer, oak forests, a splendid lake ... [Lord Derby] looks very thin and pale, but I think improved: he looks so very young [at fifty-four].

Although Lord Derby had an income of over £100,000 a year, Knowsley was 'furnished like a second-rate lodging house,' Disraeli added. 'Not from stingyness, but from sheer want of taste.'[28]

Between their visits to Wimpole and Heron Court, the Disraelis returned to London for Mary Anne to consult her doctor and 'on a debilitated frame', in her husband's words, 'she caught the London Influenza in its most aggravated form'.[29]

'We got down to the country as soon as we could,' he told Lord Londonderry, 'but she has been reduced to the last extremity, and tho' she has wonderfully rallied, at one moment the physicians hardly gave me hope. To complete my troubles, about ten days ago or so, I caught the disorder from her, for it is an epidemic ... It has been very depressing and rendered me almost incapable of business.'[30]

He soon recovered from this illness but in August, when he returned to Hughenden, he suffered from that 'state of nervous prostration' which had struck him almost 'every year' when he left London in the late summer and rendered him 'quite incapable to write the shortest letter on the most ordinary business'. 'I suppose,' he told Lady Londonderry, 'that it is the sudden cessation of excitement ... But whatever the cause, the result is most distressing. However, I will not dwell upon such egoistical twaddle. I am a little better.'

He was quite well again the following month when he and Mary Anne made another round of visits, staying with Lady Rolle, Sir Lawrence and Lady Palk and Sir John and Lady Yarde-Buller and going to Torquay for several days to see Mrs Brydges Willyams, to whom he wrote in 6 December 1854 after his return to Hughenden:

We have had very absorbing and sad times since I last wrote to you. We have lived here quite alone, reading only the ensanguined newspapers, and learning each day of the loss of our dearest friends [in the Crimea]. What tragedies!

My Parliamentary staff has suffered more than that of any of the Generals of Division. I think I told you that the chief of my staff, Sir William Joliffe, has lost his eldest son in the Guards, before Sebastopol, of cholera and that his second, and prime hope, charged with Lord Cardigan at Balaclava ... His father looks ten years older than he did last session. Colonel Hunter Blair, of the Scotch Guards, one of my most active aide-de-camps, and really invaluable both as a partisan and a friend [was] shot in the tenderest part and died in awful torments. This is a severe loss to me. My second aide-de-camp, Lord Mandeville, writes to me that he has had four cousins killed and one severely wounded.

In the midst of all this, Parliament is called suddenly together, and the pressure on me for the last week has been very great. We go up to town tomorrow, for, to complete our troubles, our house is full of workmen, and yet on the morning of the 12th I must contrive to receive two hundred members of Parliament![31]

From the first, Disraeli had been less sanguine than many about the outcome of the war. Three months earlier he had written to Mrs Brydges Willyams to say that the invasion of the Crimea was turning into another Walcheren expedition of 1809 in which a British army was withdrawn after losing four thousand men from disease. Published reports as well as private letters revealed the most appalling incompetence as well as scurvy and cholera and the lack of both provisions and clothing in the army.

Surely there must be an hour of reckoning for this hateful Government who go to war without providing for an army [Lady Londonderry, who had a son in the Crimea, wrote to Disraeli]. It is actual murder to let this little heroic wreck of an army fight those hordes and masses of barbarians who reinforce by tens of thousands while we hardly do so with hundreds ... It is all heartbreaking ... I think of nothing else even in my sleep, and if I were younger I am sure I should seize on the idea of *The Times* and get a yacht and go there. It seems so dreadful to sit at home and do nothing ... I have deplorable accounts – floating encampments on mud ... horses dying all round. There seems neither care nor thought, and a total indifference as to what becomes of this fine army and the brave spirits who seem tasked beyond human endurance.[32]

In the pages of the *Press* as well as in speeches in Parliament, Disraeli inspired and pronounced such sentiments.

I ask the House [he declared] for a moment to turn round and consider, not whether there were sufficient nurses or surgeons at Scutari, not what was the number of pots of marmalade which should be sent out to support our starving troops, but I ask the House to consider what have been the results which this Ministry, with their enormous advantages, has obtained. In the Black Sea an army had been sent out against a fortress as strong as Gibraltar, at the wrong time without any proper provision being made for its maintenance or reinforcement. It was an unpleasant surprise for Parliament and the country to find that the principal measure introduced by Ministers for the more vigorous prosecution of the war was a Bill to enable the Government to enlist 10,000 foreign mercenaries in the British army to be drilled in this country in order to vindicate the fortunes of England ... Ministers had had a unanimous Parliament and people, unlimited supplies and an overflowing exchequer, yet what had they accomplished?

This is no time to mince words, or to seek for emasculated para-phrase in place of honest English [the *Press* declared, taking up the cry of condemnation]. The nation knows that the army has been abominably treated, and that its condition at this moment is one of peril and suffering. Public indignation demands that every exertion be instantly made for the succour and solace of the troops ... There is nothing which the nation will refuse to the Administration – except confidence.[33]

BALLS AND BANQUETS

'This has been the gayest season
since 1851.'

'MAY DAY 1855 – BUT WHAT A MAY DAY!' Disraeli wrote to Mrs Brydges Willyams from Grosvenor Gate. 'No maidens, no flowers, no songs, and no sun! The sky is like an Indian-ink drawing, and the north-east blast withers everything. I hope you have escaped, tho' instead of being on the heights of Braddon, you ought to be on the warm borders of your bay. Everyone here is suffering, and everyone is gloomy in body or in mind.' The war in the Crimea dragged on its weary way.

The one more cheerful event that spring, in Disraeli's opinion, was the visit to England of the Emperor Napoleon III who had with difficulty been dissuaded from going out to the Crimea to take command of his army which was, with Piedmont, Britain's ally. The visit was, so Disraeli said, 'brilliant, exciting, successful, & never flagged'.[1]

It had not seemed likely to be so when the imperial flotilla approached the English shore in thick fog, reducing visibility at Dover to less than a hundred yards. The Queen, for whom 'these great meetings of sovereigns were always very agitating', was not looking forward to the visit; nor was the former British Ambassador, Lord Cowley, who, since he was still living in Paris, had been required by her Majesty to sail with the Emperor and who was worried that he in his smart uniform and 'the ladies in their smart toilettes' would all be seasick. Nor was the Foreign Secretary, Lord Clarendon, who had said that 'nothing could look worse, both from a military and diplomatic point of view, than the state of affairs at present'.

Clarendon need not have worried: from the moment when the Emperor walked down the pier with his beautiful, apprehensive wife, the Empress Eugénie, to be greeted with loud applause, the visit was a notable success.

The Emperor was welcomed at the State Entrance of Windsor Castle by the Queen for whom, 'against all expectations', the visit 'seemed like a wonderful dream'. She found Napoleon a 'very *extraordinary* man' with a 'great *power of fascination*', while his wife was 'so demure, so graceful, so elegant'.[2]

A grand dinner in the Castle was followed by a ball in the Waterloo Chamber, tactfully known that evening as the Picture Gallery. And how it excited the Queen to think that she, 'the granddaughter of George III, should dance with the Emperor Napoleon, nephew of our great enemy, now my dearest and most intimate ally!' Making one of his rather heavy jokes, Prince Albert had said that he would have to see that the necessary precautions were taken in the crypt of St George's Chapel in case, upon the arrival of a Bonaparte as guest at Windsor, George III should turn in his grave.[3]

Over the next few days there were concerts and operas, and military reviews, drives in the sunshine through the London streets to cheers for the Queen and cockney shouts of '*Vive le Hemperor!*' And there were several receptions, at one of which Disraeli was presented to the Emperor, who 'shook hands with me cordially,' so he told Mrs Brydges Willyams, 'and spoke some gracious words. Our Queen was on his right, the Empress next to her – Prince Albert on the left of the Emperor, the Duchess of Kent and Duchess of Cambridge, and Princess Mary – so one had to make seven reverences.'

> Altho', years ago, I had seen the Emperor, & not unfrequently, I was very much struck by the smallness of his stature. He did not seem taller than our Queen. I understood he enjoyed his visit very much, & greatly captivated Her Majesty, once so much prejudiced against him. There was immense embracing at the departure, and many tears. When the carriage door was at length closed, & all seemed over, the Emperor re-opened it himself, jumped out, pressed Victoria to his heart, & kissed her, on each cheek, with streaming eyes. What do you think of that?
>
> I was greatly disappointed with the Empress. For me she had not a charm. She has Chinese eyes, & a perpetual smile or simper

which I detest. I understand she is very natural – too natural for a sovereign, and that Napoleon looks sometimes as if he would be pleased with more reserve and dignity. She was always playing with the royal children, who doted on her, and was sometimes found sitting on the edge of a table! What do you think of that? The courtiers were horrified ... [Disraeli later changed his mind about the Empress who he decided was, after all, 'very agreeable and sparkled almost as much as her necklace of colossal emeralds and diamonds'.]

Ld. John [Russell] has come back [from an abortive Congress summoned in Vienna in the vain hope of securing peace]. He made his appearance in the House of C. last night. Everything looks very bad but I do not entirely despair of peace. I understand the siege [of Sebastopol] is certain to be raised, but what are the new plans of campaign I know not, Scarcely promising, I should think, or Napoleon would not have given up his expedition to the Crimea, on which he was quite bent. This makes me believe in peace, as nothing but that would justify his relinquishment of his announced project.[4]

Four months later the country was still at war; and Disraeli could see 'little prospect of anything happening'. He told Mrs Brydges Willyams that Lady Londonderry was 'in despair about her son who [was] now in the trenches'. And these trenches were so near the enemy that forty men a day were lost in them.[5]

Six days after this letter was written, Sebastopol fell, but Russia displayed no inclination to sue for peace. Nor did the Prime Minister, Lord Palmerston; nor did Edward Bulwer (now Bulwer-Lytton, having succeeded to the Knebworth estate); nor did most of the Tories of the Carlton Club; nor did the English public generally until Russia was thoroughly beaten; while Lord Derby declared in a letter to Disraeli, 'We cannot with honour, or even with regard to party interests, constitute ourselves a peace Opposition merely because we have a war Ministry.' Disraeli, however, pressed for an early and complete cessation of hostilities.

So did the *Press*, expressing his own views: 'We can now say that every object for which the war was originally undertaken has been conceded by negotiation or won by arms. England and France have no longer an object in maintaining the war.'[6]

The French Emperor agreed. 'He is wearied with the war,' Disraeli told Mrs Brydges Willyams, 'and is pressing our Government to accede to terms of peace which he considers satisfactory. But Lord Palmerston will not listen to these overtures and the consequences may be critical. If Lord Palmerston succeeds, the war may last as long as the Peloponnesian, or the Thirty Years of Germany.'

In the end Palmerston was obliged to give way; and on 19 January 1856 the *Week* announced: 'Lord Aberdeen's Peace Government, against its will, drifted into war, and Lord Palmerston's War Government, equally against its will, has drifted into peace ... We forced Lord Aberdeen to engage in a war necessary to the honour of England and to the security of Europe; we have forced Lord Palmerston to agree to peace now that the objects of the war are accomplished.'

The Treaty of Paris, guaranteeing the neutrality of the Black Sea, was signed on 30 March 1856; and soon afterwards, in a letter to Mrs Brydges Willyams, Disraeli described London as having gone 'quite mad – fêtes and festivities night and morn. Never were there so many balls and banquets. No roof so hospitable this year as the Palace itself. Two young Princes reconnoitring Princesses will account for this. The Prince of Prussia [the Crown Prince Frederick], fiancé to our Princess Royal, is well informed, and appears able – but more like a German student than a Prince.'

> Prince Oscar of Sweden, tho' he is a Scandinavian Prince with a Scandinavian name, is a veritable grandson of Bernadotte [the former French marshal, who became King Charles XIV, King of Sweden and Norway], dark with glowing cheeks and sparkling eyes – a veritable Gascon ... He came over to make his bow to the Princess Mary of Cambridge [the Duke of Connaught's daughter, granddaughter of George III, who was eventually to marry the Duke of Teck and became the mother of George V's consort, Queen Mary], but appears to be less absorbed in [Princess Mary's] society than is desirable; and it is thought he will quit us without making the most important speech which a man can in this world ...
>
> We were at a ball some weeks ago [in the new ballroom at Buckingham Palace] with more than 1,500 guests; but the other night Her Majesty did us the honour of inviting us to a full-dress concert, held in the same ball-room, where there is a permanent organ. There were only 500 invited, & all in costume. It seemed to me that I had never seen before in England anything which realised my idea of a splendid Court.

The orchestra was very strong; there were 125 performers – among them Johanna Wagner [adopted daughter of Richard Wagner's elder brother]. All the music was German, & the second act, entirely consisting of the Walpurgis Night of Mendelssohn. Goethe's poetry wedded to such wild harmonies – made a whole of supernatural splendour.

I enjoyed myself very much, being fond of German music, but at the same time I can't help fancying that one cause of my satisfaction was that I had a seat. In the concert room the space was so limited that gentlemen were never seated. This was very wearisome.[7]

'This has been the gayest season since 1851 [that of the Great Exhibition], so Mr Gunter [of Gunter's Tea shop, Berkeley Square] assures me,' Disraeli wrote in a letter dated 31 July 1856. 'As for politics, it is abused by the million as an uneventful session.'[8]

A few days later, suffering again from that kind of 'nervous debility' which so often oppressed him at the end of a session, Disraeli took his wife to Spa in Belgium, telling no one where they were going.

I have experienced the greatest benefit from the waters & mineral baths [he told Mrs Brydges Willyams]. I have never had recourse to such remedies ... I feel entirely renovated. Nevertheless I am about to direct my steps homeward, *via* Amsterdam which I have never seen.

Spa is extremely pretty ... a picturesque village of hotels, walks of linden trees ... dwarf oak & spruce and silver firs ... ponies and carriages of all forms, cantering & coursing about from spring to spring, & making the tour of silver fountains shrouded in sunny woods. The ghost of the eighteenth century seems to haunt its favourite watering-place, where Sovereigns and Ministers of State settled once the affairs of Europe as they walked before breakfast to drink a sparkling glass of the renovating element or hazarded some *louis d'ors* at the Redouté, still open, & much frequented.

Spa was nearly dead, having been eclipsed by its modern rivals, the German bathing places, when a railroad of late years revealed it to the 19th century. But tho' there are four or five thousand visitors here, & an unceasing round of balls, concerts, colossal riding parties, & rural festivals, you may live, as we do, in profound solitude ...[9]

Returning to England in the middle of September, the Disraelis made their annual visit to see Mrs Brydges Willyams at Torquay, then spent several months at Hughenden, 'planting and pruning and almost in perfect solitude'.

> Lord and Lady Villiers [later sixth Earl and Countess of Jersey] came here and Lady Rothschild, the only persons we have seen; and we have refused all invitations. I have myself been much engaged with the new Rural Police, which is to be established forthwith in this county. The magistrates at Quarter Sessions appointed a Committee for this purpose who chose me as chairman, and I have been as busy this autumn as if I were in the House of Commons. As I have no railroad to Aylesbury, I am obliged very frequently to travel by road between 30 and 40 miles a day, which in the decline of the year is not agreeable; but I have always risen not later than seven o'clock.
>
> All this, however, is now going to change, for in a very few days we shall proceed to Grosvenor Gate *en route* to Paris. I am now sorry to depart; the weather is so beautiful, the evergreens so bright, and planting so interesting and creative; but go I must. Affairs are very perplexed, and, as I told you at Torquay in confidence, there is someone [the Emperor Napoleon III] who wants to see me, and whom I have promised to pay my respects to.

As with King Louis Philippe, Disraeli was anxious to discuss with Napoleon III the unsatisfactory relations between England and France and to bring to his notice statesmen and politicians, other than Palmerston, who were anxious to improve these relations.

> I am supposed to be, and perhaps am, in higher favour [Disraeli wrote from Paris on 26 December 1856 to Lord Henry Lennox]. Banquets from Fould [Achille Fould, Minister of State] and Walewski [still Minister of Foreign Affairs] etc., etc. – all the diplomats on their knees; all secrets told from all sides: and Cowley confidential: but nothing from the all-commanding mind [of the Emperor] definite: it is still brooding in its unfathomable recesses.[10]

At a banquet at the Palais Royale Disraeli met Alexandre Dumas *fils* ('a very handsome man' but getting rather fat), Alfred de Vigny (also fat as well as grey-bearded), and Emile de Girardin (the journalist), a 'hideous guignol' with 'large green goggle-eyed spectacles'. Disraeli himself did not create so favourable an impression on the Emperor as he had hoped and supposed.

On New Year's Day, still in Paris, Disraeli wrote to Mrs Brydges Willyams:

> I wish you a happy New Year, from the Imperial City. It is the first letter that I have written this year, and I will accept it as a good omen that it is addressed to Mount Braddon.
>
> Ten years ago, as long as the siege of Troy, since I found myself last in this place. Everything squalid has been pulled down, or driven out of sight – a city of palaces and glittering streets, and illimitable parks and pleasure-gardens, statues and gondolas, and beautiful birds and deer.
>
> Paris is a beautiful woman, and London an ugly man: still, the masculine quality counts for something.
>
> Our reception here has not turned our heads, but has tried the strength of our constitutions; once we dined out eleven days running. The Ministers here live in palaces, with appointments and service, quite as gorgeous and stately as our own Court – very different from the position of English Ministers. Nevertheless, I don't think English gentlemen would ever feel easy under roofs which were not their own, however splendid. They would think they were too much like the Lord Mayor.
>
> Our most interesting dinner was, however, certainly at the Tuileries, for my wife sat by the Emperor, and I sat by the side of the beautiful Empress.[11]

Disraeli's political discussions with Napoleon III were disappointing. He failed in his endeavours to undermine the trust which was reposed in Palmerston by the Emperor, who dismissed the Conservatives with the remark, 'Lord Derby has no men.'[12] Disraeli still failed to impress the Emperor with his own qualities. Napoleon told Lord Malmesbury later, '[Disraeli] has not the head of a statesman'. Like all literary men, so he had found them, from Chateaubriand to Guizot, they were ignorant of the world, talking well enough 'but nervous when the moment of action arises'.[13]

The Emperor's low opinion of Lord Derby as the leader of a political party was understandable. Lord Henry Lennox went so far as to say that, 'as a leader of a party', Lord Derby was 'more hopeless than ever, devoted to Whist, Billiards, Racing, Betting, making a fool of himself with either Ladies Emily Peel or Mary Yorke . . . Bulwer Lytton came to

Bretby [Bretby Hall, Derbyshire] for three days and was in despair! Not one word could he extract from Derby about public affairs; nothing but the odds and tricks.' Disraeli was inclined to agree with Lennox that Derby 'really does not desire office, his health having of late become equal to its fatigue'.

If Lord Derby was considered inadequate as leader of the Conservative party in the House of Lords, Disraeli's unpopularity was considered a severe handicap to the Conservatives in the House of Commons. Robert Gascoyne-Cecil, later to become Prime Minister as the Marquess of Salisbury, expressed the opinion that Disraeli was an adventurer, a 'mere political gangster . . . without principles and honesty'. In a letter suggesting that Derby gave the impression of being 'tired of politics and no longer ambitious for office', Lord Malmesbury added that the unpopularity of Disraeli was 'distracting the party'.[14] Derby agreed with him. 'As to Disraeli's unpopularity, I see it and regret it,' Derby replied to Malmesbury. 'I especially regret that he does not see more of the party in private; but they could not do without him, even if there were anyone ready and able to take his place. For myself, I *never* was *ambitious* for office, and am not likely to become more so as I get older.'[15]

Despite his perceived unpopularity in his party, Disraeli was returned unopposed in the general election of 1857.

> The Conservative Party have got thro' the ordeal very well [he told Mrs Brydges Willyams]. Tho' numerically a little lessened, they are more compact and united . . . Now we have, I am assured by Sir William Jollife, the chief of my staff, 260 good men and true.
>
> We were nearly paying you a visit, but must postpone it for a while, to go thro' a series of country visits which are the inevitable consequence of a General Election . . . Tomorrow we go to Norman Court, Mr Thomas Baring's, for two or three days . . . and then to the north of the county to the Pauncefort Duncombes of Brickhill Manor, and then to Colonel Hanmer of Stockgrove Park [Great Brickhill] . . . then to the Chesters of Chicheley [Hall] and to the Lovetts of Liscombe and the Dayrells of Lillingstone Dayrell and a great many more, all of whom, by their ancestors, came in with the Conqueror, tho' Colonel Hanmer had an ancestor much more interesting, for he married a Miss Ximenes, a descendant of Cardinal X, and yet a daughter of Israel notwithstanding, so I think he must have been quite gratified proposing me as member for Bucks.[16]

26

VISITS AND VISITORS

'Nothing more striking than some
of your English gentry.'

IN A LETTER DATED 29 APRIL 1857, Disraeli told Lady Londonderry
that she would not be amused by the visits he and his wife had been
paying to some of these 'principal supporters in the north of this county'.

> They were people you never heard of before, yet living with a
> refinement and splendour quite remarkable. Nothing more strik-
> ing than some of your English gentry with châteaux, parks, and
> broad domains; greater men by a good deal than many German
> Princes, and yet utterly unknown in London society; among these
> one of our greatest Bucks squires, a Mr Pauncefort Duncombe,
> whose home was really radiant, and contrasted very much with
> Woburn Abbey, which he took me over to see, larger, but the
> most gloomy and squalid place that you can conceive.
>   One day we went out to see Mentmore, which one of the
> Rothschilds is building, or rather has built, in the midst of the
> Vale of Aylesbury, a hunting palace, which will be, to this county,
> what Belvoir is to the vale of that name. But all that even *you*
> can recall or fancy of interior taste, splendour, and magnificence
> and curiosity of art, can give you only a faint idea of the reality
> of this gorgeous palace. I have been told, for more than fifteen
> years Rothschild has had agents in every part of Europe, regardless
> of cost, collecting its contents, but the taste of their distribution
> is as remarkable as their curiosity and costliness. The hall appears
> to one the masterpiece of modern art and decoration, glowing
> with colour, lit by gorgeous Venetian lamps of golden filigree that
> once were at the head of Bucentaurs. Such chairs – Titian alone
> could paint them, such clocks of lapis lazuli, such cabinets of all

forms and colours, such marble busts of turbaned Moors, such a staircase of polished marble from this vast central saloon, for such it really is, glittering with its precious contents, and yet the most comfortable and liveable-in apartment in the world.[1]

A few days after this letter was written, sepoys of the Bengal army broke out in mutiny, shot their British officers and marched on Delhi to restore to his throne the elderly Mughal emperor.

'The Indian news is really alarming,' Disraeli told Mrs Brydges Willyams. 'It is the most serious thing of the kind that has yet happened.'[2]

Even so, life in London continued as though nothing untoward had occurred.

London is very gay: fêtes every night [Disraeli continued his letter] and the Court itself at many, for the Prince of Prussia [the Crown Prince Frederick] is here visiting his *fiancée* the Princess Royal, and young Princes and Princesses require balls . . . There is also a famous beauty here, the Comtesse Castiglione [the influential Tuscan '*divina contessa*'] who, having charmed the Emperor of the French, is now on a tour of conquest in foreign parts, and, as she is universally decried by all the grand ladies, I take it is of ravishing excellence.

The most remarkable fête of the season, and indeed of many seasons, was given by the Prussian Minister at Prussia House to the Queen and Court last Monday. We had the honour to be invited. It recalled the old days of Carlton House splendour, fanciful illuminations, and golden fish in endless fountains. There was a pavilion two hundred feet long, lined with the most splendid trees and shrubs I ever saw, araucarias and Norfolk Island pines . . .

The Queen of Holland [Queen Sophia, the accomplished consort of King William III] has been the heroine of the last fortnight – indefatigably intelligent [Disraeli continued his description of the summer season a week or two later in a letter to Lady Londonderry]. The *fête champêtre* at Orleans House [the house at Twickenham, mostly now demolished, bought by Louis Philippe's widow in 1852] has been the most considerable incident since your departure. So much royalty that our friend, Lady Jersey, seemed to be rushing about the gardens in perplexed ecstacy. The Princesses, in fantastic hats, sat under trees to receive their guests; and never was a prettier Court circle. The tables for the banquet

– a variety of round tables – were laid in a *bosquet*, surrounded with tall green trees; and, as the day was burning, the site was delicious. Everything was well done, and the whole thing successful.

The Comte de Paris and the Duc D'Aumale came to me after my Indian speech, which they heard on Monday, and dined at Bellamy's [Bellamy's Coffee House, Westminster]! What do you think of that?[3]

The horrors of the Mutiny in India continued to preoccupy both the government ministers and the public at large; but Disraeli could not 'altogether repress a suspicion that many of the details, which so enraged the sensibility of the country' were 'manufactured'. In a letter to Lady Londonderry he wrote:

The detail of all these is suspicious ... The accounts are too graphic ... Details are a feature of the Myth ... The rows of ladies standing with their babies in their arms to be massacred, the elder children clutching to their robes – who that would tell these things could have escaped? One lady says to a miscreant: 'I do not ask you to spare my life, but give some water to my child.' The child is instantly tossed in the air and caught on a bayonet! Those who invented the Skene story [the invented story of an English officer who kissed his wife goodbye then shot her to spare her from rape] might invent others. It was no rude hand that forged that tale of plaintive horror. What can there be, even in your *Copperfield*, like that?

I wish, like you, I could content myself with reading novels, or even writing them, but I have lost all zest for fiction, and have for many years.[4]

As with the Queen, who considered the shouts for a bloody revenge in India 'too horrible and really quite painful', Disraeli strongly deprecated the 'spirit of vengeance' which was being preached as though 'we were to take our enemies for our model'. He said as much in the House of Commons where he declared that 'the great body of the population of that country [India] ought to know that there is for them a future of hope. I think we ought to temper justice with mercy – justice the most severe with mercy the most indulgent.'[5]

'I protest against meeting atrocities with atrocities,' he said later at a farmers' dinner at Newport Pagnell. 'I have heard things said and seen things written of late which would make me almost suppose that the religious opinions of the people of England had undergone some sudden change, and that, instead of bowing before the name of Jesus, we were preparing to revive the worship of Moloch. I cannot believe that it is our duty to indulge in such a spirit.'

Although the news from India was still 'most grave', when he went down to Hughenden that autumn he enjoyed, as always when resting there, 'the charming scene and season'. He left the place with regret at the beginning of October, to join 'a lively party' at Ashridge Park, Hertfordshire where, in the evening, the guests 'performed charades with all the neighbours and servants assembled and admitted'. 'Nothing could be worse,' he told Lady Londonderry, 'except [Augustus] Stafford, a Member of Parliament and "master of epigram", who is capital; not a performer had the slightest dramatic talent. They all seemed to cluster round Stafford like bees, with their backs to the audience, and mumbling in a nervous whisper, occasionally a giggle.'[6]

'Our Hostess [Lady Marian Alford] who is as kind as she is agreeable, thought they were not applauded enough, and we ordered some *claqueurs*; but this finished the business. The rehearsal in the morning of a charade took three hours, and the performance could never be spun out to ten minutes! At last Mr Stafford went away in despair, and the company took refuge in a more congenial round game.'[7]

Caustic as he was about the entertainments provided there, Disraeli thought Ashridge 'a wonderful place – a castle in a forest and not thirty miles from town', built at the beginning of the century, 'a sort of Windsor restored to its present style by the same architect [Sir Jeffry Wyatville] ... No words can describe the variety and beauty and size and age of the trees at Ashridge ... ferns taller than the Life Guards, and herds of both red and fallow deer.'*[8]

Yet he had long since decided that these country house visits were, as often as not, a tiresome duty rather than a pleasure. As Mary Anne told Sir William Fraser after she and her husband had been to stay with the Duke of Rutland at Belvoir and the Marquess of Exeter at Burghley, 'Whenever we go to a country house the same thing happens: Disraeli is not only bored, and has constant ennui, but he takes on eating as a

---

* The Ashridge Estate of some 1,600 acres now belongs to the National Trust.

resource. He eats at breakfast, luncheon and dinner. The result is by the end of the third day he becomes dreadfully bilious, and we have to come away.'[9]

Disraeli was, however, as taken with Hatfield House as he had been with Ashridge. He travelled down to Hatfield towards the end of November 1857 in the same carriage as Lady Stuart de Rothesay, the mother of Lady Canning, wife of Earl Canning, the Governor-General of India.

Lady Stuart de Rothesay was 'as usual, very agreeable and chatty and told us endless tales of Calcutta, and all the adventures of this perilous crisis,' Disraeli reported to Mrs Brydges Willyams:

> One thing she said particularly amused me. She was very indignant at a statement made in Exeter Hall by Lord Shaftesbury [the social and industrial reformer], that mutilated Englishwomen were constantly arriving at Calcutta, and that he had read in a letter of Lady Canning that there were more than thirteen English ladies with their noses cut off at that moment at the Presidency. Lady Stuart said that there was not the slightest authority for this statement of Lord Shaftesbury, and that Lady Canning had never alluded to the subject in any letter.
>
> In consequence of this statement of Lord Shaftesbury, a surgeon wrote to the Ladies' Committee for the Relief of the Indian Sufferers, of which Lady Stuart de Rothesay is a member, stating that he had great experience in the formation of artificial noses, that he was ready to give all his skill, time, and devotion, to the cause, but as the machinery was rather expensive, he hoped, in accepting his services, the Committee would defray the prime cost of the springs! He then gave a tariff of prices, and offered to supply noses for English ladies by the dozen, and, I believe, even by the gross.[10]

Two months after his visit to Hatfield, Disraeli went to court again to a ball given to celebrate the engagement of the Princess Royal to the Crown Prince Frederick of Prussia. It was, he told Lady Londonderry, 'unbecomingly limited; for the new ball room was only half full, and all the other rooms were open and empty'. He quite liked it, however, for he 'got a seat'.

> There were as many Princes as at the Congress of Vienna [he continued]. The royal party did nothing but dance with each

other, and I thought, perhaps in consequence, looked bored. I saw the Princess of Prussia cram her pocket-handkerchief into her mouth to stifle a yawn. The Princess Royal, however, looked bright and gay, tho' I understand she is continually crying about leaving home; but then, they say, she is very childish and always cries . . .

One of the Princes, the Duke of Brabant [son of the King of the Belgians], a tall and otherwise good-looking young man, has so long a nose that it startles everyone who meets him, and makes the women almost scream. It is such a nose as a young Prince has in a fairy-tale, who has been banned by a malignant fairy, or as you see in the first scenes of a pantomime, or in the initial letter of a column in *Punch* . . .

A few days later we assisted at another royal party, a dinner at which we met all the illustrious exiles of France [including the duchesse d'Orléans, the comte de Paris and the Duke of Chartres, who had all sought refuge in England] . . . The circle was, however, very agreeable, the guests to meet them choice, among them, by-the-by, Cardinal Wiseman [the first Archbishop of Westminster], and the banquet not to be surpassed in splendour or *recherché* even at Windsor.[11]

In February 1858, following the fall of Palmerston's administration, Lord Derby formed his second cabinet in which Disraeli once again was appointed Chancellor of the Exchequer; and in April, in a letter to Mrs Brydges Willyams, he congratulated himself on having presented a budget which was 'said to be the most successful for a quarter of a century'.[12] This was followed by a dramatic rout of the Opposition – 'never was such a rout' – which Disraeli described in a characteristic passage:

There is nothing like that last Friday evening in the history of the House of Commons. We came down expecting to divide at 4 o'clock in the morning, and I myself, with my armour buckled on, prepared to address them, perhaps, for two hours after midnight. We were all assembled. Our benches, with their serried ranks, seemed to rival those of our proud opponents, when there arose a wail of distress, but not from us. What ensued I can only liken to that mutiny of the Bengal army with which we are all so familiar. Regiment after regiment, corps after corps, general after general, all acknowledged that they could not 'march through

Coventry' with Her Majesty's Opposition ... it was rather like a convulsion of nature than one of the ordinary transactions of human life. I can liken it only to one of those earthquakes in Calabria or Peru, of which we sometimes read. There was a rumbling murmur, a groan, a shriek, distant thunder; and nobody knew whether it came from the top or the bottom of the House.

There was a rent, a fissure in the ground. Then a village disappeared. Then a tall tower toppled down. And then the whole of the Opposition benches became one great dissolving view of anarchy![13]

In May 1858, an attempt was made to strengthen the Earl of Derby's Cabinet by making an appeal to Gladstone:

If you join Lord Derby's Cabinet, you will meet there some warm personal friends; all its members are your admirers. You may place me in neither category, but in that, I assure you, you have ever been sadly mistaken. The vacant post [of President of the Board of Control] is, at this season, the most commanding in the Commonwealth; if it were not, whatever office you filled, your shining qualities would always render you supreme, and if party necessities retain me formally in the chief post, the sincere and delicate respect which I should always offer you, and the unbounded confidence which on my part, if you choose, you could command, would prevent your feeling my position as anything but a form.

Think of all this in a kindly spirit. These are hurried lines, but they are heartfelt ...

There is [as Disraeli added with what Gladstone's biographer, Richard Shannon, described as 'exquisite ineptness'] a Power, greater than ourselves, that disposes of all this.

Gladstone's reply was not encouraging; and in the course of it, he wrote, in 'accents of guarded reprobation':

You consider that the relations between yourself and me have proved the main difficulty in the way of certain political arrangements. Will you allow me to assure you that I have never in my life taken a decision which turned upon them?

You assure me that I have ever been mistaken in failing to place you among my friends or admirers. Again I pray you to let me say that I have never known you penurious in admiration towards anyone who had the slightest claim to it, and that at no period of my life, not even during the limited one when we were in sharp political conflict, have I either felt any enmity towards you, or believed that you felt any towards me.[14]

'My life has been passed in constant combat,' Disraeli explained to Mrs Brydges Willyams that summer, when apologizing for not having written for some time. 'Morning sittings and evening sittings, with the duties of my department, Cabinet Councils, and the general conduct of affairs, engross and absorb my life from the moment I wake until the hour of rest, which is generally three hours after midnight. But I never was better. I am sorry to say I cannot aver as much of my chief and colleague. Lord Derby has a raging fit of the gout, which terribly disconcerts me.'[15]

Disraeli wrote again to Mrs Brydges Willyams the following month to apologize and to explain that that June had been a month 'of almost supernatural labour. It has, however, been successful,' he added. 'Notwithstanding all the disturbances and hostilities of the early part of the session, there has seldom been one in which a greater number of excellent measures have been passed than the present.'[16]

He was, however, still concerned by Lord Derby's indisposition which, as he said, 'very much puts me out and deranges my plans'. 'Nothing disturbs a party so much as an invalid chief,' he wrote on 11 October; 'they are always afraid he is going to die and break up the Ministry.' Derby's illness increased the amount of work he had to get through; and even at Hughenden 'business [was] very active' with 'couriers and despatch boxes [arriving] every day'. He made time, however, to ensure that his letters to Mrs Brydges Willyams were not entirely given over to politics and complaints:

> We have had a great many visitors at Hughenden of late: Lord Stanley, Sir Edward Lytton, the Rothschilds, Sir W. Jollife, Mr Baring; the greater part of them combined business with pleasure, for they settled state affairs as well as occasionally killing a bird for you . . .
> The great thing now will be the new French Ambassadress [the Duchess of Malakoff, wife of the French marshal Pélissier, commander-in-chief in the Crimea] – a Spanish lady of high degree, and very haughty, they say, scornful, and all that. We have had nothing in that style for a great many years, and I think it will be amusing. The Emperor has given her a tiara of diamonds,

and large pearls fit for the Empress; the Empress herself has given her a stomacher entirely of brilliants; the Queen of Spain a fan of diamonds and emeralds; the Duke of Malakoff himself a corbeille, according to custom, full of all sorts of dainty devices – Cashmere shawls, brilliant trinkets, lace, pocket-handkerchiefs like the petticoats of the Madonna of Loretto, and no end of fancy splendour. But what we await with the greatest interest are – her favours . . .

Today we go to Gunnersbury, Baron Rothschild's, to meet the French Ambassador and his bride, and stay there till Monday, on which morning I shall appear in Downing Street. All the Ministers will have arrived by that time – Lord Derby on Monday evening – and at 12 o'clock on Tuesday we two have our first confidential conference for three months. There will be no lack of matter to talk about.[17]

FÊTES AND FOLLIES

'With no unkindly expression on his inscrutable
old face, he shook me by the hand.'

'AN INTERESTING AND EXHAUSTING SESSION is drawing to a close,' Disraeli told Mrs Brydges Willyams on 23 July 1860. 'The hours very late, sometimes four o'clock in the morning. I have borne it very well.'

It had, he said, also been 'a very gay and brilliant social season – at least', he added, 'Mrs Disraeli tells me so, for I never go anywhere except Wednesdays off and Saturdays.' He went on, nevertheless, to describe various fêtes and other entertainments which he had attended.

The first was at the Russian Ambassador's, at Chesham House, 'and was really like a festival in a play, or a masquerade. There were a dozen servants in scarlet liveries, who never left the entrance hall, only bowing to those who arrived, and ushering you to one of the finest and most fantastical staircases in London, reaching to the roof of the house, and full of painted and gilded galleries. All the attendants, who swarmed, were in Court dresses and wore swords.'[1]

> The other entertainment which amused me was a ball given by the Duchess of Wellington at Apsley House. I had never been there since the death of the famous old Duke [on 14 September 1852]. This magnificent mansion has been entirely redecorated, and with consummate taste and splendour. The gallery, where he used to give his Waterloo banquets, is now hung with ruby silk and covered with rare pictures, the spoils of Spain and Portugal, and is one of the most effective rooms in this city. The banqueting room [the Waterloo Chamber], hung with full-length portraits

of the sovereigns and notabilities at the Congress of Vienna, most interesting at this moment, when the pact has really become history, and the famous settlement of 1815 is disturbed, and perhaps about to be superseded.

I closed my season last night by making my bow to the wife of my rival, Lady Palmerston, whose crowded saloons at Cambridge House were fuller even than usual, for she had invited all the deputies of the Statistical Congress, a body of men who, for their hideousness, the ladies declare were never equalled: I confess myself to a strange gathering of men with bald heads, and all wearing spectacles. You associate these traits often with learning and profundity, but when one sees 100 bald heads and 100 pairs of spectacles the illusion, or the effect, is impaired.[2]

Not long after this ball at Apsley House, Disraeli was in Northumberland staying at Alnwick Castle, after Windsor the largest inhabited castle in England, which has been in the possession of the Percys, Earls and Dukes of Northumberland, since 1309.

'Three hundred men for the last seven years, have been at work daily at this wondrous place, and they are to work for three years more,' he told Mrs Brydges Willyams. 'The result, that the ancient Castle of Hotspur is externally restored in perfect style; while the interior has all the refinements, fancy and magnificence of an Italian palace in the palmiest days of Italian art . . . The Duke has formed a school of carvers in wood, where there are about thirty men, chiefly youths, working like Gibbons or Cellini.'[3]

Disraeli went from Alnwick to Seaham Hall, the Londonderrys' house in County Durham where they had another property, Wynyard Park, Billingham-on-Tees, which Disraeli described as a 'palace' in a 'vast park with forest rides and antlered deer, and all the splendid accessories of feudal life. But the chatelaine [his old friend Frances Anne Emily, Lady Londonderry], a remarkable woman – the daughter and heiress of Sir Henry Vane Tempest – preferred living at Seaham Hall on the shores of the German Ocean, surrounded by her collieries, and her blast-furnaces, and her railroads, and unceasing telegraphs, with a port hewn out of the solid rock, screw steamers and four thousand pitmen under her control':

One day she dined the whole 4,000 in one of the factories. In the town of Seaham Harbour, a mile off, she has a regular office, a fine stone building with her name and arms in front, and her flag flying above; and here she transacts, with innumerable agents, immense business – I remember her five-and-twenty years ago, a mere fine lady; nay, the finest in London! But one must find excitement, if one has brains.[4]

Much as he usually enjoyed such occasions as the reception given to Giuseppe Garibaldi, the great military leader in the campaign for Italian unification, who came to London in April 1864, Disraeli declined all invitations to meet him, unwilling to see a man who threatened the authority of the Pope in Rome and who had fought to unify Italy by such 'piratical' means.

Disraeli was almost alone in his disapproval. Garibaldi dined with Palmerston, with Lord John Russell, by now the first Earl Russell, and with the Gladstones. He was welcomed by Lord Derby; exchanged walking sticks with the Foreign Secretary at Pembroke Lodge; at Cliveden he planted a tree for the Duchess of Sutherland; he was given banquets in Fishmongers' Hall and at the Reform Club; he was made an honorary freeman of the City of London; he was taken to Woolwich Arsenal, to the Britannia works at Bedford to see the new steam plough, to Barclay and Perkins's brewery at Southwark, to the Crystal Palace, to the royal farms at Windsor and to Eton College where masters and boys alike shouted 'after him as if he had just won them the match against Harrow'. Everywhere that he went crowds gathered to cheer him. He was 'the darling of the lower classes' as well as of the nobility. The courtyard of Stafford House was thronged with people hoping to catch a glimpse of him; and the Duke's servants found a ready market for bottles of soapsuds from his washbasin.

The Queen was 'half ashamed of being the head of a nation capable of such follies' and deeply regretted that honours, usually reserved for royalty, should be lavished upon one who 'openly declares his objects are to lead the attack upon Venice, Rome and Russia, with the sovereigns of which countries the government in her name professes sentiments of complete friendship and alliance'. Disraeli was in sympathy with this view. While not altogether agreeing with Karl Marx, who declared the whole excitement to be 'a miserable spectacle of imbecility', he did mock the enthusiastic welcome extended to the bearded revolutionary, going so far and so repeatedly in his derision that Lord Stanley, who had found his comments 'amusing at first', complained that his 'cynical affectation' was 'apt to grow tedious'.[5]

It was not long since that, to the Queen's overwhelming distress, her beloved husband had died of typhoid at Windsor on 14 December 1861; and Disraeli had spoken in the House of Prince Albert's 'sublime life' and of the need for a monument to commemorate it. So that the Queen should know exactly what he had said in this speech, he wrote out a copy of it which he sent to Windsor. She responded by sending him an edition of the Prince's speeches inscribed to 'the Right Honourable Benjamin Disraeli in recollection of the greatest and best of men from the beloved Prince's broken-hearted widow'.

'I think that you will agree with me,' Disraeli wrote proudly to Mrs Brydges Willyams, 'that this is the most remarkable inscription which a Sovereign ever placed in a volume graciously presented to a subject!'[6]

In a covering letter the Queen had gone on to say that she could not 'resist from expressing, personally, to Mr Disraeli her deep gratification at the tribute he had paid to her adored, beloved and great husband. The perusal of it made her shed tears, but it was very soothing to her broken heart to see such true appreciation of that spotless and unequalled character.'[7]

Disraeli responded in equal hyperbole, maintaining that his acquaintance with the Prince was 'one of the most satisfactory incidents in his life, full of refined and beautiful memories'. The Prince was 'the only person he had ever known who realized the Ideal', combining 'an union of the manly grace and sublime simplicity of chivalry with the intellectual splendour of the Attic Academe'.

It was in such terms that he spoke and wrote of Prince Albert to the Queen whenever he had occasion to refer to him thereafter, well aware that, however extravagant his words, the Queen would accept them and be grateful to him for having expressed an acknowledged truth.

18 June 1865 was the fiftieth anniversary of the defeat of Napoleon at Waterloo; and, to commemorate the event, it was planned that an

immense block of granite should be transported to the Duke of Wellington's country house, Stratfield Saye between Reading and Basingstoke, and there set up to serve as a base for a statue of the Duke by Baron Carlo Marochetti, the Italian sculptor, who had cast the four bronze lions at the foot of the Nelson column in Trafalgar Square.

There were, however, insuperable difficulties in transporting the granite block to its proposed site and the distinguished people, including *The Times*'s correspondent, William Howard Russell, waited in vain for its arrival. Disraeli, who had been asked to make a short speech on the occasion, was among them, accompanied by his friend, Lady Dorothy Nevill, who lived near the Disraelis in Upper Grosvenor Street.

> It would have made you laugh to see the Duke [Arthur Richard Wellesley, the fifty-eight-year-old second Duke of Wellington, so Lady Dorothy reported to Lady Airlie] – Dizzy – Ld Stanhope, etc., dancing a new dance, which consists in running in a ring, jumping and singing – 'What have you for supper, Mrs Bond? – Ducks in the garden, geese in the pond, etc. etc.[8]

Lady Dorothy also wrote about these jollifications to Lord Ellenborough, who replied to say that he was entertained to hear that the 'chief guest, the Pillar', had not arrived. He had, he said, always doubted 'their being able to get it there; and I think, when the Duke asked you all for this season, he must have speculated on a frost or on snow on which it might travel on a sledge.' 'The dancing of this new dance', which Lady Dorothy described in her letter, must have had its 'origins in the festivals of Pan and Bacchus,' so Lord Ellenborough presumed; 'but the Roman precedent was evidently not fully followed, for the Saltatori [pantomimic dancers] were naked. Perhaps D[israeli] in his excitement proposed this to Lord Stanhope, who would have entered into a long disquisition [upon] the Lupercalia [the ancient Roman festival of fertility].'[9]

> Dizzy was in great force after dinner [William Howard Russell reported]. Talked of Tycho Brahe [the Danish astronomer], Copernicus, Kepler, Galileo, the Ptolomaic system, to our wonder till [William] Calcraft suggested he was lecturing and John Hay [the strongly republican anti-Tory Secretary of the American legation in Paris] shrewdly hit on the real fact that he was only repeating part of the speech that he would have made had he

been elected Rector of the University of Edinburgh [an office for which he had been defeated by Thomas Carlyle, who had won 657 votes to Disraeli's 310].[10]

Disraeli's companion on his visit to Stratfield Saye, Lady Dorothy Nevill, was the thirty-eight-year-old mother of three children, an attractive, unconventional woman who smoked cigars, drank whisky, and was a well-informed botanist and gardener. She was the daughter of the Earl of Orford – a member of the family to which Horace Walpole belonged – and the wife of Reginald Nevill, grandson of the Earl of Abergavenny, a man almost ten years older than herself. Her brothers, Horatio and Frederick, were both friends and colleagues of Disraeli, who referred to Horatio, as he also referred to the due d'Aumale and others, as his best friend.

'You are dear Walpole's sister,' Disraeli said when introducing himself to Dorothy Nevill; 'and I must know you.' There were numerous other men who wanted to know her, including George Sydney Smythe, who told Disraeli that he did not care about 'family' in the least and that he would 'rather marry into a rich, vulgar family. Madness no objection.'

It was rumoured that among the several young women who had succumbed to Smythe's raffish charm was Lady Dorothy, and that the doctor who was said to be treating her for injuries sustained upon falling downstairs had, in fact, been called in for a less innocent purpose.

After her marriage to Reginald Nevill, Lady Dorothy spent much of her time in London in their house in Upper Grosvenor Street while her husband chose to remain on his estate in Hampshire, enjoying his country pursuits. In London, Lady Dorothy saw much of her friend, Mr Disraeli, to whom she referred in her letters as 'Lion', she herself being 'Mouse'.

It was further rumoured that, while her husband was in Hampshire and Mrs Disraeli at Hughenden, Disraeli and Lady Dorothy became occasional lovers and that her third surviving son, Ralph, born nine months before the fiasco at Stratfield Saye, was Disraeli's son. In later life, Ralph Nevill well remembered as a child being shown to Mr Disraeli and told to say how-do-you-do to him. 'Dressed in a shabby old paletot he [looked] at me as if I were some strange little animal, but, with no unkindly expression on his inscrutable old face, he shook me by the hand.'*[11]

---

* Disraeli may possibly have had another child, a girl who grew up to be 'strikingly' like him, by a woman whose identity is unknown. This child, whose name is given as Catherine Donovan on her birth certificate, grew up to confide in a few members of her family that her mother was French and Jewish. She was 'petite and fine-boned with wavy black hair not as ringleted as Disraeli's, yet her great pride. Like Disraeli, she kept it dyed a deep black nearly all her days. Her handwriting was well schooled and elegant . . . She claimed, as a child, to have met various persons of importance, including the Prince of Wales, who allegedly called her "my little Katey". Her favourite was Baroness Burdett-Coutts [of whom] she spoke with the greatest affection. [She also] spoke of the Rothschilds with great esteem and an air of intimacy' (Stanley Weintraub, *Disraeli: A Biography* (1993), 419–36).

28

DISTINGUISHED PERSONS
AND PRIVATE SECRETARIES

'A ceaseless flow of . . .
contemporary anecdote'

DISRAELI CONSIDERED HIS VISITS to such places as Alnwick, Knowsley, Hatfield, Seaham and Wynyard to be an essential part of the duties imposed upon him by his position. In them he was brought into contact, as he put it himself, with 'all the most distinguished persons in the country, especially of [his] own party'. 'I meet and converse with them . . . every day at dinner and in the evening which is very advantageous and suggestive,' he told Mrs Brydges Willyams. 'It allows me to feel the pulse of the ablest on all the questions of the day.'

He especially enjoyed staying at Hatfield since Lord and Lady Salisbury were 'real friends' and did not disturb him in the mornings, never expecting him to go down to breakfast and allowing him to work undisturbed in his room before joining the other guests.

He entertained a number of influential people in his own houses, too, giving a series of dinners to his 'parliamentary friends of both Houses'. 'The members of the House of Commons like very much to meet members of the House of Lords, who have themselves in their time, sat in the House of Commons.' 'It is', he explained, 'like old schoolfellows meeting; the memories of the past are interesting, and from old experience they understand all the fun of the present. The Duke of Buckingham, the Earl of Shrewsbury, and the Marquis of Normanby, who were all of them a long time in the House of Commons,

248

dine with me on Wednesday, and meet a number of the Lower House.'

He did not, however, much enjoy such gatherings at gentlemen's clubs such as Grillion's, to which his delayed election brought him little pleasure, as did his election to 'the Club', the parliamentary dining club.

'I have not dined with these gentry [the members of Grillion's] for three years,' he was to write to his friend, Lord Cairns, in December 1868, when, in fact, he had dined with them on three occasions. 'But my recollection of them is extreme dullness; no genuine and general conversation, but a dozen prigs and bores (generally) whispering to their next-door neighbours over a bad dinner in a dingy room. Not a single thing ever said at Grillion's remains in my memory.' 'I hate men parties,' he had once told his sister, 'except for eating.'

Disraeli far preferred his visits to country houses – where the company of ladies could be enjoyed – to the tedious dinners at gentlemen's clubs; and in the summer of 1865, he was a guest at Lowther Hall in Westmorland, Ashridge Castle [Park] in Hertfordshire, Woburn in Bedfordshire and Raby Castle in County Durham.

Lowther Hall he described as 'a splendid domain; parks and deer, mountains and lakes'. The house was 'convenient and handsome in the interior, but the exterior deplorable, as might be expected from the Gothic of 1800 and Sir Smirke' (*sic.*, Sir Robert Smirke, who built the castellated edifice for the first Earl of Lonsdale in 1806–11). His fellow-guests, mostly 'silent', were evidently not considered worthy of remark.

> Then we returned to the south to Ashridge Castle [Ashridge Park], Lord Brownlow's, also a modern erection by [James] Wyatt [for the 7th Earl of Bridgwater, 1808–13] but gorgeous, and in a vast park of wonderfully sylvan beauty.
>
> Lord Brownlow [the second Earl], a good deal beyond six feet high, slender, rather bent, with one lung already lost, and obliged to pass the winter at Madeira; intellectual, highly educated, with a complete sense of duty, and of a soft and amiable disposition; living, as it were, on sufferance, but struggling to perform his great part. A devoted mother [Lady Marian Alford, daughter of the second Marquess of Northampton] watches every glance and every wind; shares his annual exile, where she actually has not a single companion ...
>
> Lady Marian a woman of commanding ability. Above the common height, a fine figure, but a countenance of animation

and intelligence marred by a red and rough complexion. She always reminded me of Lady Blessington in face, when Lady B's beauty had departed; the eyes were the same – extremely speaking . . .

From Ashridge we went to Woburn Abbey [Disraeli continued his account], and paid a visit of several days to Hastings Russell [afterwards the 9th Duke of Bedford and his wife, Lady Elizabeth, sister of Lady Salisbury]. The present [8th] Duke of Bedford lives in perfect solitude, and fancies himself unable to encounter the world . . . He detests the country and country life, especially the provincial magnificence of grand seigneurs. 'Let me live always among chimney-pots,' he says . . . He must be now nearer sixty than fifty; nor is it probable, he will ever marry . . .*

Hastings is his cousin; a young man, at least he looks young, though he has been married twenty years; good-looking, graceful, though hardly the middle size, very intelligent, well-informed and well-meaning. The Duke gave him Oakley and £6,000 a year, and expressed his wish, also, that he would receive every year his friends at Woburn, which is kept up exactly as if His Grace resided there.

Woburn is fine from its greatness and completeness, everything that the chief seat of a princely English family requires. The house, though not beautiful in its exterior, is vast; the great quadrangle, when lit up at night, with its numerous and flashing windows, reminded Bright, he said when on a visit there, of a factory . . . A mass of choice and rare collections of all kinds which have been accumulating for centuries: splendid books, rare MSS.; some fine; many interesting pictures. A park of 3,000 acres . . . And all this only forty miles from town!

The Salisburys, our dear friends, were there, and Comte Pahlen, who gives the results of a life experienced in society with taste and terseness, and Odo Russell [later the first Lord Amptill] just arrived from Rome (where he is our Minister), *via* Paris. He brought the new toy, Pharaoh's serpent. Quite a miracle! A most agreeable party, which it could not fail to be with such guests and such a host and hostess, for Lady Elizabeth is quite worthy of her husband. The predominant feature and organic deficiency

---

* 'He has two mistresses,' Disraeli noted in a passage not printed in Monypenny and Buckle, 'one is his nurse; the other he visits daily and dines with her. She is not faithful to him; that's not wonderful, perhaps not necessary' (Hughenden Papers, Box 26, A/X/75, quoted in Robert Blake, 411).

of the Russell family is shyness. Even Hastings is not free from it though he struggles to cover it with an air of uneasy gaiety.[1]

Before his visit to Woburn, Disraeli and his wife had been to Raby Castle, County Durham, a 'real castle and vast', 'the general effect feudal and Plantagenet', its entrance hall so large that carriages drove into it to deposit visitors inside its imposing walls. Its chatelaine was the Duchess of Cleveland, described by Disraeli as 'a brilliant woman, sister of Lord Stanhope. She has the quickest, and the finest, perception of humour I know, with extraordinary power of expression, and the Stanhope wit; her conversation . . . a wondrous flow of drollery, information, social tattle, eloquence; such a ceaseless flow of contemporary anecdote I never heard. And yet she never repeats.' Her son, Lord Dalmeny, the future Prime Minister, Lord Rosebery, then a boy at Eton, was intrigued by his mother's guests:

> Mama came in from riding when they were all in the library [Dalmeny recorded]; so she said, 'I was sorry to be so rude as not to be here to receive you, but the fact is that I had such a bad headache that I was obliged to go and take a ride.' To which Dizzy replied with an air, 'The pleasure of seeing Your Grace in your riding habit makes up for the loss of your society' – the sort of compliment in fact that one sees in *Coningsby*.
>
> I sat next to Mrs Disraeli at dinner. May I have memory and strength to write down some of our conversation . . . 'I have many people who call themselves my friends, yet I have no friend like him. I have not been separated from him since we have been in the country except when I have been in the woods, and I cannot lose him' (here her voice trembled touchingly) . . . I think this half-crazy warm-hearted woman's talk is worth setting down, for she is an uncommon specimen. Parts are very touching . . . *September 1st*. Mrs Disraeli greeted me at breakfast with 'We have been talking about you.' 'I am indeed honoured, Mrs Disraeli.' 'Oh, but I did not say it was very good.' 'But to be talked about by you is enough honour.' I cannot help quizzing her by talking in this way, though I really like her. She praised me in her own and her husband's name very warmly this evening. *September 2nd*. After breakfast Dizzy came up and asked me how much we had shot. I said that partridges were scarce and that we intended, therefore, to kill nothing but time today. 'Then you have a certain bag.'

During the visit Disraeli took Dalmeny for a long walk in the park [according to Rosebery's biographer, Robert Rhodes James] and they discussed politics.

> In spite of all that has been written about him, the secret of Disraeli's extraordinary fascination still eludes us. But part of the admiration he evoked in young people was due to his interest in their doings, the apparent seriousness with which he considered their sayings, and his complete lack of condescension. Although most people laughed at his extravagant language and studied courtesy, they were secretly flattered, and young people in particular were very receptive to his kindly interest in their affairs. Dalmeny returned from his walk excited and impressed.[2]

Here at Raby one day that summer of 1865, while writing in his room, Disraeli was disturbed by the sound of music and laughter downstairs. He went down, opened the drawing-room door and found an embarrassed young man surrounded by the laughing girls of the house party who had insisted upon his dancing a riotous dance while singing a comic song. Disraeli stood in the doorway gazing upon the scene in that expressionless way of his which could be so unnerving.

The young man was Montagu Corry, then twenty-seven years old, the son of Henry Thomas Lowry Corry (Conservative Member for Tyrone County and First Lord of the Admiralty, a grandson of the Earl of Shaftesbury). Montagu Corry had been at Harrow and, after graduating at Cambridge, he had been called to the bar. He was extremely popular in society and was often to be seen at country house parties where his charm and wit, his handsome looks and easy manners, made him a most welcome guest. Recognizing his qualities and beguiled by his attractive personality, it was not long before Disraeli – still susceptible as always to the charm of handsome men younger than himself – asked him to become his private secretary, a position he was to occupy, as a lifelong bachelor, until his master's death.[3]

One of Montagu Corry's predecesors in this appointment was Ralph Earle, who had become Disraeli's private secretary in 1858 and a Member of Parliament the next year. An ambitious and plausible man, he 'appealed', in Sarah Bradford's words, 'to the less attractive side of Disraeli's nature, and was to exercise a malign influence over him in the following decade'. Jealous of this influence, and of Disraeli's evident fascination with Earle, Lord Henry Lennox, protesting that he was too ill to carry on, resigned from his post at the Admiralty; and when he was later offered and had accepted office with the Board of Works in Disraeli's first administration, he made it only too evident that he was deeply offended not to be in the Cabinet; and although Disraeli later attempted to rekindle their close friendship – and would have appointed the touchy Lennox Chief Civil Service Commissioner had he not been advised against it as too obviously a favour to an unsuitable candidate – his fond intimacy with Lennox was never resumed.

Nor did Ralph Earle's friendship with Disraeli survive the arrival of Montagu Corry in their lives. Jealous of Corry, Earle quarrelled with Disraeli who, in a letter to Lord Beauchamp, lamented the fact that he had ignored the warnings that had been given him about the man, ascribing these warnings to prejudice and misapprehension. Disraeli was, he admitted, 'ashamed at [his] want of discrimination'. With Montagu Corry there were to be no such misapprehensions and no such quarrels.

Corry served as Mrs Disraeli's secretary also and clearly became as fond of her as he was of her husband. Soon after his appointment, there were riots in Hyde Park close to the Disraelis' house in Grosvenor Gate, when protesters calling for parliamentary reform had been forbidden to hold a meeting there. Disraeli, who could not get away from the House of Commons, relied on Corry to see that no harm came to his wife. 'No mob outside your house now,' Corry wrote to reassure him. 'The Inspector in charge at Grosvenor Gate tells me that while the crowd was at its worst here your house was never mentioned as obnoxious – though the house of Mr Walpole [Spencer Walpole, the Home Secretary] and Lord Elcho and others have come in for some threats. The soldiers have moved away to Marble Arch, and Mrs Disraeli wishes me to add that the people in general seem to be thoroughly enjoying themselves; and I really believe she sympathises with them. At any rate I am glad to say she is not in the least alarmed – nor do I think you need be at all.'[4]

Devoted as Corry was to Disraeli, it could not be denied that, on occasions, he found him an exasperatingly fussy employer. A series of long letters, written between 2 September and 21 December 1866, is an example of this:

HUGHENDEN, Sept. 2, 1866 ... When letters come from any colleagues marked 'Private', it is unnecessary to open them, as no action can be taken on them until they are forwarded to me. Nothing, therefore, is gained by the process, which is not necessary, and which my correspondents under such circumstances, dislike.

My hand is by no means so bad as my handwriting would imply; the scrawl is the consequence of the wretched, cheap huckster's ink, supplied by that miserable department, the Stationery Office.

The ink is not so bad on my own paper, of which I enclose a specimen; but it soon gets so. I can't think it is the pen's fault. Bad stationery adds much to the labour of life; and whether it be the ink, the pens, or the paper, it seems to me, when in office, I never can write like a gentleman. It's a serious nuisance ...

Sept. 26 ... We must not make another mistake about our paper. I observe the 'Hughenden' sheet, which I sent you yesterday, is part of a lot which I did not much approve of at the time. I thought it too austere.

Now I write on some 'Grosvenor Gate' paper, which I think perfectly satisfied me in town; but whether it be the office ink or the office pens, my calligraphy has a cheese-mongerish look ... The whole subject will employ your vacant hours till I return to town, as I shall certainly lose my temper, when real business commences, if my tools are not first-rate ...

Dec. 21 ... I think the time has arrived when the Patronage Secretary of the Treasury (of all men in the world!) should at least learn the office which his master fills, and his due title. Give him at the earliest opportunity a gentle educational hint. Somebody has instructed Hunt long ago – I suppose Hamilton. The manners of D[owning] S[treet] are getting quite American. The tradition of the old etiquette must be gradually revived.

We ought to have made the F. O. Press print all their labels over again, and I think you had better order the circular one. I did insist upon it in the case of 'Earl Derby'! I dare say Colonel Taylor addresses the Lord Chancellor as Lord Chelmsford!

As though in apology for the fuss he was making he added, 'You do your business very well.'

Impatient as he could be on occasions, and, from time to time, harassed by money-lenders and debt collectors, Disraeli, for most of the time, succeeded in presenting to the world an appearance of what a colleague described as 'sublime equanimity'. This appearance, so far as money was concerned, was, by the later 1860s, beginning to reflect a more genuinely settled and relieved state of mind.

In the recent past his debts had risen to about £60,000 (in today's money some £2½ million). But since then a rich Yorkshire Conservative had offered to buy Disraeli's debts and charge a very low rate of interest; a second mortgage had been arranged on Hughenden; then Mrs Brydges Willyams had died, leaving Disraeli about £40,000 on condition that she was buried in his vault at Hughenden Church.

He was now able to allow Mary Anne to have her way with her planned alterations and redecoration at Hughenden, the creation of the formal garden and what she called 'the walks' as well as the embellishment of the terrace with large marble vases. The alterations and redecoration of the interior of the house were, however, not altogether a success: Lord Ronald Gower, for instance, in his *Reminiscences*, described the gloomy drawing-room as 'wonderfully hideous'.[5]

THE 'POTENT WIZARD'

'We come here for fame.'

AFTER HIS RETURN TO LONDON from his latest succession of country house visits, Disraeli learned that Lord Palmerston was gravely ill. The Prime Minister was now over eighty years old, and had maintained his vigour to the end. The Speaker, John Evelyn Denison, told Disraeli of a dinner at which Palmerston had recently been present and after which Denison had said to a young Member of Parliament who had been sitting on his left:

> Now you are a very young man, and if I were you, when I went home tonight, I would make a memorandum of what happened today; something in this fashion: Mem. – Dined with the Prime Minister, who was upwards of eighty years of age. He ate for dinner two plates of turtle soup; he was then served very amply to a plate of cod and oyster sauce; he then took a paté; afterwards he was helped to two very greasy-looking entrées; he then despatched a plate of roast mutton; there then appeared before him the largest, and to my mind the hardest, slice of ham that ever figured on the table of a nobleman, yet it disappeared, just in time to answer the enquiry of his butler, 'Snipe, my Lord, or pheasant?' He instantly replied 'Pheasant', thus completing his ninth dish of meat at that meal.[1]

A few days after Palmerston's death, on 18 October 1865, Mrs Disraeli wrote to Lady Cowper, Lady Palmerston's daughter-in-law: 'Mr Disraeli had a great regard for Lord Palmerston and, although circumstances prevented them from acting politically together, there had existed between them for twenty years, a mutual confidence which often removed difficulties.'

Disraeli himself declared in the House of Commons that Palmerston, who was succeeded by Earl Russell, left behind him 'not merely the memory of past achievements, but also the tender tradition of personal affection and social charm'.

Every year, usually at Greenwich, a banquet known as a Whitebait Dinner was spread before a distinguished assembly including a number of Cabinet Ministers. At the Dinner of 1866 both Disraeli and Lord Derby were in what John Delane described as 'high spirits', Disraeli, in particular, 'pouring forth a perfect avalanche of puns'. He was in better health that year and apparently contented. Charlotte de Rothschild, when he called upon her one day, found him 'brilliantly eloquent' and 'wonderfully agreeable', so much so, indeed, that she was 'quite sorry to be his only listener and when [her] father came back from Gunnersbury' she made 'the great man' repeat his anecdotes.

It was beginning by now to be widely accepted in Parliament, even by those who were prejudiced against him, that Disraeli was, indeed, a 'great man', that there was no one in his Party, as Lord Lonsdale said, who could take 'Ben Dizzy's' place.

His motives might well be questioned. John Bright, for example, the great orator and Radical Member for Birmingham, wrote in his diary that Disraeli did not seek to 'preach and act the truth' but 'to distinguish himself'. 'We come here for fame,' he once said to Bright; and, as Bright conceded, he 'did distinguish himself'.

Samuel Wilberforce, the Bishop of Oxford, was ready to make the same concession. Disraeli was 'not a bit of a Briton', but 'all over an Eastern Jew'; yet he was, undeniably, a 'marvellous man'.

Well-known marks of royal favour had played their due part in improving Disraeli's reputation in the Conservative party, which noted also his election to the Athenaeum and to a Trusteeship of the British Museum. And when, in October 1865, Palmerston's successor, Earl Russell, had brought in an ill-framed Reform Bill which was condemned by some for going too far and by others for not going far enough, Disraeli's skill in helping to bring about Russell's resignation had been widely admired.

Increasingly respected as he was in the House of Commons, Disraeli was also by now becoming more sound financially. When Mrs Brydges Willyams died in 1863, Philip Rose suggested that her bequest to Disraeli should be publicly known. 'I wish you would consider whether some paragraph might not be advantageously put in the newspapers,' he wrote. 'These things are catching and the great probability is that the example would be followed if properly made known.'[2]

Unsurprisingly, this did not prove to be the case; but by now Disraeli was less in need of such windfalls than ever before in his career. By the beginning of 1866, his income had risen to about £4,500 a year and his wife had a similar amount. In today's terms, their joint income would be worth about £360,000.

In June 1866, Derby formed his third Cabinet, in which Disraeli became Chancellor of the Exchequer yet again. It was a far stronger Cabinet than Derby had been able to assemble in the past; and Disraeli, who had played a leading part in the choice of Ministers – including Derby's son, Lord Stanley, as Foreign Secretary – was acknowledged to be its dominant member.

The most urgent problem which the new government had to face was that of Reform, the extension of the franchise to a larger and more representative section of the community. Up till now Disraeli's attitude towards Reform had been largely dictated by his determination to force the Whigs out of office. It was now largely dictated by a determination to stay in office himself.

The question of Reform could clearly no longer be shelved or ignored. Derby, who would have preferred to do nothing about it, was convinced by the strength of feeling in the country that the matter would have to be settled. And Disraeli was equally convinced that the matter would have to be seen to be settled by the Conservatives: any idea of a settlement in co-operation with other parties would be fatal. When the Queen offered to intercede with the Liberals, he quickly condemned the 'royal project of gracious interposition' as a 'mere phantom', the 'murmuring of children in a dream'. The Conservatives must take the initiative, ride on the surf to shore and land in the leading boat. As it happened, this entailed bringing in a far more wide-ranging Bill than either Derby or Disraeli would have liked; but it did 'dish the Whigs', which is how Disraeli, borrowing a phrase of Derby's, is said to have described his principal object all along.

In later years Disraeli attempted to demonstrate that he had consistently had this goal in view, that his recurrent retreats had been advances towards that goal, and that his skilful negotiation of crisis after crisis had been in accordance with a predetermined policy rather than improvised to meet the needs of the hour. In fact, he was consistent only in his determination to bring in a Bill which would leave the Government in power and the Opposition in disarray. But he achieved this with such marvellous parliamentary skill, such masterly improvisation, that the Reform Bill of 1867 established Disraeli as the hero of the party, which he had always wanted to be. *Punch* published a caricature entitled 'D'Israeli in Triumph', depicting him as the Egyptian Sphinx being pulled along in triumphant state to the Temple of Reform by a team of well-known politicians. His speech on the second reading of the Bill was generally considered to be a masterly performance. 'Its exuberance caught the House,' wrote Sir Edward Russell in *Belgravia*. 'Men who have heard Mr Disraeli throughout his career agree that never did he show such mastery over his audience, such boundless histrionic resource.' From all sides came such praise and congratulations.

'The speech of last night pleased all our friends,' wrote Lord Stanley, never a man to be given to exaggeration. 'I think it one of the best you ever made.' Stanley's father thought so, too, and said so in almost the same words: 'I hear from all quarters that it was the finest speech you ever made; and you seem to have carried the House bodily away with you. In fact you have won the game for us; and in writing to the Queen this morning to announce your "triumphant success" I told H.M. that I now, for the first time, entertain a sanguine hope of carrying a Bill through in the course of the present session.'

Disraeli's success was, of course, not greeted with universal acclaim. One day, soon after the passing of the Reform Bill, he encountered Lady Cowper, whom he had not seen for some time.

'Oh, Mr Disraeli,' she said to him, 'I haven't seen you since you ruined the country.'

'I assure you,' he replied, 'if that is so it is your own fault.'

'Why, I had nothing to do with it.'

'No; but I called several times at St James's Square to take your ladyship's advice on political affairs, and it is to my never having found you in that I attribute any defect that this may have had in the [Reform] Bill.'[3]

He was equally debonair when he sat next to Princess Louise – the Queen's fourth daughter – at a dinner party at Windsor. He found her 'very good-looking and vivacious', while she, responding to his ready charm and wit, reminded him that she had been one of the little girls who had to knock on the door when he was talking to their father to remind them that 'dinner was waiting'.

Contented as he appeared, however, Disraeli was only too well aware that, the more successful he became, the more often it was suggested that the nation, in the words of Benjamin Jowett – Master of Balliol College, Oxford and Regius Professor of Greek – was now being run by 'a wandering Jew'. To another Oxford scholar, the historian, Edward Freeman, he was a 'loathsome Jew'.[4] Henry James described him as 'the tawdry old Jew'.[5]

Lord Cranborne was not alone in calling him a 'rogue', while Gathorne Gathorne-Hardy described him as 'unscrupulous'. Thomas Carlyle observed: 'Dizzy is a charlatan and knows it', adding that Gladstone was a charlatan and did not know it.

Yet no one could deny Disraeli's brilliance, nor suppose that anyone else could become an effective leader of the Conservative Party when the ailing Lord Derby retired at last.

Disraeli returned home in the early hours of 13 April 1867, delighted by the cheers which had greeted a splendid speech and by a decisive vote that had ensured the Government's success. On his way, he called in at the Carlton Club where a member rose in the crowded dining-room to propose a toast to the man who 'rode the race' and 'did the trick!' He was loudly cheered again and pressingly invited to sit down and join the celebrations. But he declined the invitation, disliking clubs as he did and exclusively male society never having been much to his taste. Besides, he wanted to get home to his wife. He found her, as he had expected, waiting up for him. She had ordered him his favourite pie from Fortnum and Mason's and a bottle of champagne. 'Why, my dear,' he said to her with deep affection, 'you are more like a mistress than a wife.'

The older they grew the more devoted to each other they appeared to be, and the more extravagant became the display of the husband's devotion. On more than one occasion he was seen to go down on one knee before her and to kiss her hand. 'He often caresses her,' Lord

Ronald Gower wrote disapprovingly, 'even before the servants'; and once he knelt before her in the drawing-room after dinner, covered her hand with kisses and asked fondly, 'Is there anything I can do for my little wife?'

Numerous stories were told of the eccentricities of her conversation. 'You think he looks splendid now,' she said to someone who had commented upon his appearance during a debate in the House. 'Some people think he is ugly, but he's not. He is very handsome. I should like them to see him when he is asleep.' She was said to have confided in the Queen that she always slept with her arms round her husband's neck. And in the company of ladies who were discussing the handsome appearance of a nearly nude Greek god in a painting, she protested, 'Oh! You should see my Dizzy in his bath.' He had, she said, such a wonderfully white skin. And at breakfast in a country house where they were staying, a house renowned for its fine art collection, she complained to her hostess, 'Your house is full of indecent pictures! There is a most horrible picture in our bedroom. Disraeli says it is Venus and Adonis. I have been awake half the night trying to prevent him from looking at it.'[6]

In a conversation with her at a dinner at Raby Castle, Dalmeny mentioned that he was shortly going up to Oxford.

'"Oh yes, I love Oxford," she said. "They are all so fond of Mr Dizzy there. They all applaud him so."

'"I suppose Mr Disraeli took an Honorary Degree there?"

'"Yes," said she [adding, with what Robert Blake called "that engaging touch of dottiness seldom absent from her utterances"], "he was made D.T.C.L. or something of the sort."'

She then asked if he were fond of reading, and after a little talk, she said that the only novels she liked were those that improved and instructed her. '"I think *Coningsby* is that," I hinted. "Of course," she said, "written by a clever man like him" . . .

'"Do you care for politics, Mrs Disraeli?"

'"No, I have no time. I have so many books and pamphlets to read and see if his name is in any of them, and I have everything to manage, and write his stupid letters."'[7]

'Mrs Disraeli, who was a very great friend of mine, was just as talkative in society as her husband was silent,' commented Lady Dorothy Nevill. 'She was, indeed, a most vivacious woman. I remember her indignation with reference to a photographer suggesting a pose to her "dear Dizzy" (so she always called him). The man said he wanted to take him leaning on a chair, but I soon settled that, for I said, "Dizzy has always stood alone, and he shall continue to do so!" She adored her husband and used to chatter away nineteen to the dozen when with him, whilst he, silent and preoccupied, did not, I fancy, listen to a word. He took good care, however, not to let her know it.'[8]

One day, Bernal Osborne, the rudely outspoken Member of Parliament, told Disraeli that he had seen him and the elderly and oddly dressed Mrs Disraeli walking together in the Park. 'I cannot for the life of me understand what sentiments she can possibly inspire you with,' Osborne commented.

A sentiment quite foreign to your nature, Bernal,' Disraeli replied. 'Gratitude.'[9]

She became increasingly eccentric in her behaviour and odd in her appearance. Sir William Gregory, admittedly not the most unprejudiced of witnesses, went so far as to describe her as 'a most repulsive woman, flat, angular, underbred with a harsh grating voice';[10] while Constance de Rothschild wrote of her: 'she was getting old and not at all at her best, going to sleep after dinner in the drawing-room and asking all manner of random questions. [Young people were inclined to] make fun of the gallant old lady, and of her queer wig, so often awry, and her flame-coloured dresses, her vain attempts at a somewhat youthful appearance.'[11]

By the 1860s Disraeli's distressing differences and quarrels with his wife were long since in the past; and after his exertions over the Reform Bill, he would have liked to take her on holiday, perhaps abroad. But he was engaged to attend a dinner and make a speech in Edinburgh, where he was also to receive an honorary degree from the University and to attend a meeting of working men in the Music Hall. For the first few days of his visit he and his wife stayed with the Dundases of Arniston; and Mrs Dundas later told him that she overheard a man, 'a radical servant', who had gone to the meeting, say that 'he knew plenty of fellows who had gone to make a row'. 'But,' the man said, 'I came away *almost* a Tory. I was prejudiced against the Chancellor; but you know he . . . made us all think like him.'[12]

Sir John Skelton, the Scottish author who published a sympathetic sketch of Disraeli the following year, described how old Lady Ruthven and Mrs Disraeli sat 'over the fire with their feet on the fender, making between them the funniest pair – the witches in *Macbeth* or what you will'.

> And the potent wizard himself, with his olive complexion and coal-black eyes, and the mighty dome of his forehead (no Christian temple to be sure), is unlike any living creature one has met. I have never seen him in daylight before, and the daylight accentuates his strangeness. The face is more like a mask than ever, and the division between him and mere mortals more marked. I would as soon have thought of sitting down at table with Hamlet, or Lear, or the Wandering Jew. He was indeed more than cordial; especially appreciative of the Scottish allies who had stood by him through thick and thin.
>
> 'I fancied, indeed,' Disraeli said, 'until last night that north of the border I was not loved, but last night made amends for much. We were so delighted with our reception, Mrs Disraeli and I, that after we got home we actually danced a jig (or was it a hornpipe?) in our bedroom.'
>
> They say, and say truly enough, 'What an actor the man is!' and yet the ultimate impression is of absolute sincerity and unreserve. Grant Duff will have it that he is an alien. What's England to him, or he to England? That is just where they are wrong. Whig or Radical or Tory don't matter much, perhaps; but this mightier Venice – this Imperial Republic on which the sun never sets – that vision fascinates him, or I am much mistaken. England is the Israel of his imagination, and he will be the Imperial Minister before he dies – if he gets the chance.[13]

After the Disraelis' return to London from Scotland, Gladstone had referred sympathetically to Mrs Disraeli's illness in a speech in the House. He liked Mrs Disraeli, who told T.E. Kebbel, author of a life of her husband, that Gladstone would go round to Grosvenor Gate to 'show he bore no malice' after a sharp encounter in the House of Commons. Disraeli responded with tears in his eyes to Gladstone's graceful recognition that the two men's animosity did not extend to their wives and he wrote to Gladstone to say, 'My wife has always had a strong personal regard for you and, being of a vivid and original character, she could comprehend and value your great gifts and qualities.'[14]

Gladstone replied with similar feeling: 'I have always been grateful for, and have sincerely reciprocated, Mrs Disraeli's regard . . . But, even if I had not had the pleasure of knowing her, it would have been impossible not to sympathise with you at a moment when the fortitude necessary to bear the labours and trials of your station was subjected to a new burden of a character so crushing and peculiar.'[15]

In his distress and anxiety, Disraeli himself fell ill. 'When I got home on Wednesday morning in the cab into which you kindly tumbled me,' he told Lord Derby on 30 November, 'I could not get out and the driver, I fancy, thought I was drunk.' His doctor told him that his complaint was sciatica; and this, he told Montagu Corry, 'frightens me: James, my man, says his mother has the *sciatics* and they last a year at least. But, though depressed, I still have faith in my star.' It was gout, however, not sciatica; but he was confined to bed all the same; and, prevented from visiting his wife's sick-room across the bedroom corridor, he took to writing her letters and notes. She preserved them all carefully, as she preserved the strands of dyed hair she cut from his head, wrapping the papers up in a packet labelled, 'Notes from dear Dizzy during our illness when we could not leave our rooms.'

'Being on my back, pardon the pencil,' he wrote in the first of several of these notes.

> You have sent me the most amusing and charming letter I ever had. It beats Horace Walpole and Mme. de Sévigné.
>
> Grosvenor Gate has become a hospital, but a hospital with you is worth a palace with anybody else . . .
>
> I have had a sleepless night, and in agony the whole time. This morning the pain in the foot became greatly mitigated, and I dozed a little from 6 to 8. I have been nearly a week in bed, and am much worse than when I took to it . . . My only consolation is that you are better and stronger. I never felt worse or more desponding. I am so irritated at the blundering manner in which I have been treated [having been prescribed wine and brandy for his agonizing attack of gout].[16]

Mary Anne's letters to him were more stoical and helpful: 'Pray put a strip of Flanl rd yr waist it would not be seen Flanl drawers is not enough when you go out of yr warm room . . . Dr Gull says yr illness proceeds from coming up & down so often the night I was so ill & agitation of mind combined.'

'Mrs Disraeli must not leave her room,' her husband told Sir Stafford Northcote on 7 December 1867, 'tho' getting on well ... My dinner, consisting, I am sorry to say, of a tapioca pudding, need not have prevented us meeting yesterday; but my butler is a pompous booby.'[17]

30

A GUEST AT
BALMORAL AND OSBORNE

'He is vy peculiar ... most singular ... but I did not find
him so to talk to.

'I AM SELFISH IN HOPING you will not quit public life,' Disraeli had
written disingenuously to Lord Derby on 14 September 1867, 'as my
career will terminate with yours.'

At the beginning of the following year, suffering increasingly debilitating attacks of gout, and, as he put it, 'lying here [at Knowsley] like a
useless log', the Prime Minister confessed that he had been aware for
some time that 'the increased frequency of [his] attacks of illness would,
at no distant period, incapacitate [him] for the discharge of [his] public
duties.' He had, he continued, communicated this to no one except the
Queen, who 'particularly pleased' him by declaring that she 'by no
means contemplated the break-up of the present government as the
result' of his retirement. 'And I am sure,' he added, 'that as far as she
is concerned, you, with the aid of our present colleagues, will receive
the same cordial support which I have enjoyed.'

A few days later Derby's condition had deteriorated so sharply that
Lord Stanley was summoned to Knowsley, where he found his father
resigned to what his doctors described as the indispensability of 'absolute
repose of mind and body'.

On 19 February 1868 Derby wrote again to Disraeli:

> You may be assured of receiving from me all the support which,
> out of office, it is in my power to give ... And I cannot make

this communication without gratefully acknowledging your cordial and loyal co-operation with me, in good times and in bad
... nor, above all, the courage, skill, and judgement, with which
you triumphantly carried the Government through all the difficulties and dangers of the past years.[1]

In his reply, Disraeli again maintained that he 'never contemplated
nor desired' taking Derby's place. 'I was', he wrote, 'entirely content with
my position, and all that I aspired to was that, after a Government of
tolerable length, and, at least fair repute, my retirement from public
affairs should have accompanied your own.' However, he 'would not
shrink from the situation'; nor did he 'underrate its gravity', and counted
upon Lord Derby's guidance and support.[2]

'And I do, even solemnly, entreat you never to permit any sentiment
of estrangement to arise between us,' he added in a later letter, 'but to
extend to me for ever that [which] has persisted so long between us;
which has been the pride and honour of my life, and which it will ever
be my constant effort to cherish and deserve.'

The Queen had already made it clear that she would welcome
Disraeli as Lord Derby's successor. Towards the end of January he had
been summoned to Osborne, the Queen's house on the Isle of Wight,
and, as he reported to his wife, it was the most successful visit he had
ever had there.

> All that I could wish and hope. She spoke of everything without
> reserve or formality. A brilliant day here. The Queen ordered a
> vessel at Portsmouth to be at my disposal ... M[ontagu] Corry,
> lucky fellow, had to come down here yesterday on some business,
> and Her Majesty, hearing of it, invited him to dine with the
> household and sleep here![3]

Corry had arrived on the island before Disraeli and the Queen's
Private Secretary, General the Hon. Charles Grey, had come to his room
to inform him that Her Majesty intended 'to make Mr Disraeli her First
Minister. Mr D[israeli] was much struck by the fact that his old rival
at Wycombe [where Grey had stood as candidate in 1832] should become
the bearer of such a message'.

> I have not written to the Queen, [Disraeli wrote to Grey] because
> I thought you could keep HM *au fait*, and it would be better for
> me to keep silent. Cairns has accepted the Great Seal [as Lord

Chancellor] and all my colleagues have placed themselves at my disposal, except Walpole [the former Home Secretary]. I am deeply considering the question of the Chancellor of Exchequer [eventually to be G. Ward Hunt] but have done nothing: the more so, as about two hours ago I received a serious intimation not to precipitate affairs in this direction, as 'a most important and influential adhesion' was possible. I conclude it can't be Gladstone![4]

The following day, 26 February 1868, Disraeli wrote to the Queen the first of that series of fulsomely flattering letters which were to please her so much:

Mr Disraeli with his humble duty to Your Majesty.

He ventures to express his sense of your Majesty's most gracious kindness to him, and of the high honour which your Majesty has been graciously pleased to confer on him.

He can only offer devotion.

It will be his delight and duty to render the transaction of affairs as easy to your Majesty as possible: and in smaller matters he hopes he may succeed in this; but he ventures to trust that, in the great affairs of state, your Majesty will deign not to withhold from him the benefit of your Majesty's guidance.

Your Majesty's life has been passed in constant communion with great men, and the knowledge and management of important transactions. Even if your Majesty were not gifted with those great abilities, which all now acknowledge, this rare and choice experience must give your Majesty an advantage in judgement which few living persons, and probably no living prince, can rival.

He whom your Majesty has so highly preferred presumes to trust to your Majesty's condescension in this behalf.[5]

To this letter the Queen replied by return of post from Osborne:

The Queen thanks Mr Disraeli very much for his kind letter received today, and can assure him of her cordial support in the arduous task which he has undertaken. It must be a proud moment for him to feel that his own talent and successful labours in the service of his country have earned for him the high and influential position in which he is now placed.

The Queen has ever found Mr Disraeli most zealous in her service, and most ready to meet her wishes, and she only wishes her beloved husband were here now to assist him with his guidance.

The Queen rejoices to see how much unanimity he has found amongst his colleagues. She will be glad to see Mr Disraeli tomorrow, but does not ask him to stay overnight, as she knows how precious every moment must be to him.[6]

Later that day Disraeli arrived at Osborne and wrote to his wife to describe his reception by the Queen, who 'came into her closet with a very radiant face and saying "You must kiss hands", which I did immediately, and very heartily, falling on my knee. Then she sat down, which she never used to do, and only does to her First Minister, and talked over affairs for half an hour (I standing) so that I had scarcely time to dress for dinner.'[7]

> Mr Disraeli has achieved his present high position entirely by his ability [the Queen reported contentedly to Queen Augusta of Prussia], his wonderful, happy disposition and the astounding way in which he carried through the Reform Bill, and I have nothing but praise for him. One thing which has for some time predisposed me in his favour is his great admiration for my beloved Albert and his recognition of and respect for his great character.[8]

This had not always been so: in the early days of her relationship with Mr Disraeli she had described him as 'detestable, unprincipled, reckless & not respectable', while Prince Albert had dismissed him as having 'not one single element of the gentleman in his composition'. Disraeli had, however, taken care to heap high praise upon Prince Albert himself when talking about him to the Queen. He had, she remembered, paid a most admirable public tribute to her husband, whose acquaintance, he privately assured her, was 'one of the most satisfactory incidents of his life'.

Mr Disraeli had also spoken most movingly about the Albert Memorial, and, when he had become Chancellor of the Exchequer and Leader of the House of Commons under Derby, he had impressed the Queen by the clarity and vividness of the parliamentary reports which it was his duty – his 'pleasure', he said – to send her. But he was a very odd person; so was his wife; and, while she felt assured of his devotion to herself and the Crown, she had never been quite at ease in his presence.

This had quite changed by the time he became Prime Minister, 'a proud thing for a man "risen from the people" to have obtained', a remarkable achievement, as he put it himself, to have reached 'the top of the greasy pole'.*

He was, as the Queen acknowledged, undoubtedly an outsider in the hierarchy of his party, and she was well aware that the Marquess of Salisbury was far from being the only man of influence who referred to him disparagingly. Salisbury himself, indeed, was positively insulting. Years ago he had declared that there was 'no escape on earth for men from taxes, toothache or . . . from Mr Disraeli'; and when in 1868 Disraeli invited him to rejoin the Cabinet from which he had resigned the year before on the issue of parliamentary reform, he replied insultingly that he had the greatest respect for every member of the administration except one, but that he did not think his honour safe in the hands of that person. And when, in 1874, he did agree to join Disraeli's Cabinet, he told his wife that the prospect of having to serve with this man was 'like a nightmare'.[9] Other members of the Cabinet, while not going nearly so far, could not but be conscious of the fact that Disraeli was an outsider and in many ways a mysterious one. His appearance and tastes and manner, even his education, separated him from his colleagues: in Lord Derby's Cabinet – apart from the Lord Chancellor, Lord Chelmsford, who had been educated at a naval school at Gosport – he was the only member who had not attended a well-known public school: two had been to Rugby, one to Shrewsbury, the remaining nine to Eton, a school upon which Disraeli looked with a mixture of envy and respect and which features in his novel *Coningsby* in a guise in which Old Etonians found much to criticize, despite his enlistment of George Smythe's old tutor in an attempt to present an accurate picture.

*   *   *

* 'Leaving aside Disraeli, every nineteenth-century prime minister came from a family whose circumstances had been changed and improved between the 1780s and the 1830s. Of those from old and august dynasties: Lord John Russell was a Bedford, and his father benefited greatly from the development of Bloomsbury; Lord Derby depended on the coals and ground rents of Lancashire; and the Salisbury money and Marquesate had been obtained during precisely this period. Two more were Anglo-Scottish: Lord Aberdeen, who fought so hard for the UK peerage in the 1800s, and Lord Rosebery, whose UK title dated from 1828. Two were Anglo-Irish: Wellington . . . and Palmerston . . . Two were Whigs . . . of recent title: Melbourne . . . and Grey . . . And two were descendants of businessmen whose forbears had bought their way into the landed elite during the classical phase of the Industrial Revolution: Sir Robert Peel . . . and Mr Gladstone' (David Cannadine, *Aspects of Aristocracy: Grandeur and Decline in Modern Britain*, 1994, 35).

From the beginning, Disraeli set out to woo and flatter the Queen with an infallible instinct for the phrase, the gesture, the compliment, the overture that would most delight her. He was later to tell a colleague who had asked for advice as to how to handle the Queen, 'First of all, remember she is a woman.' He never forgot this himself. She responded by sending him a valentine card depicting cherubs lying on clouds.

'The present man will do well,' she told her daughter, the Crown Princess of Prussia, with complacent satisfaction, 'and will be particularly loyal and anxious to please me in every way. He is vy peculiar . . . most singular . . . thoroughly Jewish-looking, a livid complexion, dark eyes and eyebrows and black ringlets. The expression is disagreeable, but I did not find him so to talk to. He has a very bland manner, and his language is very flowery . . . but he is vy clever and sensible and vy conciliatory. He is full of poetry, romance and chivalry. When he knelt down to kiss my hand wh[ich] he took in both of his – he said: "In loving loyalty and faith."'[10]

Disraeli himself recognized that he did lay it on 'rather thick' with her. When he received a box of primroses from Windsor, for example, he told her that 'their lustre was enhanced by the condescending hand which [had] showered upon him all the treasures of Spring'. As he said to Matthew Arnold, 'You have heard me called a flatterer, and it is true. Everyone likes flattery; and when you come to royalty, you should lay it on with a trowel.'[11] But he never underestimated the Queen's astuteness; he grew genuinely fond of her; in treating her with elaborate courtesy and deferential flirtatiousness he was behaving towards her as he did towards all women he liked. In writing those long, amusing, informative, gossipy letters which meant so much to her, he was indulging a whim to please her rather than performing a necessary and arduous duty.

Disraeli's letters certainly delighted her. She told Lady Stanley, who told Lord Clarendon: 'Dizzy writes daily letters to the Queen in his best novel style, telling her every scrap of political news dressed up to serve his own purpose, and every scrap of social gossip cooked to amuse her. She declared that she has never had such letters in her life, which is probably true, and that she never before knew *everything*!'

'No Minister,' she wrote, 'since Sir R. Peel (excepting poor dear Lord Aberdeen) has ever shown that care for my personal affairs, or that respect and deference for me which he has.'

There were, of course, things she was not told, but Disraeli was always anxious to ensure that she was given the impression of constantly being consulted except on trivial matters not worth her consideration. On suggesting, for example, that the Duke of Atholl might be appointed a Knight of the Order of the Thistle, he wrote, 'Your Majesty is a much better judge of these matters than himself; and indeed there are very few public matters on wh[ich] he feels more and more every day Your Majesty is not much more competent to advise than be advised.' 'I never deny,' he once said, explaining his method of dealing with her. 'I never contradict. I sometimes forget.'

Attentive towards her in his fulsome correspondence, Disraeli was as careful to charm her whenever they met. He did not much like going to Windsor, that 'castle of the winds' as he called it, remembering with a shudder the icy draughts that blew under doors and through ill-fitting window frames; but he never showed his discomfort to her. He resented having to go to Balmoral, being forced to travel so many miles from London to a place where it rained almost continuously throughout his first visit and where he had been ill on his second: he never paid a third. But he displayed no irritation. He 'seemed delighted with his visit,' the Queen wrote of the first occasion, '& made himself most agreeable'.

On a subsequent visit to Osborne it was the Queen who made herself most agreeable to him.

> Osborne was lovely [Disraeli told a friend], its green glades refreshing after the fervent glare of the voyage, and its blue bay full of white sails ... [The Queen] sent for me the instant I arrived. I can only describe my reception by telling you that I really thought she was going to embrace me. She was wreathed in smiles, and, as she tattled, glided about the room like a bird. She ... said, 'To think of your having gout! How you must have suffered! And you ought not to stand now! You shall have a chair!'
>
> Only think of that! I remember Lord Derby after one of his severest illnesses, had an audience of her Majesty, and he mentioned it to me, as a proof of the Queen's favour, that Her Majesty had remarked to him 'how sorry she was she could not ask him to be seated'.[12]

There were, of course, many who could not share the pleasure which the Queen took in having Disraeli as her Prime Minister. 'Disraeli Prime

Minister!' the Earl of Shaftesbury expostulated, expressing a common enough opinion. 'He is a Hebrew ... He is a man sprung from an inferior station ... a good thing in these days, as showing the liberality of our institutions ... But he is a leper, without principles, without feeling, without regard to anything, human or Divine, beyond his personal ambition.'[13]

Lady Palmerston expressed herself more succinctly: 'We are all dreadfully disgusted at the prospect of having a Jew for our Prime Minister.'[14]

MINISTER IN ATTENDANCE

'I am sustained by the speedy prospect
of our being again together, and talking over
1,000 things.'

'WILL YOU LEND YOUR RECEPTION-ROOMS [at the Foreign Office] to my wife for a couple of nights or so?' Disraeli asked the Foreign Secretary, Lord Stanley, early in March 1868. 'According to the Whips there must be some high festivals on a very extensive scale; and she can do nothing with D[owning] S[treet], it is so dingy and decaying.'

Stanley readily agreed; and on the night of 26 March, a stormy night of wild wind and sleet, the Disraelis greeted 'an immense gathering both of society and of the Conservative Party, with a sprinkling of Liberal friends'. The Bishop of Oxford, Samuel Wilberforce, was also there and described 'Dizzy in his glory, leading about the Princess of Wales [Princess Alexandra, daughter of King Christian IV of Denmark, to whom the Prince had been married for five years]. Mrs Disraeli looking very ill and haggard. The impenetrable man low.'

Disraeli sent the Queen copies of his books; and she herself sent him, in return, a copy of her *Leaves from the Journal of our Life in the Highlands* which had been published by Smith, Elder and Co. and which Disraeli, of course, praised extravagantly, unlike some members of her family such as the Crown Princess Frederick, who was gently reprimanded for never having said 'one word about [her mother's] poor little book'. Disraeli, on the contrary, wrote to her to say that it possessed 'a freshness and fragrance like the heather amidst which it was written'. It gave him the opportunity to delight the Queen, so it was said, with his celebrated flattery – 'We authors, Ma'am!'

The Queen's grumpiness that spring was exacerbated by her failing health which, she thought, might deteriorate to such an extent that she would be unable to continue working. A holiday in Switzerland was proposed; and so, travelling as the Countess of Kent, she left for Lucerne by way of Paris where, in the words of Lord Cairns, the Lord Chancellor, 'Our dear Peeress did not return the visit of the Empress [Eugénie, consort of the Emperor, Napoleon III]. This is to be deplored, particularly as they had named a Boulevard after her and she went to see it.'

This discourtesy on the part of the Queen required a most tactful reproof which Disraeli framed in his practised and carefully worded style:

> There is no doubt that your Majesty acted quite rightly in declining to return the visit of the Empress at Paris. Such an act on your Majesty's part would have been quite inconsistent with the incognito assumed by your Majesty, for a return visit to a Sovereign is an act of high etiquette; for which incognito is invented to guard against.
>
> Nevertheless there is, Mr Disraeli would ask permission to observe, perhaps no doubt that your Majesty was scarcely well advised in receiving the visit, as such a reception was equally inconsistent with incognito.
>
> Certain persons, M. de Fleury notably among them, made a great grievance of the visit not being returned, but Mr Disraeli hoped the matter would have blown over and been forgotten. The Empress, who is far from irrational, was not at first by any means disposed to take M. de Fleury's view, but everybody persists in impressing on her she has been treated with incivility; and there is no doubt that it has ended by the French court being sore.
>
> Mr Disraeli thought it his duty to lay this matter before your Majesty; as your Majesty perhaps on your return, with your Majesty's happy judgement, might by some slight act gracefully dissipate this malaise.[1]

The Queen did not make the call which Disraeli recommended; but Lady Ely, her timid and nervous Lady of the Bedchamber, wrote to him to say:

The Queen desired me to tell you that H.M. has written to the Empress herself to express all her regrets, but to say H.M. has given up paying visits now and had declined going to her own relations, but hoped at some future time when she passed through Paris to call and see the Empress.[2]

Soon after the Queen's return from France, Disraeli set out for Balmoral Castle where, for ten days, he was to act as Minister in Attendance. His wife did not go with him; but he wrote to her every day to tell her what life at Balmoral was like:

My darling wife [he wrote to her from Perth on 18 September],

I telegraphed to you this morning that all was well. Within an hour of this place, where we ought to have arrived a little after eleven o'clock, it was signalled that something had gone wrong with a goods train, and that the road was blocked up: and we had to sit in the dark for two hours and more! However, this was better than being smashed. Everything, otherwise, has gone very well.

You provided for me so admirably and so judiciously, that I had two sumptuous meals; a partridge breakfast, and a chicken and tongue dinner; and plenty of good wine! I did not slumber on the road, but had a very good night here, and have got up early, quite refreshed, to send you a telegram, and write a few letters, this particularly, which you will get tomorrow.

There was a great mob at Carlisle who cheered me very much, but I profited by our experience during our Edinbro' visit, and would not get out: so they assembled on the platform round the carriage. It was an ordeal of ten minutes; I bowed to them and went on reading; but was glad when the train moved.

I was greatly distressed at our separation, and when I woke this morning, did not know where I was. Nothing but the gravity of public life sustains me under a great trial, which no one can understand except those who live on the terms of entire affection and companionship like ourselves; and, I believe, they are very few.

Write to me every day, if it is only a line to tell me how you are; but you, with your lively mind and life, will be able to tell me a great deal more. Montagu [Corry] will have discovered by this time the best mode of communication. The Queen's messenger goes every day by the same train I did – 10 o'clock Euston. Adieu, with a thousand embraces, my dearest, dearest wife. D.[3]

The next day Disraeli continued his account:

BALMORAL CASTLE, Sept. 19, '68. – Arrived here last night, ½ past nine; the household at dinner. The Queen sent a considerate message, that I need not dress, but I thought it best, as I was tired and dusty, not to appear: particularly as I found some important letters from Stanley on my table. They served me a capital little dinner in my room, and I had a very good night ... I thought it right to appear at breakfast today, as I had not presented myself last night.

Lady Churchill in attendance and Miss Lascelles, and Lord Bridport.

Bridport told me that I need not wear frock coats, 'which, as a country gentleman, I know in the country you must abominate.'

Sept. 20. – I write to you whenever I can snatch an opportunity, and they are so frequent here, but so hurried, that I hardly know when I wrote to you last, or what I said. Yesterday, I dined with the Queen, a party of eight. H.M., the Prince and Princess Xtian, Princess Louise, the Duke of Edinburgh, and myself, Lord Bridport and Lady Churchill.

We dined in the Library, a small, square room, with good books – very cosy; like dining with a bachelor in very good rooms in the Albany.

Conversation lively, though not memorable ... Yesterday morning I went out walking with Lord Bridport, and made a tour of the place: so I quite understand the situation and general features: I much admire it. Mountains not too high; of graceful outline and well wooded, and sometimes a vast expanse of what they call forest, but which is, in fact, only wild moor, where red deer congregate ...

Sept. 21. – The Queen sent for me yesterday afternoon. Her rooms are upstairs ... I dined with the household, and, between ourselves, was struck, as I have been before, by the contrast between the Queen's somewhat simple, but sufficient, dinner, and the banquet of our humbler friends.

Sept. 22. – The weather here, instead of being cold as they predicted, has been wet and warm.

Yesterday, after a hard morning's work – for the messenger goes at 12 o'clock, and I rise exactly at seven; so I get four hours' work – Lord Bridport drove me to see some famous falls – of Garrawalt: and though the day was misty and the mountains veiled, the cataract was heightened by the rain. I never in my life saw anything more magnificent . . .

Sept. 23. – Yesterday we went on one of those expeditions you read of in the Queen's book . . . We went to the Castle of Braemar, where, every year, the contiguous clans assemble, and have Highland games. I was very glad there were no games . . . The party was very merry: all the courtiers had a holiday. Lady Churchill said that, when she asked the Queen, through the Princess Louise, whether she was wanted this morning, the Queen replied 'No; all the ladies are to go, to make it amusing to Mr Disraeli.'

Returning we went to Mar Lodge, and took tea with Lady Fife. There we found Sylvia Doyle, looking more absurd than any human being I can well remember. The Highlanders call her 'The coloured lady'. Her cheeks were like a clown's in a pantomime, and she had a pile of golden hair as high as some of the neighbouring hills. However, she smiled and cracked her jokes as usual, and gave me, as usual, a long list of places she was going to.

Sept. 24. – The Queen gives her Minister plenty to do: but I will write every day, however briefly . . .

Sept. 26. – Only a line to keep up the chain . . . The Queen has got a photographer and insists upon my being *done* . . .

Sept. 26. – The bag has brought me no letter from you this morning, which greatly distresses me: for although all goes on well here, I am extremely nervous, my health being very unsatisfactory . . . I have never tasted one of your dear peaches, which I much wished to do for your sake, and have drunk nothing but sherry.

I leave this on Monday, and get to Perth to sleep, and the next morning to Knowsley, as I must see Lord Derby. On Thursday I propose to be at Grosvenor Gate, after an absence of a fortnight! . . .

This morning the Queen has sent me two volumes of views of Balmoral; a box full of family photographs, a very fine whole-length portrait of the Prince, and 'a Scotch shawl for Mrs Disraeli, which H.M. hopes you will find warm in the cold weather'. Today I am resolved to keep in my room.

Adieu, my dearest love; though greatly suffering, I am sustained by the speedy prospect of our being again together, and talking over 1,000 things.

Sept. 27. – The Queen sent for me yesterday after she came home from her ride: but said, when I left H.M., 'This is not your audience before leaving.'

Sept. 28. – A very rapid letter before departure. The joy at our soon meeting again is inexpressible.

Princess Christian said yesterday that they were all very sorry I was going, but she knew who was glad, and that was Mrs Disraeli . . .

I had a long audience of the Queen at four o'clock, and shortly afterwards was invited to dine with H. Majesty again.[4]

Disraeli confessed to feeling social life at Balmoral – as well as to finding time to work there – too much of a strain, and he determined to go there in future as infrequently as he could. 'Carrying on the Government of a country six hundred miles from the metropolis doubles the labour,' he told Bishop Wilberforce. He could not, however, escape another visit.[5]

When Disraeli relinquished office as Prime Minister after the Conservatives' defeat in the general election of 1868 – 'a strange and unfortunate result' – he was sixty-four years old; and he told the Queen that it had been his 'original intention' to close his political career and to 'humbly solicit' Her Majesty to bestow upon him 'some mark of Her Majesty's favour'. Yet he had subsequently felt that if he could serve her as leader of her Opposition, he would be quite content to do so, 'even if he were never to be Minister again'.

But next to your Majesty there is one to whom he owes everything [he wrote to her on 23 November 1868] . . . Might Mr Disraeli therefore, after 31 years of Parliamentary toil . . . humbly solicit your Majesty to grant those honours to his wife which perhaps under ordinary circumstances your Majesty would have deigned to bestow on him . . . Mrs Disraeli has a fortune of her own adequate to any position in which your Majesty might deign to place her. Might her husband then hope that your Majesty would be graciously pleased to create her Viscountess Beaconsfield, a town which Mr Disraeli has been long connected with and which is the nearest town to his estate in Bucks which is not yet ennobled?[6]

Disraeli's request caused some consternation in the Royal Household. General Grey warned that 'attacks and endless ridicule' would

'surely follow' Mrs Disraeli's elevation. But the Queen, with some reluctance, assented to the request; and, while there were snide remarks in
various newspapers, there was general approval of the honour bestowed
on a lady of seventy-six. Gladstone, now Prime Minister, wrote to
Disraeli asking him to present his best compliments 'on her coming
patent to (I suppose I must still say, and never can use the name for
the last time without regret) Mrs Disraeli'.[7]

Lord Derby also sent his congratulations to Disraeli: "Lady Beaconsfield" will, I am sure, receive it as a graceful acknowledgement, on the
part of the Crown, of *your* public service, unaccompanied by the drawback of removing you from the House in which your presence is indispensable.'[8]

His work in the House was taking its toll, however. Two months later
Disraeli told Lord Henry Lennox that he had been feeling 'unwell all this
year'. 'I am afraid', he added, 'I have thought too much of myself. Illness
makes one selfish and disgusts one's friends.' 'I can't say much for myself,' he complained to Sir Stafford Northcote. 'I have been to the seaside;
but it has brought me no relief, and I still suffer, which is disheartening.'

By the middle of August, however, he was feeling much better, 'quite,
quite myself', he told Lord Derby; and to Lord Cairns he wrote, 'I have
entirely cured [my gout] by giving up sugar, burgundy and champagne
– almost as great a surrender as Sedan [where France had been defeated
in the Franco-Prussian War].'

By the beginning of 1871, he had recovered his former spirits and,
in a debate in the House, he trounced Gladstone with all the flair and
confidence of the past. 'The Premier was like a cat on hot bricks,' wrote
an observer of the scene, 'and presented a striking contrast to Disraeli,
for Disraeli cuts up a Minister with as much *sang-froid* as an anatomist
cuts up a frog. Gladstone could hardly keep his seat. He fidgeted, took
a quire of notes, sent for blue books and water, turned down corners
and "hear-heared" ironically or interrupted his opponent to make a
denial of one of his statements, or to ask the page of a quotation so
frequently that Disraeli had to protest once or twice by raising his
eyebrows or shrugging his shoulders. And when Gladstone rose, you
could see that every stroke of Disraeli's had gone home. He was in a
white passion, and almost choked with words, frequently pausing to
select the harshest to be found.'[9]

In March that year, Reginald Brett, the future Lord Esher, then an undergraduate at Trinity College, Cambridge, wrote to his father to concede that 'Dizzy's speeches [had been] brilliant enough, but not earnest'. He never would 'frame a great Opposition' for he failed to 'convince'. 'He is', Brett thought, 'a critic, and a capital one of a bad government but not the counter-theorist who by dint of facts and perseverance can gain his end.'[10]

32

THE WIDOWER

'There is nothing happier than
a happy marriage.'

WITH RETURNING HEALTH came further demonstrations of regard and popularity. In the autumn of 1871, Disraeli was preferred to John Ruskin as Lord Rector of Glasgow University; and in February the following year, when the Prince of Wales gave public thanks at St Paul's Cathedral for his recovery from typhoid fever, while Gladstone's progress was watched with indifference, Disraeli – who had declared with familiar fulsomeness that the people's devotion to the Prince must 'make a man of his sweet disposition and noble character, happier and prouder' – was greeted with the greatest enthusiasm.

> On returning from St Paul's, Disraeli met with an *overpowering* 'ovation', I should say 'triumph' for he was in his chariot [wrote his biographer Sir William Fraser]. This not only continued from the City to Waterloo Place; but his carriage, ascending Regent Street, turning along Oxford Street, and thence back to the Carlton Club, the cheers which greeted him from all classes convinced him that, for the day at least, a more popular man did not exist in England. Soon after his return I happened to pass into the morning room of the Carlton Club. Disraeli was leaning against the table immediately opposite to the glass door, wearing the curious white coat which he had for years occasionally put on over his usual dress. Familiar as I was with his looks and expression, I never saw him with such a countenance as he had at that moment. I have heard it said by one who spoke to Napoleon I that his face was as that of one who looks into another world: that is the only description I can give of Disraeli's look at the moment I speak

of. He seemed more like a statue than a human being: never before nor since have I seen anything approaching it ... In the afternoon I said to Mr Sclater Booth, now Lord Basing, 'What was Disraeli talking about when I came into the room?' He replied, 'About some country business; I wanted his opinion.' I said, 'I will tell you what he was thinking about: he was thinking that he will be Prime Minister again!' I had no doubt at the time; nor have I ever doubted it since.[1]

Disraeli was greeted with similar enthusiasm in the provinces. At Manchester during the Easter holiday, for example, his carriage was drawn through the streets by a crowd of workmen on holiday; and in the pouring rain of the next day an immense parade of deputations from all the Conservative Associations of the country marched past him; and 'for each deputation the leader had an apt word, as one after the other, with banners flying and laudatory addresses in their hands, the deputies defiled before Disraeli and Lady Beaconsfield filling the vast hall of the Pomona Gardens, a building reckoned to hold thirty or forty thousand people.'

Disraeli was equally well received at the Free Trade Hall in Manchester on 3 April where he spoke to 'an enthusiastic audience with unflagging spirit for three hours and a quarter'. In this effort, 'so tremendous for a man never very robust and in his sixty-eighth year, he was sustained', according to H. C. Raikes, the Member for Chester, 'by two bottles of white brandy, indistinguishable by onlookers from the water taken with it, which he drank in doses of ever-increasing strength till he had consumed the whole!'[2]

Disraeli enjoyed another triumph at the Crystal Palace in June when he addressed the National Union, the central society of the Conservative and Constitutional countrywide associations; and further proof of his popularity was given at a dinner at the Literary Club where the demonstration after his speech, so he told Montagu Corry, was 'equal to Manchester. The mob consisting of Princes [Leopold II, King of the Belgians, was in the chair], Ambassadors, wits, artists – and critics!'[3]

Disraeli's speeches at this time, and his reception at Manchester, 'placed his leadership beyond question,' wrote his biographer, G. E. Buckle, 'and proved the reality of Conservative reaction.'

The editor of The Times, J. T. Delane, remarked to Lord Henry

Lennox that Disraeli now stood in 'the highest position in which any statesman has ever stood for many years, that [he] had given proof of the very highest order of statesmanship, both unselfish and patriotic ... that he had displayed a judgement and a spirit of which Gladstone would be utterly incapable.' For the first time in his life Disraeli himself felt fully assured of his popularity. 'It is all well and good now,' he said to Lady Dorothy Nevill, 'I feel my position assured.'[4]

As a writer, however, he was not so highly regarded by many of his contemporaries in the literary world. Nor was he on the best of terms with several of those fellow authors with whom he came into contact. Thackeray, who lampooned him as Rafael Mendoza in 'Codlingsby, by B. de Shrewsbury, Esq.', was not forgiven. John Hollingshead, the journalist and theatre manager, witnessed the two men at an exhibition fifteen years later. 'They saw each other but showed no signs of recognition.'

Anthony Trollope, six years older than Thackeray, also offended Disraeli by inventing the character of Ethelbert Stanhope in *Barchester Towers* who goes to the Holy Land to convert the Jews but is himself converted to Judaism. Trollope also introduced the Disraeliesque figure of Daubeny in *Phineas Finn*, a Tory politician, a clever man without principle who would 'give his fingers and toes' to remain in office. 'You think exactly about Dizzy as I do,' Trollope's publisher, John Blackwood, said to him. 'You know I would be very glad to hear he had been up for – for shoplifting.' When standing (unsuccessfully) as a Liberal parliamentary candidate at Beverley, Trollope took the opportunity of abusing Disraeli roundly in his speeches to the electors; his fellow novelist and political opponent was, he said, 'a conjuror and a charlatan'. It would be 'unnatural' for them to vote Tory; it would, indeed, be 'a sin which they must expiate'.[5]

Trollope and Lord Houghton, the former Monckton Milnes, wondered how much Thomas Longman had paid Disraeli for *Lothair*, his novel of 1870. Houghton suggested £10,000. Why, only Dickens was worth that, Trollope protested.* He himself considered *Lothair* the 'very bathos of story-telling', while Houghton observed of the

---

* In fact, *Lothair* earned Disraeli at least £10,600 (Robert Blake, *Disraeli*, 520.)

book, 'His wisest friends think it must be a mistake, and his enemies hope that it will be his ruin.' Recent critics and biographers have been much kinder: Robert Blake commended it as 'perhaps the best of all Disraeli's novels';[6] while A.N. Wilson wrote of it, 'Lothair has fizz, and like the best satire it delights in what it mocks.'[7] Certainly, it could not be denied that there are memorable characters and portraits in it, particularly Cardinal Grandison, unmistakably a portrait of Cardinal Manning, the Bishop (Samuel Wilberforce), the Duke, equally unmistakably the rich Duke of Abercorn, and Lothair himself the third Marquess of Bute who 'devoted a comparatively short life to the pleasures of aestheticism, who translated the Roman Breviary into English and employed William Burges as architect of a transformed Cardiff Castle.'[8]

There are also memorable aphorisms: 'When a man fell into his anecdotage it was a sign for him to retire from the world ... Every woman should marry – and no man ... You know who the critics are? The men who have failed in literature and art ... "My idea of an agreeable person," said Hugo Bohun, "is a person who agrees with me." ... St Aldegonde had a taste for marriages and public executions ... Every day he looked into the glass, and gave the last touch to his consummate toilet, he offered his grateful thanks to Providence that his family was not unworthy of him ... [A hansom cab] the gondola of London ... London: a nation not a city ... "English," said Mr Pinto to St Aldegonde, "is an expressive language, but not difficult to master ... It consists, so far as I can observe, of four words: 'nice', 'jolly', 'charming' and 'bore'."'

Dickens's low opinion of Disraeli was well known; while Disraeli, for his part, claimed in a letter to Lady Londonderry that he had 'never read anything of Dickens, except for an extract in a newspaper'.*

*   *   *

* Oscar Wilde also maintained that he disliked Dickens's novels, preferring, so he said, those of Disraeli, 'a man who could write a novel and govern an empire with either hand'. When Wilde met Disraeli, however, the meeting was not a success. Wilde said, 'I hope you are very well.' Disraeli responded dismissively, 'Is one ever very well, Mr Wilde?' (Richard Ellman, *Oscar Wilde*, 1987, 25, 104).

'Marriage is the happiest state in the world, where there is, on each side, a complete knowledge of the characters united,' Disraeli wrote to the fifteenth Earl of Derby, as Lord Stanley had become on his father's death in 1869. 'Next to yourself [who was shortly to marry the Marquess of Salisbury's young widow, with whom he was obviously much in love]; by what you tell me, no man, perhaps, will be happier, than I am. Under this roof, we have long and fondly wished that this should happen. The lady I have ever loved; and if fine intelligence, a thoughtful mind, the sweetest temper in the world, and many charms, can make a man happy, your felicity is secured . . . To all the many blessings wh. distinguish you in life, rank, wealth and, above all, great abilities, you have had the wisdom to add the only element wh. was wanting to complete the spell. Lady Beaconsfield sends you her congratulations thro' her tears – of joy.'

'There is no greater risk, perhaps, than matrimony,' Disraeli later wrote to Queen Victoria upon the engagement of her daughter Princess Louise to the Marquess of Lorne, 'but there is nothing happier than a happy marriage.'[9]

His own marriage was as happy as ever; though clouded by the thought that it would not last much longer. Lady Beaconsfield was now eighty years old; and while her husband continued to speak confidently of her health – to the Queen he wrote in October 1870 that she was, he was 'happy to say, quite well'; and to his private secretary, Montagu Corry, he wrote in September the following year, 'Milady is very well indeed' – in fact she was far from being as well as he protested and hoped. He loved her now as deeply as he had ever done. Others might deride her as an oddity, and suggest that her illness – which was probably cancer of the womb – had affected her brain, repeating such stories as that related by the Earl of Rosebery, who recorded her behaviour at a reception at the Foreign Office when he was showing her through the rooms: 'I am afraid she is very ill,' Rosebery said. 'She insisted on introducing me to the Burmese Ambassador as her son.'

Her husband ignored her crankiness. He valued her good sense, her loyalty, her discretion and her stoicism, once demonstrated by an episode, later to become widely known, when she painfully trapped her finger in a carriage door as she and her husband were on their way to a meeting and she gave no indication that she had been hurt in case she disturbed him before an important engagement. She had displayed a similar concern for his peace of mind in 1856 when staying with the Salisburys at Hatfield House while recovering from a fall which had left her with blackened eyes and a bruised face. So as not to alarm her husband, who was due to arrive at Hatfield the next day, when he had a 'great speech' to make, she asked Lady Salisbury to tell the other guests that she had a headache and stayed in her room. When the following day she appeared late for dinner, Disraeli had no opportunity to see her at close quarters. 'He has lost his eyeglass,' she had told Lady Salisbury, 'and if you put me a long way from him at dinner he will never see what a condition I am in.'

In some ways Disraeli was almost as odd as his wife. He made it a practice, for example, to treat her pearls in the manner described as being practised by Mr Ruby, the Bond Street jeweller in *Lothair*:

> Pearls are troublesome property, my Lord. They require great care; they want both air and exercise; they must be worn frequently; you cannot lock them up. The Duchess of Havant has the finest pearls in the country, and I told her Grace, 'Wear them whenever you can, wear them at breakfast'; and her Grace follows my advice, she does wear them at breakfast. I go down to Havant Castle every year to see her Grace's pearls, and I wipe every one of them myself, and let them lie on a sunny bank in the garden, in a westerly wind, for hours and days together. Their complexion would have been ruined had it not been for this treatment.*

Having recovered from the illness which beset her in 1868, Mary Anne fell ill again in May 1872, as her husband told Montagu Corry:

> Milady went to Lady Waldegrave's last night but was obliged to come home almost immediately. But, as she boastfully says, her illness was not found out. She delighted Fortescue [Chichester Fortescue, later Lord Carlingford] by telling him that she had heard him very much praised. He pressed her very much when and where. She replied, 'It was in bed.'

* The jeweller, Richard Ogden, tells me that this treatment is not quite as strange as it sounds: 'This way of treating pearls seems a little odd, but essentially it is very practical. Cleaning pearls by wiping them with a slightly damp cloth is a very good way of removing any dirt. Laying the pearls in a sunny and airy place would also help dry out the silk on to which the pearls would be strung ... A natural pearl is a very hard substance but they do have a vulnerability when they have been drilled and strung on to silk.'

Sir William [Gull, the physician] gives a good account of her today, and seems to think he has remedied the pain, which is all we can hope for, and has sanctioned, and even advised, her to go to Court: but I don't think he allows enough for her extreme weakness. However, I shall be with her today; last night she was alone, which I think fearful.

'The visit to Court was not successful,' Disraeli told Corry the next day. 'She was suffering as she went and was taken so unwell there, that we had to retreat precipitately, but . . . knowing the haunts of the palace a little, I got hold of some female attendants who were very serviceable.'

Nothing encouraging at home [Disraeli continued his account to Corry on 14 May]. To see her every day weaker and weaker is heartrending. I have had, like all of us, some sorrows of this kind: but in every case, the fatal illness has been apparently sudden, and comparatively short. The shock is great under such circumstances no doubt, but there is a rebound in the nature of things. But to witness this gradual death of one, who has shared so long, and so completely, my life, entirely unmans me.

For herself, she still makes an effort to enter society: and Sir William approves and even counsels it: but it is impossible the effort can be maintained.[10]

It was not maintained for long. A few days later she was taken to Hughenden where she could not 'bear the slightest roughness in the road'. She went for a ride in the grounds; but 'suffered afterwards'. So she was pushed about in a perambulator, which seemed 'to amuse her'.

She made a brief recovery in the summer and began to resume her social life, having been taken back to London; but on 17 July at a reception to meet the Duchess of Cambridge, wife of the Queen's cousin, she was taken ill and, as at Lady Waldegrave's, had to be taken home to Grosvenor Gate where her husband wrote her a brief note:

'I have nothing to tell you, except that I love you, which, I fear, you will think rather dull. Natty [Baron de Rothschild] was very affectionate about you, and wanted me to come home and dine with him; quite alone; but I told him you were the only person now whom I could dine with.'

'My own dearest,' Mary Anne managed to reply the next day in what seems to have been the last letter which she was able to write to him. 'I miss you sadly. I feel so grateful for your constant tender love and kindness. I certainly feel better this evening . . . Your own devoted Beaconsfield.'[11]

In the middle of August, however, she had 'more than one return of haemorrhage'.

'We have not been separated for three and thirty years,' Disraeli told Lord Cairns on 17 August. 'And in all that time, in her society I never have had a moment of dullness. It tears the heart to see such a spirit suffer, and suffer so much! May you, my dear Cairns, never experience my present feelings!'[12]

As well as from Cairns, Disraeli received letters of sympathy from several other friends. On 12 September the Duchess of Cleveland wrote from Raby Castle:

> One privilege you have which is not granted to all. No two people surely can look back upon a life of such loving and perfect companionship. One of my sons once spoke to Lady Beaconsfield in wonder of the youthful energy and high spirits she preserved, and said something of the courage and force of character it showed. 'No,' she said, 'it is not that. It is that my life has been such a happy one. I have had so much affection, and no troubles.'[13]

Four days later Disraeli replied to a 'kind letter' from Gathorne-Hardy, who was told that Lady Beaconsfield had for some time been suffering from 'a total inability to take any sustenance yet was talking of endeavouring to get down from London to Hughenden'. In the meantime, Disraeli took her on drives through parts of London which they had never seen before, past 'miles of villas throwing out their antennae in every direction, and beautiful churches and all sorts of architecture and gorgeous gin-palaces and a real feudal castle which turned out to be the new City prison in Camden Road'.[14]

Towards the end of September, Lady Beaconsfield's condition showed a slight improvement and she resolved 'to try a change of air' at Hughenden where her health improved daily, so her husband said, and there was 'a sustained revival of appetite which had altogether ceased'. 'You know her buoyancy of spirit,' he wrote to Lady Ely. 'She says she is now convinced that everybody eats too much.'

The improvement was maintained for a time; but on 8 November Disraeli wrote to Montagu Corry:

... Affairs have been going very badly, so badly, that I telegraphed, yesterday, for Leggatt and he came down immediately: but he took a different view from us, I am glad to say: and persisted that, if sustenance could be taken, no immediate danger was to be apprehended. But how to manage that? The truth is, she never has even tasted any of the dishes, that the Rothschilds used to send her in London, and anxious as she was to partake of the delicacies you so kindly provided for her, and which touched her very much, it has ended with them as with the feats of Lionel's *chef*![15]

Yet once again she rallied; and from 21 to 25 September she was sufficiently recovered to enjoy a small house party consisting of Lord and Lady John Manners and, for the first two days, Lord Rosebery, and, for the second two, Lord Ronald Gower and Sir William Harcourt (who, on his return to Trinity College, Cambridge sent Lady Beaconsfield a consignment of Trinity audit ale).[16]

She bore up well during the visit of these guests, although the face of her husband, generally so emotionless, as Lord Ronald Gower said, 'was filled with a look of suffering and woe that nothing but the sorrow of her whom he so truly loves would cause on that impassive countenance'.

Gower, who sat next to Mary Anne at dinner, recalled that she ate nothing, while her husband, deeply concerned, ate little himself. 'Although occasionally flashing out into conversation,' Lord Ronald recalled, 'with all his curious action of arms & shrugging of shoulders, [he was] evidently very much depressed at her state ... His attention to her was quite touching, and "Mary Anne", as he sometimes calls her, was constantly appealed to. We did not sit long over our wine after the ladies had left.'

After dinner it was equally distressing to 'have to sit by and hear much of the poor old [eighty years old] lady's twaddle & little of Mr D's talk'.[17]

'The poor old soul was sadly altered since London in looks,' Gower added. 'Shrunk and more like an anointed corpse than ever, but dressed in her usual gorgeous mode, a black velvet sort of cushion on her poor old wig, with a huge star on one side, banded with a circle of gold, her poor old shoulders covered with a gaudy crimson velvet & tinselled shawl.'

When their guests had departed, Mary Anne's sufferings increased, so her husband told Montagu Corry, and he was obliged to send for her doctor. It was suggested that he should also send for a clergyman, who urged her to put her trust in Jesus Christ. 'I couldn't,' she protested. 'You know *Dizzy* is my J.C.'[18]

'Affairs are most dark here,' Disraeli wrote to Philip Rose on 5 December. 'I tremble for the result . . . My poor wife has got congestion on her lungs, and with her shattered state, it seems to me almost hopeless that . . . we should again escape. I entirely trust to your coming to me, if anything happens. *I am totally unable to meet the catastrophe.*'[19]

Just over a week later, on 15 December 1872, the end came after Mary Anne, in her delirium, railed against her husband who listened to her ravings outside the door, tears in his eyes;[20] and, during the following days, letter after letter of condolence to the distraught widower was delivered at Hughenden. Among these were letters from the Prince and Princess of Wales, from the King of the Belgians, the Queen of the Netherlands and the Empress of Austria, from Lord Russell and Lord Rosebery, and from William Gladstone, who wrote to say:

> You and I, as I believe, married in the same year. It has been permitted to both of us to enjoy a priceless boon through a third of a century. Spared myself the blow which has fallen on you, I can form some conception of what it must have been and be. I do not presume to offer you the consolation which you will seek from another and higher quarter. I offer only the assurance which all who know you, all who knew Lady Beaconsfield, and especially those among them who like myself enjoyed for a length of time her marked though unmerited regard, may perhaps render without impropriety; the assurance that in this trying hour they feel deeply for you, and with you.[21]

The Queen, who had made constant enquiries about the course of Lady Beaconsfield's illness, wrote again immediately upon learning of her death:*

> The Queen knew and admired as well as appreciated the unbounded devotion and affection which united him to the dear partner of his life, whose only thought was him. And therefore

---

* The Queen sent six telegrams between 11 and 20 December; and, upon learning of Lady Beaconsfield's death, she wrote to one of the Ladies-in-Waiting characteristically requesting a full account of the patient's last hours (Hughenden Papers, Helen Langley, 130).

the Queen knows also *what* Mr Disraeli has lost and what he must suffer. The only consolation to be found is in *her* present peace and freedom from suffering, in the recollection of their life of happiness and in the blessed certainty of eternal reunion.

May God support and sustain him is the Queen's sincere prayer.[22]

33

FEMALE FRIENDS

'A female friend, amiable, clever, and devoted,
is a possession more valuable than
parks and palaces.'

Sᴉxᴛᴇᴇɴ ʏᴇᴀʀs ʙᴇғᴏʀᴇ ʜᴇʀ ᴅᴇᴀᴛʜ, on the eve of their departure
for a course of the baths and mineral waters at Spa, Mary Anne had
written a letter to her 'own dear husband'.

> If I should depart this life before you, leave orders that we may
> be buried in the same grave at whatever distance you may die
> from England. And now, God bless you, my kindest, dearest! You
> have been a perfect husband to me. Be put by my side in the
> same grave. And now, farewell, my dear Dizzy. Do not live alone,
> dearest. Some one I earnestly hope you may find as attached to
> you as your own devoted MARY ANNE.[1]

Lady Beaconsfield was buried in the vault in the churchyard at
Hughenden where the body of Mrs Brydges Willyams already lay. For
almost a quarter of an hour after the funeral Disraeli stood, bareheaded,
looking down upon the coffin as a strong wind blew and rain fell from
a grey sky.

Having lost his wife as well as his house in London, the lease of which
had belonged to her and reverted to the Wyndham Lewis estate, Disraeli
had to move – the poorer by the £5,000 a year which she had brought
to their marriage – to Edward's Hotel in George Street, which became,
for the time being, his headquarters when in London. 'My friends admire
my rooms,' he told Corry. 'I cannot say I agree with them.' He was, he

293

confessed, in a 'miserable state', overwhelmed by melancholy. 'I hope some of my friends will take notice of me now in my great misfortune, for I have no home and when I tell my coachman to drive home I feel it is a mockery.'[2]

Various friends and colleagues did take notice of him, and called upon him to keep him company in his distress – among them Northcote, Barrington and Hardy. But he was in no mood to face large parties; and when he himself called upon Lionel de Rothschild, he was annoyed to find there several people whom he had no wish to see.

He preferred solitude; and, when he ventured from Edward's Hotel to the Carlton Club, he was thankful that other members there were inclined to leave him alone. He was, however, plied with invitations which he did not want.

> The John Manners asked me again tomorrow which I declined [he told Montagu Corry, who had been called away to the bedside of his dangerously ill father]. On Thursday I am to dine with the Cairns and meet the Hardys, and, on Friday, alone with the Stanhopes: Saturday alone with my Countess [Lady Chesterfield]. So all my plans of absolute retirement are futile. I regret this, for every visit makes me more melancholy – though hotel life in an evening is a cave of despair ... *Adieu! mon très cher.* I never wanted you more, but it is selfish to say so.[3]

As an antidote for grief, Disraeli now threw himself into the political struggle. From 1872 onward, he had 'taken charge of his party with a firm hand,' Lord Blake wrote. 'On three broad issues he sharply differentiated Conservative from Liberal policy. In a speech in April 1872 he defended the monarchy, the House of Lords and the Church against the radical threat that he claimed to discern in Gladstone's policy. He later asserted for the first time the Conservative belief in consolidating the Empire ... and dwelled on the importance of social reform ... which touched the real interests of the masses more effectively than most of Gladstone's measures. Disraeli was at last able to show that Tory democracy was not a mere phrase.'[4] Exercising great restraint and shrewdness, he refused to form a government in 1873, when Gladstone's administration was defeated in the House of Commons; on the grounds that he could not dissolve Parliament for some time because of the large amount of unfinished business and that a minority government could not but damage his party's prospects.

Disraeli sensed that, if he waited, the dissatisfactions and divisions in the Liberal party would become more pronounced; that the people would become even more tired than they already were of what he called the Liberals' 'incessant and harassing legislation'; and that the Conservatives, standing on a patriotic platform and promising gradual reform rather than continual upheaval, would win a clear victory. He was encouraged in this belief by the enormous improvement he had helped to bring about in the party's organization. Some years before he had entrusted John Eldon Gorst, a clever young barrister and former Fellow of St John's College, Cambridge, with the task of ensuring that every constituency was contested by a candidate selected in advance. Gorst and Major Charles Keith-Falconer, as Secretary, also efficiently administered the reformed National Union of Conservative Working Men's Associations, dropping the 'Working Men's' from the Association's title at the suggestion of Disraeli, who considered the words laid unnecessary emphasis on the class of its members.

Disraeli's faith in victory after this organization of the party's machinery was fully justified. In the general election of 1874 the Conservatives gained a majority of almost a hundred seats over the Liberals. Disraeli's triumph was complete when Lord Salisbury, formerly one of his most influential critics, was prevailed upon to join his Cabinet.

In this Cabinet, as in Lord Derby's Cabinet in 1866, Disraeli was a prominent outsider, both in race and manner as also in his education. Apart from Lord Cairns, the Lord Chancellor, who had been educated at Belfast Academy, he was the only member who had not been at a well-known public school. Five members had been to Eton, two to Rugby, one to Westminster and one to Shrewsbury.

The Queen, of course, was delighted to have Disraeli back in office as her Prime Minister. 'You will see that instead of being a Govt. of Dukes as you might imagine,' she told her daughter in Germany, 'it will contain 1 [the Duke of Richmond] and he a very sensible, honest, and highly respected one. The others are all distinguished and able men not at all retrograde.'[5] Indeed, it was a highly promising government, well qualified to keep the Liberals in their now subordinate place.

Its task was much eased by the retirement of Gladstone, who 'deeply desired', as he put it himself, 'an interval between Parliament and the grave'. And so, with the Opposition in disarray and with a large majority, Disraeli was able to carry with ease several major measures of social reform, including an Artisans' and Labourers' Dwellings Improvement Act, a Public Health Act and a number of factory and trade union acts.

He was not, however, as much concerned with the details of these various Acts, as he was with the pursuit of general policies. At Cabinet meetings he spoke little; and outside the Cabinet he left his Ministers to run their departments in their own way, reluctant to dismiss the failures, loyally taking the responsibility for their errors. Yet he was by no means a weak Prime Minister. There was never any doubt that he was in charge. Conciliatory and approachable, polite and even-tempered, he was nevertheless inflexible when his mind was made up, always ready to exercise his power in the realization of important aims. He kept Ministers on a loose rein, but they were always aware that the rein was there and that he would tighten it when necessary.

Over the Queen he could not exercise the same dominion. On occasions, indeed, he was obliged to defer to the wishes of the Faery – as he referred to her in allusion, less ironic than affectionate, to Spenser's *Faerie Queene*. His personal relationship with her grew closer and closer: she permitted him to sit down during audiences and to write to her in the first person letters couched in the most outlandishly romantic terms. And she allowed herself to be persuaded by cajoling flattery to do things no one else could have induced her to do. 'He has got the length of her foot exactly, and knows how to be sympathetic,' commented the Queen's Secretary, Henry Ponsonby. 'He seems to me always to speak in a burlesque . . . with his tongue in his cheek. But are not her woes told in the same manner? . . . He communicates . . . boundless professions of love and loyalty. He is most clever . . . In fact, I think him cleverer than Gladstone with his terrible earnestness.'[6]

'A female friend, amiable, clever, and devoted, is a possession more valuable than parks and palaces,' Disraeli had written in *Henrietta Temple*; 'and, without such a muse, few men can succeed in life, none be content.'

His sister had been such a friend; so had his wife and so had been

Mrs Brydges Willyams. Now, after his beloved wife's death, he turned
to other women to fulfil his need for female company. He renewed his
friendship with the extremely rich Angela Burdett-Coutts, whom he had
had vague thoughts of marrying when he was young; and when Miss
Burdett-Coutts became engaged to a man so very much younger than
herself he was to be as intrigued and surprised as everyone else. 'Next
to Afghanistan,' he was to write to the Queen, 'I think the greatest scrape
is Lady Burdett's marriage. I thought Angela would have become classical
and historical history, and would have been an inspiring feature in your
Majesty's illustrious reign. The element of the ridiculous has now so
deeply entered her career that even her best friends can hardly avoid a
smile by a sigh!'[7]

There was also something of the ridiculous in the pursuit of Disraeli
by the eccentric Adelina de Horsey, who married the Earl of Cardigan
and, after his death, a Portuguese nobleman, the Condé de Lancastre.

'I have had 12 offers of marriage since Lord Cardigan's death,' she
told Disraeli, and was now convinced that a union between herself and
'the greatest man we have in genius & intellect' would suit both parties.
Disraeli did not think so; and his rejection of her offer prompted her
to give a biased and misleading account of the matter in her *Recollections*:

> I was riding my famous horse 'Dandy' . . . and that morning I
> was much exercised in my mind about a proposal of marriage I
> had just received from Disraeli. My uncle, Admiral Rous, had said
> to me, 'My dear, you can't marry that d-d old Jew', but I had
> known Disraeli all my life & liked him very well. He had, however,
> one drawback as far as I was concerned, and that was his breath
> . . . I was wondering whether I could possibly put up with this
> unfortunate attribute in a great man, when I met the King [then
> the Prince of Wales] who was graciously pleased to ride with me.
> In the course of our conversation I told him about Disraeli's
> proposal and asked him whether he would advise me to accept
> it, but the King said he did not think the marriage would be a
> very happy one.[8]

Disraeli's relationships with two other women were to go far to fulfilling
that need for 'a female friend' so essential to his contentment during
the later years of his life. These women were two of the five daughters
of the first Lord Forester.

One of these daughters married Robert John Smith, eldest son of Lord Carrington of Wycombe Abbey; another married General the Hon. Sir George Anson, Commander-in-Chief in India at the time of the Mutiny; a third was the wife of Lord Albert Conyngham, a grandson of the Marchioness of Conyngham, the stately mistress of King George IV. The two daughters who were Disraeli's intimate friends were the eldest sister, Anne, Countess of Chesterfield, and the youngest, Selina, Countess of Bradford.

Lady Chesterfield was a widow two years older than Disraeli. Lady Bradford, seventeen years younger than her sister, was the wife of the third Earl of Bradford who had served as Lord Chamberlain and was soon to be appointed Master of the Horse. Both sisters were intelligent and sympathetic, ready to respond to Disraeli's need for female company and sympathy.

In March 1874 – using the black-banded mourning paper which, in memory of his dear wife, he was reluctant to abandon – he told them that they were the 'two persons' he loved 'most in the world'; and so much did he want to bind these 'matchless sisters' to him that, although she was over seventy years old, he asked Lady Chesterfield to marry him. She refused him, of course, well aware that he would have asked her sister instead, had not Lady Bradford been married already.

It was to Lady Bradford, a grandmother in her mid fifties, that he wrote most of the fifteen hundred letters to the sisters which have survived, sometimes writing twice, even three times, a day, having a messenger wait at her house for her replies, keeping her informed not only as to his social activities but also, as the Duke of Richmond told Lord Cairns, everything 'down to the most minute details' of all that passed in the political world 'and assuring her of his undying devotion'.

'The most fascinating of women was never more delightful than this afternoon,' he wrote one day (when she was about to leave London for her country house, Weston Park in Shropshire), using phrases much like those he addressed on the same day to Lady Chesterfield, who was also leaving London for Bretby Park in Derbyshire: 'I could have sat for ever, watching every movement that was grace, and listening to her sparkling words – but alas! the horrid thought, ever and anon, came over me – "Is it a farewell visit?" It seemed too cruel! . . . Constant separations! Will they never cease . . . I am certain that there is no greater misfortune than to have a heart that will not grow old . . ."[9]

There were occasions when Lady Bradford was exasperated by the barrage of paper which Disraeli dispatched to her, and the fulsome compliments which he bestowed upon her. Yet, when she made this clear, he would write her long, pained letters of explanation and apology:

> Your view of correspondence, apparently, is that it should be confined to facts, and not admit feelings. Mine is the reverse; and I could as soon keep a journal, wh. I never could do, as maintain a correspondence of that kind.
>
> The other day you said it was wonderful that I cd. write to you, with all the work and care I have to encounter. It is because my feelings compel me to write to you. It was my duty and delight: the duty of my heart and the delight of my life.
>
> I do not think I was very unreasonable. I have never asked anything from you but your society. When I have that I am content, which I may well be, for its delight is ineffable. When we were separated, the loneliness of my life found some relief in what might have been a too-fond idolatry.[10]

Such letters would elicit responses, prompted as much by pity as by affection; and Disraeli, having been despondent enough to suppose that 'all was over between' them, was relieved and delighted to receive a reply which took such a load off his heart that he pressed it to his lips.

Then all would go well between them for a time until Disraeli felt compelled to write such a letter as this:

> I am distressed at the relations which have arisen between us, and, after two days' reflection, I have resolved to write once more.
>
> I went to Montagu House on Friday with great difficulty, to see you, and to speak to you on a matter of interest to me. I thought your manner was chilling: you appeared to avoid me, and when . . . I suggested some mode by which we might recognise each other at the ball, you only advised me not to go!
>
> Your feelings to me are not the same as mine have been to you. That is natural and reasonable. Mine make me sensitive and perhaps *exigeant*, and render my society in public embarrassing to you, and therefore not agreeable. Unfortunately for me, my imagination did not desert me with my youth . . . The only person whom you seem neither to care to see, nor to please, is myself.

And when you come to town it will only, I fear, be to tell me, as you usually do, that you are going again into the country.[11]

As before, a letter of contrition from Lady Bradford arrived and he replied, 'Your note had just reached me. It was unexpected and delightful. I am touched by your writing so spontaneously, for my stupid words did not deserve a response . . .'[12]

This letter was followed soon afterwards by another, prompted by one of their numerous tiffs:

> To love as I love, and rarely to see the being one adores, whose constant society is absolutely necessary to my life; to be precluded for ever from the only shadowy compensation for such a torturing doom . . . is a lot which I never could endure and cannot . . . This is rather a long scribblement; pardon that, for it is probably one of the last letters I shall ever send you. My mind is greatly disturbed and dissatisfied. I require perfect solitude or perfect sympathy. My present life gives me neither of these ineffable blessings. It may be brilliant, but it is too fragmentary. It is not a complete existence.[13]

And so the letters went on, protesting utter devotion. It was 'absolutely necessary' to his existence to hear from her every day; he had lived to know that the 'twilight of love' had 'its splendour and its richness'. With reference to her name, Selina, Greek for the moon, he wrote: 'It is not a "slice of the moon" I want; I want it all.'

'You said in one of your letters that I complained that you did not appreciate me. Never! Such a remark, on my part, wd. have been, in the highest degree, conceited and coxcombical. What I said was: You did not appreciate my love, that is to say you did not justly estimate either its fervour or its depth.'

Some months later there was another quarrel, during which Disraeli wrote another similar letter:

> I should grieve if the being to whom I am entirely devoted shd. believe for a moment that I am unreasonable and capricious. Therefore I will condense in a few lines a remark or two on a topic to which I hope never to recur.
>
> You have said that I prefer your letters to your society. On the contrary, a single interview with you is worth a hundred even of your letters, tho' they have been, for more than a year, the

charm and consolation of my life. But I confess I have found a contrast between yr. letters and yr. general demeanour to me, which has often perplexed, and sometimes pained, me: and it is only in recurring to those letters that I have found solace . . .

I will not tell you how much I have suffered. I became quite dejected, and could scarcely carry on public affairs.

But the sweetness of your appeal to me yesterday, and the radiant innocence of yr. countenance, entirely overcame me; and convinced me that I had misapprehended the past . . .

In March 1875, after a period of amity, there was a further quarrel:

Last year, I said I cd. not contemplate life without seeing you every day . . . It is misery: that horrible desolation wh. the lonely alone can feel . . . I have given this morning the Constableship of the Tower to General Sir Chas. Yorke. I keep the Isle of Man still open: open till you have quite broken my heart.

'I hardly had a word with you today,' he wrote some time later. 'I wonder if I shall see you tomorrow! Not to see you is a world without a sun.'

I wonder whom you will sit bet[wee]n today, and talk to, and delight and fascinate. I am always afraid of your dining at houses like Gerard's, in my absence. I feel horribly jeal[ous]; I cannot help it.

In such moods I sometimes read what was written to me only a year ago – tho' that's a long time – words written by a sylph, 'Have confidence in me, believe in me, believe that I am true – oh! how true!'

Even if one cannot believe these words, it is something to have them to read – and to bless the being who wrote them.[14]

Disraeli's letters to his 'dearest, dearest Lady Chesterfield', his 'dear darling', his 'darling friend', were quite as affectionate but more restrained. She scattered 'flowers and fruit over [his existence]'. He recalled meeting her at Wycombe Abbey and falling in love with her 'brilliant eyes' which, he told her, 'cd. hardly spare a glance, then, to poor me. But now I am rewarded for my early homage, and, amid the cares of empire, can find solace in cherishing your sweet affections.'

His letters to Lady Chesterfield, however, contain little of the passion and occasional despair which characterize those to Lady Bradford; nor do these letters to Lady Bradford contain any suggestion that he felt for the elder sister the feelings he had conceived for the younger.

> I am sorry your sister is coming to town [he wrote to Lady Bradford one day]. She will arrive when I am absorbed with affairs, and will apparently be neglected and will probably think so. This will add to my annoyance, for I have a great regard for her. I love her, not only because she is your sister and a link between us, but because she has many charming qualities.

Devoted as he was to these two sisters, he remained faithful to the memory of Mary Anne. One day while supervising with Lord Redesdale the Queen's arrangements for a banquet on her Majesty's birthday, 'he turned round all of a sudden,' Lord Redesdale said, 'and his eyes were dim and his voice husky, as he said, "Ah! my dear fellow, you are happy, you have a wife." '[15]

While going through his own wife's papers, an undertaking which he had long postponed, he discovered, so he told Montagu Corry, that she had not 'destroyed a single scrap' he had ever written to her, before and after marriage. 'Nor,' he added, 'does she appear ever to have cut my hair – which she did every two or three weeks for 33 years – without garnering the harvest; so, as you once asked for some of an early date, I send you a packet, of which I could not break the seal . . . The business of my life is a most melancholy one. I only finished arranging her personal papers yesterday; and she has died for me 100 times in the heartrending, but absolutely inevitable, process.'[16]

34

PRIME MINISTER AGAIN

'The sense of power is delightful.'

'I HAVE LIVED IN SUCH A WHIRL during the last month, that I can hardly distinguish the places where I met persons, and attribute the wrong sayings to the wrong folk,'[1] Disraeli told Lady Chesterfield on the first anniversary of his wife's death. He had been to Glasgow where, on being installed as Rector of the University, he had been welcomed with what he declared to be 'without exaggeration, the greatest reception ever offered to a public man: far beyond Lancashire even!' He had subsequently been to Keir, just outside Dunblane in Perthshire, to Bretby and to Weston, to Lamington and to Ashridge Park in Hertfordshire, to Crichel House in Dorset and to the Earl of Malmesbury at Heron Court in Hampshire.

He had also been to stay with the Prince of Wales at Sandringham, which he described as 'both wild and stately', and where he fancied he was 'paying a visit to the Dukes and Princes of the Baltic'; and he had been a guest of the Marlboroughs at Blenheim Palace. From there, one day, he went to Oxford for lunch with the Dean of Christ Church and 'saw in the flesh' Benjamin Jowett, Master of Balliol and Regius Professor of Greek, John Ruskin, Slade Professor of Fine Art, and Max-Müller, Professor of Comparative Philology – 'that *was* something!'

While staying at Weston he rode to hounds for what seems to have been only the third time in his life. He was in the saddle for well over three hours and was so tired at the end of the hunt that he almost fell against the stable wall.

It was during his days at Weston that he confessed to Lord Henry Lennox, 'Visiting does not suit me, and I have pretty well made up my mind, after this year [1873], to give up what is called society, and confine myself solely to public life ... I linger on here, boring and bored, notwithstanding a charming hostess.'

A few days before Christmas, he moved on to Hemstead Park, Staplehurst, where he wrote to Lady Bradford to say that he 'never was a great admirer of a merrie Xmas, even when a boy. I always hated factitious merriment, in the form of unnecessary guzzlement, and those awful inventions, round games, worse even than forfeits if that be possible.'[2]

He spent Christmas that year at Trentham Hall, the Staffordshire seat of the Duke and Duchess of Sutherland, 'a captive in the enemy camp' as he described himself to Selina Bradford, the Duke having been a Liberal Member of Parliament. 'But,' he added, 'they treated me with great humanity and spared my life, which was valuable to me as I had a prospect of seeing you. They wished me to remain a week but I gave them only two days. I do not stay a week except with those I love.'[3]

Upon his return to London, Disraeli took rooms at Edward's Hotel, George Street, Hanover Square, where he had stayed before, 'merely a couple of rooms on the ground floor,' he told Lady Bradford, 'but they are a sort of headquarters until I get a house, or commit some other folly.' A few weeks later he found a suitable place, Number 2, Whitchall Gardens, convenient for both the Houses of Parliament and Downing Street, where he could 'live again like a gentleman'.

It was here that Sir Henry Ponsonby, the Queen's Private Secretary, delivered a letter from Her Majesty after Gladstone's humiliating defeat in the general election of February 1874, an election shrewdly engineered by Disraeli, who had declined to take office after the Conservatives' less impressive victory the previous year on the grounds that he could not dissolve Parliament when there was so much important business to complete.

'The Queen has just seen Mr Gladstone, who has tendered his resignation and that of his colleagues, which she has accepted. She therefore writes to Mr Disraeli to ask him to undertake to form a government.'*

---

* Mrs Gladstone was as distressed by her husband's defeat in the election as the Queen was delighted. She wrote to her son, Herbert Gladstone: 'Is it not disgusting after all Papa's labour and patriotism and years of work to think of handing over ... to that Jew' (Battiscombe, *Mrs Gladstone*, 158; Hoppen, 606).

Ponsonby had met Disraeli on several occasions before: notably when Disraeli had declined to form a government in March 1873.

> During the first part of the interview [at Edward's Hotel, where Ponsonby had gone to discuss Disraeli's refusal] he sat at a table and spoke with eagerness. There was something in his over civil expressions about the Queen or 'my dear Colonel' which made me think he was playing with me, and I felt once or twice a difficulty in not laughing; but when he developed the reasons of his policy he rose and stood much more upright than I have ever seen him, spoke in a frank and most straightforward manner, and with a sharpness and decision which was different from his early words ... He was far easier to speak to than Gladstone, who forces you into his groove, while Disraeli apparently follows yours and is genial, almost too genial, in his sentiments.
>
> I could scarcely help smiling [Ponsonby added a few months later]. How anyone can put faith in Dizzy is what I don't understand.
>
> What I saw of him here [at Balmoral] made me think him clever and bright in sparkling repartee but indolent and worn out. He did not seem ever to take up any question or to discuss any problem.
>
> I so fully believe that Disraeli really has an admiration for splendour, for Duchesses with ropes of pearls, for richness and gorgeousness, mixed I also think with a cynical sneer and a burlesque thought about them. When he formed the Government he spoke in the highest delight of the great names he had selected for the household offices and the minor offices – 'sons of great Dukes'. His speech here on the Palatial Grandeur, the Royal Physician who attended on him, the Royal footmen who answered his beck and nod, the rich plate, etc. – all was worked up half really, half comically into an expression of admiration for Royalty and the Queen. Yet there might have been a sarcasm under it all.[4]

'My dear mistress will be very happy to see you again,' the Queen's Lady of the Bedchamber, Lady Ely, wrote to Disraeli on his becoming Prime Minister for the second time, 'and I know how careful and gentle you are about all that concerns her. I think you understand her so well, besides appreciating her noble fine qualities.'

'He expressed great surprise at the result of the elections,' the Queen, highly pleased, wrote in her journal. 'He had thought there might have been a very small majority for them; but nothing like this had been anticipated . . . a majority of almost a hundred!! It justified, he said, the course he had pursued last March in declining to take office.'

Two days later the Queen saw Disraeli again. 'He reported good progress,' she wrote in her journal. 'He knelt down and kissed hands, saying: "I plight my troth to the kindest of Mistresses!" Mr Gladstone came at 6, and delivered up his seals. He was very grave, and little disposed to talk.'

Although Disraeli complained to Lady Bradford of the 'crowd of interviews' which he had to undertake in the formation of his government and of the 'endless letters' he had to write when the 'only lines which really interested' him were those he wrote to her, it was clear that Disraeli was 'much excited' by the 'whirl' into which he was plunged; and he later admitted as much: 'After all, it is affectation to talk of the bore and bother of patronage and all that. The sense of power is delightful. It is amusing to receive the letters I do . . . I had no idea I was the object of so much esteem, confidence, public and private, and respectful affection.'

'The truth is forming a Government is a very severe trial.' But, when the work was done, he was satisfied that he had created a 'very strong' administration as well as one in which the great families of England were well represented and the 'minor places' were filled by 'representative' men, that was to say 'every person who might be troublesome'.

As in Derby's third Cabinet, members of the House of Lords were well represented; so were Old Etonians. The Lord Chancellor, the Lord Privy Seal, the Foreign and Colonial Secretaries and the Chancellor of the Exchequer were all earls or shortly to be so.

There were, inevitably, some 'terrible disappointments'; but the Prime Minister had written 'soothing letters' which, on the whole, had 'not been without success'.

When it was all over, he felt quite exhausted and only too conscious of the fact that, as he lamented more than once, the power, which he had for so long and so ardently desired, had come too late. And, in the process of attaining it, his health had suffered grievously: as well as bronchial trouble, he had endured debilitating attacks of gout in his foot and hand; and, while expressing the fondest love for Lady Bradford and Lady Chesterfield, he was still and for ever grieving the loss of his wife, melancholy in his quiet moments, always conscious, as he told his friend the duc d'Aumale, of being 'now alone in the world'. Later that year he confessed to Lady Bradford that he was 'wearied to extinction and profoundly unhappy'.

In the summer he was seized by a particularly painful attack of gout which, as he said, 'quite overpowered' him. He had 'left the H. of C.' with the intention of going to Montagu House, he said, but, when he began to dress, he found that he hobbled 'and a P. Minister hobbling wd. never do', so he gave it up. 'After a night of unceasing suffering', he had been obliged to ask Gathorne-Hardy, the Secretary for War, to take his place as it was 'physically impossible' for him to get to the House.

When he was able to get there, however, he had lost little of his former power.

> Never did the peculiar genius of Disraeli shine more transcendently than during the past session [wrote Sir Henry Lucy in his *Diary of Two Parliaments*]. He has at no period of his career risen higher as a Parliamentary speaker, while his management of the House is equalled only by that of Lord Palmerston. Not in the zenith of his popularity after the election of 1868 did Gladstone come near his great rival in personal hold upon the House of Commons . . . Disraeli's slow, deliberate rising in the course of a debate is always the signal for an instant filling up of the House and a steady settling down to the point of attention, the highest compliments that can be paid to a speaker.
>
> At the outset of his current Premiership, Disraeli fixed upon a policy of polite consideration, to which he was the more drawn as certain members of the Ministry he succeeded were notorious for the brusqueness of their manner. The addition of a bit of banter and of a dash of serio-comicality lent a spiciness to his speech which was always relished, and was never allowed to reach the proportion at which the mixture left an unpleasant taste upon the parliamentary palate . . . Suffering acutely from gout, Disraeli has stuck to his post with Spartan-like patience; and one of his most successful speeches . . . was delivered after he had been sitting for four hours with folded arms on the Treasury Bench, visibly tortured by twinges from his slippered and swollen feet.[5]

That summer of 1874, his gout less troublesome, Disraeli went to stay at Osborne on the Isle of Wight where 'the Faery' sent for him the instant he arrived.[6]

From Osborne, Disraeli went on to Longleat, undergoing a tedious journey which entailed a wait of two hours at both Southampton and Salisbury railway stations.

> They had telegraphed along the line to keep compartments for me [he told Lady Bradford], so wherever I stopped there was an enthusiastic group – 'Here he is' being the common expression, followed by [cheers] and little boys running after me. You know how really distressed I am at all this. And I had a headache and wanted a cup of tea and made fruitless efforts to get one ... I got a cup at Salisbury, however, from apparently a most haughty young lady; but I did not do her justice. She not only asked me for an autograph, but to write it in her favourite work, *Henrietta Temple*! I could have refused the Duchess of Manchester, but absolutely had not the pluck to disobey this Sultana. I never felt more ashamed of myself in my life.
>
> At Salisbury, I found [Walpurga] Lady Paget, who was going to Longleat with her son, a very young Etonian. Sir Augustus had travelled by an earlier train with the luggage. I cd. not avoid giving her a place in my compartment, and she talked, and with her usual cleverness, the whole way: an hour of prattle on all subjects.[7]

Disraeli did not enjoy his visit to Longleat where he was disappointed in his hopes of seeing Selina Bradford. First of all he had occasion to complain about the writing paper – a frequent cause of his displeasure – about the muddy ink and the pens, 'made from the geese on a common', which entirely destroyed 'any little genius' he had and 'literally annihilated' his 'power of expression'.

> We did not get to L[ongleat] till 9 [Disraeli continued his account of this unpleasant evening], and tho' we dressed in ten minutes, people who dine at 8 don't like dining at 9. We were seven at table ... I sat by Lady B[ath] but with a racking headache, rare with me, and not in very good spirits ... A more insipid and stupid and gloomy dinner I never assisted at, and I felt conscious I added my ample quota to the insipidity and the stupidity and the gloom. Lady P[aget] tried to rally the scene, but she had exhausted her resources bet[wee]n Salisbury and Warm[inste]r.

It was only two hours before we all retired, and had I been younger, and still in the days of poetry, I shd. have gone away in the night, wh. I used to do in my youth, when I was disgusted ... I am wearied to extinction and profoundly unhappy.[8]

Lord Bath found Disraeli as boring a guest as Disraeli found him a host. Indeed, Bath told George Russell that Disraeli was the dullest guest he had ever had at Longleat.

The next day, however, 'things [were] a little brighter'. The chatelaine went out of her way to entertain him.

She is very kind [he wrote] and has offered more than once, and unaffectedly, to be my secretary, and copy things for me. Bath says she writes an illegible hand. I rather admire it. It reminds me somewhat of missals and illuminated MSS.... She drove me to Frome to see Bennett's famous church with a sanctuary where 'lay people' are requested not to place their feet. The church is marvellous; exquisitely beautiful ...

The priest or sacristan, or whatever he was, who showed us over the church, and exhibited the sacred plate, etc., looked rather grimly upon me after my anti-ritualistic speeches ... But I praised everything, and quite sincerely, and we parted, if not fair friends, at least fair foes. The world found out who was there, and crowded into the church.[9]

Disraeli was in a sad mood that summer. He could not bear being alone, he told Lady Bradford in a self-pitying letter; but when he joined others he was 'wearied'. 'I do not think there is really any person much unhappier than I am and not fantastically so. Fortune, fashion, fame, even power may increase and do heighten happiness, but they cannot create it ... I am alone, with nothing to sustain me, but, occasionally, a little sympathy on paper, and that grudgingly. It is a terrible lot, almost intolerable.'[10]

In August he went down to Bretby Park feeling very much out of sorts; but the kindly, methodical life led there, the regular hours and the presence of Lady Chesterfield 'combined much to restore' him. He was still discontented though; and on three occasions his hostess drew him aside to ask 'if anything had happened': he 'looked so unhappy'.

From Bretby he went on to the Bradfords' house on Lake Windermere where all 'went on pretty well on the whole', even though his hostess called him a 'humbug' and was – if generally charming as usual – 'fitful'.

From Windermere he went back to Bretby, then on to Balmoral by way of Lord John Manners's house at Birnam.

> The Faery here is more than kind [he wrote to Lady Bradford from Balmoral]. She opens her heart to me on all subjects, and shows me her most secret and most interesting correspondence. She asked me here for a week, but she sent today to say that she hoped I wd. remain at least to the end of next week, and so on . . .
>
> The Derbys dined here yesterday, and with Princess Beatrice [the Queen's youngest daughter] and Lady Churchill and the Duke and Duchess of Edinburgh [her second son and daughter-in-law] made up the 8. The Dss. of Edinburgh [the Grand Duchess Marie of Russia] was full of life, asked the Queen at dinner whether she had read *Lothair*. The Queen answered, I thought, with happy promptitude, that she was the first person who had read it. Then the Duchess asked her Gracious Majesty, whether she did not think Theodora a divine character; the Queen looked a little perplexed and grave. It wd. have been embarrassing, had the Dss. not gone on, rattling away, and begun about Mr. Phœbus and the 'two Greek ladies', saying that for her part she shd. like to live in a Greek isle.[11]

Disraeli was not feeling well, and thought that had it not been for the ministrations of the Queen's doctor, Sir William Jenner, he 'might have been very ill'. 'I felt queer on Wednesday, tho' I dined with the Queen on that day,' he told Lady Bradford.

> Thursday Sir William kept me to my room. I have never left the Castle once. On Friday the Queen sent for me, and I had a very long and most interesting audience. She told me that Sir Wm. had reported to her that I had no fever, and therefore she had sent for me; otherwise she wd. have paid me a visit . . . Free from all shyness she spoke with great animation and happy expression, showed not only perception, but discrimination, of character, and was most interesting and amusing. She said I looked so well that she thought I cd. dine with her.
>
> But when Sir William came home from his drive with P. Leopold and paid me his afternoon visit, he said the symptoms were not at all good; put me on a mustard poultice on the upper part of my back, gave me some other remedies and said I must not think of dining, or of leaving my room.

'This morning the Queen paid me a visit in my bedchamber,' Disraeli continued. 'What do you think of that? . . . I am a sort of prisoner of state in the tower of a castle; royal servants come in and silently bring me my meals; a royal physician two or three times a day to feel my pulse etc., and see whether I can possibly endure the tortures that await me. I am, in short, the man in the Iron Masque.'[12]

He was still feeling unwell when he left Balmoral to go back to Bretby where, as he put it, he 'fell into the gout and that very badly', so badly indeed that he was quite incapable of paying a visit to Ireland which had been planned for the following month.

35

TROUBLES AT COURT

'It would give me real pain to be considered
by Your Royal Highness wanting in dutiful
and affectionate respect.'

'I AM TOO ILL TO WRITE EVEN TO YOU,' Disraeli told Lady Bradford
in a letter written in pencil at Bretby Park on 21 September 1874. 'A
severe attack of gout has been the culmination of my trials, and tho' it
has removed, or greatly mitigated dangerous symptoms, it adds to my
suffering and my prostration. The dear angel here [Lady Chesterfield]
is more than kindness, but that only makes me feel what an enormous
outrage on her hospitality is the whole affair . . . I sit in silence quite
unable to read, musing over the wondrous 12 months that have past
since this time last year. I have had at least my dream . . . I have at any
rate reached the pinnacle of power.'[1]

'What I am suffering from is not gout, but incipient affection in
my throat,' he wrote the following month from Hughenden, 'tho' I doubt
not real gout is at the bottom of it . . . L. [Leggatt, his doctor] says I
ought to go to Buxton, or at least to the sea, and so on, and not live,
as I am doing, among decomposing woods.'

As well as from Leggatt, Disraeli received typical advice from the
Queen, who strongly advised him not to accustom himself to very hot
rooms, 'for nothing gives people more cold than sitting over a large fire
and then going out'.

She herself at Balmoral had the big windows opened on all but the
iciest days and, there as elsewhere, she had thermometers placed in all
the principal rooms so that she could ensure that they never became

what she herself considered overheated by the reluctantly permitted fires of beechwood – almost always wood, since the Queen had 'the same rooted objection to coal as to gas'.

Lord Clarendon complained that the house was so fearfully cold that his toes were frost-bitten as he was having dinner, while in the drawing-room the two little sticks in the fireplace hissed at the man who was trying to light them and the Queen, thinking, Clarendon supposed, that they were in danger of catching fire, had a large screen placed between the royal nose and the unignited wood.

Ministers abhorred having to go to Balmoral, not only because they wasted so much time travelling there when required to attend upon the Queen, but also because they were so uncomfortable when they did get there.

Having endured appalling weather on his earlier visit to Balmoral as Minister in Attendance, and, having fallen ill on his second, Disraeli determined not to go there again. But he was careful not to show his reluctance to do so. He 'seemed delighted with his visit,' the Queen had written of the first occasion.

When he was ill in England he assured the Queen that he obeyed all her commands with regard to his health, in particular those dealing with the temperature of his rooms.

'He never sits over a fire,' he told her, 'and he has a thermometer in every room, with instructions never to exceed 63 ... What details for a servant of the Crown to place before a too gracious mistress! His cheek burns with shame. It seems almost to amount to petty treason.'

The Queen advised him to try 'the very salubrious air of Bournemouth'. His doctors agreed that the sea air should help to 'burn the gout poison' out of his blood. So, in December 1874, to Bournemouth he went, staying at the Bath Hotel where he wrote ill-tempered letters of complaint: 'I detest the place, it is a large overgrown watering-place, almost as bad as Torquay'; and the hotel was comfortless and the food 'frightful'. Had it not been for the fogs in London, he would have done far better staying there. As it was, he trudged gloomily through the snow on Montagu Corry's arm, returning to find letters from well-wishers recommending various doctors. He had gone to Bournemouth 'to get rid of doctors', he said.

Angela Burdett-Coutts invited him to stay at her new house at Hesketh Crescent at Torquay, he told Lady Bradford. Perhaps he should have married her. At least he might not have been so 'unhappy as [he] was now'.

But then, on reflection, he had much to be thankful for. By the end of the year he had begun to feel better and that year, after all, had been a 'wondrous 12 months'.

He went so far as to tell the Queen that his visit to Bournemouth, which her Majesty had 'deigned to recommend', would turn out to be 'a great success'.

While at Bournemouth Disraeli had written to seek the Queen's advice, presuming to lay before Her Majesty a subject on which, so he told her in a characteristic phrase, 'he should much like to be favoured with her Majesty's judgement'.

Her government, he said, was 'in favor with the scientific world', but 'could nothing be done for Literature'? He knew of only two authors 'who were especially conspicuous at this moment': Tennyson and Carlyle. He believed Mr Tennyson would like a baronetcy; but for Carlyle, who was old, childless, poor, very popular and respected, 'would a G. C. B. [Grand Cross of Bath] be too much?'[2]

So the offer to Carlyle was made and refused by him on the grounds that 'titles of honor, of all degrees' were out of keeping with the 'tenor of [his] poor life'. All the same, he was 'grateful that the offer had been made' by the man whom he had described as a 'Hebrew conjurer', the only man, so he told his wife, of whom he had almost never spoken except with contempt and who now came with a pan of hot coals for his 'guilty head'. The feeling was transient; Disraeli, after all, was 'an accursed being, the worst man who ever lived', 'a cursed Jew'. A Jew was 'bad enough, but what was a sham-Jew?' he asked, 'a Quack-Jew? And how could a real Jew ... try to be a Senator, or even citizen, of any country, except his own wretched Palestine?'[3]

Disraeli's general health had much improved by the beginning of 1875, though he was still suffering from a persistent cough and Sir William Jenner was required to give regular reports to the Queen on his patient's condition, her great anxiety being occasioned, so Jenner said in his blunt way, 'not so much from love of her Prime Minister as from dread of somebody else'.

In any event Disraeli was well enough that winter to give a series of political dinners to which ambassadors and royal princes, as well as Members of Parliament, were invited. At one of these, so he told Lady Bradford, he sat between the German ambassador and the Duke of Manchester, who was 'silly but not dull'; next to him was Lothair [the Marquess of Bute], who had travelled up from the wilds of Scotland 'to show his gratitude for the Thistle'. It being Lent, Bute 'could eat nothing but fish; but he managed pretty well, for he instructed his attendant to secure for him a large dish of well-sauced salmon, and that sustained him during all the courses'.

'Everybody talked,' Disraeli said. 'I think it was the most noisy party, without being boisterous, I well recollect ... I found Münster [the German Ambassador] a very capable man with great conversational powers. The cold proud Duke of Northumberland sat next to him, but was grim and acid.'

Other banquets followed and by 17 April, so he told Lady Chesterfield, he had 'dined 242 members of the House of Commons and sixty peers'. 'I had hoped to finish this campaign by the end of April,' he added; 'but I shall hardly be able to do it, as there are 112 members of the Commons to be invited and they are not contented unless they meet a certain portion of swells.'

He accepted almost as many invitations as were issued in his name. At the end of June he dined at the Malmesburys' – 'a Duke of Cambridge banquet, good company', so he reported to Lady Chesterfield:

> On my other side an Australian. I thought her an underbred minx, affecting artlessness, and trying it on me! I cd. only see Selina [Lady Bradford] at a distance, but after dinner, when the D. of Cambridge had done with her, I got my turn, and she was delightful – made a rather dull dinner a success ... Three great houses were open that night, Grosvenor, Apsley and Stafford. But I was firm and went home at once. This getting to bed before midnight answers very well ...
>
> Yesterday I dined at 43 Bel[grave] Square – a brilliant and amusing party. I took down the Dss. of Westminster to dinner and sat next to Pss. Mary [of Cambridge, afterwards Duchess of Teck]. The Duchess said as we walked in, 'You are going to sit

between the two fattest women in London.' That might be true; and yet they have both grand countenances, and are agreeable and extremely intelligent. Indeed Princess Mary has wit. The Abercorns were there also: the beautiful Viceroy [Lord-Lieutenant of Ireland] in goggles! having been struck on his eyes by a cricket ball. He excels in the game, as in everything ... The party was very successful, the guests wd. not go, but stayed till nearly midnight, the test of an agreeable dinner party ...

Yesterday I dined at Holland House; a banquet, 4 and 20 at least. As they were all grandees, I went out, as usual, last, and feared I shd. be badly off, and dine between two men; but, as I entered, a faithful groom of the chamber took me under his care, and deposited me, by the instructions of the lady of the house, next to – S[elina]. She had been taken out by Lord Stanhope. It was a most delightful dinner, and a most charming evening. We had Mr Corney Grain [Richard Corney Grain, the entertainer] to amuse us, with his songs and mimicry, and some were quaint and good. S. immensely enjoyed them. The Grand Mecklenburgs were there, the blind Duke in fits of laughter; Duke of Sutherland, the Ilchesters who, by an arrangement, accede to Holland House on the demise of its present genial lady; the Malmesburys; some distinguished foreigners, of course, who knew me years ago.[4]

*   *   *

I had a dreadful accident to my brougham in the evening and I fear I shall lose my beautiful horse, the Baron, for whom I gave 300 gu[ine]as, four years ago, and who has never been ill a single hour.

Bradford was most kind, as, I must say, he always is to me, and took me home with S. It was such a happy day that I did not care much for any accident.[5]

During the summer and autumn of this year Disraeli made, as in the past, a round of country house visits. He went to Sandringham where the Prince of Wales, in his bantering way, teased him for having lost money on the St Leger at Doncaster races. He went to stay with the Bradfords at Weston, then on to Wortley Hall in Yorkshire, then on to Sandbeck Park, and then to Duncombe Park, 'a place of high character', then to see Lady Harlowe at Gopsall Hall in Leicestershire.

While dining at Longleat as a guest of the Baths, he much impressed

Reginald Brett, the future Lord Esher, then an undergraduate at Trinity College, Cambridge, with the fluency and drollery of his talk.

> Dizzy talked a great deal [Brett wrote in his journal]. He kept us in roars of laughter and maintained his reputation for being, when he chooses, the best talker, the best mimic, the best actor, and the most agreeable companion it is possible to contemplate ... His silence even is unutterably droll ... The evening was spent very agreeably. The dinner excellent, the management perfect. Everything is done most nobly ...
>
> Dizzy's account of his visit to Brighton at a time of year when he thought no one would be there ... took the air of a performance. He described how he wandered about the town stopping to listen to bands, strolling into the Aquarium, and finally going to hear the Christy Minstrells, who all got up and made him a low and ceremonious bow ... Then he went on to describe three dinners. First with the Brunnows (for she had seen him in the street), with the feast and gorgeous footmen; then the Sturts, with Lady A. insisting in the middle of the meal on having a special train to go up to town ... Third with the Clanricardes who gave him roast mutton and dry sherry, 'because,' they said, 'you said this morning that was what you liked!' 'I had said so' [Dizzy said]; 'one does say foolish things sometimes; but if there is one thing I never eat, it is roast mutton, and one thing I never drink it is dry sherry; so I dined on Selzer Water.'[6]

Upon his return to Hughenden, Disraeli was immediately occupied with the problem of the new vicar, a young and dedicated High Church incumbent, Henry Blagden, whose wealthy wife had contributed to the restoration and enlargement of the Early English church under the direction of Sir Arthur Blomfield.

Mr Blagden was a man of decided views whom Disraeli described in a letter to Lady Bradford, not entirely flippantly, as a 'rebellious priest' whose taste for ceremonial was not shared by his principal parishioner and patron of the living. Disraeli's claim to his manorial right to a seat in the chancel was at the same time disputed, unsuccessfully, by the parson.

After the restored church was opened, Disraeli 'said a few words' which drew attention to the need to show to the country the possibility of combining 'the beauty of holiness' with the profession of the 'pure *Protestant* faith of the Church of England'.

The sacerdotal procession was tremendous [Disraeli reported], not only a banner but the Bishop's crosier, borne, and certainly nearer a 100 than 50 clergymen in surplices and particoloured scarves. I was resolved not to be betrayed into a formal speech, and especially an ecclesiastical speech; but I was obliged to bring in a Protestant sentiment by way of protest. Everything was intoned and the high altar and its rich work absolutely emblazoned with jewels. One lady in Warwickshire sent a string of pearls, and not mean ones, to enrich the altar cloth.[7]

'I do not breakfast in public,' Disraeli told Lady Bradford, describing his routine at Hughenden at this time. 'I only did that in the summer to see you, as I thought it was perhaps the only opportunity (and it often was) of seeing you in the course of the day, or of speaking to you, wh. you always seemed to grudge me.'

I always rise at ½ pt. 7, go thro' my bag [he continued], and after my toilette, saunter on the terrace, if the sun shines, and review the peacocks; then I go up to my little room (my cabinet) for my correspondence, and work at that till one. Then déjeûner; and at ½ past one, the messenger arrives, and as now I am not at home to any human being, I change the scene after déjeûner, and work at my boxes in the library. It is a favourite room of mine, and I like to watch the sunbeams on the bindings of the books.

Now that you are more knowing in such things, I shd. like to show you some of my Renaissance books. My Guicciardini and my Machiavelli are, as becomes such writers, modern editions; but there are many volumes, of less use no doubt, but of more rarity, wh. wd. charm your eye and taste.

Some day when I have time, wh. I really have not now, for only to you cd. I write this, I will tell you about *Somnium Poliphili*, the dream of Poliphilus, one of the most beautiful volumes in the world, and illustrated throughout by Giovanni Bellini . . .[8]

Disraeli's influence with the Queen was demonstrated in May 1875 when Tsar Alexander II, the Duke of Edinburgh's father-in-law, was on a visit to England. It was proposed that the visit should be prolonged for two days beyond the date which had been fixed for the Tsar's departure; but the Queen declined to postpone her spring holiday at Balmoral and insisted upon leaving for Scotland while the Tsar was still in England.

Lord Derby, the Foreign Secretary, whose relationship with the

Queen was never of the best, and whose 'very peculiar' personality was 'very difficult to manage', wrote Disraeli a letter of strong protest:

> The more I think of the matter, and the more I hear what is said, the stronger becomes my conviction that the Queen's going away during her guest's stay in England will really make a serious trouble. It will be talked of everywhere as an instance of incivility so marked as to appear intentional: It will be resented by the Russians, who are as touchy as the Yankees, and for the same reason it will entirely destroy whatever good result may be expected from the marriage and the visit: in India it will be taken up by the native press – much of which is nearly as seditious as that of Ireland – as a proof that the two countries are not really on good terms; and what possible excuse can we make? Not health, for if the great lady can bear 5 days of ceremonies she can bear 7; not public business, for what has she to do at Balmoral? It is ... the less excusable because, of all persons connected with the reception, she will have the least personal trouble.
>
> As a rule, I try always to keep matters which concern the Government, and matters which concern the Court, as far apart as possible: but it is not always possible: and if there is a row, part of the blame will fall on us.
>
> Do try what you can to set this business right. Nobody can have managed the lady better than you have; but is there not just a risk of encouraging her in too large ideas of her personal power, and too great indifference to what the public expects? I only ask: it is for you to judge.[9]

Disraeli agreed with Derby and set about trying to persuade the Queen to remain in London, using that combination of cajolery and flattery of which he was a master. Others, including the Prince of Wales, had tried to change the Queen's mind and had failed to do so; and when Disraeli approached the Queen she let it be known that he, too, offended her by making the unwelcome suggestion, however diffidently and skilfully presented. At a subsequent drawing room he fancied that she 'averted her head' from him and he 'had no doubt' that he was 'not in favor'. He was soon forgiven, however: his head, as he put it, remained on his shoulders. Lord Salisbury, Secretary of State for India, said he had 'saved an Afghan War'; and Derby complimented him on his 'unrivalled triumph'.

'It is for Mr Disraeli's sake and as a return for his great kindness,' the Queen wrote, 'that she will stop [in England] to the 20th ... The Queen thinks Lord Derby and Lord Salisbury have little knowledge of what is the etiquette between Sovereigns.'

Five days later there was 'a grand festival at Windsor'. 'St George's Hall was a truly great scene,' Disraeli told Lady Chesterfield. 'I have never seen it equalled ... The Russian Emperor is high-bred: dignified, but soft in his manners, not that *ton de garrison* wh. offends me sometimes in the Russian princes, particularly the Cesarevitch and the Grand Duke Constantine.'

> I only arrived from Windsor today at noon [he continued his account]. At 3 o'clock I am to have an audience of the Emperor at Buckingham Palace. I dine at Marlboro' House to meet him; and I close with a ball at Stafford House in his honour! And at ½ past four I must be at the House of Commons! It is difficult to get thro' such a day, and I have to change my dress as often as an actor! ...
>
> May 16 ... At three o'ck. the Emperor held a levée of the Diplomatic Body and our Ministry at Buckingham Palace. There I had an audience which was an audience rather of phrases, but nothing but friendliness to England and hopes that my Government wd. cherish and confirm those feelings. The Emperor's mien and manners are gracious and graceful but the expression of his countenance, wh. I now could very closely examine, is sad.
>
> Whether it is satiety, or the loneliness of despotism, I know not, but it was a visage of, I should think, habitual mournfulness.*[10]

Having satisfactorily settled the matter of the Queen and the Tsar's visit to England, Disraeli was required the next year to deal with the difficult question of the Prince of Wales's visit to India.

When the Queen was approached about this visit, she thought an Indian tour was not at all a good idea. It was 'quite against [her] desire', she told her daughter, the Crown Princess Frederick. There might be some political advantage but not much; it was not as if there were any particular crisis in Indian affairs. Besides, if Bertie's health were up to the strain, he ought not to leave his family for so long; and there could be

---

* Having survived several attempts on his life by revolutionaries, Alexander was mortally wounded by a terrorist's bomb in 1881.

no question of his wife going. In any case, who was to pay for it all?[11]

'Where is the money to come from?' Disraeli also wanted to know after 'our young Hal' had induced his mother to give her assent to the scheme 'on the representation that it was entirely approved by her ministers'.

> He has not a shilling. She will not give him one. A Prince of Wales must not move in India in a *mesquin* manner. Everything must be done on an imperial scale etc., etc. This is what she said. [She also said] that nothing will induce her to consent to the Princess going and blames herself bitterly for having mentioned the scheme without obtaining on the subject my opinion and that of my colleagues.[12]

In fact the Prince had never suggested to his wife that she should accompany him; and Lord Derby, for one, was thankful that he had not done so. For not only would there be extremely difficult problems of protocol to overcome if she were to visit the courts of Indian princes; but, so Derby said, '"Hal" is sure to get into scrapes with women whether she goes or not, and they will be considered more excusable in her absence.'[13]

When she discovered what her husband's intentions were, Princess Alexandra was much put out, protesting, years later, that she could '*never* forget *or* forgive' him for having left her behind. The Prince, himself, was much annoyed when he learned that his mother – who was already pestering him with advice about the food he should eat, the time he ought to go to bed each night, the way he must behave on Sundays – insisted on supervising all the arrangements, including the composition of his suite.

She had written to the Prime Minister with 'positive directions that the detailed arrangements should be considered by the government as an official question'. 'At the same time,' so Lord Salisbury told the Prince, 'the Queen was pleased to lay especial stress upon the number and composition of your Royal Highness's suite as a matter of public importance.' But it had been '*entirely*' his own idea, the Prince protested, and it was only natural that he should wish 'to keep the arrangements connected with it in his hands'. During an interview with Disraeli at Downing Street, he 'manifested extraordinary excitement' as he angrily declined to make any alterations in the names he had chosen. He would certainly not leave behind his friends, the Duke of Sutherland and Lord Carrington, simply because the Queen disapproved of them.

In the face of the Prince's obduracy, Disraeli felt compelled to give way, afterwards assuring the Queen that he would caution Carrington 'against larks', and that, apart from the Prince's secretary, Francis Knollys, who was admittedly not always as well behaved as he might be, there could be no real objection to the other members of the suite. As well as various equerries, aides-de-camp, a lord-in-waiting, a secretary, a chaplain, a physician and other attendants, the Prince's retinue was to include a page, a stud-groom and valet, three chefs and twenty-two other servants as well as a piper; and there was in addition to be an artist, a botanist, and Clarence Bartlett, Assistant Superintendent of the Zoological Gardens, who was both a zoologist and a taxidermist. The Prince's French poodle, 'Bobêche', was to be taken, as well as three handsome horses from the Sandringham stables. So as to accustom them to the sight of wild beasts and reptiles, the horses were taken regularly to look at the animals in the zoo.

Naturally there was trouble over the amount of money to be provided for the expedition as well as over its composition. All over England hostile demonstrations were held. Outraged orators demanded to know why the country was being asked to pay for presents to Indian princes, while the gifts offered in return would become the Prince's personal property. Banners and placards were waved in protest against the Indian visit, and during his travels that summer the Prince himself was made aware of the strong feelings which had once more been roused against him.

Even in royal circles people spoke slightingly of his mission. At Balmoral, after a Sunday morning service, Lady Errol, a Presbyterian attendant of the Queen, remarked to Henry Ponsonby how beautiful was the prayer which had been said for the Prince of Wales. 'Well,' Ponsonby replied, 'I don't know that it was a bad one, but I didn't understand what he meant [by] "Oh bless abundantly the objects of his mission."' Lady Errol replied, 'Oh, all the good he may do.' Ponsonby sharply observed, 'The object of his mission is amusement.' 'Yes,' agreed Lord Salisbury. 'And to kill tigers. Perhaps he meant to bless the tigers.'[14]

In spite of all the criticism, however, and in face of strong objection from the Radicals and many members of the Liberal Party, Disraeli persuaded the House of Commons to approve the expenditure of £52,000 by the Admiralty for the transport of the Prince's suite to and from India, and of a further £60,500 by the Treasury for the Prince's personal expenditure, including presents to Indian rulers. An additional £100,000 was subsequently contributed by the Indian Government. Yet the Prince maintained that this was far from enough: the Indian princes would present their guest with gifts far more lavish than any that he would be able to afford to give them in return. And, as if confident that the amount of his allowances would be increased when the importance of his mission was realized, he spoke carelessly to his 'creatures', so Disraeli recorded, 'of spending, if requisite, a million, and all that'. But although 'a thoroughly spoilt child' who could not 'bear being bored', he was also, in Disraeli's opinion, 'the most amiable of mortals'; and he soon reconciled himself to the amount which the Prime Minister had raised for him without further protest.

Irritated by quarrels over the number and quality of his companions and over the amount of money to be allowed him, the Prince was also piqued by the attitude of his wife, who, refusing to accept her husband's explanation that this was an all-male party and that 'it was difficult for ladies to move about' in India, continued to complain bitterly about being left behind and appeared to Disraeli as though she were preparing to commit suttee. The Princess was also very upset because the Queen refused to allow her to take the children to Denmark while their father was in India. Although she later relented, the Queen insisted that a decision given by the judges in the reign of George II gave her the right to prevent the royal children from leaving the country. Taking pity on the Princess, Disraeli consulted the Solicitor-General, who gave it as his opinion that the precedent was a bad one, that the Queen ought not to exercise it even if it existed, and that 'to force the Princess to live in seclusion . . . six months in England [was] a serious matter'.[15]

Before leaving England, the Prince wrote the Prime Minister what Disraeli described as a 'touching' letter of thanks for what he had done as an intermediary with the Queen, sending with it a signed photograph and giving 'the fatal date of his departure'.

'I am touched by your kind letter and good wishes,' the Prince wrote, 'and I thank you for your advice which I shall always be most ready to accept . . . It will always give me the greatest pleasure to hear from you, and I know that you will always be a good friend to me.'[16]

With the utmost reluctance Disraeli accepted an invitation to Sandringham before the departure of the amiable Prince for India.

The horseplay indulged in by the Prince's circle was not at all to his taste; nor was the lack of companionable female guests. 'It is a dull house – for me,' he wrote to Lady Bradford, to whom he also complained of the 'buffoons, & butts & parasites, and nameless toadies amongst the other guests'.

He felt quite out of place, as he had done earlier at a costume ball held at Buckingham Palace in honour of the Russian Emperor. On that occasion he and the Duke of Cambridge, as Commander-in-Chief, were the only two guests not in fancy dress, Disraeli considering that 'Commanders-in-Chief and Prime Ministers ought not to figure in Charles II wigs and false moustachios'.

He was bothered at this time by having to find a replacement as Viceroy of India for Lord Northbrook, who wanted to resign. He offered the post to Lord John Manners, who, to his annoyance, declined it.[17] 'The fact is,' he wrote grumpily, 'Manners is corpulent & uxorious & he has destroyed a fine intelligence & finer spirit with middle-class vices + eating & drinking & marrying vulgar women.'[18]

In the event, to Disraeli's relief, the Prince's visit to India was, as *The Times* maintained, a 'notable success'; but, after his return to England, there arose an issue which threatened to cause further trouble between himself and his mother. This was the Royal Titles Bill, which passed its third reading in the House of Commons on 7 April 1876 and proposed to confer on the Queen the additional title of Empress of India. Neither his mother nor the government had troubled to let the Prince know of this measure; and, 'as the Queen's eldest son', he felt he had 'some right to feel annoyed' that the 'first intimation he had had of the subject should have come from a column in a newspaper instead of having received some intimation on the subject from the Prime Minister'. Shown this letter, Ponsonby wrote to Disraeli to say that the Queen 'blamed herself' for not having written to the Prince about the Titles Bill, adding, however, that 'she certainly thought she had done so'. The Prime Minister

himself made the equally lame excuse that His Royal Highness's movements in India 'rendered any communication by post most difficult'.
Disraeli went on to say: 'It would give me real pain to be considered
by Your Royal Highness wanting in dutiful and affectionate respect.'

To this letter the Prince replied: 'While thanking you for having
kindly stated your reasons why you did not let me know previously of
the intention of H.M. Government to add the name of Empress of India
to the Queen's style, I feel bound to say that I do not feel that the facts
of the case are altered.'

However, the Prince accepted the apologies offered him on what
the Duke of Cambridge described as an '*incomprehensible* and really too
outrageous' insult and he assured his mother that he had 'not the
slightest wish but to receive Mr Disraeli in the kindest manner possible';
and although subsequently he assumed the title of Emperor of India
himself, the slight to which he had been subjected rankled with him to
such an extent that on his mother's death he initialled documents 'E.R.'
rather than follow the example of the Queen, who had written 'V.R.I.
[Victoria Regina et Imperatrix]'.[19]

The Prince was far from being the only critic of Disraeli's ready
agreement to the Queen's assumption of the title of Empress without
proper consultation. Gladstone was outraged and made his feelings only
too clear. So vehement, indeed, was his objection that Disraeli remarked
contentedly to Lord Derby that only posterity could now 'do justice to
that unprincipled maniac ... extraordinary mixture of envy, vindic-
tiveness, hypocrisy, and superstition, and with one commanding characteristic – whether preaching, praying, speechifying, or scribbling – never
a gentleman'.[20]

36

EARL OF BEACONSFIELD
AND VISCOUNT HUGHENDEN
OF HUGHENDEN

'He looks like one of those stone figures
of Ancient Egypt that embody the idea
of motionless quiescence for ever.'

THE ROYAL TITLES BILL had not been passed without strong opposition which the Queen found 'quite inexplicable'. She had, so Lady Ely told Disraeli, 'quite *entre nous* been much upset by this debate and had taken the opposition very badly to her title, personally and for the sake of you, as the Queen says, "her kind, good and considerate friend". She fears you have been much annoyed but her displeasure is very great with those who have opposed it.'[1]

By the end of the year all opposition had been overcome; and the Queen gave Disraeli her portrait by Heinrich von Angeli for him to hang at Hughenden. He knelt down before her and said, 'I think I may claim, Madam, the privilege of gratitude.' She held out her hand and he kissed it three times 'very rapidly' and 'she actually gave [him] a squeeze'.

He was asked to dine at Windsor with the Empress of India. 'It is New Year's Day when she is proclaimed in Hindustan,' he told Lady Bradford, 'and she wishes the day to be celebrated, and "marked" hereafter ... The Faery is much excited about the doings at Delhi. They have produced great effect in India, and indeed throughout the world, and vindicate triumphantly the policy of the measure wh. was so virulently, but so fruitlessly, opposed. Our poetical Viceroy [the first Earl of

Lytton] is doing justice to the occasion. The Faery is so full of the great incident, and feels everything about it so keenly that she sent me a Xmas card and signed her good wishes *Victoria Regina et Imperatrix*.'[2]

Disraeli went down to Windsor with Lord George Hamilton, the Under-Secretary of State for India, who was acting as Secretary while the Marquess of Salisbury was attending a conference in Constantinople. The Queen appeared at dinner in a 'mass of oriental jewellery, mostly consisting of very large uncut stones and pearls', presents from Indian princes given to her after the Mutiny when the Crown had taken over the government of India from the East India Company. After dinner the Queen's son, the Duke of Connaught, proposed the toast of his mother as 'Queen and Empress of India', using far less extravagant words than those employed by Disraeli when, on a later occasion, he 'broke through all etiquette by rising and proposing the health of the Empress of India with a short speech as flowery as the oration of a Maharajah'. The Queen responded with a 'pretty smiling bow, half a curtsey'.[3]

So far in his career Disraeli had had little chance of displaying his formidable gifts in what a character in one of his books describes as 'real politics: foreign affairs'. Indeed, he did not seem particularly well suited to deal with them; he could speak no foreign language except French; and that not well; and although always ready to attack the Liberals for what he condemned as their responsibility for England's decline as a great power, neither in opposition nor in office did he seem to have any constructive ideas on foreign policy: on what was now the main issue of the day, the problems created by the slow collapse of the Turkish Empire, his views were at variance with public opinion in the country as a whole. Having little sympathy with nationalist movements, he did not share the general feelings of outrage at reports of the cruel misrule of the Christian subjects of the still huge, though ramshackle Turkish Empire. He would have preferred, in fact, to let the Eastern Question alone, and was only anxious lest the Dreikaiserbund, the League of the Three Emperors (of Austria, Germany and Russia), would steal a march on him. If there were capital to make out of the Question, he was determined to make it himself.

As it happened, he stole a march on his rivals over a matter only indirectly concerned with the Turkish Empire – the Suez Canal. In October 1875 the Sultan's bankruptcy led to the ruin of the Khedive of Egypt, who was thereby forced into negotiations with two competing French syndicates, neither of which in the end could raise the money. As soon as he heard of these negotiations, Disraeli made up his mind that the British, not the French, must have the Khedive's shares. The Cabinet did not agree with him. But he persuaded them that 'the thing *must* be done'; and Montagu Corry was dispatched post-haste to Baron Rothschild to borrow the money which could not be raised in Parliament as it was in recess. According to Corry, Rothschild asked only two questions, 'When?' and, after eating a grape and spitting out the skin, 'What is your security?' The next day £4,000,000 (in today's terms about £160,000,000) was lent to the British government at an interest of 2½ per cent. The Rothschilds earned £100,000 and the British government acquired the Khedive's shares.

'It is just settled; you have it, Madam,' Disraeli wrote proudly to the Queen, who was reported to be 'in ecstasies'. 'The French Government has been out-generalled. They tried too much, offering loans at an usurious rate, and with conditions which would have virtually given them the government of Egypt.'

'This is, indeed, a great and important event,' the Queen replied. 'When it is known it will, the Queen feels sure, be most popular in the country. The great sum is the only disadvantage. The Queen will be curious to hear all about it from Mr Disraeli when she sees him today.'[4]

The *coup* was not as immediately significant as Disraeli made it out to be; the purchased shares represented less than half the total and were, in any case, mortgaged until 1895. But it certainly proved to be a profitable investment: before the century was out the shares were worth well over six times as much as at the time of their purchase and were increasing in value year by year. Disraeli's reputation for financial acumen, though resting on rather shaky foundations, was secure.

'The Faery is in ecstasies about "this great and important event"', he told Lady Bradford. 'She was in the 10th heaven, having received a letter of felicitations from the King of the Belgians on "the greatest event of modern politics" . . . What she liked most, she said, [was that] it was a blow against [the German Chancellor, Prince Otto von] Bismarck.'

Disraeli believed, he told her, that the coup would be 'looked upon as a great unparalleled success', which was 'greatly owing', he added with characteristic flattery, 'to the sympathy and support which Mr Disraeli received from your Majesty, and to the clear-sightedness which your Majesty evinced in the affair from the outset'.[5]

'I have had the illness of a month crammed and compressed into 8 and 40 hours,' Disraeli told Lady Bradford one day in January 1876. He had just come from the Cabinet where his colleagues had found him looking extremely ill and, judging from their expression, they evidently thought, so he said, that the Burials Bill which they were discussing 'was rather a fitting subject for their chief'. For much of the time lately he had been looking and feeling ill. In May, Arthur Munby, the poet, 'met him on foot' in Green Park and thought that he looked 'worn and gaunt'.[6] That month he wrote a series of letters to Lady Bradford detailing his various complaints and intermittent recoveries:

> I could not call yesterday and was very unwell with my throat
> ... I sat through the debate in great suffering ... and went home
> very late and rather hopeless ... If I cd. have stayed at home, I
> shd have been all right. But that is impossible ... I am dreadfully
> weak ... The Faery keeps telegraphing for bulletins ... She is
> very anxious ... I ought to drive a little, or I shall become a
> confirmed invalid ... Writing requires a degree of energy and
> precision of wh. I am now quite incapable ... The N.E. blast has
> returned and this is my direst foe ... I can't give a good account
> of myself, as I had a fresh attack last night ... a senseless line
> from the solitary. You cannot expect much.[7]

'I could not write yesterday, being so very ill, and quite incapable of thought and expression,' he reported at the beginning of July. 'What irritates me is that Gull [Sir William Gull, the physician], who has now been tinkering me for a week and making a series of conceited mistakes – ordering me, for example, to drink port wine, wh. I have not done for ten years, and wh. has nearly killed me – keeps telling Monty that I am better.'*[8]

---

* Gull and the Queen's doctor, Sir James Reid, were but two physicians who received baronetcies in the Queen's reign. One of the characters in Disraeli's *Sybil* says that 'a baronetcy has become the distinction of the middle classes, a physician, our physician, for example, is a baronet, and I dare say some of our tradesmen; brewers, or people of that class' (J. V. Beckett, *The Aristocracy in England, 1660–1914*, 1986, 115).

Montagu Corry in turn reassured the Queen, who nevertheless remained anxious.

'She was very sorry to hear from General Ponsonby that [Mr Disraeli] was feeling the fatigue of his work,' she had written at the beginning of June. 'Should he feel that the fatigue of the House of Commons is too great, she would be happy to call him up to the other House, where the fatigue would be *far less* and where he would be able to *direct* everything. No one, no doubt, can replace him in the House of Commons; still, if he felt it too much for his health, something must be done, and he has some excellent men – especially Sir S[tafford] Northcote [Chancellor of the Exchequer] – who could no doubt work under him. The Queen throws this out, as she feels the immense *importance* he is to the Throne and country and now – more than ever now – she wishes and hopes his Govt. may be long maintained.'[9]

Faced with the possibility of going to the House of Lords, as the Queen proposed, Disraeli consulted his principal colleagues, most of whom agreed with Lord Derby, the Foreign Secretary, that his continuance in the Commons was a sacrifice that should not be asked of him and that he could still lead his Cabinet colleagues as a member of the House of Lords.

The Duke of Richmond, the Lord President, considered that his having a peerage conferred upon him was 'by far the best arrangement that could be made'. Lord Salisbury, the Secretary for India, considered the problem as 'a choice of evils'; but it was infinitely better that he should 'come to the House of Lords' and give life to the 'dullest assembly in the world', than retire. Lord Cairns, the Lord Chancellor, and Gathorne-Hardy, the Secretary for War, were equally convinced that Disraeli should choose to go to the Lords; while the Queen 'absolutely protested' against the idea of his retirement. And, when Disraeli announced his decision, Lord John Manners, the Postmaster-General, told him, 'You have acted in this supreme crisis as you have ever acted in public affairs: rightly, wisely, dutifully.' Manners was confident that the Queen, his colleagues, and the country as a whole would approve the decision at which he had arrived.

It pained him to make the decision and it pained Lord George Hamilton to hear it. Hamilton was, so he said, 'not the only Under-Secretary who would miss the Prime Minister's "kindly advice"' and who would feel he was 'in a different place' now that their leader was 'no longer in it'.[10]

When making the announcement of his retirement from the House of Commons, in August 1876, there were tears in Disraeli's eyes.[11]

The 'deep feeling of regret' was 'quite universal throughout every corner of the House', one Member, Sir William Hart Dyke, wrote in a letter to the Prime Minister. 'Your constant kindness, assistance and advice to me here I shall never forget; always the kind word, when mistakes have been made; and work which might have been dull and laborious has been made ever bright and pleasant.'[12]

Another Member, Thomas Burt, was in the House of Commons when the Prime Minister left it for the last time. He watched him walking slowly down the chamber to the Bar where he turned and gazed for a few moments on the House which had become so familiar to him. He then walked back, passing the Treasury bench and going out behind the Speaker's chair.[13]

Outside he was seen talking to several Members who came up to shake his hand. It was late on a summer evening; and it was noted that the Prime Minister was as dandiacally clothed as he had been when first entering the House as Member for Maidstone in 1837. His long white overcoat hung from his shoulders; and on his hands, one of which was resting on his secretary's arm, was a pair of lavender kid gloves.

The next day it was announced that Mr Disraeli was to go to the House of Lords as the Earl of Beaconsfield* and Viscount Hughenden of Hughenden.

When it became known that Disraeli had left the House of Commons for ever, there was, so Sir William Hart Dyke said, 'much surprise and general consternation. The deep feeling of regret [was] quite universal throughout every corner of the House.'†

* Disraeli eschewed the common pronunciation Beckonsfield, choosing to call himself *Beacons*field. It meant, he said, the field of the beacon. In fact, it appears as Bekensfeld in the Pipe Rolls of 1185 (Eilert Ekwall, *Concise Oxford Dictionary of English Place Names*, Oxford, 1960).
† 'The different analyses of Disraeli's motives in becoming a peer which we got in the newspapers are entertaining,' Reginald Brett wrote in his diary. 'A subtle correspondent suggests that it was his desire to glorify the Hebrew race, by admitting one of the chosen people to the hitherto untasted honours of the English peerage ... I for my part think he was quite right in becoming a peer ... His great merit is that he is a perfect captain of a

The Prime Minister had become a kind of institution in Parliament, or, as he put it himself, 'a sort of favourite', always in his place, listening and watching, his attentive colleagues around him. He was almost invariably neatly dressed in a black frock coat and double-breasted waistcoat in winter and a blue frock-coat in summer, refusing to put papers in his pockets for fear lest they put the cloth out of shape, slipping out for a quiet dinner or a hurried snack in the brougham in which his wife had been waiting for him in a nearby court.

> You never see him gazing around him [an observer had written of him in rather earlier times], or lolling back in his seat, or seeking to take his ease as other men do in the intervals of political excitement. He sits with his head rigid, his body contracted, his arms closely pinned to his side, as though he were an automaton. He looks like one of those stone figures of ancient Egypt that embody the idea of motionless quiescence for ever.[14]

'He invariably sat with one knee over the other,' wrote another observer, Sir William Fraser, 'his arms folded across his breast, leaning against the back of his seat, his hat slightly over his brows. The more vehement the attack of his adversary became, the more he affected somnolence; when it waxed very hot indeed, he, without removing his pendant leg, brought his body round towards the west. Placing the glass in the breast pocket of his coat, he again relapsed into simulated sleep.'[15]

He had presented a similarly impassive appearance as he glided about the House of Commons, 'more like the shadow than the substance of a man, seemingly oblivious of his surroundings and, for the most part, oblivious also of his fellow-Members.' In later years, however, he was more often to be seen in the company of younger men, standing with his back to a fireplace, 'interested in any little piece of gossip or rumour relating to current events' and anxious 'to learn what was going on outside Parliament.'[16]

When he spoke in the House he did so with evident confidence and the benefit of a remarkable memory, still employing occasional and unobtrusive mannerisms to emphasize a point or to ensure the attention

---

side . . . [Unlike Gladstone] Dizzy possesses self-control. He is without hatred, and never appears to bear malice. This together with his wit, and the air of mystery that is about him, captivates men' (Brett, *Journals and Letters*, i, 37, 42).

of the House. Once, while Gladstone was making a speech in the Commons, he took a piece of paper from his pocket, examined it carefully through his eyeglass, appearing to read it with marked attention, before tearing it up and dropping the pieces to the floor. A Member, curious to know what Disraeli had been reading, later picked the pieces up only to discover that they were bits of a blank sheet of paper.[17]

He spoke with conviction, sometimes with controlled passion, enunciating his words carefully, pronouncing business with three syllables, for example, Parliament with four. Dispensing for the most part with notes, he still delivered his speeches with occasional shafts of humour. Ironical, satirical, sometimes derisive, sarcastic or mocking, they were quite without the spurious oratorical tricks, gestures and sudden changes of tone of the demagogue.

> He began slowly and very deliberately [wrote Sir William Fraser]. Whenever he was about to produce a good thing, and his good things were very good, anyone in the habit of watching him knew precisely when they were coming. Before producing the point he would always pause, and give a nervous cough: the action of his hands was remarkable. He carried a cambric handkerchief, of spotless whiteness, in his left skirt pocket. He would place both hands in both pockets behind him; then bring out the white handkerchief, and hold it in his left hand before him for a few seconds; pass it to his right hand: then with his right hand pass the handkerchief lightly under his nose, hardly touching it; and then with his left hand replace the handkerchief in his pocket, still holding his hand, with the handkerchief in it, in his pocket, until a fresh topic arose.[18]

'Disraeli had a perfectly melodious voice [quite without the regional accents of north countrymen such as the Old Etonian, Gladstone,* and of many West Country Members] and what is rare, a voice increasing in beauty of tone the more loudly he spoke. He had the proud consciousness of having a master-mind; and a masterly power of influencing men.'

---

* A future Prime Minister, Herbert Henry Asquith, also spoke with a north country accent, in his case Yorkshire, until his second wife, Margot Tennant, persuaded him to speak as she did (Colin Clifford, *The Asquiths*, 2002). In his younger days Peel, the Old Harrovian son of a rich Lancashire cotton manufacturer, also had the traces of a north country accent, as had Lord Stanley, an old Etonian like Gladstone, who spoke in what Disraeli described as a 'Lancashire patois'.

'He was not only brilliant himself,' Sir Henry Lucy wrote in his *Diary of Two Parliaments*, 'but the cause of brilliancy in others. He wound up the House to a certain pitch, at which it was constantly kept going. His mere presence supplied a focus towards which the minds of speakers was bent.'

Above all, he took the trouble to make himself master of the subjects upon which he spoke. 'I cannot read now what are called "works of fiction",' he said at this time. 'Such compositions entirely with me depend upon their style; and that seems a quality quite unknown to the present generation of critics. Something very fine like *Wilhelm Meister*, or the earlier works of George Sand, might not only attract but absorb me; but I require nothing short of those great masters. Fiction must be first rate or it is nothing.' Indeed, he claimed that, when he 'wanted to read a novel', he 'wrote one'. He also claimed, however, that he had read Jane Austen's *Pride and Prejudice* 'at least sixteen times'.

Yet, if he rarely read works of fiction, he made a study of history and biography, politics and economics, blue books and Parliamentary papers, official reports and works of reference; and he sought to discover in conversation what he could not discover in print. Lord Derby once exclaimed ruefully, on learning that Disraeli was to join a shooting party at Lord Malmesbury's house, Heron's Court, 'Ah! Now we shall be obliged to talk politics.'

37

BERLIN

'Der alte Jude, das ist der Mann!'

'WE SATE UNDER BOWERY TREES surrounded by cooing doves,' Lord Beaconsfield wrote to Montagu Corry while paying a short visit to the Bradfords at Castle Bromwich Hall, Warwickshire, soon after his last appearance as a commoner in the lower house. 'At six o'clock we went for some amusing drives and Miladi generally drove me alone. I visited Drayton [Sir Robert Peel's House near Tamworth], a very fine place full of art and all on a great scale.'[1]

On the day of his departure, 22 August 1876, the Bradfords took him to Birmingham, where he was 'cheered through the streets' to the railway station. 'The people were very tumultuous after we separated,' he wrote to Lady Bradford, 'perhaps you heard them. And there was a party collected at every station till we got to Banbury with vociferous ejaculations to the "noble Hurl of Beaconsfield"'.[2]

'I continue to receive innumerable letters of congratulation,' he added later, 'occasionally mixed with 1 or 2 of menace.'

Back at Hughenden Manor he was soon 'tied to his post', as he put it to Lord Salisbury. 'I ought to be at Whitehall, but really in August and September that would be too dreary. Even Derby gets back every night to his "placens uxor". But still even here with endless telegrams and ceaseless messengers, I find myself, every now and then, behindhand.'[3]

The heavy, almost unremitting work proved too much for his increasingly poor health. He was seventy-two, and in the next few months he was to suffer from a variety of lowering complaints: attacks of extremely painful gout, debilitating bronchitis, asthma, what he called 'feverish catarrh', and an intermittent cough which, he said in April 1877, 'harassed me, more or less, for three months . . . My eyes trouble me much, and I think my retirement from society a necessity. Whe[ther] I can go on steering the ship, I hardly know, but I may be turned out of office, wh. will solve that diffi[cult]y.'

He did not think much of his doctors. Sir William Gull, he now complained, was 'all froth and words . . . Yesterday he was evidently perplexed and disappointed and came twice. They are all alike. First of all, they throw it on the weather: then there must be change of scene. Sir W. Jenner, after blundering and plundering in the usual way, sent me to Bournemouth, and Gull wants to send me to Ems. I shd. like to send both of them to Jericho . . . The only thing in all these troubles is that I am to drink port wine. After 3 years of plebian tipples this amuses me.'

'I have been very ill and am really quite incapable of walking upstairs,' he complained in August. 'Gout and bronchitis have ended in asthma, the horrors of wh. I have never contemplated or conceived . . . Sometimes I am obliged to sit up all night, and want of sleep at last breaks me down.'[4]

Ill as he often felt, he considered it advisable occasionally to appear at certain dinner parties; and, on occasions, contrived to be good company. Lady Randolph Churchill, comparing his conversation with that of Gladstone, said, 'When I left the dining-room after sitting next to Gladstone, I thought he was the cleverest man in England. But when I sat next to Disraeli, I left feeling that I was the cleverest woman!'*[5]

'It is sometimes necessary to show oneself, or else the *Daily News* says I am dead,' he told Lady Chesterfield; and to the Queen he wrote, 'Lord Beaconsfield assures your Majesty that he is prudent in his social movements. He never goes out in the evening and only to such dinners where it is necessary for him to appear. There is a certain tact in the management of even great affairs which only can be acquired by feeling the pulse of society.' So it was that he went to dine, for example, at the

---

* This was not a universal opinion. He made Anthony de Rothschild's wife, so she said, feel '*lamentably stupid*'; and she added that he was liable to become grave and even sulky when he was not the centre of attention. She conceded, though, that it pleased her to reflect that this remarkable man 'belonged to us' as one of Israel's sons (Lucy Cohen, *Lady de Rothschild and her Daughters*, 1935, 44–5).

French embassy, which proved to be 'a menagerie', although he 'sat next to Pss. Mary'.[6]

'The dinner yesterday at P[ercy] Wyndham's was of an aesthetical character,' he told Lady Bradford, 'Pss. Louise, [Viscount and Viscountess] De Vescis, of course, etc. etc., and [Robert] Browning, a noisy, conceited poet; all the talk about pictures and art, and Raffaelle, and what Sterne calls the Corregiosity of Correggio.'[7]

He now particularly disliked dinners at which he had to make a speech as, for instance, on that 'fatal day', the Lord Mayor's Day:

'It always makes me ill,' he wrote to Lady Bradford. 'It is about as nervous an affair as can fall to the lot of man – particularly when it is to be accomplished in a heated hall, full of gas and aldermen and trumpeters, after talking slipslop to a defunct Lady Mayoress, and with every circumstance that can exhaust and discomfort man. I think I will never do so again, and should not be able to do it now, were it not for the hope of seeing you tomorrow.'

In the summer of 1877, he decided that his own house should become, as he put it, 'the headquarters of the Government'. 'I can't be away for more than an hour or two even if I wished,' he wrote. 'It rains telegrams, morn, noon and night, and Balmoral is really ceaseless.' Indeed, so worried was the Queen about her Prime Minister's hard work and poor health, and the dreaded prospect of having to deal once more with the detested Gladstone, that the Faery, so he said, 'writes every day and telegraphs every hour. This is almost literally the case.'

Even his beloved peacocks at Hughenden 'got on his nerves'. 'I am almost thinking of perpetrating a sort of atrocity here, and massacring the peacocks,' he declared. 'They make a sorry show at this time of the year [early September], with[ou]t their purple trains; a "ragged regiment" on the terrace every morning, and all the flower-beds full of their moulting plumage.'

In October 1877 he contrived to get away for three weeks with Montagu Corry to Brighton, a 'bustling, idle place' as he called it, where, to his 'great annoyance', Corry, 'who says he is ill', left him. 'I certainly shd. not have come here had I not understood he was to remain with me,' he complained to Lady Bradford. 'One requires someone [here] to guard one from "third parties" who are ever attacking and invading you in every form . . . I have no substitute for him. The other two are faithful and able, and gentlemen, but I can't live with them, as I do with Monty.'[8]

'I leave this place in no degree better as regards the main suffering – asthma,' he added. 'I am now inhaling night and day; a last desperate effort, and futile. I am very ill . . . If only I could face the scene wh. would occur at headquarters if I resigned, I would do so at once; but I never cd. bear the scene, and have no pluck for the occasion.'

A few days after this letter was written, he left Brighton to stay with the Duke of Bedford at Woburn Abbey for a few days:

> The Duke, whom I always like, and who received me with cordial ceremony, soon suggested that I might like to go to my rooms, but I had not had my tea, and did not want to be dismissed for two hours. Still he hung about me, and would insist upon showing me to my room. It seems the State suite was prepared for me, wh. is very gorgeous, and he wished, I suppose, personally to witness the effect produced upon his guest. I sleep in a golden bed, with a golden ceiling.[9]

The visit was not as tedious as he had feared it might be; but, when it was over, he felt – and felt every year more strongly – that country-house visiting was 'very irksome'.

This did not apply so much to Hatfield, where he usually felt quite at home.

'All the Cecil family seem wonderfully clever but natural,' he told the Queen in April 1878. 'There are two daughters, Ladies Maud and Gwendolen (20 and 18). Lord Beaconsfield has rarely met more intelligent and agreeable women, for they are quite women though in the wild grace of extreme youth.'

They 'keep everyone alive,' he told Lady Bradford a few months later, 'always on horseback, and in scrapes, or playing lawn tennis even in twilight. The evening passes in chorus singing – all the airs of *Pinafore*. It's a distraction both for Salisbury and myself from many cares.'[10]

He invited them to join the Order of the Bee (B standing for Beaconsfield) which, with a bee-shaped brooch, he bestowed upon privileged women friends, including the Queen's youngest daughter, Princess Beatrice, as well as Lady Bradford and Lady Chesterfield.[11]

Towards the end of that year, Beaconsfield decided to leave Whitehall Gardens, where the stairs were so 'terribly steep' that he could not manage them. Instead, he moved into 10 Downing Street, which was to be his London residence so long as he remained Prime Minister. Here he consulted a new doctor, Joseph Kidd, a homeopath whom he liked, considering him 'the best medical man' he had ever known. Having examined the patient 'as if [he] were a recruit', Kidd diagnosed bronchial asthma, 'more distressing than bronchitis but curable', and Bright's disease, 'congestion of the kidneys'. He advised his patient to give up port, which aggravated his gout, to give up pastry and puddings also, and to take more exercise. He was also recommended to take small doses of arsenic 'to clear the tubes', to spend more time over his evening meal, to have a vapour bath before going to bed to help him sleep; and to wear warm clothes in bed to make him sweat. To this he objected. 'You say you want me to perspire,' he said. 'I never did since I was born. I have had a dry skin all my life.'[12] However, since he trusted Kidd, he did as he was told.[13]

After spending a few days in London, Beaconsfield went home again to Hughenden where he was to act as host to the Queen, who had proposed coming to see him for luncheon on a most unfortunate day, the anniversary of Lady Beaconsfield's death, a choice of date for which she apologised when 'it was too late to alter it' and which 'annoyed her very much'.[14]

She travelled with her youngest child, Princess Beatrice, and a few members of her Household to High Wycombe where she was greeted by Disraeli, by Corry, now recovered from his illness, by the mayor and by dense and cheering crowds. 'It took us hardly a quarter of an hour to reach Hughenden which stands . . . rather high, and has a fine view,' the Queen wrote in her journal. 'Lord Beaconsfield met me at the door, and led me into the library, which opens on to the terrace, and a pretty Italian garden. We went out at once, and Beatrice and I planted each a tree.'[15]

The following day her host wrote a characteristically fulsome letter to the Queen: 'Lord Beaconsfield hopes he may be permitted to take this occasion of offering to your Majesty his grateful, and heartfelt, thanks for the honour, which your Majesty conferred on him, yesterday, by deigning to visit his home: where your Majesty left a dream of dignified condescension and ever-graceful charm.'*[16]

* The visit of the Queen to Hughenden did not pass without adverse comment. E. A. Freeman, Regius Professor of Modern History at Oxford, who had already referred to 'the Jew's drunken insolence', now described the Queen as having gone ostentatiously to eat with the Prime Minister 'in his ghetto' (Robert Blake, 607; A. N. Wilson, 402–3).

Six months after this visit of the Queen to Hughenden, on 8 June 1878, Beaconsfield, his health somewhat improved, left for Berlin to attend an international conference under the presidency of Prince von Bismarck, which had been called to discuss the problems presented by the gains Russia had made by the treaty of San Stefano at the end of the recent Russo-Turkish war.

The Queen had been opposed to Lord Beaconsfield's going to Germany, since he was 'far from strong' and seventy-three years old. 'He is the firm and wise head and hand that rules the Government and my great support and comfort,' she told the Prince of Wales, who had written to her to say that the Prime Minister was 'not only the right man to represent us at a Congress but the only man who can go'.

'You cannot think how kind he is to me,' she protested, 'how attached! His health and life are of immense value to me and the country and should on no account be risked. Berlin is decidedly too far.'[17]

Beaconsfield himself wrote to the Queen, explaining the reasons why he and Derby's successor as Foreign Secretary, Lord Salisbury, should attend the conference, and that he would take four days over the journey so as to 'arrive quite fresh'. To this letter the Queen replied that there was no doubt that no one else had 'such weight and such power of conciliating men, and no one [else had such] firmness or a stronger sense of the honour and interests of his Sovereign and Country. If only the place of meeting could be brought nearer!'[18]

Promising that, 'in all his troubles and perplexities', he would 'think of his Sovereign Lady', and that the thought of her would 'sustain and inspire him', he and Corry sailed for Calais where they spent the first night. From there, sending couriers '*en avant*' to 'arrange about hotels and other botherations', they moved on to Brussels, where the King and Queen of the Belgians entertained them 'right royally', then on to Cologne, arriving at eight o'clock in the evening in Berlin, where they were to stay at a hotel, the Kaiserhof.

While they were having dinner that evening, Bismarck's chief secretary arrived at the hotel to invite Lord Beaconsfield to visit his master immediately.

Accordingly [Beaconsfield told the Queen], at a quarter to ten o'clock Lord Beaconsfield waited on the Chancellor. They had not met for sixteen years; but that space of time did not seem adequate to produce the startling change which Lord B. observed in the Chancellor's appearance. A tall, pallid man, with a wasplike waist, was now represented by an extremely stout person with a ruddy countenance, on which he is now growing a silvery beard. In his manner there was no change, except perhaps he was not quite so energetic, but frank and unaffected as before. He was serious throughout an interview which lasted one hour and a quarter, and apparently sincere. He talked a great deal, but well and calmly: no attempt at those grotesque expressions for which he is, or has been, celebrated.[19]

'I should not have recognized him,' Beaconsfield added in a letter to Lady Bradford. Formerly 'he was a very tall man . . . with a waist like a wasp. Now he is a giant, his face ruddy . . . enormously stout.'

Beaconsfield was clearly intrigued by the man, his enormous appetite, his idea of a strict diet consisting of a mere five courses – smoked herrings, pickled salmon, oysters, potato salad and caviare – his consumption of large doses of beer and champagne as well as cigars, his Rabelaisian monologues 'and endless revelation of things he ought not to mention'. Yet he was clearly a man of 'immense consequence'. Also of discernment: he shared Beaconsfield's abomination of Gladstone.

The favourable impression which Beaconsfield gained of Bismarck was warmly reciprocated. '*Der alte Jude,*' Bismarck was soon to declare, '*das ist der Mann!*' 'In spite of his fantastic novel writing he is a capable statesman,' Bismarck decided. 'It was easy to conduct business with him: in a quarter of an hour you knew exactly where you stood with him, the limits to which he was prepared to go were exactly defined.' Bismarck would not have been so impressed had Disraeli fulfilled his original intention and addressed the Congress in French, the language of diplomacy in which, despite his claim that he spoke it with 'great ease and some elegance', he was far from fluent and which he spoke with a scarcely comprehensible accent – so atrocious an accent indeed that Lady Randolph Churchill said she found it difficult not to burst out laughing, all the more so since he had a fondness for using French words whenever opportunity offered.[20]

Lord Odo Russell, the British Ambassador in Berlin, so the rather doubtful story goes, was asked to intervene to prevent Lord Beaconsfield attempting to speak French, it being a matter which the other members

of the English delegation did not dare raise. Russell approached Beaconsfield just as he was going to bed, and told him that he had heard a
rumour that he was going to deliver his speeches in French. This would
be a great disappointment to the other delegates, Russell said, for they
knew that he was 'the greatest living master of English oratory' and that
they were looking forward to his speech 'as the intellectual treat of
their lives'. Susceptible to such flattery, Lord Beaconsfield said he would
consider the matter, and Montagu Corry and the other members of his
staff were profoundly relieved when next day he spoke in English.*[21]

For the duration of the Congress Lord Beaconsfield was kept occupied to the point of exhaustion, making speeches, taking part in prolonged discussions, going to dinners, having lengthy conversations with
Bismarck, writing long letters to Lady Bradford, Lady Chesterfield, Sir
Stafford Northcote, who was acting as head of the Government in the
Prime Minister's absence and, most often, and most exhaustively, to
the Queen, who was not only kept informed as to the progress of the
Congress, but also constantly assured of Lord Beaconsfield's undying
admiration:

> He hopes his most beloved Sovereign is well and happy. Distant
> from your Majesty in a foreign land, and with so awful a responsi-
> bility, he feels more keenly than ever, how entirely his happiness
> depends on his doing his duty to your Majesty, and on your
> Majesty's kind appreciation of his efforts.

'The Crown Princess [the Queen's daughter] encouraged him by
many kind glances,' he continued in a description of a banquet held in
the White Hall of the old Palace, 'and the C[rown] Prince and Princess
drank to the health of the Queen of England, which Lord B. acknowledged with some agitation. It was the health of one of whom he was
almost always thinking ... He will try to say how deeply and finely he
feels the privilege of being the trusted servant of a Sovereign whom he
adores.'[22]

As the days passed, Beaconsfield found the entertainments and
business of the Congress utterly exhausting and some of his colleagues
not very satisfactory. They were, he said, 'all middle-class men and I

---

* Lord Salisbury, however, spoke in French, in what the Russian plenipotentiary, Prince
Gorchakov, termed 'Foreign Office French' (Brett, *Journals and Letters*, i, 54).

have always observed through life that middle-class men are afraid of responsibility'. 'It was consequently absolutely necessary' for himself to attend these receptions, he said, 'but the late hours tire me. I begin to die at ten o'clock, and should like to be buried before midnight.'

'Where do you dine today?' Bismarck asked him one day.

'At the English embassy.'

'I wish you would dine with me. I am alone at 6 o'clock.'

'I accepted his invitation,' Beaconsfield told the Queen, 'sent my apology to Lady Odo, and dined with Bismarck. He was very agreeable, made no allusion to politics, and tho' he ate and drank a great deal, talked more.' He smoked 'countless cigars', Beaconsfield joining him and, thereby, giving the 'last blow' to his 'shattered constitution'.[23]

Before the final document was signed in Berlin, Beaconsfield had to agree to Turkey's loss of more territory than he would have liked; but he returned to England having gained Cyprus for the Queen and having thus secured what he termed a *place d'armes* from which Russian designs on the crumbling Turkish empire could be resisted.

He arrived back in England to a hero's welcome. Large crowds cheered him enthusiastically as he drove from the railway station to Downing Street. The poet A.J. Munby was among them. 'He sat in an open barouche,' Munby wrote, 'and was vociferously cheered by thousands of people, who filled the streets. Thus the Great Panjandrum attains his highest: soon, probably, to have his works undone or at least vilified.'[24]

'High and low are delighted,' the Queen assured him, 'except Mr Gladstone who is frantic.' She offered Beaconsfield a dukedom, which he refused, and repeated her offer of the Garter which he accepted on condition that Lord Salisbury was also thus honoured.*[25]

Crowds cheered him once again as he drove to the Guildhall to receive the freedom of the City of London; and three days later he had to address hundreds of representatives of Conservative Associations;

---

* He had by now become a convinced admirer of Lord Salisbury. Never until now, at the end of his life, so he told Lady Gwendolen Cecil, had he known what it was to work with 'a man of nerve'. 'You will find as you grow older,' he said, 'that courage is the rarest of all qualities to be found in public men. Your father is the only man of real courage that it has ever been my lot to work with' (Lady Gwendolen Cecil, *Life of Robert, Marquis of Salisbury*, ii, 204–5).

and then, although suffering from a bad attack of asthma, he agreed reluctantly to go to see a performance of a Gilbert and Sullivan opera, 'some nonsense which everyone is going to see,' he complained to Lady Bradford, 'Parasol or Pinafore – a burlesque – the sort of thing I hate'. As he had feared, he did hate it. In fact, 'except at Wycombe Fair not long ago', he had 'never seen anything so bad as *Pinafore*'.[26]

He was now at the height of his fame and popularity. Attitudes towards him had been changing for some time. His unscrupulous past and cynical opportunism were being largely forgotten or forgiven. He was gradually becoming recognized not only as the prophet of a new Conservatism, at once compassionate at home and positive abroad, but as a great statesman whom the Queen did well to honour. Power had brought responsibility. The transformation of public attitudes towards him was complete.

As he walked down Whitehall leaning on Montagu Corry's arm, straightening his back with an effort when he felt himself being watched, the black curls carefully arranged in the centre of his forehead, one of his eyelids drooping now, his tired, pale face gently rouged, rings worn over the fingers of his white or lavender gloves, men respectfully raised their hats to him as he passed.

38

THE 'GUARDIAN ANGEL'

'I love the Queen – perhaps
the only person left to me in
the world that I do love.'

WITHOUT TROUBLING THE QUEEN with the immensely detailed
reports on Government measures which Gladstone was inclined to press
upon her, Lord Beaconsfield was careful to ensure that she was kept
well informed of all important questions which the Cabinet had to
consider and of the views which both he and individual Ministers held
on them. Indeed, as the Queen told her daughter, the Crown Princess
Frederick, she had never, since the days of Lord Melbourne, had a Prime
Minister who took such trouble to guide and instruct her and to ensure
that she 'knew everything'.

There were those, indeed, who believed she was indulged too much
and that, as Lord Derby suggested, there was 'a risk of encouraging her
in too large ideas of her personal power'. Certainly Lord Beaconsfield
spoke often of Government policy as 'your Majesty's'.

There were occasions, of course, when the Queen's opinions and
those of Beaconsfield did not coincide. One example of this was the
attitude to be adopted towards Lord Chelmsford, commander of British
forces in Zululand, who, having been taken unawares and seen his army
overwhelmed by Zulus on 22 January 1879 at Isandhlwanda, defeated
the Zulu King Cetewayo at Ulundi on 4 July.

The Queen shared the general enthusiasm at Chelmsford's victory
at Ulundi and urged Lord Beaconsfield to receive him at Hughenden.
This Beaconsfield was disinclined to do, believing Chelmsford to be as

incompetent as Sir Bartle Frere, High Commissioner in South Africa, was self-opinionated. In a letter to the Queen, he wrote of Chelmsford's having invaded Zululand with a light heart, 'no adequate knowledge of the country he was attacking, and no precaution or preparation. A dreadful disaster occurred in consequence and then Lord Chelmsford became panic-struck; appealed to yr. Majesty's Govt. frantically for reinforcements, and found himself at the head of 20,000 of yr. Majesty's troops in order to reduce a country not larger than Yorkshire.'

'It is most painful for Lord Beaconsfield to differ from yr. Majesty,' he added in characteristic style, 'not merely because he is bound to yr. Majesty by every tie of duty and respectful affection but because he has a distinct and real confidence in yr. Majesty's judgement, matured, as it is, by an unrivalled political experience, and an extensive knowledge of mankind.'

The Queen replied immediately and crossly from Balmoral to say that the Prime Minister's letter 'grieved and astonished her'. How, she asked, '*can* civilians decide in a Cabinet on the causes for movements and the reasons for defeat? ... The Queen does not pretend to say that Lord Chelmsford has not made mistakes, but she cannot bear injustice, a want of generosity towards those who have had unbounded difficulties to contend with, and who ought to be supported from home and not condemned unheard.'[1]

Beaconsfield replied to say that he was grieved that any remarks he had made should have disquieted the Queen 'in any degree but the system he had hitherto pursued of communicating everything to her Majesty without reserve might be pleaded, he hoped, to some extenuation of his indiscretion'.[2]

He wrote also to Lady Ely, confident, no doubt, that the letter would be shown to the Queen: 'I am grieved, and greatly, that anything I should say, or do, should be displeasing to Her Majesty. I love the Queen – perhaps the only person in the world left to me that I do love – and therefore you can understand how much it worries and disquiets me, when there is a cloud between us.'[3]

Beaconsfield, however, persisted in his refusal to see Lord Chelmsford at Hughenden even after – having received Chelmsford at Balmoral – the Queen pressed him to do so. But their disagreement was soon forgotten; and before long Beaconsfield was again treating the Queen with that elaborate courtesy and extravagant protestation of affection and regard that so pleased her.[4]

The Queen was too astute to take seriously the more extreme forms of flattery with which Beaconsfield sprinkled his letters to her; but, as with Queen Elizabeth I, Queen Victoria was delighted by the romantic ardour with which her chief Minister chose to address her, by the respect he accorded to her views and the pliancy of his manner.

He never forgot, he might have added, that she was a susceptible and romantic woman. One day, so he told her, as a guest at a banquet where decorations, ribbons, stars and orders glittered on the breasts of other guests, 'he could not resist the temptation, by placing some snow-drops on his heart, of showing that he, too, was decorated by a gracious Sovereign'.

Having admitted him to the Order of the Garter, she granted him – 'as a mark of personal regard and friendship' – the right to wear the Windsor uniform, a uniform designed by George III and worn at Windsor by the Royal Family and certain members of the Royal Household. Lord Beaconsfield welcomed the honour as connecting him 'permanently with [your] Majesty's service. It [would] always be a link.'

The link had become closer than ever when the Queen's daughter, Princess Alice, died of diphtheria after kissing her young son who had contracted the disease. Lord Beaconsfield made a speech in the House of Lords on the Vote of Condolence which the writer, George Russell, described as one of 'inconceivable bathos' but which touched the Queen's heart:

'It became [Princess Alice's] lot to break to her son ... the death of his youngest sister, to whom he was devotedly attached. The boy was so overcome with misery that the agitated mother, to console him, clasped him in her arms – and thus received the kiss of death. My lords, I hardly know an incident more pathetic. It is one by which poets might be inspired, and in which the artist in every class, whether in picture, in statue or in gem, might find a fitting subject for commem-oration.'[5]

In thanking the Queen for her Christmas letter which, as usual, she sent him this year, Beaconsfield wrote, 'Ever since he has been intimately connected with your Majesty, your Majesty has been to him a guardian Angel, and much that he has done that is right, or said that was appropriate, is due to you, Madam. He often thinks how he can repay your Majesty, but he has nothing more to give, having given to your Majesty his duty and his heart.'[6]

Devoted as he always professed to be to 'the Faery', Beaconsfield contrived to be on excellent terms with her eldest son, whom, in allusion to Shakespeare's *Henry IV*, he referred to as 'Prince Hal'. He also got on well with the Princess of Wales, who enjoyed his company as much as he enjoyed hers. He told Lady Bradford of a dinner party at which he sat next to Princess Alexandra, who, he said, had the 'accomplishment of being gracious without smiling; she has repose'. She remembered with gratitude Lord Beaconsfield's help in persuading Queen Victoria to allow her to accompany the Prince of Wales on his visit to Ireland, a journey the Queen had at first strongly opposed.

'Is it not worth Your Majesty's gracious consideration,' he had suggested, '[whether the good of the visit] might not be doubled if His Royal Highness were accompanied by the Princess? Would it not add to the grace, and even the gaiety of the event?'[7] And it was, he said, because of his devotion to Alexandra that he had supported the claims of Greece, of which her brother was King, at the Congress of Berlin. 'I did something yesterday for Greece,' he had said. 'It was very difficult but it is by no means to be despised. It was all done for Her Royal Highness's sake. I thought of Marlborough House all the time.'

The friendly relationship between Beaconsfield and Princess Alexandra was illustrated by a story he told Lady Bradford of a dinner at the Hertfords' at which he sat next to her.

'I said something about her "orders" all of which she wore. She said it was a shame I had no decoration, and she gave me her menu, which was a pretty one, to wear instead. I said "Your Royal Highness will not be able to select your dinner." She replied, "We will exchange menus, and I will wear yours as an additional order".'[8]

Some time later the Prince of Wales hinted that he would like to go to stay as Beaconsfield's guest at Hughenden. The visit was a success, Beaconsfield assured the Queen, the Prince 'maintaining his part with the other guests' with 'felicity and even distinction'. 'He praised the house, praised his dinner, praised the pictures, praised everything,' his host added in a letter to Lady Bradford; 'was himself most agreeable in conversation, said some good things, and told more ... We played at whist in the evening – his own choice ... He beat us, which does not displease him.'

'Yes, I am far from well,' Beaconsfield told Lord George Hamilton, in the early winter of 1880. 'But I have a clever doctor who looks me up when I have anything public to do. I then manage to crawl to the Treasury Bench; and when I get there to look as fierce as I can.'

'Terribly knocked down' with gout, and suffering from nephritis and uraemia, he had felt incapable of carrying the sword of state at the opening of Parliament on 5 February. He also had difficulty in speaking and confessed that what he did say, he 'said badly'.

Lord Ronald Gower, who called to see Beaconsfield that winter at Hughenden, found him sitting on the south veranda in a long fur coat. He looked older and weaker as he smoked what he claimed was the first cigar he had had since Gower's previous visit two months before. He spoke of the past and his youth and of the three attractive Sheridan sisters and of their wit and gaiety – 'dreams! dreams! dreams!' As on Gower's previous visit, Beaconsfield spoke also of his 'dear wife', several portraits of whom hung in the house. Life, he concluded gloomily, was full of troubles and anxieties. He seemed as bitter about Gladstone as ever. Referring to a letter from him in *The Times*, thanking its readers for their sympathy during his recent illness, he commented disdainfully, 'Did you ever hear anything like that? It reminds one of the Pope blessing all the world from the balcony of St Peter's.'[9]

Staying at Hatfield House during the general election of 1880, Beaconsfield was shocked by the overwhelming defeat of his party which, despite agricultural distress and an industrial slump, surprised even his most pessimistic supporters. He blamed 'six bad harvests in succession' and told Gower that, 'like Napoleon', he had been 'beaten by the elements'.[10] Yet he accepted the defeat with apparently calm equanimity, while Gladstone wrote exultantly of the 'downfall of Beaconsfieldism' being like the 'vanishing of some vast magnificent castle in an Italian romance'.[11]

*   *   *

The Queen, by contrast, was distressed beyond measure as she contemplated with horror having now to deal with 'that half mad firebrand', Mr Gladstone, who 'wd soon ruin everything & be a Dictator'. Others might 'submit to his rule, but not the Queen'.[12] 'The grief to her ... at having to part with the kindest & most devoted as well as one of the wisest Ministers the Queen ever had, is not to be told,' she wrote to Lord Beaconsfield. 'You must not think it is a real parting ... I shall always let you know how I am & what I am doing, & you must promise me to let me hear from & about you ... I often think of you – indeed constantly & rejoice to see you [his portrait] looking down from the wall after dinner ... Oh, if only I had you, my kind friend & wise counsellor & strong arm to help and lean on! I have *no one*.'[13]

She comforted herself with the thought that she might not have to deal with the dreaded Gladstone for long: she was not displeased to note, he looked 'very ill, old and haggard'.[14]

In the meantime, by way of a leaving present, she presented her departing Prime Minister with statuettes of her dog 'Sharp', her favourite pony, herself and her indulged ghillie, the overbearing John Brown.

At Hughenden, Lord Beaconsfield settled down to finish a novel which he had begun several years before. This was *Endymion*, the story of the twins, Endymion and Mya, who survive the misfortune of their father's impoverishment and death to rise to prominence in the social world. It is a book full of well-drawn characters, of entertaining social and political comment. But its contents were not of primary concern to the publisher, Thomas Norton Longman, whose firm had done very well with Disraeli's previous novel, *Lothair*. The publisher was so confident of selling large numbers of any new novel by Lord Beaconsfield that he offered for *Endymion* a sum which, so its author told Lady Bradford, had never before been given for a work of fiction.

Negotiations for the sale had been entrusted to Montagu Corry, who, having settled the price with Longman, sat down beside the author as he was listening to a speech by the Duke of Argyll in the House of Lords. Seeing that Disraeli was attending to the Duke, Corry left the chamber to write him a note:

There are things too big to impart in whispers! so I leave your
side, just to write these words – Longman has today offered *Ten
Thousand Pounds* for *Fndymion*.

I have accepted it! I cannot tell you what a pleasure it is to
me to see my ardent ambition for you gratified![15]

In September 1881, Longman went over to Hughenden to collect the
manuscript. He found Lord Beaconsfield in 'capital spirits', with a whim
to invest a simple transaction with an air of intrigue and mystery. His
host, speaking in hushed tones, led him up to the study where he insisted
on short-sightedly lighting the candles himself as he did not wish to
excite the suspicions of the servants. He produced the three handwritten
volumes, each 'carefully tied up in red tape', and laid them in three red
despatch boxes. These boxes were then carried to Longman's bedroom
with such care and silence that the publisher felt as though he and the
author were 'about to rob a church'.

'What are you going to do with them?' Beaconsfield whispered,
having closed the door 'with extra precaution'.

'A happy thought flashed across my mind,' Longman recorded. '"My
Glad—" I luckily stopped in time – "bag". So the boxes were secreted
in his Gladstone bag, to be removed from the house the next morning.'[16]

'Having at last accomplished the solemn task of formal delivery of the
MS. we returned to his Lordship's room and in a very few minutes finished
my part of the business by paying him a cheque and taking his receipt.

'On sitting down for our tête-à-tête dinner, the first thing his Lordship said was, "Now, Mr Longman, we will be like two gentlemen at
their Club. Pray take your time and do not hurry your dinner. I often
wait a quarter of an hour between the courses." I knew exactly what he
meant – don't you bore me with talking, and I will not bore you. The
soup came, the fish came, not a word passed between us . . .'[17]

Less than three months later the novel was published; and so nervous
was Beaconsfield that it would not justify the huge amount which Longman had paid for it that he offered to cancel the agreement in exchange
for a fixed royalty on each copy sold. But he need not have worried.
The critics were kind; and, although the original edition did not sell as
many copies as *Lothair*, a subsequent cheap edition enabled the publishers 'to make a profit out of the bargain'.

Much of the success of the book, as in Disraeli's earlier novels, was due to the reader being presented with recognizable sketches of men in public life, as, for instance, of Palmerston as Lord Roehampton, Cardinal Manning as Penruddock, Cobbett and Cobden combined in Job Thornberry, George Smythe as Waldershare, Napoleon III as Prince Florestan, the Rothschilds as the Neuchatels, Bismarck as Count Ferroll, Thackeray as St Barbe, 'the vainest and most envious of men', and Dickens as 'Gushy' of whom St Barbe says, 'I am as much robbed by that fellow Gushy as men are on the highway.'

Encouraged by Longman's faith in *Endymion*, Beaconsfield immediately started to write another novel in which, in the character of Joseph Toplady Falconet, he intended to satirize Gladstone, that 'wicked man' of 'maniacal vanity' for whom he had recently conceived a far greater dislike than he had ever felt in the earlier years of their rivalry. Like Falconet, in the author's opinion, Gladstone, while clever enough, suffered from 'complete deficiency' in a sense of humour. He was, again, in Beaconsfield's view, 'essentially a prig'. In fact, so Beaconsfield told Lady Bradford, the man was 'a vindictive lunatic'.

Beaconsfield worked on the new book with evident relish, and completed the first few chapters during the pleasant Indian summer of 1880. But it was never finished. The mild autumn was followed by a harsh winter of snowstorms and bitterly cold east winds. Beaconsfield attended the House of Lords in January to attack the Government for its 'perpetual and complete reversal of all that has occurred'; but he did not feel strong enough to say all that he wanted to say and sat down exhausted.

39

THE LAST ACT

'Quite alone with his peacocks'

ON 1 MAY 1880, LORD BEACONSFIELD HAD LEFT LONDON for Hughenden where he was to spend most of the remaining months of his life, travelling up to Westminster from time to time when his presence there was needed and when he felt up to the journey. One day Sir William Fraser encountered him in the Carlton Club, peering about as though lost. 'I know you wish someone to speak to you,' Fraser said, approaching him. 'I am very much obliged to you,' Lord Beaconsfield replied. 'I am so blind, I come here, I look round, I see no one; I go away.'

Having given up the house in Whitehall Gardens for 10 Downing Street, which was now at the disposal of Mr Gladstone, he was grateful to accept the offer of a suite of rooms in Alfred de Rothschild's house at No 1 Seymour Place, 'the most charming house in London,' as he described it in a letter to Lady Chesterfield, 'the magnificence of its decorations and furniture equalled by their good taste'.

He was feeling out of sorts at Hughenden, having arrived there in what he described as a 'state of coma' and later suffering from a return of asthma and then of gout. He spent days on end in solitude, so he told Lady Bradford, the peacocks being his only company. 'There are ½ doz peacocks now basking at full length on the lawn, motionless,' he told her one day in June. 'I prefer them in these attitudes to their flourishing their unfurled tails. They are silent as well as motionless, and that's something. In the morning they strut about, and scream, and make love or war.'

In July Sir Stafford Northcote went to see him and found him 'very well' though 'quite alone with his peacocks'. 'I am quite alone,' he had also told Lady Bradford, '& unless I have the companionship of those I love wh: I never shall have, alone I wish to remain.' Corry had fallen in love with a daughter of the Earl of Ilchester and was frequently going to Melbury to see her; and, when he was at Hughenden, he was so dull and lovelorn, sighing as he took dictation and between the courses at meals, that he was a depressing companion.

Sir Stafford Northcote found Beaconsfield less depressed in his library.

> After dinner [Northcote wrote] we chiefly talked about books; the Chief is always at his best in his library, and seemed thoroughly to enjoy a good ramble over literature. He was contemptuous over Browning (of whom, however, he has read very little) and the other poetasters of the day, none of whom he thought would live except Tennyson . . . He talked of Lord Derby's translation of Homer and said he had given his opinion against rendering him in blank verse. It was Ballad poetry. Pope's style was better suited to it . . . Walter Scott would have done it better than anyone . . . The Chief considered that everything Gladstone had written on Homer was wrong . . . Ben Jonson he did not care for. I did battle for him and he promised to read him again . . .
>
> We lamented the disuse of classical quotations in the House of Commons. He said he had at one time tried to revert to them but the Speaker [Evelyn Denison] had asked him not to. 'Why? Do you think they don't like it?' 'Oh, no, but you are making John Russell restless, and I am afraid of his taking to it too. Russell gave us six or seven lines of Virgil the other night, which had not the smallest connection with his speech or with the subject.'[1]

That autumn Lord Beaconsfield fell ill again, suffering at first from asthma, then from 'a fit of gout' which attacked him with 'ferocity' and reminded him of 'poor Ld. Derby'. After five weeks 'of imprisonment' at Hughenden, he went up to Seymour Place to consult his doctor, since, as he complained to Lady Bradford, if the man continued his visits to Hughenden his patient would 'have to execute a mortgage' on his estate.

In fact, his financial situation had by now been much improved. The money he received for *Endymion* helped him to buy a seven years' lease of a house, 19 Curzon Street. He had conducted the negotiations for this purchase himself since Montagu Corry, by then granted a peerage as Baron Rowton of Rowton Castle in Shropshire, was in Algiers where he had taken his sister for a recuperative holiday. 'Your absence is a calamity,' he had complained; and to Lady Bradford he wrote grumpily: 'Sisters should marry & not require such a sacrifice.' He had soon found a temporary replacement in George Barrington, who had 'good talents, great experience of the pol. world, having been priv. secy. to Lord Derby, and [was a man upon] whose honour and devotion' he could rely. But Barrington was 'not a Monty'.

Accompanied on occasions by his new secretary, Beaconsfield ventured out, when he felt well enough, to the dinner parties he had so much enjoyed in years gone by and still often did so. 'One is struck by the sheer pleasure in society which his great position gave him,' Robert Blake observed. 'Of course, he grumbled about the food at one dinner party, the wine at another, the company at a third, the cold rooms at a fourth. Although his own table was notoriously bad, and had been so even in Mary Anne's time, he was a critical gourmet when it came to other people's hospitality . . . But his complaints, which were largely designed to elicit sympathy, somewhat unforthcoming from Lady Bradford, seldom resulted in any interruption in his social round of receptions and dinner parties during the season and country-house visits when it was over.'[2]

> I dined at Granville's, a pleasant party [he described one such]. I sat next to Pss. Louise who never looked prettier; and on Sunday I dined with Lady Lonsdale, my lord away – very amusing. Louise and Harty-Tarty [Marquess of Hartington] were there – the Cadogans, H[enry] Chaplins, Sir Charles Dilke, all very good company and talked well, Harty T. particularly, who is a clever fellow, and with some humour. I am suffering, however, very much from asthma, wh. is detestable.[3]

Three weeks later he dined out on three consecutive evenings, on the first at Lady Airlie's, where he met Matthew Arnold whom he complimented upon being the only living Englishman who had become a classic in his own lifetime, on the second at Lady Stanhope's, and on the third at Alfred de Rothschild's with the Prince of Wales and Sir Charles Dilke, the model for Endymion, who found him 'very polite and pretty in all his ways and in all he said' and who recorded that, when Beaconsfield was offered a cigar, he said, in allusion to Sir Walter Raleigh, 'You English once had a great man who discovered tobacco, on which you English now live; and potatoes on which you Irish live; and you cut off his head.'[4]

As well as attending parties in other houses, Beaconsfield gave a grand one of his own on 10 March in his new house in Curzon Street. In addition to his friends, Lady Chesterfield and Lord Bradford – Lady Bradford was out of town – he invited Henry Manners, Lord John's eldest son, later eighth Duke of Rutland, the Barringtons and the Cadogans, Alfred de Rothschild, the Duke and Duchess of Sutherland, Lady Dudley, wife of the first Earl, Lady Lonsdale, afterwards Marchioness of Ripon, and Sir Frederick Leighton, President of the Royal Academy.

It had seemed for a time that Beaconsfield's gout would oblige him to cancel the party, as he did, in fact, cancel a sitting for the unfinished portrait by Sir John Millais; but, having been confined to bed for two days, he had recovered sufficiently on the third to act as host at the dinner which, so he said, went very well, even though he had to greet his guests leaning heavily on a walking-stick.

Five days later he hobbled into the House of Lords for the last time and spoke eloquently in support of a vote of condolence to the Queen on the assassination of the Tsar Alexander II in St Petersburg two days before. But thereafter his appearances at dinner parties sometimes shocked his fellow-guests. To Henry Ponsonby he seemed 'indolent and worn out ... He shot little arrows into the general discourse, pungent and lively, and then sat perfectly silent as if it were too much trouble to talk.'[5] These shafts of wit grew more and more rare; and sometimes he would sit slumped in his chair throughout an entire meal, apparently heedless of the conversation being held around him, peering and poking at the food on his plate. The travel writer, Augustus Hare, who encountered Disraeli at several parties and dinners, described him as 'absorbed'; he 'scarcely noticed anyone, barely answered his hostess when spoken to'. At Gorhambury House 'it was amusing *seeing* Lord Beaconsfield ... *hear* him I never did, except when he feebly bleated out some brief and ghastly utterance'.[6]

Lady Randolph Churchill said that he resembled 'a black sphynx'; Lytton Strachey described him as an 'assiduous mummy' stumbling from 'dinner party to dinner party'.

George Joachim Goschen's wife, who spoke to him at a dinner in March, thought that he had lost all his former spirit and appeared very aged. 'I only live for climate,' he told her that evening in a cold and windy month, 'and I never get it.'[7] On the sixteenth he wrote to Monty Rowton who was still abroad: 'Barrington is very kind and sedulous, but I want you. My health has been very bad, and I have really been fit for nothing.' His gout was so painful on occasions that his manservant, Baum, and Baum's wife, had to carry him up and down stairs.

A week after writing his letter to Rowton he went to bed with a chill and another severe attack of asthma to be nursed by the Baums, supervised by Barrington who, encountering Sir Charles Dilke in Curzon Street, took him to No 19 to see the invalid whom they found lying on a sofa and breathing with difficulty, yet 'still the old Disraeli' with what Dilke called 'his pleasant spitefulness about Mr G[ladstone] not in the least abated'.*

Given worrying reports about her friend's illness, the Queen told Barrington, who had been invited to dinner at Buckingham Palace, that he ought to call in another doctor and not rely on the advice of the homeopath, Dr Kidd. This was also the opinion of Sir Philip Rose, who called at 19 Curzon Street the next morning. So application was made to Dr Richard Quain, a specialist in diseases of the chest and soon to be elected President of the General Medical Council. Another doctor was also called in to relieve Kidd in the night.

Their patient was not hopeful that they could cure him. 'I shall never survive this attack,' he told Rose. 'I feel it is quite impossible ... I feel this is the last of it ... I feel I am dying. Whatever the doctors may tell you, I do not believe I shall get well.'[8]

Concerned by the violent spasms that overcame him at intervals, the doctors decreed that he should be kept as quiet as possible and receive few visitors. It comforted him, however, to receive old friends. 'It does me good,' he said, 'and distracts me and helps me to get through the day.'

---

* Beaconsfield would, no doubt, have been exasperated to learn that Catherine Walters, the delectable courtesan known as 'Skittles', compared him unfavourably with Gladstone. Beaconsfield, she told her admirer, Wilfrid Scawen Blunt, was 'a kind old fellow, but very dull'. 'I loved old bully Gladstone far more than Dizzy. Old G. had a lot of fun in him and was a more powerful man to me than old Dizzy' (Elizabeth Longford, *A Pilgrimage of Passion: The Life of Wilfrid Scawen Blunt*, 1979, 376).

Although bulletins were issued every day, enquiries, letters and tele-
grams poured ceaselessly through the letter box at 19 Curzon Street.
Several of these were from the Queen, who also sent flowers from
Windsor and Osborne and who wrote on 30 March:

> I meant to pay you a little visit this week but I thought it better
> you should be quite quiet and not speak. And I beg you will be
> very good and obey the doctors ... Hoping to hear a good report
> of you tonight ... Everyone is so distressed at your not being
> well. Beatrice wishes I should say everything kind to you ...'

'You are very constantly in my thoughts,' she wrote in another letter,
'and I wish I could do anything to cheer you and be of the slightest use
or comfort. With earnest wishes for your uninterrupted progress in
recovery, Ever yours affectionately, V.R.I.'

He replied to these letters as best he could with a pencil that shook
in his hand; and when he was asked if he would like the Queen to visit
him, he replied, making a last, sad joke, 'No, it is better not. She would
only ask me to take a message to Albert.'[10]

When Lord Rowton arrived back from Algiers, Beaconsfield was, at
first, reluctant to see him also. 'I cannot see him,' he said repeatedly,
while Barrington gently pressed him to do so: 'Surely Monty, who is so
fond of you – you would like to see when he arrives.'

'You and Rose must arrange it gradually,' the dying man said. 'It
would be too great a shock.' So, for three days after his arrival, Rowton
did not see him. 'He still shrinks from seeing me,' Rowton told Lady
Bradford. 'He knows I am always here day and night, and I have begged
him to give no thought to me till we can meet without effort to him.
The doctors wish him to be as quiet as possible ... He does not try to
read letters ... The weakness! How can we overcome it? He is being
wonderfully nursed, and, they say, is so gentle and clear and kind. All
about him are charmed. He begs to be told the worst – if it is to be:
and I have told the doctors they must do so, should it become evident.
He talks of death without a shadow of fear.'

Soon after this letter was written, Rowton was admitted to his
friend's room and thereafter shared with Barrington and Rose the painful
duty of watching over him.

On 17 April, Rose proposed that, since it was Easter Day, his friend might want to receive the Sacrament. Barrington and Rowton agreed; but Dr Quain firmly opposed the suggestion, maintaining that his patient would consequently suppose that his case was hopeless and give up the struggle to live. 'I had rather live,' he had said; 'but I am not afraid to die.'[11]

It was clear that the end was now near. Rowton and Barrington on one side of the bed and Dr Kidd on the other held his hands as he struggled to rise as though he believed himself to be in the House. His lips moved but no words came.

At half past four in the morning of 19 April, he calmly 'passed away without suffering, as if in sleep,' Rose told his son. 'We kissed his fine noble forehead . . . I never saw anything more fine and impressive than his peaceful and tranquil expression.'

'The last days and hours were distressing,' Rowton reported to Lady Bradford, 'but the last minutes and moments were very quiet and evidently quite painless . . . The very end was strikingly dignified and fine, and as I looked on his dear face, just at the moment when his spirit left him, I thought that I had never seen him look so triumphant and full of victory. In all those last days he was so brave and gentle, so wonderfully considerate and good to all that I felt I should have loved him more than ever, had he lived . . . I am very unhappy! but I won't dwell on that. My life is dreadfully changed. But I have often thought of you and Lady Chesterfield and known how your dear kind hearts were aching. Would you give her my love and ask her to forgive my not writing to her?'

The Queen, who confessed that she was 'heart-broken', asked Lord Rowton to come to Osborne to tell her 'everything'. She had always, so one of her ladies said, taken 'the keenest interest in death and all its horrors'; and she told Lord Rowton that she found his report in 'a sad and touching letter', 'so painfully interesting'.

'She feels very keenly not having seen him, or even looked at him once more, but then she feared the great agitation for him, and it might have been painful for all. And she grieves now to think one cannot see him even in his last sleep . . . Words are too weak to say what the Queen feels; how overwhelmed she is with this terrible, irreparable loss . . . His kindness and devotion to the Queen on all and every occasion – his anxiety to lighten her cares and difficulties she never can forget, and will miss cruelly . . . Never had I *so* kind and devoted a Minister and very few such devoted friends. His affectionate sympathy, his wise counsel – all were so invaluable even out of office. I have lost *so* many dear and valued friends but none whose loss will be more keenly felt.'[12]

Only a few hours after his opponent's death, Gladstone proposed that he should be granted a state funeral; but Lord Beaconsfield had left instructions that he was to be buried quietly at Hughenden as his wife and Mrs Brydges Willyams had been. Even so, the funeral was an impressive ceremony attended by the Prince of Wales and other members of the Royal Family, by European ambassadors, the American ambassador, the poet and critic, James Russell Lowell, by numerous distinguished figures not only from his own political party, but also from that of his opponents, by Sir Frederick Leighton, President of the Royal Academy, by Sir John Millais, who had been painting the dead man's portrait before his last illness, by his two executors, Sir Philip Rose and Sir Nathan Rothschild, and by the only two surviving members of his immediate family, his brother, Ralph Disraeli, Clerk Assistant in the House of Lords, and Ralph's son, his uncle's heir, Coningsby.*

The coffin was carried by tenants of the Hughenden estate to the vault, where the bodies of Mary Anne and Mrs Brydges Willyams already lay. On it were piles of wreaths – among them one of primroses, bearing the legend: 'His favourite flowers, from Osborne, a tribute of affection from Queen Victoria.'†

Thomas Norton Longman, the publisher, was 'one of the select band of followers . . . who had the honour of accompanying the great man's coffin' to the grave by the west wall of Hughenden Church.

---

* Coningsby Ralph D'Israeli, the heir to Hughenden, was then fourteen years old. After school at Charterhouse, he went up to New College, Oxford. He became a major in the Royal Buckinghamshire Hussars and a conscientious alderman and justice of the peace and, from 1892 to 1906, an undistinguished Member of Parliament for Altrincham. He died childless at the age of sixty-eight in 1936 when the male line of the family became extinct.
† 'The primrose is generally supposed to have been Lord Beaconsfield's favourite flower,' Lady Dorothy Nevill wrote. 'But I cannot say for certain that I ever heard him express any partiality for it . . . I sat next to Mr Gladstone at a dinner some time after Lord Beaconsfield's death, and in the course of conversation he suddenly said: "Tell me, Lady Dorothy, upon your honour, have you ever heard Lord Beaconsfield express any particular fondness for the primrose?" I was compelled to admit that I had not, upon which he said: "The gorgeous lily, I think, was more to his taste."' (*Reminiscences of Lady Dorothy Nevill*, 210–11).

On our return to the Manor [Longman recorded] about fifty of us went into the drawing-room to hear the will read. I waited behind a little for the three Princes to move first; and, much to my surprise, the Duke of Connaught turned round, and took me by the hand. This little incident made it all a peculiarly interesting and eventful day. We all returned to town together . . . and I think I may safely say that a train never arrived at Paddington Station with a more distinguished company on board.

As I walked from the church I could not help thinking that the last time I walked up the hill I had poor Lord B. on my arm. The demand for *Endymion* is very great, and, in fact, the demand for all his novels is greater than we can meet. We are printing night and day to keep the trade supplied.[13]

Four days after the funeral, the Queen came to Hughenden where the vault was opened so that she could lay some china flowers upon her friend's coffin and see the church in which she was to have a marble monument placed above his seat in the chancel, inscribed: 'To the dear and honoured memory of Benjamin, Earl of Beaconsfield, this memorial is placed by his grateful Sovereign and Friend, Victoria R.I.' She asked also to be taken to her friend's study where she spent some time alone. She had tea in the drawing-room, where she 'seemed to hear his voice and the impassioned, eager way he described everything'.

She could 'scarcely see' for her 'fast-falling tears', she told Lord Rowton. 'To England (or rather Great Britain) and to the *World* his loss is immense.'

Her people shared her grief. Walking past the drawn blinds of the Carlton Club, one of them thought that England would 'always regret the passing of the greatest statesman of his time: there was no one left to take his place'.

'A WISE AND WORLDLY MAN'

*'Zeal for the greatness of England
was the passion of his life'*

THE QUEEN DID NOT ATTEND THE FUNERAL, custom preventing her. The Prince of Wales was there, however, and so were all but one of Beaconsfield's former Cabinet. Gladstone was not, making the public excuse that he was too busy, and privately suggesting, through his secretary, that he would be accused of being 'a humbug' had he been present and that the 'private character of the funeral would render his presence *de trop*'. Besides, he considered that the manner in which the ceremony was to be conducted was a characteristic show of conceit: 'as he had lived, so he died', 'all display without reality or genuineness'.[1] Yet in the Commons he spoke charitably of Lord Beaconsfield's 'great qualities' and 'parliamentary courage'; and, in his diary, on learning of his rival's death, he had written:

> At 8 a.m. I was much shocked on opening a telegram to find it announced the death of Ld Beaconsfield, 3½ hours before . . . It is a telling, touching event. There is no more extraordinary man surviving him in England, perhaps not in Europe.[2]

In the House of Lords further tributes were expressed. Lord Salisbury spoke of the fine qualities of the great man under whose leadership he had been proud to serve, of his 'patience, gentleness, unswerving and unselfish loyalty'. The people of his country, who had come to love and revere him, well knew that one burning desire 'dominated his actions': 'Zeal for the greatness of England was the passion of his life.'

It was a fitting epitaph. No one doubted the depth and honesty of

Disraeli's patriotism. Unmoved as he was by nationalist movements in other countries, he never wavered in his fervent support of English nationalism and of England's Empire, in his belief in the greatness of a country in which he seemed so alien a figure. Of Disraeli's other motives and beliefs it was, and is, difficult to be so sure. There will always be argument about him, about the extent to which he was guided by opportunism and ambition rather than by principle, about the true feelings which lay beneath those sardonic features, that inscrutable irony.

Sir Robert Ensor wrote of the enigmatic nature of Disraeli: 'His party came to trust him, to idolize, and even to love him; but they never understood him. And he, with his passion for England, remained deeply un-English. Idealist and cynic, prophet and tactician, genius and charlatan in one, men took him for a flaunting melodramatist until they experienced him as a deadly fighter. A radical by origin and instinct, he remade the conservative party, but though he ruled its counsels so long, it was only warily and within limits that he ever shaped them to his ideas.'[3]

There is surely little doubt that until 1846, when he helped to engineer the resignation of Peel, Disraeli was driven by an ambition to make his mark rather than by any consistent political purpose, and that his attacks on Peel would not have been so mounted as they were had his ambition been satisfied by his being given in 1841 the office for which he craved.

Very slowly after 1846, however, a rational and realistic policy can be discerned through the fog which he chose to cast over it with his romantic Tory philosophy and his fanciful interpretations of history. He believed that, although the greatness of England depended upon the ascendancy of the landed classes, the Conservative Party must associate itself more closely with the business and commercial interests of the middle class, and that, in fact, while Peel himself had been destroyed, Peel's beliefs and policies must not die with him but be restored and refreshed. That Disraeli, a Jew, with a far from respectable past, heavy debts and a dubious reputation, became and remained the leader of the Conservative Party in the Commons at such a time was itself proof of his courage and parliamentary genius.

Yet, if Disraeli's origins were by no means obscure and his family never poor, he was undoubtedly an outsider in the hierarchy of his

Party. Not only his race and tastes and manner, but even his education separated him from his colleagues. There is no doubt, too, that in the earlier years of his influence he had had to struggle constantly against a degree of both dislike and prejudice which would have overborne a less determined, brave and resilient man, and against a fierce resentment occasioned by the fact that the Conservatives could not manage without his great talents – as many of them would have liked to do – since he was the only man who possessed them in such multiplicity, on his side of the House.

It was his triumphant achievement to use these abilities not only ultimately to provide his party with an efficient organization but also to provide it with a policy of social reform combined with imperialism which appealed to the country's new electorate and brought forward the Conservatives as an acceptable and practical alternative to the Liberals.

His bitter rivalry with Gladstone after the death of Palmerston was an important factor in this. In sharp contrast to the stern and moralistic Gladstone – whose radical reforms caused widespread alarm – Disraeli was able to present himself as a wise and worldly man of moderation and common sense, a believer in measures to alleviate the plight of the poorer classes, but above all as the leader of a national party with a concern for the interests of every class, and a determination to ensure that the ideals of the Empire were sustained and the greatness of England in the world enhanced. As he said in a speech at the Guildhall, in the year that he brought back what he had described as 'peace with honour' from Berlin, 'One of the greatest of Romans, when asked what were his politics, replied, "*Imperium et Libertas*". That would not make a bad programme for a British Ministry.'

'How will Lord Beaconsfield be judged by posterity?' Reginald Brett wrote in his diary on being told by his manservant that the great man had died – 'not unexpectedly and very quietly' – in the night. 'No more curious figure ever appeared in English political life. He inspired affection, as well as admiration, in his friends and adherents. By all but his bigoted opponents he was held in regard and respect. He was the most magnanimous statesman of our time. He captivated the imagination of the English people, and triumphed over their not unnatural prejudices.'[4]

REFERENCES

SOURCES

INDEX

REFERENCES

For full biographical details see Sources, pp. 377–83.

Abbreviations

M & B   Monypenny and Buckle
BDL   Benjamin Disraeli Letters
RB   Robert Blake (*Disraeli*)
HL   Helen Langley (*Scenes*):
        Bodleian Library, Oxford

CHAPTER 1 : *Boyhood*

1 Weintraub, 17–18.
2 M & B, i, 6; Ridley, 9–10.
3 M & B, i, 13.
4 Ridley, 12–13.
5 M & B, 18.
6 Prothero, *Byron's Letters and Journals*, iv, 274.
7 Ridley, 16.
8 M & B, i, 20.
9 The *Standard*, 24 April 1887.
10 *Jewish Chronicle*, 28 April 1887.
11 Quoted in RB, 14.
12 M & B, i, 30–33.
13 Ibid., 41–2.

CHAPTER 2 : *A Young Man of High Fashion*

1 M & B, i, 36–7.
2 Ibid., 37.
3 Meynell, *The Man Disraeli*, 21.
4 RB, 20; BDL, 29 July 1824, 9.
5 BDL, i, 14, 19 August 1824.
6 Ibid., i, 10, 29 July 1824.
7 Ibid., i, 11, 2 August 1824.
8 Ridley, 29.
9 M & B, i, 57; BDL, 'Mutilated Diary', i, 445.

10 *Vivian Grey*, i, Chs. 7 and 8.
11 BDL, i, 27, 18 September 1825.
12 M & B, i, 71, 25 September 1825.
13 Ibid., i, 70.
14 Lockhart Papers, 3 October 1825, quoted in M & B, i, 29.
15 Johnson, 898–900.
16 M & B, i, 77.
17 Quoted in Weintraub, 62; Ridley, 41; *Vivian Grey*, v, Ch. 14.
18 Murray Papers, quoted in RB, 45–6.
19 Cyrus Redding, quoted in RB, 37.
20 *Vivian Grey*, ii, Ch. 16.
21 *Contarini Fleming*.
22 RB, 36; Ridley, 50.
23 BDL, i, 49, July 1826.

CHAPTER 3 : *A Continental Holiday*

1 M & B, i, 99, 9 August 1826.
2 Ibid., i, 100–02.
3 M & B, i, 100–02, 21 August 1826; BDL, i, 51.
4 Ridley, 53.
5 M & B, i, 103; BDL, 2 September 1826.
6 Lord Rowton's Note, M & B, i, 106.
7 M & B, i, 104–5, 2 September 1826.

8 M & B, i, 104–5, 2 September 1826; BDL, i, 52, 2 September 1826.
9 BDL, i, 53, 13 September 1826.
10 M & B, i, 108.
11 BDL, i, 55, 29 September 1826.
12 M & B, i, 111, 20 September 1826.
13 BDL, i, 56, 29 September 1826.
14 M & B, i, 115; Ridley, 58.
15 BDL, i, 56, 29 September 1826.
16 M & B, i, 115.
17 Layard, *Autobiography*, i, 18.
18 M & B, i, 113, 10 October 1826; HL (*Scenes*), 35.

CHAPTER 4 : *Mental Breakdown*

1 Morley, *Gladstone*, ii, 499.
2 *Vivian Grey*, viii, Ch.5.
3 Ridley, 62.
4 M & B, i, 120, 11 June 1827.
5 M & B, i, 120, March 1828.
6 Ridley, 64.
7 Ibid., 65.
8 Ibid., 68; M & B, i, 120, January 1829.
9 *Endymion*, Ch. 11.
10 M & B, i, 127.
11 Ibid., i, 132.
12 Ibid., i, 126, 8 December 1829.
13 Ibid., i, 126–7, 7 March 1830.
14 Meredith's Diary, 29 March 1830, quoted in M & B, i, 128; Weintraub, 87.
15 M & B, i, 130, 9 May 1830.
16 BDL, i, 81, 9 May 1830.

CHAPTER 5 : *Travels and Adventures*

1 M & B, i, 141, 1 July 1830; BDL, i, 90.
2 Ibid.
3 Ibid.
4 Ibid., i, 147.
5 Ibid., 143; BDL, i, 90.
6 BDL, i, 96, 20 August 1830.
7 Sultana, 19; Weintraub, 92; BDL, i, 92.
8 BDL, i, 94, 1 August 1830.
9 Ibid., 1, 98, 14 September 1830.
10 Ibid., i, 149.
11 Ibid., i, 95, 20 August 1830.

12 Ibid., i, 92, 14 July 1830.
13 Ibid., 157; Weintraub, 93.
14 Ibid., i, 161, 14 September 1830.
15 Ibid., i, 100, 10 October 1830.
16 Blake, *Disraeli's Grand Tour*, 22.
17 BDL, i, 97, 25 August 1830.
18 Quoted in Weintraub, 95; Ridley, 86.
19 Gregory, *Autobiography*, 95.
20 BDL, i, 97, 25 August 1830; M & B, i, 160, 29 August 1830.
21 M & B, i, 162.
22 M & B, i, 163; BDL, i, 101, 25 October 1830.
23 Blake, *Disraeli's Grand Tour*, 36–7; BDL i, 101, 25 October 1830; Sultana, 55.
24 M & B, i, 168.
25 BDL, i, 104, 23 December 1830.
26 M & B, i, 171.
27 Ibid., i, 172.
28 Blake, *Disraeli's Grand Tour*, 53, 55.
29 *Life of Bulwer*, ii, 323.
30 Blake, *Disraeli's Grand Tour*, 67.
31 M & B, i, 176–7.
32 Blake, *Disraeli's Grand Tour*, 95; Ridley, 98.
33 BDL, i, 112, 28 May 1831; Blake, *Disraeli's Grand Tour*, 91.
34 Ibid., i, 115, 20 July 1831; 'Mutilated Diary', BDL, i, 446; M & B, i, 181, 30 July 1831.
35 M & B, i, 182; BDL, i, 114, 20 July 1831.
36 HL, 66.
37 M & B, 1, 184.
38 Quoted in Ridley, 103–4.
39 RB, 71–3; Ridley, 102–3.
40 RB 73; BDL, i, 132.
41 M & B, i, 140.

CHAPTER 6 : *The Jew d'Esprit*

1 M & B, i, 195, 26 May 1832.
2 BDL, i, 194, 23 May 1832; M & B, i, 195, 28 May 1832.
3 Ibid., 5 July 1832.
4 Ridley, 115.
5 M & B, i, 203.
6 RB, 87; M & B, i, 209, 15 May 1832; BDL, 192, 24 May 1832.
7 Fraser, 187.

8 'Mutilated Diary', BDL, i, 447, Appendix 111.
9 BDL, i, 159, 26 March 1832.
10 Ibid., i, 159, 26 March 1832.
11 M & B, i, 207.
12 BDL, i, 169, 2 April 1832; M & B, i, 208.
13 RB, 82.
14 BDL, i, 242, 2 March 1833.
15 Waterfield, 18.
16 Devey, 412.
17 RB, 155.
18 Ibid., 114; Ridley, 130.
19 Diary of B.R. Haydon, iv, 51, 58; Ridley, 130.
20 RB, 87; BDL, i, 198, 2 June 1832; Ridley, 117.

CHAPTER 7 : *The Candidate*

1 Quoted in A.N. Wilson, 381.
2 M & B, i, 216.
3 BDL, i, 201, 10 June 1832; M & B, i, 217.
4 M & B, i, 223.
5 Ridley, 118.
6 Ibid., i, 224.
7 BDL, i, 233, 7 February 1833; M & B, i, 221.
8 *Quarterly Review*, January 1889.
9 M & B, i, 235, 21 February 1833.
10 Ibid.
11 *Motley's Correspondence*, i, 264, quoted in M & B, i, 236.
12 M & B, i, 236.
13 Ibid., i, 237.
14 'The Mutilated Diary', 1 September 1833, Appendix 111; BDL, i, 445–50.
15 M & B, i, 242.
16 Preface to *Revolutionary Epic*.
17 M & B, i, 243; BDL, i, 297, 1 December 1833.
18 *Quarterly Review*, January 1889.
19 Bradford, 71–2.
20 M & B, i, 244.
21 BDL, i, 307, 7 March 1834.
22 N.P. Willis, *New York Mirror*, 11 August 1838.
23 Bradford, 76.
24 M & B, i, 257–60, quoted in Bradford, 52.

25 Ibid.
26 Ibid., i, 263, 24 October 1834.

CHAPTER 8 : *Affairs*

1 M & B, i, 250, 13 February 1834; BDL, i, 307.
2 Jerman, 187–8.
3 BDL, i, 276, 5 June 1833.
4 RB, 98.
5 BDL, i, 362, 6 June 1833.
6 BDL, i, 377, 17 June 1833.
7 RB, 99; HL, 75.
8 RB, 100.
9 Ibid., 103.
10 Ibid., 106.
11 Ibid., 107; Ridley, 142.
12 Ridley, 143.
13 Ibid., 194.
14 RB, 110.
15 'The Mutilated Diary', BDL, Appendix 111, i, 448.
16 BDL, 411; RB, 117–19.
17 RB, 118.
18 BDL, 659, Note 3.
19 Ridley, 203.
20 RB, 141.

CHAPTER 9 : *The Reforming Tory*

1 M & B, i, 266, 4 November 1834.
2 Ibid., i, 271, 17 November 1834.
3 Ibid., i, 272.
4 BDL, i, 360, 30 December 1834.
5 M & B, i, 279.
6 BDL, i, 363, 7 January 1835.
7 *Pen and Ink Sketches of Poets, Preachers and Politicians, 1846.*
8 M & B, i, 286.
9 *Pen and Ink Sketches of Poets, Preachers and Politicians, 1846.*
10 *The Courier*, 6 May 1835.
11 BDL, i, 396, 5 May 1835.
12 M & B, 296; Ridley, 160.
13 BDL, i, 399, 6 May 1835.

CHAPTER 10 : *Debts and Duns*

1 BDL, i, 408, 27 June 1835.
2 M & B, i, 308, 20 August 1835.
3 Ibid., i, 310, 23 December 1835.

4 BDL, i, 459, 1 December 1824.
5 BDL, i, 477, 5, February 1836.
6 M & B, i, 324–5.
7 'The Mutilated Diary', BDL, ii, 416.
8 M & B, i, 327.
9 Ibid., i, 331.
10 BDL, i, 368, 19 November 1835; HL, 83.
11 Ridley, 193.
12 BDL, 505, 31 May 1836.
13 M & B, i, 342.
14 Ibid., i, 352.
15 Ridley, 188.
16 M & B, i, 357, 8 January 1837.
17 BDL, 601, 16 January 1837.
18 Ibid., 573, 7 February 1837.

CHAPTER 11 : *The Member for Maidstone*

1 'The Mutilated Diary', M & B, i, 371.
2 Healey, *Lady Unknown*, 60.
3 M & B, i, 375, 20 June 1837.
4 Ibid., i, 376, 30 June 1837.
5 Ibid., i, 377.
6 BDL, i, 629, 1 July 1837.
7 M & B, i, 377.
8 Ibid., i, 379.
9 Sir John Hollams, *Jottings of an Old Soldier*, 1900, 2–8.
10 Sykes, 35–42.
11 M & B, i, 382.
12 Ibid., i, 383, 24 October 1837.
13 Ibid., i, 384–5.
14 Ibid., i, 399, 15 November 1837.
15 BDL, 676, 21 November 1837.
16 M & B, i, 405.
17 Hitchman, *Public Life of the Earl of Beaconsfield*, i, 134.
18 M & B, 408–9.
19 Greville, iii, 404.
20 BDL, 686, 8 December 1837.
21 Ibid.
22 M & B, i, 410.
23 BDL, 686, 8 December 1837.
24 Ibid., 688, 11 December 1837.

CHAPTER 12 : *'Most Brilliant and Triumphant Speeches'*

1 BDL, 690, 15 December 1837.
2 M & B, i, 414.

3 Ibid.
4 Ibid., i, 417.
5 Ibid., 418.
6 Ibid.
7 Ibid., i, 419.
8 BDL, 748, 19 March 1838.
9 Ibid., 747, iii, 36–8, 16 March 1838.
10 Ibid., 766, iii, 51, 26 April 1838.
11 Ibid., 770, iii, 56, 5 May 1838.
12 Ibid., 790, iii, 69–70, 29 June 1838; 791, iii, 70–71, 2 July 1838 and 796, iii, 74–5, 10 July 1838.

CHAPTER 13 : *'A Pretty Little Woman, a Flirt and a Rattle'*

1 Hardwick, 17–18.
2 Ibid., 29.
3 Ibid., 23.
4 M & B, i, 381.
5 BDL, 30 July 1837, 644.
6 Ibid., 1 September 1837, 660.
7 M & B, i, 383, 8 September 1837.
8 BDL, 5 January 1838, iii, 4, 698.
9 M & B, 27 April 1838, 425.
10 BDL, 796, iii, 75, 10 July 1838; Ridley, 218.
11 BDL, 802, iii, 78, 26 July 1838; iii, 79, 27 July 1838.

CHAPTER 14 : *A Troubled Courtship*

1 Hardwick, 81.
2 RB, 155.
3 Hardwick, 96.
4 BDL, iii, 88, 816; Ridley, 219–20.
5 BDL, iii, 124, 861.
6 Ibid., iii, 858–66.
7 Ibid., iii, 882.
8 M & B, i, 451.
9 BDL, iii, 885.
10 Hardwick, 102–3.
11 Sykes, 53–4.

CHAPTER 15 : *A Happy Marriage*

1 M & B, i, 436, 7 and 9 October 1838.
2 BDL, 965, iii, 197, 13 July 1839.
3 M & B, i, 448, 26 December 1838.
4 Ibid., i, 444, 29 December 1838.
5 Ibid., i, 453–4, 25 February 1839.

6 BDL, 918, iii, 166, 19 April 1839.
7 M & B, i, 462, 13 July 1839.
8 BDL, 961, iii, 195, 11 July 1839.
9 Ibid., 951, 952, 953, 961, 6 and 8 July 1839.
10 Ridley, 237.
11 M & B, i, 469, 2 October 1839.
12 Ibid., i, 470, 4 November 1839.
13 Ibid., i, 471, 22 November 1839.

CHAPTER 16 : *The Brilliant Orator*

1 M & B, i, 488, 23 January 1840.
2 Ridley, 240.
3 Ibid., 239.
4 Ibid., 268, 272.
5 M & B, i, 488.
6 Ibid., i, 20 April 1840.
7 BDL, 1092, iii, 294, 7 September 1840.
8 Ibid., 666, 25 October 1837.
9 M & B, i, 494, 22 October 1840.
10 Ibid., i, 494, 26 December 1940.
11 Ibid., i, 512, 7 July 1841.
12 Ibid., i, 494, 21 November 1840.
13 BDL, 1170, 30 June 1841, iii, 346; Sykes, 66–71.
14 M & B, i, 513.
15 BDL, 1108, 1 November 1840, iii, 304.
16 Ibid., 1153, 6 May 1841, iii, 333.
17 *Letters of Queen Victoria*, i, 280, 18 May 1841.
18 BDL, 1186, 5 September 1841, iii, 356.
19 M & B, i, 516–17.
20 Ibid., i, 517–18.
21 Ibid., i, 520.
22 Ibid., i, 521.
23 BDL, 1224, 9 March 1842, iv, 25–6.

CHAPTER 17 : *Young England*

1 M & B, i, 545.
2 Ibid., i, 546.
3 BDL, 1268, 21 November 1842, iv, 64; M & B, i, 546–51.
4 M & B, 547–57, 22 November 1842–4 February 1843.
5 Ibid., i, 580, 17 July 1843.
6 Edgar Johnson, *Dickens*, ii, 597.

7 RB, 177; Jennings, *Croker*, iii, 9; Weintraub, 210.
8 Parker, *Peel*, iii, 425; M & B, i, 583.
9 M & B, i, 584.
10 Ibid., i, 585.
11 Ibid., i, 591.
12 Greville, v, 162–5.

CHAPTER 18 : Coningsby *and* Sybil

1 BDL, 1335.
2 Ibid., 1343, 10 May 1834, iv, 121.
3 M & B, i, 598.
4 Ibid., i, 623.
5 *Fraser's Magazine*, February, 1847.
6 M & B, i, 649.
7 *Sybil*, Book III, Ch. 1.
8 Ibid., Book III, Ch. 2.

CHAPTER 19 : *Damning Attacks*

1 BDL, 1441, iv, 189–90, 6 September 1845.
2 Ibid., 1443, iv, 190–91, 8 September 1845.
3 Ridley, 312–13; Bradford, 164–6; Weintraub, 243–5.
4 BDL, iv, 1444–8, 17 September 1845.
5 M & B, i, 735–6.
6 Ibid., i, 737–8.
7 Ibid., i, 777–8.
8 Ibid., 785–6, 15 May 1846.
9 Broughton, vi, 170.
10 Greville, v, 32.

CHAPTER 20 : Tancred

1 M & B, i, 827.
2 BDL, 2107, 2 August 1851, v, 461.
3 M & B, i, 864.
4 BDL, vi, 275, Note 3; M & B, 865.
5 M & B, i, 865.
6 Ibid., i, 869.
7 Ibid., 869–70.

CHAPTER 21 : *The Jockey and the Jew*

1 M & B, i, 830.
2 Ibid., i, 835.
3 *Fraser's Magazine*, February 1847.
4 Greville, vi, 2–3.

5 M & B, i, 902.
6 *Croker Papers*, iii, 2 March 1848.
7 BDL, 1700, 30 August 1848, v, 72.
8 Ibid., 1703, 31 August 1848, v, 74.
9 Ibid., 12 June 1846, vi, 233.
10 Ibid., 1762, 6 January 1849, v, 120.

CHAPTER 22 : *The Country Gentleman*

1 M & B, i, 929.
2 Ibid., i, 932; BDL, 23 September 1848, 1718, v, 85, 1720–21.
3 Ibid., i, 936–7.
4 Ibid., i, 941.
5 Ibid., i, 940.
6 Ibid., i, 938.
7 Ibid., i, 951.
8 BDL, 31 January 1849, 1782, v, 141.
9 M & B, i, 955.
10 BDL, v, 1753, Note 3.
11 Ibid., 1758, v, 122, 31 December 1848.
12 M & B, i, 963–79.
13 Ibid., i, 979.
14 Ibid., i, 980.
15 BDL, 1711, v, 81, 6 September 1848.
16 Ibid., 25 January 1849, v, 137–8.
17 Rhodes James, *Rosebery*, 45.
18 Lang, *Northcote*, 98.
19 *Cornhill Magazine*, January 1912.
20 Quoted in Weintraub, 307.
21 M & B, i, 1269.
22 RB, 414–15.
23 M & B, i, 1271, 2 August 1851.
24 Ibid., i, 1271, 4 August 1851.
25 Ibid., i, 1274, 28 February 1853.
26 Ibid., i, 1274, 29 September 1853.
27 Ibid., i, 1270–1288.
28 Bradford, 248.

CHAPTER 23 : *The Chancellor*

1 M & B, i, 1160.
2 Ibid.
3 Ibid., i, 1159–60.
4 Ibid., i, 1162.
5 M & B, i, 1166; Weintraub, 314.
6 William Fraser, 49.
7 *Letters of Queen Victoria*, ii, 372.
8 Ibid.
9 Ibid., 30 March 1852.
10 Ibid., 1 April 1852.

11 M & B, i, 1171, 17 March 1852.
12 Bradford, 215–17.
13 Weintraub, 319.
14 Bradford, 216.
15 M & B, i, 1187.
16 Ibid., i, 1190, 16 June 1852.
17 Greville, vi, 337, 20 March 1852.
18 Ibid., vi, 338.
19 Greville, vi, 337.
20 *The Leader*, 25 September 1852.
21 M & B, i, 1210.
22 BDL, 2442, 20 November 1852, vi, 183.

CHAPTER 24 : *Marital Difficulties*

1 M & B, i, 1325.
2 Ibid., i, 1325–6.
3 RB, 359.
4 M & B, i, 1325.
5 RB, 358.
6 *The Press*, 21 May 1853.
7 Ibid., 11 June 1853.
8 Hansard, 3rd Series, 136.
9 Magnus, *Gladstone*, 119.
10 Pemberton, 227.
11 Ibid.
12 BDL, 18 July 1849, v, 197.
13 Ibid., 18 July 1849, v, 198.
14 Ibid., 1871, 25 August 1849, v, 208.
15 Ibid., 1915, 4 November 1849, v, 248.
16 Ibid., 1965, 23 January 1850, v, 297.
17 Ibid., 2170, 23 August 1851, v, 463.
18 Ibid., 2195, 7 November 1851, v, 488.
19 Ibid., 2196, 11 November 1851, v, 489.
20 Bradford, 285.
21 Ibid., 242.
22 RB, 284.
23 Quoted in Weintraub, 299.
24 Northcote, 279.
25 F.V. Keneally, *Memoirs*, 192.
26 *Passages From the English Notebooks of Nathaniel Hawthorne* (1870).
27 M & B, i, 1249.
28 Ibid., i, 1344.
29 Ibid., i, 1349.
30 Ibid., i, 1350.
31 BDL, 2705, 6 December 1854, vi, 387.
32 M & B, i, 1367–8.
33 *The Press*, 25 November 1854.

CHAPTER 25 : *Balls and Banquets*

1 BDL, 2747, 1 May 1855, vi, 419.
2 *Letters of Queen Victoria*, iii, 122–4.
3 Aronson, 102.
4 BDL, 2747, 1 May 1855, vi, 419–20.
5 M & B, i, 1417, 2 September 1855.
6 *The Press*, 29 September 1855.
7 BDL, 2856, 7 July 1856, vi, 494.
8 M & B, i, 416.
9 BDL, 2862, 30 August 1856, vii, 497–8.
10 M & B, i, 1455.
11 Ibid., 1456, 1 January 1857.
12 Ibid., i, 1457.
13 Malmesbury, *Memoirs of an Ex-Minister*, 19 April 1859.
14 M & B, i, 1458.
15 Malmesbury, *Memoirs of an Ex-Minister*.
16 M & B, i, 1476, 13 April 1857.

CHAPTER 26 : *Visits and Visitors*

1 M & B, i, 1477.
2 Ibid., i, 1486, 13 July 1857.
3 Ibid., i, 1494–5.
4 Ibid., i, 1496, 16 September 1857.
5 Ibid., i, 1491.
6 Ibid., i, 1497–8, 8 October 1857.
7 Ibid., i, 1498.
8 Ibid., i, 1498.
9 Sykes, 102.
10 M & B, i, 1501.
11 Ibid., i, 1508–9, 23 January 1858.
12 Ibid., i, 1536.
13 Ibid., i, 1552.
14 Morley, *Gladstone*, i, 387–9; Richard Shannon, i, 356–7; RB, 384.
15 M & B, i, 1565, 16 June 1858.
16 Ibid., i, 1568–9, 26 July 1858.
17 Ibid., i, 1587, 11 October 1858.

CHAPTER 27 : *Fêtes and Follies*

1 M & B, ii, 16, 23 July 1860.
2 Ibid., ii, 15–16.
3 Ibid., ii, 38, 24 November 1861.
4 Ibid.
5 Hibbert, *Garibaldi and His Enemies*, 1965, 339–50.

6 M & B, ii, 127.
7 Ibid., ii, 128.
8 Dorothy Nevill, 127–8.
9 Ibid., 128.
10 Atkins, *Life of Sir William Howard Russell*, ii, 202.
11 Weintraub, 428.

CHAPTER 28 : *Distinguished Persons and Private Secretaries*

1 M & B, ii, 154–5.
2 Rhodes James, *Rosebery*, 43–4.
3 Bradford, 263.
4 M & B, ii, 186; Weintraub, 438.
5 Gower, *Reminiscences*, i, 321.

CHAPTER 29 : *The 'Potent Wizard'*

1 Jasper Ridley, *Palmerston*, 529.
2 RB, 424.
3 Rhodes James, *Rosebery*, 62.
4 Weintraub, 568.
5 Ibid., 590.
6 Sykes, *passim*.
7 Rhodes James, *Rosebery*, 43; RB, 412.
8 Dorothy Nevill, *Reminiscences*, 205–6.
9 Weintraub, 354.
10 Gregory, *Autobiography*, 271.
11 Constance de Rothschild, *Reminiscences*, 194.
12 M & B, ii, 292.
13 Skelton, *Table Talk of Shirley*, 247.
14 M & B, ii, 304.
15 Ibid.
16 Ibid., ii, 306.
17 Ibid.

CHAPTER 30 : *A Guest at Balmoral and Osborne*

1 M & B, ii, 318.
2 Ibid., ii, 319.
3 Ibid., ii, 320.
4 Ibid., ii, 323.
5 Ibid., ii, 325.
6 Hibbert, *Queen Victoria . . . Letters and Journals*, 203.
7 M & B, ii, 326, 28 February 1868.

8 Hibbert, *Queen Victoria . . . Letters and Journals*, 203.
9 Rose, *The Later Cecils*, 36.
10 Hibbert, *Queen Victoria . . . Letters and Journals*, 203.
11 Longford, *Victoria R*, 401.
12 Quoted in Hibbert, *Queen Victoria . . . Letters and Journals*, 319.
13 Quoted in Weintraub, 462.
14 Ibid.

CHAPTER 31 : *Minister in Attendance*

1 M & B, ii, 390–91.
2 Ibid., ii, 391.
3 Ibid., ii, 391–2.
4 Ibid., ii, 392–5.
5 Hibbert, *Queen Victoria . . . Letters and Journals*, 318.
6 M & B, 438–40.
7 Shannon, *Gladstone: Heroic Minister*, 45; Morley, ii, 158.
8 Sykes, 122–7.
9 M & B, ii, 475–6.
10 Brett, *Esher*, i, 2.

CHAPTER 32 : *The Widower*

1 Fraser, *Disraeli and His Day*, 374–6.
2 M & B, ii, 527.
3 Ibid., ii, 537.
4 Ibid., ii, 558.
5 Glendinning, *Trollope*, 389–90.
6 RB, 518.
7 Wilson, *The Victorians*, 379.
8 Ibid., 380.
9 M & B, ii, 469.
10 Ibid., ii, 562.
11 Ibid., ii, 564.
12 Ibid.
13 Ibid.
14 Ibid., ii, 565–6.
15 Ibid., ii, 567.
16 Ibid., ii, 568.
17 Quoted in Bradford, 298.
18 Ibid., 299.
19 M & B, ii, 568.
20 Bradford, 299.
21 Quoted in Bradford, 300.
22 Hibbert, *Queen Victoria . . . Letters and Journals*, 229.

CHAPTER 33 : *Female Friends*

1 Sykes, 64.
2 M & B, ii, 574.
3 Ibid., ii, 575.
4 Blake, *Encyclopaedia Britannica*, 1974, 900.
5 Quoted in RB, 540.
6 Ponsonby, 245.
7 Healey, 202–3.
8 Countess of Cardigan and Lancaster, *Recollections*, 223.
9 Zetland, i, 57.
10 M & B, ii, 584, 17 March 1874.
11 Zetland, i, 109; ii, 42.
12 M & B, ii, 586.
13 Ibid., ii, 586–7, 3 August 1874.
14 Ibid., ii, 587–8.
15 Ibid., ii, 590.
16 Sykes, 64.

CHAPTER 34 : *Prime Minister Again*

1 M & B, ii, 609, 12 December 1873.
2 Ibid., ii, 610, 19 December 1873.
3 Ibid., 28 December 1873.
4 Ponsonby, 244–5.
5 Lucy, *Diary of Two Parliaments*, i, 40.
6 M & B, ii, 679, 7 August 1874.
7 Ibid., ii, 679–80, 7 August 1874.
8 Ibid., ii, 680.
9 Ibid., 8 August 1874.
10 Ibid., 14 August 1874.
11 Ibid., 10 September 1874.
12 Ibid., M & B, ii, 685.

CHAPTER 35 : *Troubles at Court*

1 M & B, ii, 687.
2 Ibid., ii, 696.
3 Weintraub, 413–14.
4 M & B, ii, 729–30.
5 Ibid., 731.
6 Brett, *Esher*, i, 17–18.
7 M & B, ii, 743.
8 Ibid., ii, 744–5.
9 Ibid., ii, 754.
10 Ibid., ii, 755–6.
11 Hibbert, *Edward VII*, 125.
12 M & B, ii, 768.

13 Hibbert, *Edward VII*, 126.
14 Ibid., 127.
15 Ibid., 128.
16 M & B, ii, 771.
17 Ibid., ii, 775–6.
18 Bradford, 326.
19 Longford, 405–6; Ponsonby, 137–8; St Aubyn, *Edward VII*, 434; Bradford, 330–31; M & B, ii, 803–9; RB, 562–3.
20 Magnus, *Gladstone*, 244–5; Hoppen, 630.

CHAPTER 36 : *Earl of Beaconsfield and Viscount Hughenden of Hughenden*

1 M & B, ii, 809, 21 March 1876.
2 Ibid., ii, 826.
3 Ibid., ii, 827.
4 RB, 582–7; Longford, 407; St Aubyn, 428 & 433–4; Queen Victoria's Journal, 24 November 1875.
5 M & B, ii, 793.
6 Munby, 383.
7 M & B, ii, 830.
8 Ibid., ii, 835.
9 Ibid., ii, 831.
10 Ibid., ii, 838.
11 RB, 566.
12 M & B, ii, 837.
13 Ibid., ii, 828.
14 *Fraser's Magazine*, 18 February 1847.
15 Ibid.
16 Lord George Hamilton, *Parliamentary Reminiscences*, 60.
17 M & B, ii, 849.
18 Fraser, *Disraeli and his Day*, 401–2.

CHAPTER 37 : *Berlin*

1 M & B, ii, 922.
2 Ibid.
3 Ibid., ii, 923–4.
4 Ibid., ii, 1040–41.
5 Lady Randolph Churchill, *Reminiscences*, 207.
6 M & B, ii, 1155.
7 Ibid.
8 Ibid., ii, 1059.
9 Ibid., ii, 1061.
10 Rose, *The Later Cecils*, 37.

11 Ibid.
12 M & B, ii, 1062.
13 Bradford, 347; M & B, ii, 1063.
14 Hibbert, *Queen Victoria . . . Letters and Journals*, 248.
15 Ibid., 248–9.
16 M & B, ii, 1075.
17 Ibid., ii, 1178.
18 Hibbert, *Queen Victoria . . . Letters and Journals*, 252.
19 M & B, ii, 1186.
20 Bradford, 386.
21 RB, 648.
22 M & B, ii, 1189–90.
23 Ibid., ii, 1196.
24 Munby, 394.
25 Bradford, 354.
26 Ibid., 356.

CHAPTER 38 : *The 'Guardian Angel'*

1 M & B, ii, 1332.
2 Ibid., ii, 1333.
3 Ibid., ii, 1334; Meynell, *Disraeli*, 539.
4 M & B, ii, 1335.
5 Ibid., ii, 1342.
6 Ibid.
7 Battiscombe, *Queen Alexandra*, 93.
8 M & B, ii, 1343.
9 Gower, *Reminiscences*, ii, 353.
10 Ibid., ii, 354–5.
11 RB, 712.
12 Ponsonby, *Henry Ponsonby*, 184.
13 M & B, ii, 1400.
14 Ibid., ii, 1411.
15 RB, 733–4.
16 M & B, 1423–6.
17 T.N. Longman, 'Memories Personal and Various', quoted in HL, 145.

CHAPTER 39 : *The Last Act*

1 Lang, *Life and Letters of Lord Northcote*, Ch. 16; M & B, ii, 1454–6.
2 RB, 681.
3 M & B, ii, 1473.
4 Jenkins, *Dilke*, 292.
5 Ponsonby, *Henry Ponsonby*, 221.
6 Barnes, *Augustus Hare*, 153.
7 Eliot, *Life of Lord Goschen*, i, 247–8.
8 M & B, ii, 1483.

9 Ibid., ii, 1485.
10 Bradford, 388.
11 RB, 748; Bradford, 389.
12 RB, 750.
13 Thomas Norton Longman,
  'Memories: Personal and Various',
  quoted in HL, 149.

CHAPTER 40 : 'A Wise and Worldly
Man'

1 Jenkins, *Gladstone*, 459.
2 Ibid., 458–9.
3 Ensor, 70–71.
4 Brett, *Esher*, i, 81.

SOURCES

Aldburgham, Alison, *Silver Fork Society* (1983)

Anderson, W.E.K. (ed.), *Journal of Sir Walter Scott* (1972)

Archer Shee, William, *My Contemporaries* (1893)

Argyll, Duke of, *Autobiography and Memoirs* (2 vols, 1906)

Aronson, Theo, *Victoria and Disraeli* (1977), *Heart of a Queen: Queen Victoria's Romantic Attachments* (1991)

Bagehot, Walter, *Biographical Studies* (1980)

Bamford, Francis and the Duke of Wellington, *The Journal of Mrs Arbuthnot* (2 vols, 1950)

Barnes, Malcolm, *Augustus Hare: Victorian Gentleman* (1984)

Battiscombe, Georgina, *Mrs Gladstone: The Portrait of a Marriage* (1956), *Queen Alexandra* (1969)

Beckett, J. V., *The Aristocracy of England 1660–1914* (1986)

Beeley, Sir H., *Disraeli* (1936)

Bell, H.F.C., *Lord Palmerston* (1936)

Benjamin Disraeli Letters (University of Toronto Press):
  Vol. 1. 1815–1834, eds. J.A.W. Gunn, John Matthews, Donald M. Schurman, M.G. Wiebe (1982)
  Vol. 2. 1835–1837, eds. J.A.W. Gunn, John Matthews, Donald M. Schurman, M.G. Wiebe (1982)
  Vol. 3. 1838–1841, eds. J.B. Conacher, John Matthews, Mary S. Millar, M.G. Wiebe (1987)
  Vol. 4. 1842–1847, eds. J.B. Conacher, John Matthews, Mary S. Millar, M.G. Wiebe (1983)
  Vol. 5. 1848–1851, eds. J.B. Conacher, John Matthews, Mary S. Millar, M.G. Wiebe (1993)
  Vol. 6. 1852–1856, eds. Mary S. Millar, Ann P. Robson M.G. Wiebe (1997)

Benson, A.C. and Viscount Esher (eds.), *The Letters of Queen Victoria* (3 vols, 1907)

Blake, Robert, *Disraeli* (1966), *Disraeli's Grand Tour: Benjamin Disraeli and the Holy Land 1830–31* (1982), 'The Rise of Disraeli' in H.R. Trevor-Roper (ed.), *Essays in British History Presented to Sir Keith Feiling* (1964)

Bradford, Sarah, *Disraeli* (1982)

Braun, Thom, *Disraeli the Novelist* (1981)

Bresler, Fenton, *Napoleon III: A Life* (1999)

Brett, Maurice V. (ed.), *Journals and Letters of Reginald, Viscount Esher* (2 vols, 1934)

Briggs, Asa, *Victorian People* (1954)

Broughton, Lord, *Recollections of a Long Life* (6 vols, 1909–11)

Buckle, G.E. (ed.), *The Letters of Queen Victoria, Second Series, 1862–86* (3 vols, 1926); *see also* Monypenny, W.F.

Campbell, Lord, *Lives of the Lord Chancellors* (vol. 8, 1869)

Cannadine, David, *Decline and Fall of the British Aristocracy* (1992), *Aspects of Aristocracy: Grandeur and Decline in Modern Britain* (1994)

Cecil, Lady Gwendolen, *The Life of Robert, Marquis of Salisbury* (1921)

Charlot, Monica, *Victoria: The Young Queen* (1991)

Churchill, Lady Randolph, *Reminiscences of Lady Randolph Churchill* (1908)

Cline, C.L., 'Disraeli at High Wycombe: The Beginnings of a Great Political Career', University of Texas Studies in English, vol. xxii (1942)

Cohen, Lucy, *Lady de Rothschild and her Daughters* (1935)

Connely, Willard, *Count D'Orsay: The Dandy of Dandies* (1952)

Cowles, Virginia, *The Rothschilds: A Family of Fortune* (1973)

Cowling, Maurice, *Disraeli, Gladstone and Revolution* (1967)

Croker, *see* Pool

Dasent, A.I., *John Thadeus Delane, Editor of the Times* (2 vols, 1908)

Davis, R.W., *The English Rothschilds* (1983)

Devey, Louisa, *Life of Rosina, Lady Lytton* (1887)

Disraeli, Benjamin, *Lord George Bentinck: A Political Biography* (1852); *and see Benjamin Disraeli Letters*

Disraeli, Ralph (ed.), *Home Letters, 1830–31* (1885), *Lord Beaconsfield's Correspondence with his Sister, 1822–52* (1886)

Edelman, Maurice, *Disraeli in Love* (1972)

Ellmann, Richard, *Oscar Wilde* (1987)

Ensor, R.C.K., *England 1870–1914* (1987)

Esher, *see* Brett

Feuchtwanger, F.I., *Disraeli, Democracy and the Tory Party* (1968)

Foot, M.R.D. and H.C.G. Matthew (eds.), *The Gladstone Diaries* (vols 1–3, 1968–74)

Francis, George Henry, *The Rt. Hon. Benjamin, Disraeli, M.P. A Critical Biography* (1852)

Fraser, Sir William, *Disraeli and his Day* (1891)

Froude, J.A., *Life of the Earl of Beaconsfield* (1914)

Fulford, Roger, *Darling Child: Private Correspondence of Queen Victoria and the Crown Princess of Prussia, 1871–78* (1976)

Gardiner, A.G., *Life of Sir William Harcourt* (2 vols, 1923)

Gash, Norman, *Politics in the Age of Peel* (1953); *Sir Robert Peel* (1972)

Gathorne Hardy, A.E. (ed.) *Gathorne Hardy, 1st Earl of Cranbrook* (2 vols, 1910)

Glendinning, Victoria, *Trollope* (1992)

Gower, Lord Ronald, *My Reminiscences* (2 vols, 1895)

Gregory, Sir William, *An Autobiography* (1894)

Greville, C.F., *The Greville Memoirs, 1814–60*, eds. Roger Fulford and Lytton Strachey (8 vols, 1938)

Grierson, H.J.C. *Letters of Sir Walter Scott* (vol. ix, 1935)

Hardwick, Mollie, *Mrs Dizzy: The Life of Mary Anne Disraeli, Viscountess Beaconsfield* (1972)

Healey, Edna, *Lady Unknown: The Life of Angela Burdett-Coutts* (1978)

Hibbert, Christopher, *Queen Victoria in her Letters and Journals* (1984)

Hoppen, K. Theodore, *The Mid-Victorian Generation* (1998)

Hudson, Derek, *Munby: Man of Two Worlds* (1974)

James, Robert Rhodes, *Rosebery* (1963)

Jenkins, Roy, *Sir Charles Dilke: A Victorian Tragedy* (1958); *Gladstone* (1995)

Jennings, L.J., *The Croker Papers* (3 vols, 1885)

Jerman, B.R., *The Young Disraeli* (1960)

Johnson, Paul, *A History of the Jews* (1987); *The Birth of the Modern: World Society, 1815–1830* (1991)

Kebbel, T.E., *Selected Speeches of the Late Rt. Hon. the Earl of Beaconsfield* (2 vols, 1882); *Lord Beaconsfield and Other Tory Memories* (1907)
Kidd, Joseph, 'The Last Illness of Lord Beaconsfield', *Nineteenth Century* (1889)
Kitson Clark, G., *The Making of Victorian England* (1962)

Lamington, Lord, *In the Days of the Dandies* (1890)
Lang, Andrew, *Life and Letters of J.G. Lockhart* (2 vols, 1896)
Langley, Helen (ed.), *Benjamin Disraeli: Scenes from an Extraordinary Life* (2003)
Layard, Sir Henry, *Autobiography and Memoirs* (2 vols, 1905); 'The Early Life of Lord Beaconsfield', *Quarterly Review* vol. 168 (1889)
Londonderry, Marchioness of (ed.), *Letters of Benjamin Disraeli to Frances Anne, Marchioness of Londonderry, 1837–61* (1938)
Longford, Elizabeth, *Victoria R.I.* (1964); *Pilgrimage of Passion: The Life of Wilford Scawen Blunt* (1979)
Lytton, Earl of, *The Life, Letters and Literary Remains of Edward Bulwer, Lord Lytton by his son* (2 vols, 1883)

Madden, R.R., *The Literary Life and Correspondence of the Countess of Blessington* (1855)
Magnus, Sir Philip, *Gladstone: A Biography* (1951); *King Edward VII* (1964)
Malmesbury, the Earl of, *Memoirs of an Ex-Minister* (2 vols, 1884)
Martin, Sir Theodore, *A Life of Lord Lyndhurst* (1883)
Maurois, André, *Disraeli: A Picture of the Victorian Age* (1928)
Maxwell, Sir H., *Life and Letters of George William Frederick, Fourth Earl of Clarendon* (2 vols, 1913)
Meynell, Wilfrid, *Benjamin Disraeli: An Unconventional Biography* (2 vols, 1903); *The Man Disraeli* (1927)
Mitchell, Leslie, *Bulwer Lytton: The Rise and Fall of a Victorian Man of Letters* (2003)
Moers, Ellen, *The Dandy* (1960)
Monypenny, W.F. and G.E. Buckle, *The Life of Benjamin Disraeli, Earl of Beaconsfield* (revised edition, 2 vols, 1929)
Morgan, Lady, *Lady Morgan's Memoirs* (2 vols, 1862)
Morley, John, *Life of W.E. Gladstone* (3 vols, 1903)

Morton, Frederic, *The Rothschilds* (1961)

Munby, Arthur, *see* Hudson

National Trust, *Guide to Hughenden Manor*

Nevill, Lady Dorothy, *Under Five Reigns* (1910)

Nevill, Ralph (ed.), *Reminiscences of Lady Dorothy Nevill* (1906); *Leaves from the Note-Books of Lady Dorothy Nevill* (1907); *My Own Times by Lady Dorothy Nevill* (1890)

Northcote, Sir Stafford, *Life, Letters and Diaries of Sir Stafford Northcote, First Earl of Iddesleigh* (2 vols, 1890)

Ogden, James, *Isaac D'Israeli* (1969)

Oman, Carola, *The Gascoyne Heiress: The Life and Diaries of Frances Mary Gascoyne Cecil 1802–39* (1968)

Parker, C.S. (ed.), *Sir Robert Peel From his Private Papers* (3 vols, 1891–9)

Paston, George, *At John Murray's* (1932)

Pemberton, W. Baring, *Lord Palmerston* (1964)

Phipps, the Hon. E., *Memoir of Robert Plumer Ward* (2 vols, 1850)

Pinney, T. (ed.), *Letters of T.B. Macaulay*, (6 vols, 1974–81)

Ponsonby, Arthur, *Henry Ponsonby: Queen Victoria's Private Secretary: His Life From His Letters* (1942)

Ponsonby, Sir Frederick, *Recollections of Three Reigns* (1951)

Pool, Bernard (ed.), *The Croker Papers, 1808–85* (1967)

Pope, W.B. (ed.), *Diary of Benjamin Robert Haydon* (5 vols, 1960–63)

Pope-Hennessy, James, *Monckton Milnes: The Years of Promise* (1949); *The Flight of Youth* (1951)

Prothero, R.F. (ed.), *Byron's Letters and Journals*

Redding, Cyrus, *Fifty Years' Recollections* (3 vols, 1858)

Reid Wemyss, T., *The Life, Letters and Friendships of Richard Monckton Milnes, First Lord Houghton* (2 vols, 1890)

Rhodes James, Robert, *Rosebery* (1963)

Ridley, Jane, *The Young Disraeli, 1804–1846* (1995)

Ridley, Jasper, *Lord Palmerston* (1970)

Rose, Kenneth, *The Later Cecils* (1975)

Roth, Cecil, *Benjamin Disraeli* (1952)

Rothschild, Constance de, *Reminiscences* (1922)

Russell, G.W.E., *Collections and Recollections* (1904); *Portraits of the Seventies* (1916)

Sadleir, Michael, *Bulwer and his Wife: A Panorama, 1803–36* (1931); *Blessington-D'Orsay: A Masquerade* (1933)

Saunders, C.R., K.J. Fielding, C.D. Ryalls (eds.), *The Collected Letters of Thomas and Jane Welsh Carlyle* (21 vols, 1970–93)

Schwarz, Daniel R., *Disraeli's Fiction* (1979)

Seton-Watson, R.W., *Disraeli, Gladstone and the Eastern Question* (1935)

Shannon, Richard, *Gladstone: Peel's Inheritor, 1809–65* (1982); *Gladstone: Heroic Minister, 1865–1898* (1999)

Sichel, W., *Disraeli: A Study in Personality and Ideas* (1904)

Smiles, Samuel, *Memoirs and Correspondence of the Late John Murray* (2 vols, 1891)

Smith, Paul, 'Disraeli's Politics', *Transactions of the Royal Historical Society*, 5th series, vol. 37 (1987); *Disraelian Conservatism and Social Reform* (1967)

Somervell, D.C., *Disraeli and Gladstone* (1938)

Stanley, Lady Augusta, *Later Letters, 1864–76* (1929)

St Aubyn, Giles, *Queen Victoria: A Portrait* (1991); *Edward VII: Prince and King* (1979)

Strachey, Lytton and Roger Fulford (eds.), *The Greville Memoirs* (8 vols, 193)

Sultana, Donald, *Benjamin Disraeli in Spain, Malta and Albania, 1830–32* (1976)

Sutherland, John, *Victorian Novelists and Publishers* (1976)

Swartz, Helen M. and Marvin (eds.), *Disraeli's Reminiscences* (1975)

Sykes, James, *Mary Anne Disraeli: The Story of Viscountess Beaconsfield* (1928)

Thompson, G.C., *Public Opinion and Lord Beaconsfield, 1876–80* (1886)

Torrens, W.M., *Memoirs of . . . Viscount Melbourne* (1890)

Toynbee, William (ed.), *The Diaries of William Charles Macready* (1912)

Trevor Roper, H.R. (ed.), 'The Rise of Disraeli' in *Essays in British History Presented to Sir Keith Feiling* (1934)

Trewin, J.C., *Journal of W.C. Macready* (1967)

Trollope, Anthony, *An Autobiography* (1946 edition)

Vincent, John, *Disraeli* (1990)

Waterfield, Gordon, *Layard of Nineveh* (1961)

Weintraub, Stanley, *Disraeli: A Biography* (1993); *Victoria* (1987)

Whibley, Charles, *Lord John Manners and His Friends* (2 vols, 1925)

Wilberforce, Reginald, *Life of The Right Reverend Samuel Wilberforce*
    (3 vols, 1881)

Wilson, A.N., *The Victorians* (2002)

Wolf, Lucien, 'The Disraeli Family', *Transactions of the Jewish Historical
    Society of England*, vol. 5 (1902–5)

Woodham-Smith, Cecil, *Queen Victoria: Her Life and Times, 1819–61*
    (1972)

Woodward, Llewellyn, *The Age of Reform, 1815–70* (1962)

Young, G.M. (ed.), *Early Victorian England, 1830–65* (2 vols, 1934)

Zetland, the Marquis of (ed.), *The Letters of Disraeli to Lady Bradford and
    Lady Chesterfield* (2 vols, 1929)

Ziegler, Philip, *Melbourne* (1987)

INDEX

Disraeli's name is abbreviated to BD, his wife's, throughout her life, to Mary Anne, and Queen Victoria's to QV.